Travel Discount Coupon

This coupon entitles you to special discounts when you book your trip through the

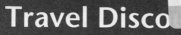

TRAVEL NETWORK®
RESERVATION SERVICE

Hotels ♦ Airlines ♦ Car Rentals ♦ Cruises
All Your Travel Needs

Here's what you get: *

♦ A discount of $50 USD on a booking of $1,000** or more for two or more people!

♦ A discount of $25 USD on a booking of $500** or more for one person!

♦ Free membership for three years, and 1,000 free miles on enrollment in the unique Travel Network Miles-to-Go® frequent-traveler program. Earn one mile for every dollar spent through the program. Redeem miles for free hotel stays starting at 5,000 miles. Earn free roundtrip airline tickets starting at 25,000 miles.

♦ Personal help in planning your own, customized trip.

♦ Fast, confirmed reservations at any property recommended in this guide, subject to availability.***

♦ Special discounts on bookings in the U.S. and around the world.

♦ Low-cost visa and passport service.

♦ Reduced-rate cruise packages and special car rental programs worldwide.

Visit our website at http://www.travelnetwork.com/Frommer or call us globally at 201-567-8500, ext. 55. In the U.S., call toll-free at 1-888-940-5000, or fax 201-567-1838. In Canada, call at 1-905-707-7222, or fax 905-707-8108. In Asia, call 60-3-7191044, or fax 60-3-7185415.

---

* To qualify for these travel discounts, at least a portion of your trip must include destinations covered in this guide. No more than one coupon discount may be used in any 12-month period, for destinations covered in this guide. Cannot be combined with any other discount or promotion.

**These are U.S. dollars spent on commissionable bookings.

***A $10 USD fee, plus fax and/or phone charges, will be added to the cost of bookings at each hotel not linked to the reservation service. Customers must approve these fees in advance. If only hotels of this kind are booked the traveler(s) must also purchase roundtrip air tickets from Travel Network for the trip.

Valid until December 31, 1998. Terms and conditions of the Miles-to-Go® program are available on request by calling 201-567-8500, ext 55.

WDW234

Frommer's 98

Walt Disney World & Orlando

by Mary Meehan

with coverage of the Best Beach Vacations near
Orlando by Victoria Pesce Elliott
& Bill Goodwin

Macmillan • USA

ABOUT THE AUTHOR

From opening day at Universal Studios Florida to the first plunge down Tower of Terror, **Mary Meehan** has been on hand as travel options have exploded in Central Florida. As an Orlando-based writer whose award winning work appears in regional and national publications, Meehan has an insider's view of the best things to see and do in Central Florida—and the best things to avoid.

MACMILLAN TRAVEL

A Simon & Schuster Macmillan Company
1633 Broadway
New York, NY 10019

Find us online at **http://www.mgr.com/travel**
or on America Online at Keyword: **Frommer's**

ISBN 0-02-861648-0
ISSN 1082-2615

Editor: Douglas Stallings
Production Editor: Lori Cates
Design by Michele Laseau
Digital Cartography by Ortelius Design and Roberta Stockwell
Page Creation by Tammy Ahrens, Dana Davis, Toi Davis, CJ East, David Faust, Joy Dean Lee, and Heather Pope

SPECIAL SALES

Bulk purchases (10+ copies) of Frommer's and selected Macmillan travel guides are available to corporations, organizations, mail-order catalogs, institutions, and charities at special discounts, and can be customized to suit individual needs. For more information write to: Special Sales, Macmillan General Reference, 1633 Broadway, New York, NY 10019.

Manufactured in the United States of America

Contents

List of Maps

AN INVITATION TO THE READER

In researching this book, we discovered many wonderful places—hotels, restaurants, shops, and more. We're sure you'll find others. Please tell us about them, so we can share the information with your fellow travelers in upcoming editions. If you were disappointed with a recommendation, we'd love to know that, too. Please write to

Mary Meehan
Frommer's Walt Disney World & Orlando '98
Macmillan Travel
1633 Broadway
New York, NY 10019

AN ADDITIONAL NOTE

Please be advised that travel information is subject to change at any time—and this is especially true of prices. We therefore suggest that you write or call ahead for confirmation when making your travel plans. The authors, editors, and publisher cannot be held responsible for the experiences of readers while traveling. Your safety is important to us, however, so we encourage you to stay alert and be aware of your surroundings. Keep a close eye on cameras, purses, and wallets, all favorite targets of thieves and pickpockets.

WHAT THE SYMBOLS MEAN

✪ Frommer's Favorites

Hotels, restaurants, attractions, and entertainment you should not miss.

The following abbreviations are used for credit cards:

AE	American Express	EU	Eurocard
CB	Carte Blanche	JCB	Japan Credit Bank
DC	Diners Club	MC	MasterCard
DISC	Discover	V	Visa

Introducing Walt Disney World & Orlando

Orlando was a sleepy Southern town ringed with sparkling lakes, pine forests, and citrus groves until Walt Disney turned 43 square miles of swampland into a Magic Kingdom. He sparked an unprecedented building boom, as hotels, restaurants, and scores of additional attractions arose to take advantage of the tourist traffic he had generated.

The world's most famous mouse changed central Florida forever. Though the citrus industry still exists here, orange groves have largely given way to high-rise apartment complexes, vast hotels and resorts, and shopping malls. Many national firms have relocated their headquarters to this thriving Sunbelt region, and it has become one of the fastest growing high-tech centers in the country with one of the most active downtowns in the country.

For travelers, Orlando represents a vacation from stressful reality to a world of make-believe—one where there are parades every day and fireworks every night. Forget all your problems but one: How are you possibly going to cram so many attractions into one short vacation?

And that's a tough one. But never fear. I've checked out every square inch of all the parks, ridden every ride, and inspected every hotel and restaurant. In the pages that follow, I'll share my discoveries and tips with you and help you create your own itinerary so that you can get the most out of your trip and minimize the time you spend standing in line.

Though in recent years Disney has been marketing itself aggressively as a vacation spot for adults traveling alone (personally, without the kids, I'd rather go to Paris), Orlando is obviously America's number-one destination for families—the vacation your kids clamor for. Much of what is available here is geared toward kids, and I'm not just talking about the parks. Many hotels, some whimsically themed, have video-game arcades and other child-pleasing features, and just about every restaurant in town has a low-priced children's menu.

In this city, visitors are the real VIPs. The major players are vying for your business, as they engage in an ongoing high-stakes game of one-upmanship. Disney's innovative movie-magic motif MGM Studios theme park was countered a year after it opened by Universal Studios Florida, which brought in Steven Spielberg as a creative consultant. When Church Street Station, a single-price–admission entertainment complex, opened in downtown Orlando, Disney responded with Pleasure Island (see chapter 10). And now Universal is getting into the act with a slick nightlife park of its own called City Walk and plush themed resorts that will rival Disney's. Wet 'n' Wild in town? Disney has three water parks of its own and provides free transportation to them for its vast numbers of on-premises resort guests. Busch Gardens in nearby Tampa has an animal park? Well, by gosh, Disney will have an Animal Kingdom.

It's rather fascinating, this battle of the titans that sometimes degenerates into the laughable. If Universal has a 3-D attraction, Disney–MGM ups its wattage to 4-D (whatever that means).

But make no mistake, we are the spoils. Now that Universal is building a Jurassic Park attraction, will Disney have to create real dinosaurs from DNA found in amber?

1 Frommer's Favorite Orlando Experiences

- **Splash Mountain.** This Magic Kingdom attraction combines gorgeous scenery with Disney magic and a theme-park thrill—a five-story splashdown! Don't chicken out. It's great.
- **The Daily Parade and SpectroMagic.** The daily 3pm parade at the Magic Kingdom is enchanting. And SpectroMagic, which takes place after dark, adds high-tech dazzle to Disney's genius for spectacle. The Hercules Parade at Disney–MGM Studios is also a delight.
- **The Making of Me.** Martin Short teaches the facts of life in this very charming 15-minute film at Epcot's Wonders of Life pavilion.
- **Cranium Command.** Another Wonders of Life feature, this hilarious multimedia attraction is one of Epcot's best. It stars a handful of "Saturday Night Live" actors and other comedians.
- **Wonders of China.** This 360° Circle-Vision film at Epcot's China pavilion explores 6,000 years of Chinese history and ranges the country's landscape in stunning cinematography.
- **Sports Activities.** Though most people come for the rides and attractions, Walt Disney World and the surrounding area offer numerous sporting options for the whole family—great golfing, tennis, boating, fishing, waterskiing, cycling. . . you name it.
- **Tower of Terror.** A terrifying plunge that lives up to the unparalleled Disney hype. The drop leaves even the hardiest of thrill seekers a little weak in the knees.
- **Universal Studios.** Universal combines cutting-edge, high-tech effects with great creativity. Adults will find Universal—A Day in the Park with Barney notwithstanding—a more hip and sophisticated park, not afraid to poke fun at itself or the mouse down the road. Not-to-be-missed attractions here: Back to the Future, Jaws, Terminator 2: 3-D Battle Across Time, and Earthquake—The Big One.
- **Cypress Gardens.** Two hundred acres of gorgeous botanical gardens punctuated by lakes and lagoons, waterfalls, and sculpture. A very laid-back attraction; popular with seniors.
- **Church Street Station.** Dance halls, old-fashioned saloons, dining rooms, and shopping make this the prime non-Disney attraction in Orlando. Top-flight musicians provide entertainment amid this downtown renovated train depot spanning across real cobblestone streets.
- **The Orlando Science Center.** Opened in 1997 after a $40-million expansion, this is a wonderful real-world alternative to the go-go pace of the theme parks. It's educational and entertaining fun for both parents and kids. Located in Loch Haven Park near downtown Orlando.

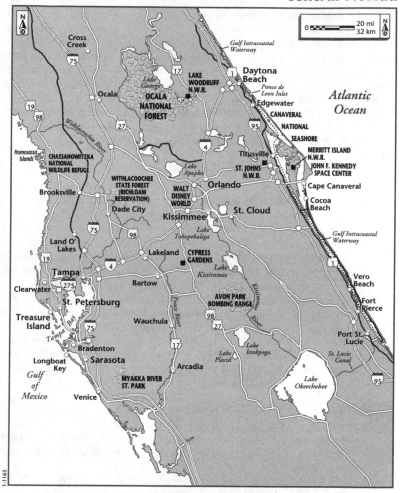

Central Florida

- **Sea World.** With the addition of a roller coaster, Sea World has added a little thrill, but enjoy what this park does best—hands-on encounters with dolphins and stingrays and up-close views of everything from polar bears to killer whales. Not to be missed is "Mermaids, Myths & Monsters," a thrilling nighttime multimedia spectacular at Sea World where images appear to dance, hop, and stomp across a 60-foot screen of water.

2 Orlando Today & Tomorrow

In the 1990s, Orlando enjoys the best overall business climate in the state of Florida. In addition to tourism, its dynamic economy thrives on diverse industry, thousands of technology-related companies, and agriculture. The only remnant of Orlando's slow-paced, pre-Disney Southern image is its down-home friendliness. This burgeoning Sunbelt metropolis looks forward to the future with unbounded optimism.

For the observant visitor, this part of Florida is very different from the rest of the state. Indeed, the parts of town most tourists see are unlike any others on the planet. Mile after mile of perfectly manicured landscape (courtesy of Disney and other major players here), in an area consisting largely of strip malls and spotless theme parks, creates a kind of sterile "Twilight Zone" quality. And this plastic presence is only going to increase as Walt Disney World and other parks continue to expand. Disneyesque street signs have within the last few years begun to appear downtown. There's even a whole Disney town—Celebration. Just 20 or so miles in any direction from the tourist mecca you'll find a real town, like anywhere else. But most attractions builders recognize that people coming to Orlando aren't looking for reality.

Recent major developments include the following:

- **Universal Studios** also has multibillion-dollar expansion plans. Utilizing 600 presently undeveloped acres, the company is creating competition for Disney with five movie- and television-theme resorts comprising more than 4,300 rooms; a golf-villa community centered on an 18-hole championship course; a top-of-the-line tennis complex; a series of lakes, winding rivers, canals, and other waterways that will be traversed by water taxis and ferries; a streamlined people-mover system; and a 12-acre entertainment park (details on the latter in chapter 8). But perhaps the biggest news is Universal's Islands of Adventure, billed as a "21st-century theme park set among the exotic coastlines of the oceans." Among numerous rides, shows, and attractions, it will include a Jurassic Park ride, and attractions based on Dr. Seuss and Marvel Comics. Islands of Adventure is scheduled to open in 1999.

- **Universal's City Walk,** a 12-acre entertainment complex, could easily be renamed theme-restaurant heaven. Not only is it home to the world's largest Hard Rock Cafe—the grande dame of all theme restaurants—but also the Nascar Cafe, the Motown Cafe, and Marvel Mania, a theme send-up to villains and superheroes. The City Walk, which opens in 1998, also contains a hearty dose of Cajun spice with Pat O'Brien's, a re-creation of the famous New Orleans bar, and Emeril's of New Orleans, featuring the Creole-based cuisine of chef Emeril Lagasse. If that's not enough to keep you busy, there is the Down Beat Jazz Hall of Fame, a tribute to reggae *mon* Bob Marley, and a 5,000-seat Cineplex Odeon Megaplex movie theater.

- **Disney's Animal Kingdom,** an exotic "live-animal adventure park," will be five times the size of the Magic Kingdom, at 500 acres. Centering on a 14-story "tree," it will combine thrill rides, exotic landscapes, and close encounters with great herds of wild animals, divided into three "regions."

  In addition to real animals, guests will meet up with unicorns and dragons, storybook animals, and dinosaurs. It will be interesting to see Disney go head-to-head with the eco-entertainment offered by Sea World and, to a lesser extent, Busch Gardens. Much of the preopening buzz has, in a very un-Disney manner, centered more on the serious zoological work to be done there, not the traditional Mouse Magic.

- **Disney Cruise Lines** offers park vacations in conjunction with Caribbean cruises. Aboard ships reminiscent of classic luxury liners, guests will enjoy a choice of theme restaurants, nightclubs, family entertainment, supervised children's activities, and much more. Maiden voyages are scheduled for early 1998.

- **Celebration, Florida,** a 4,900-acre planned community (surrounded by a protected greenbelt of almost equal size)—with 8,000 residences, a prototype Disney-influenced public school, a downtown retail area with many buildings on a lakefront promenade, a Michael Graves–designed post office, a vast adjoining office complex, comprehensive health-care facilities, and extensive recreational facilities including an 18-hole championship golf course. Residents were chosen through a lottery system, but regular folks have access to the public areas in this new Disney "world."

3 History 101, or How a Sleepy Southern Town Met a Mighty Mouse

It would almost seem that the history of Orlando could be condensed into two terse sentences: (1) There were orange groves. (2) Walt Disney came. There is, however, considerably more juice to be squeezed from the story. The modern metropolis of Orlando began as a rough-and-tumble Florida frontier town.

SETTLERS VS. SEMINOLES: THE ROAD TO STATEHOOD

Florida history dates back to 1513—more than a century before the Pilgrims landed at Plymouth Rock—when Ponce de León, in search of the fabled "fountain of youth," spied the beaches and lush greenery of Florida's Atlantic coast. He named it *La Florida*—"the Flowery Land." After years of alternating Spanish, French, and British rule, the territory was ceded (by Spain) to the United States in 1821. Lost in the international shuffle were the Seminoles, who, after migrating from Georgia and the Carolinas in the late 18th century to settle on some of Florida's richest farmlands, were viewed by the Americans as an obstacle to white settlement. After a series of compromise treaties that left both sides dissatisfied, the federal government threw down the final gauntlet with the Indian Removal Act of 1830, stipulating that all eastern tribes be removed to reservations west of the Mississippi. This cruel edict sparked the Second Seminole War (1835–42). At a treaty conference at Payne's Landing in 1832, a young warrior named Osceola strode up to the bargaining table, slammed his knife into the papers on it, and, pointing to the quivering blade, proclaimed, "The only treaty I will ever make is this!"

Guerrilla warfare thwarted the U.S. army's attempt to remove the Seminoles for almost 8 years, during which time many of the resisters drifted south into the interior of central Florida. In what is today the Orlando area—on a small, triangular parcel of land formed by Lake Gatlin, Lake Gem Mary, and Lake Jennie Jewell—the Americans built Fort Gatlin in 1838 to offer protection to pioneer

Dateline

- **1817–18** The First Seminole War. Aligned with refugee Creeks from Georgia, native Appalachees, and runaway slaves, the Seminoles battle Andrew Jackson's troops while Florida is still a Spanish territory.
- **1843** Mosquito County in central Florida is renamed Orange County.
- **1856** Orlando becomes the official seat of Orange County.
- **1861** Florida secedes from the Union. The demise of slavery sounds the death knell for the area's burgeoning cotton industry.
- **1870** Cattle ranching and citrus growing replace cotton as the bulwark of Orlando's economy.
- **1875** Orlando is officially incorporated as a municipality under state law.
- **1880** The South Florida Railroad facilitates the expansion of Orlando's agricultural markets.
- **1884** Fire rages out of control, destroying much of Orlando's fledgling business district.
- **1894–95** Freezing temperatures destroy 2 years of citrus crops and wreck orchards. Many growers lose everything.
- **1910–25** A land boom hits Florida. Fortunes are made overnight.
- **1926** The land boom goes bust. Fortunes are lost overnight.

continues

- **1929** An invasion of Mediterranean fruit flies devastates Orlando's citrus industry. Its ruined economy is capped by the stock-market crash.
- **1939–45** World War II revives Orlando's ailing economy. The city becomes "Florida's Air Capital."
- **1964** Walt Disney begins surreptitiously buying up central Florida farmland, purchasing more than 28,000 acres at a cost of nearly $5.5 million.
- **1965** Disney announces his plan to build in Orlando the world's most spectacular theme park.
- **1971** The Magic Kingdom opens its gates.
- **1972** A new 1-day attendance mark is set on December 27, when 72,328 people visit the Magic Kingdom. It will be broken almost every year thereafter.
- **1973** Shamu ventures into Orlando waters. Sea World opens.
- **1979** Mickey Mouse welcomes the Magic Kingdom's 100-millionth visitor, 8-year-old Kurt Miller from Kingsville, Maryland.
- **1982** Epcot opens to the public with vast hoopla. Participating celebrities include everyone from Richard Nixon to George Steinbrenner.
- **1984** Donald Duck's 50th birthday is celebrated with a special parade down Main Street that includes 50 live Peking ducks.
- **1988** Walt Disney World celebrates Mickey Mouse's 60th birthday. A special parade *does not* include 50 live mice!
- **1989** WDW launches Disney-MGM Studios Theme Park (offering a

continues

homesteaders. The fort, sited near an ancient oak tree where followers of Osceola frequently met to discuss strategies, was the scene of many skirmishes. The Seminoles kept up a fierce rebellion until 1842, when, undefeated, they accepted a treaty whereby their remaining numbers (about 300) were given land and left in peace. The same year, the Armed Occupation Act offered 160 acres to any pioneers willing to settle here for a minimum of 5 years. The land was fertile: Wild turkeys and deer abounded in the woods, grazing land for cattle was equally plentiful, and dozens of lakes provided fish for settlers and water for livestock. In 1843, what had been Mosquito County was more invitingly renamed Orange County. And with the Seminoles more or less out of the way (though sporadic cattle rustling and bloody uprisings still occurred), the Territorial General Legislature petitioned Congress for statehood. On March 3, 1845, President John Tyler signed a bill making Florida the 27th state in the Union.

Settlements and statehood notwithstanding, at the middle of the 19th century the Orlando area (then named Jernigan for one of its first settler families) was comprised largely of pristine lakes and pine-forested wilderness. There were no roads, and you could ride all day (if you could find a trail) without meeting a soul. The Jernigans successfully raised cattle, and their home and stockade, which was granted a post office in 1850, became a way stop for travelers and the seat of future development. Farmers and cattle ranchers were drawn to the area's verdant grasslands. Before long, a sawmill went up (on the site of today's Orlando Public Library) and a trading post was opened. Other merchants followed, and farms and ranches—which would grow to vast agricultural dynasties—were carved out of the wilderness. In 1856, the boundaries of Orange County were revised, and, thanks to the manipulations of resident James Gamble Speer, a member of the Indian Removal Commission, Fort Gatlin (Jernigan) became its official seat. How the fledgling town came to be named Orlando is a matter of some speculation. Some say Speer renamed the town after a dearly loved friend, whereas other sources say he named it after one of his favorite Shakespearean characters from *As You Like It*. But the most accepted version is that the town was named for prominent plantation owner Orlando Reeves (or Rees), who died in battle with the Seminoles in 1835. The site where he was buried on the shores of

Lake Eola came to be known as "Orlando's Grave." Speer is reported to have said, "This place is often spoken of as 'Orlando's Grave.' Let's drop the word 'grave' and let the county seat be called Orlando."

THE 1860s: CIVIL WAR/CATTLE WARS

Throughout the early 1860s, cotton plantations and cattle ranches became the hallmarks of central Florida. Orlando was ringed by a vast cotton empire. Log cabins went up along the lakes, and the pioneers eked out a somewhat lonely existence, separated from each other by miles of farmland. But there were troubles brewing in the 31-state nation that would soon devastate Orlando's planters. By 1859, it was obvious that only a war would resolve the slavery issue. In 1861, Florida became the third state to secede from the Union, and the modest progress it had achieved came to a standstill. The Stars and Bars flew from every flagpole, and local men enlisted in the Confederate army, leaving the fledgling town in poverty. A federal blockade made it difficult to obtain necessities, and many slaves fled. In 1866, the Confederate troops of Florida surrendered, the remaining slaves were freed, and a ragtag group of defeated soldiers returned to Orlando. They found a dying cotton industry, unable to function without slave labor or transport to markets. In 1868, Florida was readmitted to the Union.

behind-the-scenes look at Tinseltown), Typhoon Lagoon (a 56-acre water theme park), and Pleasure Island (an adult-nightclub theme park).

- **1990** Universal Studios opens, offering visitors thrilling encounters with E.T. and King Kong.
- **1993** Sea World continues a major expansion. Universal Studios unleashes the fearsome *Jaws*.
- **1997** Disney begins its own cruise line. Universal Studios opens City Walk, a vast new entertainment complex.

Its untended cotton fields having gone to seed, Orlando now concentrated on cattle ranching, a business plagued by heavy taxation on herds by the occupation government and one that ushered in an era of lawlessness and violence. Cattle rustling, widely practiced, generated vicious feuds, clogging courtroom calendars and igniting long-running hostilities between warring parties. Like frontier cattle towns out West, post–Civil War Orlando was short on civilized behavior; gunfights, brawls, and murders were commonplace. But as the 1860s drew to a close, large-herd owners from other parts of the state moved into the area and began organizing the industry in a less chaotic fashion. Branding and penning greatly reduced rustling, though it never totally eliminated the problem; even a century later, soaring beef prices brought on a rash of cattle thievery as late as 1973!

AN ORANGE TREE GROWS IN ORLANDO

In the 1870s, articles in national magazines began luring large numbers of Americans to central Florida with promises of arable land and a warm climate. In Orlando, public roads, schools, and churches appeared to serve the newcomers, many of whom replanted defunct cotton fields with citrus groves. Orlando was officially incorporated under state law in 1875, setting up definitive boundaries, a city government complete with a mayor, laws and ordinances, a city hall, a jail, and other adjuncts of a municipality. New settlers poured in from all over the country, businesses flourished, and by the end of the year the town had its first newspaper, the *Orange County Reporter*. The first locomotive of the South Florida Railroad chugged into town in 1880, representing a major step toward growth and prosperity and sparking a building and land boom—the first of many. Orlando got sidewalks and its first bank in 1883—the same year the town voted itself "dry" in hopes of averting the fistfights and brawls that ensued when cowboys crowded into local saloons every Saturday night for rowdy R&R. For many years the city continued to vote itself alternately wet and dry, but in actuality, it made very little difference. Legal or not, liquor was always readily available.

FIRE & ICE

In January 1884, a grocery fire that started at 4am wiped out blocks of businesses, including the offices of the *Orange County Reporter*. But 19th-century Orlando was a bit like a Frank Capra movie. The town rallied 'round, providing a new location for the paper and presenting its publisher, Mahlon Gore, with $1,200 in cash to help defray losses and $300 in new subscriptions. The paper not only survived but flourished. And the city, realizing the need, created its first fire brigade. By August 1884, a census revealed that the population had grown to 1,666. That same year 600,000 boxes of oranges were shipped from Florida to points north—most of those boxes originating in Orlando. By 1885, Orlando was a viable town boasting as many as 50 businesses. It was dubbed the "Phenomenal City," after a South Florida Railroad booklet called the city's growth "phenomenal." Which is not to say it was New York. Razorback hogs roamed the streets, and alligator wrestling was a main form of entertainment.

Disaster struck a week after Christmas in 1894, when the temperature plummeted to an unseasonable 24°. Water pipes burst, and orange blossoms froze, blackened, and died. The freeze continued for 3 days, wrecking the citrus crop for the year. Karl H. Abbott, son of the owner of the San Juan Hotel, where Northern buyers met to bid on citrus crops, later described the pandemonium that broke out as the thermometer began dipping shortly after noon:

> *The buyers hurriedly left the lunch tables and went out of doors to view the weather. The big thermometer in front of the hotel indicated unusual cold. By 2pm the San Juan was in an uproar. Prices had dropped to "no sale." Commission merchants were frantically trying to get out of options and heated debates and fistfights started in the lobby. . . . About nine that night a fine-looking gray-haired gentleman in a black coat and Stetson hat walked up the street in front of the hotel and looked at the thermometer, groaned "Oh my God!" and shot himself through the head.*

Many grove owners went bust, and those who remained were hit with a second devastating freeze the following year. Tens of thousands of trees died in the killing frost. Small growers were wiped out, but large conglomerates that could afford to buy up their properties at bargain prices and wait for new groves to mature assured the survival of the industry.

SPECULATION FEVER: GOOD DEALS, BAD DEALS . . .

As Orlando entered the 20th century, citrus and agriculture had surpassed cattle ranching as the mainstay of the local economy. Stray cows no longer had to be shooed from the railway tracks. Streets were being paved and electricity and telephone service installed. The population at the turn of the century was 2,481. In 1902, the city passed its first automobile laws, which included an in-town speed limit of 5 miles per hour. In 1904, the city flooded. And in 1905 it suffered a drought that ended—miraculously or coincidentally—on a day when all faiths united at the local First Baptist Church to pray for rain. By 1910, prosperity had returned and Orlando, with a population of nearly 4,000, was, in a small way, becoming a tourism and convention center. World War I brought further industrial growth and a real-estate boom, not just to Orlando but to all of Florida. Millions of immigrants, speculators, and builders descended on the state in search of a quick buck. As land speculation reached a fever pitch, and property was bought and resold almost overnight, many citrus groves gave way to urbanization. Preeminent Orlando builder and promoter Carl

Dann described the action: "It finally became nothing more than a gambling machine, each man buying on a shoestring, betting dollars a bigger fool would come along and buy his option."

Quite suddenly, the bubble burst. A July 1926 issue of the *Nation* provided the obituary for the Florida land boom: "The world's greatest poker game, played with lots instead of chips, is over. And the players are now. . . paying up." Construction slowed to a trickle, and many newcomers who had arrived in Florida to jump on the bandwagon returned to their homes in the north. Though Orlando was not quite as hard hit as Miami—scene of the greediest land grabs—some belt-tightening was in order. Nevertheless, the city managed to build a municipal airport in 1928. Then came a Mediterranean fruit-fly infestation that crippled the citrus industry. Hundreds of thousands of acres of land in quarantined areas had to be cleared of fruit and vast quantities of boxed fruit were destroyed. The 1929 stock market crash that precipitated the Great Depression seemed almost an afterthought to Florida's ruined economy.

. . . AND NEW DEALS

President Franklin D. Roosevelt's New Deal helped the state climb back on its feet. The Works Progress Administration (WPA) put 40,000 unemployed Floridians back to work—work that included hundreds of public projects in Orlando. Of these, the most important was the expansion and resurfacing of the city's airport. By 1936, the tourist trade had revived somewhat, construction was up once again, and the state began attracting a broader range of visitors than ever before. But the event that finally lifted Florida—and the nation—out of the depression was World War II.

Orlando had weathered the Great Depression. Now it prepared for war with the construction of army bases, housing for servicemen, and training facilities. Almost all new business was geared toward defense. Enlisted men poured into the city, and the airport was again enlarged and equipped with barracks, a military hospital, administration buildings, and mess halls. By 1944, Orlando had a second airport and was known as "Florida's Air Capital"—home to major aircraft and aviation-parts–manufacturing factories. Thousands of U.S. servicemen did part of their hitch in Orlando, and when the war ended, many returned to settle there.

POSTWAR PROSPERITY

By 1950, Orlando—with a population of 51,826—was the financial and transportation hub of central Florida. The city shared the bullish economy of the 1950s with the rest of the nation. In the face of the Cold War, the Orlando air force base remained and grew, funneling millions of dollars into the local economy. Florida's population increased by a whopping 78.7% during the decade—making it America's 10th most populous state—and tourists came in droves, nearly 4.5 million in 1950 alone. One reason for the influx was the advent of the air conditioner, which made life in Florida infinitely more pleasant. Also fueling Orlando's economy was a brand-new industry arriving in nearby Cape Canaveral in 1955—the government-run space program. Cape Canaveral became NASA's headquarters for the Apollo rocket program that eventually blasted Neil Armstrong heavenward toward his famous "giant

In the Words of Walt Disney

Why be a governor or a senator when you can be king of Disneyland?

You can dream, create, design, and build the most wonderful place in the world. . . but it requires people to make the dream a reality.

Animal Kingdom

Disney's fifth and newest park combines animals, elaborate landscapes, and rides to create yet another reason not to venture outside of the Disney world.

Slated to open in early 1998, Animal Kingdom is divided into three "regions," one dedicated to the wildlife in Africa today, one to mythical creatures such as unicorns and dragons, and one focusing on extinction. The park covers more than 500 acres.

At the heart of it all is a 14-story "Tree of Life," an intricately carved free-form representation of animals handcrafted by Disney artists. This impressive landmark is nearly as tall and as imposing as the silver golf-ball dome, also known as Spaceship Earth, that has come to best symbolize Epcot.

Things are hush-hush about the exact nature of the wildlife and exhibits, but it is obvious from the heavy emphasis on conservation and education that Disney is directly entering into competition with the other animal parks, Sea World and Busch Gardens. The preopening publicity has centered on the heavily credentialed experts who have been brought in to run the park, and the emphasis has been on its zoological value over its entertainment value.

Although it's uncertain whether Animal Kingdom can immediately challenge those parks, which over the years have honed their eco-entertainment theme, it will be interesting to see how Disney integrates the wonders of nature with the magic of make-believe.

leap." During the same decade, the Glenn L. Martin Company (later Martin Marietta), builder of the Matador Missile, purchased 10 square miles for a plant site 4 miles south of Orlando. Its advent sparked further industrial growth, and property values soared. More than 60 new industries located in the area in 1959 alone. But even the most optimistic Orlando boosters could not foresee the glorious future that was the city's ultimate destiny.

THE DISNEY DECADES

In 1964, Walt Disney began secretly buying up millions of dollars worth of central Florida farmland. As vast areas of land were purchased in lots of 5,000 acres here, 20,000 there—at remarkably high prices—rumors flew as to who needed so much land and had so much money to acquire it. Some thought it was Howard Hughes; others the space program. Speculation was rife almost to the very day, November 15, 1965 ("D" Day for Orlando), when Disney himself arrived in town and announced his plans to build the world's most spectacular theme park ("bigger and better than Disneyland"). In a 2-year construction effort, Disney employed 9,000 people. Land speculation reached unprecedented heights, as hotel chains and restaurateurs grabbed up property near the proposed parks. Mere swampland sold for millions. Total cost of the project by its October 1971 opening was $400 million. Mickey Mouse personally led the first visitor into the Magic Kingdom, and numerous celebrities—everyone from Bob Hope to Julie Andrews—took part in the opening ceremonies. In Walt Disney World's first 2 years, the attraction drew 20 million visitors and employed 13,000 people. The sleepy citrus-growing town of Orlando had become the "Action Center of Florida" and the fastest-growing city in the state. A 1972 referendum revitalized downtown Orlando.

Additional attractions multiplied faster than fruit flies, and hundreds of firms relocated their businesses in the area. Sea World, a major theme park, came to town in 1973. Walt Disney World has continued to grow and expand, adding Epcot in 1982 and Disney–MGM Studios in 1989, along with water parks, over a dozen "official" resorts, a shopping/restaurant village, campgrounds, a vast array of recreational facilities, and several other adjuncts that are thoroughly described in this book. Universal Studios, which also continues to expand, opened in 1990. In 1998, Disney opens yet another theme park, this one dedicated to zoological entertainment and aptly called Animal Kingdom.

At the same time, Universal continues to become more of a player. In 1998 they will unveil a new entertainment district, City Walk, and in 1999 Universal plans to open Islands of Adventure, a second theme park including, among other things, attractions dedicated to Dr. Seuss, Marvel Comics, and Jurassic Park. Also scheduled to open in 1999 is the Portofino Bay Resort at Universal City Florida, a 750-room Loews hotel. Universal is to open three more hotels by 2005.

4 Behind the Scenes

- Known for going to great lengths to protect its image and name—even removing unofficial Disney pictures from murals on the wall of a day-care center—Disney recently lost the name game. Originally dubbed Wild Animal Kingdom, Disney's latest park was renamed after complaints that the moniker too closely mirrored the televised "Wild Kingdom," starring Marlin Perkins and his faithful sidekick Jim Fowler.
- Many have tried but few have succeeded in trying to replicate even a piece of the Disney magic. One of the more unusual plans was put forth in 1989 by magician Doug Henning and Indian spiritual leader Maharishi Mahesh Yogi. What they had up their sleeves was a mystically themed park called Vedaland that was announced with much fanfare in 1989 and then—*poof*—seemed to vanish into thin air.
- Plenty of shiny coins are dropped in Disney fountains as visitors pick a scenic location and make a wish. To literally squeeze every dime out of its operations, Disney has devised an elaborate mechanized system to get that change out of the fountains and back into the tills of its restaurants and stores—dried, sorted, and rolled—sometimes before the end of the day.
- Disney, the epitome of family-friendly entertainment, is not without conservative critics. In 1996, the Southern Baptist Convention, the nation's largest Protestant denomination, threatened to boycott the parks and all Disney-related businesses because of less-than-family–oriented films produced by subsidiaries. That same year the Catholic church sent memos nationwide saying it no longer approved of priests performing ceremonies in Walt Disney World's Wedding Pavilion. Weddings ought to be performed in churches, leaders said, not theme parks. No word on the impact on the number of Catholic weddings, but in spite of the rhetoric, Baptists seemed willing to put their money where the mouse is. Night of Joy, an annual Christian music concert, was a sellout in 1996. Tickets were even sold at bookstores owned and operated by the Southern Baptist Convention.
- Disney and Universal aren't the only central-Florida attractions with film stars on the rolls. Klondike and Snow, the polar-bear twins at Sea World, became the darlings of Denver after they were discovered abandoned by their mother. Their pre–Sea World life is the subject of a documentary often seen on public broadcasting stations.

In the Words of Walt Disney

I only hope we never lose sight of one thing. . . that it was all started by a mouse.

- Disney, where employees are "cast members," continued to create its own lexicon with the opening of its school in the new Disney-designed town of Celebration. Although this is a public school, Disney has imposed a private language. Students are known as "learners," teachers are "specialists," and the principal is called the "director." And Celebration has not a school but "a community of learners."
- If you're thinking of being part of one of the upcoming opening days, you may want to think again. If history is any indication, the grand openings scheduled over the next several years will be filled with glitches. The most recent example? When Universal Studios opened in 1990, several of the major rides didn't work, prompting a minor insurrection as dozens of irate visitors gathered in front of guest services demanding their money back. Actor Charlton Heston, one of dozens of stars flown in for the gala, said it was the first time he'd ever seen an entire limo motorcade turn around because it was headed the wrong way.
- It's a story even Disney couldn't make up. The Osbornes of Arkansas apparently took to heart the old hymn that says, "you can't be a beacon if your light don't shine." Their Christmas-light collection of 2 million-plus blinkers, twinklers, and strands shone so bright that neighbors complained about the incredible lightness of being near. There were rumors that air traffic was even disrupted, as well as the flow of faithful in cars, causing mile-long backups in a mostly rural area where a couple of pickups in front of the feed store was considered a major delay. The neighbors, finally seeing the light, went to court in what became a nationally known battle. Disney came to the rescue and in 1995 moved the whole thing to Orlando, adding a million or so additional bulbs. It's now known as the Osborne Family Christmas Lights. No complaints, yet.
- The Twilight Zone Tower of Terror was originally designed with a single, swooshing drop straight down 13 floors. Riders apparently felt a little cheated that the free fall was over so quickly, so Imagineers divided it into two shorter drops.
- Ever wonder why you never catch a glimpse of, say, Mickey relaxing with his head off or Pluto taking a cigarette break? The people inside the characters at Disney do have a very strict code of conduct: Absolutely no talking; Minnie Mouse must always sign her name in cursive. But, beyond that, the characters and their keepers, along with all the Disney "cast," travel around the park through an intricate system of underground tunnels that are strictly off-limits to the public.
- Disney's hidden Mickey mania probably hit some kind of peak in 1994 with the opening of Disney's Wilderness Lodge. There are 16 hidden Mickeys within the resort. Eight are carved in the balconies of guest rooms. Eight are in public areas. (Hint: One is hidden in the screen of the 82-foot fireplace in the lobby.)
- Disney annually gives away dozens of T-shirts during the unofficial "Gay Day" on June 6. Those supporting homosexuals are encouraged to wear red during this loosely organized celebration of gay pride. Disney traditionally provides dozens of T-shirts to unwitting tourists who wear red that day but feel strongly about not being identified as part of the "Gay Day" crowd.
- *BOOOOMMMMM, BOOOOMMMMM.* Tourists may find themselves occasionally awakened by window-rattling double booms. Don't worry; it's not part of the rumored American crime culture—it's the space shuttle landing. The twin sonic booms are produced as the shuttle reenters the atmosphere. The loud, thunderous sound can be heard from Cape Canaveral on the coast throughout Orange, Seminole, and Osceola counties, including the tourist areas.

Planning a Trip to Walt Disney World & Orlando

Orlando is so packed with attractions that advance planning is crucial. In this chapter, I've compiled everything you need to know before you go. In addition to the information below, see chapters 5 (for accommodations), 7 (for Walt Disney World), and 8 (for other attractions in the Orlando area) for other tips.

1 Visitor Information

As soon as you know you're going to Orlando, write or call the **Orlando/Orange County Convention & Visitors Bureau,** 8723 International Dr., Suite 101, Orlando, FL 32819 (☎ **407/363-5871**). The bureau can answer all your questions and will be happy to send you maps, brochures (including the informative *Official Visitors Guide,* the *African-American Visitors Guide,* the *Area Guide* to local restaurants, and the *Official Accommodations Guide*). The packet includes the "Magicard," good for discounts of 10% to 50% on accommodations, attractions, car rentals, and more.

For general information about Walt Disney World—and a copy of the informative *Walt Disney World Vacations* brochure—write or call the **Walt Disney World Co.,** Box 10000, Lake Buena Vista, FL 32830-1000 (☎ **407/934-7639**).

Also contact the **Kissimmee–St. Cloud Convention & Visitors Bureau,** 1925 E. Irlo Bronson Memorial Hwy. (U.S. 192), Kissimmee, FL 34744, or P.O. Box 422007, Kissimmee, FL 34742-2007 (☎ **800/327-9159** or 407/847-5000). They'll send maps, brochures, discount coupon books, and the *Kissimmee–St. Cloud Vacation Guide,* which details the area's accommodations and attractions.

For information about the entire state—including Orlando and Kissimmee—write or call the **Florida Department of Commerce,** Division of Tourism, Visitor Inquiry, 126 Van Buren St., Tallahassee, FL 32399-2000 (☎ **904/487-1462**).

For information about the Winter Park area, contact the **Winter Park Chamber of Commerce,** 150 New York Ave., P.O. Box 280, Winter Park, FL 32790 (☎ **407/644-8281**).

WEB SITES

If you have Internet access, you can visit Walt Disney World's own web site at **http://www.disneyworld.com**, which has extensive, entertaining, and regularly updated information, including a live-action look from video cameras perched throughout the various parks. (This is mostly long-distance shots of tourists walking about, but is still a chance to see those blue Orlando skies and dream ahead to vacation time.) There are dozens of web pages devoted to Disney, especially Disney trivia. But one is a very informative newsgroup on Usenet called **rec.arts.disney**.

Information about Universal Studios can be found at **http://www.usf.com**, and Sea World information is available at **http://4adventure.com**. Both sites offer maps and a basic description of rides, shows, and ticket information. The city newspaper, the *Orlando Sentinel,* also produces *Orlando Sentinel Online* at **http://www.oso@aol.com**. Once there, click into "Theme Park Central" for a variety of information and updates on what is going on at local attractions.

2 Money

Disney parks, resorts, shops, and restaurants (but not fast-food outlets) accept the three major credit cards—American Express, MasterCard, and Visa. Disney offers some resort guests a debit card that can be used in park shops and restaurants.

You can also purchase Disney dollars (currency bearing the images of Mickey, Goofy, and Minnie), available in $1, $5, and $10 denominations; they're good at shops, restaurants, and resorts throughout the Disney realm, as well as Disney stores everywhere. I don't suggest you buy these Disney dollars, because you'll have to cash in leftover bills for real currency upon leaving (a bother), or you'll be stuck with something, as they say in New York, that with a token will get you on the subway.

You can get cash advances on MasterCard and Visa, cash traveler's checks, cash personal checks of $25 or less (drawn on U.S. banks, upon presentation of a valid driver's license and a major credit card), and exchange foreign currency at branches of the **SunTrust** on Main Street in the Magic Kingdom (open 9am to 4pm daily; ☎ 407/828-6102) and at 1675 Buena Vista Dr., across from the Disney Village Marketplace (open weekdays 9am to 4pm, until 6pm on Thursday; ☎ 407/828-6106).

ATM machines are conveniently located on Main Street and in Tomorrowland in the Magic Kingdom; at the entrances to Disney–MGM Studios and Epcot; at Pleasure Island; at Disney Village Marketplace; at the All-Star Sports Resort; and at the Crossroads Shopping Center.

There are also ATM machines near the entrance to Sea World and at Universal located in the First Union National Bank inside the main entrance, near guest services.

It may come as a surprise to foreign tourists just how prevalent ATM machines are in central Florida. Most malls have at least one ATM and they can even be found in many convenience stores, namely 7-11s and Circle Ks. There may be an extra charge for using these nonbank machines. Depending on your institution, charges usually range from $1 to $1.50 per transaction. The fee may sometimes be higher in areas with heavy tourist traffic.

Tourists should exercise caution with accessing ATM machines, especially at night and in areas that are not well-lit and heavily traveled. When entering your ATM Personal Identification Number, be sure to shield the keyboard from anyone who may be in line or observing from a distance. Also, keep all doors locked when accessing a drive-through ATM. The common ATM networks are Cirrus, Honor, MasterCard, Plus, and Van.

What Things Cost in Orlando	U.S. $
Taxi from airport to WDW area	38.00
Bus from airport to WDW area (adult fare)	25.00
Double room at Disney's Grand Floridian Beach Resort (very expensive)	290.00–365.00
Double room at Marriott's Orlando World Center (expensive)	159.00–219.00
Double room at Disney's Port Orleans Resort (moderate)	95.00–129.00
Double room at Disney's All-Star Music Resort (inexpensive)	69.00–79.00
Double room at Comfort Inn Maingate, Kissimmee (inexpensive)	39.00–69.00
Seven-course prix-fixe dinner for one at Victoria & Albert's, not including tip or wine (very expensive)	80.00
Three-course dinner at L'Originale Alfredo di Roma in Epcot, not including tip or wine (expensive)	30.00
All-you-can-eat buffet dinner at Akershus in Epcot, not including tip or wine (inexpensive)	17.95
Bottle of beer (restaurant)	2.25
Coca-Cola (restaurant)	1.25
Cup of coffee	1.25
Roll of ASA 100 Kodacolor film, 36 exposures, purchased at Walt Disney World	7.35
Adult 4-Day Value Pass admission to Walt Disney World	136.74
Four-Day Value Pass admission to Walt Disney World for children ages 3–9	109.18
Adult 1-day admission to Sea World	39.95
One-day admission to Sea World for children ages 3–9	32.80
Adult 1-day admission to Universal Studios	40.81
One-day admission to Universal Studios for children ages 3–9	32.85

3 When to Go

Orlando is essentially a theme-park destination, and its busiest seasons are whenever kids are out of school—summer (early June to about August 20), holiday weekends, Christmas season (mid-December to mid-January), and Easter. Obviously, the whole experience is more enjoyable when the crowds are thinnest and the weather is the most temperate. Hotel rooms are also priced lower off-season. Best times: the week after Labor Day until Thanksgiving, the week after Thanksgiving until mid-December, and the 6 weeks before and after school spring vacations. Worst time: summer, when crowds are very large and weather is oppressively hot and humid. I probably shouldn't say this, but I would pull the kids out of school for a few days around an off-season weekend to avoid long lines.

Central Florida Average Temperatures

	Jan	Feb	Mar	Apr	May	June	July	Aug	Sept	Oct	Nov	Dec
High °F	71.7	72.9	78.3	83.6	88.3	90.6	91.7	91.6	89.7	84.4	78.2	73.1
°C	22.0	22.7	25.7	28.7	31.3	32.5	33.2	33.1	32.0	29.1	25.7	22.8
Low °F	49.3	50.0	55.3	60.3	66.2	71.2	73.0	73.4	72.5	65.4	56.8	50.9
°C	9.6	10.0	12.5	15.7	19.0	21.8	22.7	23.0	22.5	18.6	13.8	10.5

ORLANDO AREA CALENDAR OF EVENTS

January

✪ **CompUSA Florida Citrus Bowl.** January kicks off with this football event, located in downtown Orlando and featuring two of the year's top college teams. Tickets ($28) go on sale in late October or early November. Call ☎ 407/423-2476 for information; 407/839-3900 for tickets.

✪ **Walt Disney World Marathon.** This 26.2-mile marathon winding through the resort and theme park areas is open to all, including the physically challenged. The $50 entry fee is included in the room price with some Disney resort packages. Preregistration is required. Call ☎ 407/824-4321 for details.

✪ **The Zora Neale Hurston Festival.** This 4-day celebration in Eatonville, the first incorporated African-American town in America, highlights the life and works of author Zora Neale Hurston and is usually held the last weekend in January. Eatonville is about 25 miles north of the theme parks. Call ☎ 800/352-3865 for details.

February

✪ **The Silver Spurs Rodeo,** featuring real cowboys in contests of calf roping, bull and bronco riding, barrel racing, and more, is a celebration of the area's rural, pre-Disney roots. It's held at the Silver Spurs Arena, 1875 E. Irlo Bronson Memorial Hwy. (U.S. 192) in Kissimmee, on the third weekend in February. Call ☎ 407/847-5000 for details. Tickets $15.

March

• **Kissimmee Bluegrass Festival.** Major bluegrass and gospel entertainers from all over the country perform at this 4-day event, beginning the first weekend of March at the Silver Spurs Arena, 1875 E. Irlo Bronson Memorial Hwy. Tickets are $12 to $20; multiday packages are available. Call ☎ 800/473-7773 for details.

• **The Central Florida Fair.** During 11 days in early March (some years beginning late February), the fair, held at the Central Florida Fairgrounds, 4603 W. Colonial Dr., features rides, entertainers, 4-H and livestock exhibits, a petting zoo, and food booths. Adults pay $6, children 6 to 10 are charged $3, and children 5 and under enter free. Call ☎ 407/295-3247 for details.

✪ **Bay Hill Invitational.** Hosted by Arnold Palmer, this PGA Tour event is held in mid-March at the Bay Hill Club, 9000 Bay Hill Blvd. Daily admission is $28; week-long admission, $50. Call ☎ 407/876-2888 for details.

• **The Spring Flower Festival.** From March to May at Cypress Gardens, the festival features more than 30,000 brightly colored bedding plants and flowers creating beautiful topiaries shaped as butterflies, birds, and animals. You have to pay admission to the park to get into the festival: adults $29.50, children $24.95, seniors $24.50. Call ☎ 941/324-2111 for details.

• **The Sidewalk Art Festival.** Held in Winter Park's Central Park, this exhibition draws artists from all over North America during the third full weekend in March. The festival is consistently named one of the best in the nation by the national magazine *Sunshine Artist.* Call ☎ 407/623-3234 or 407/644-8281 for details. Admission is free, although you may have to pay for parking.

April

✪ **Fringe Festival.** Over 100 diverse acts from around the world participate in this eclectic event, held for 10 days at various stages in downtown Orlando. Entertainers perform drama, comedy, political satire, and experimental theater. Everything, from sword swallowers to actors doing a 7-minute version of Hamlet performed on outdoor stages, is available to Fringe-goers free after they purchase a festival button for under $5. Ticket prices vary, but individual performances are generally under $12. Call ☎ 407/648-1333 for details.

- **Orlando Rays Baseball Season.** The Chicago Cubs farm team plays at Tinker Field, 287 Tampa Ave. S., from April to early September. Admission is $3 to $7. Call ☎ 407/245-2827 for details.

- **Easter Sunrise Service.** An interdenominational service, with music, is presented at the Atlantis Theatre at Sea World, 7007 Sea World Dr. It is hosted by a well-known person each year, most recently Elizabeth Dole. Admission is free. Call ☎ 407/351-3600 for details.

- **Easter Sunday** is celebrated in Walt Disney World with an old-fashioned Easter Parade and early opening/late closing throughout the season. Call ☎ 407/824-4321 for details.

May

- **Epcot International Flower and Garden Festival.** A month-long event with theme gardens, topiary characters, special floral displays, speakers, and seminars.

June

✪ **Gay Weekend.** The first weekend in June has become known for attracting tens of thousands of gay and lesbian travelers to central Florida. In 1997, Universal City Travel offered a "Gay Weekend" tour package including tickets to Universal Studios, Sea World, and Church Street Station. This is all grown out of "Gay Day," which has been held unofficially at Walt Disney World for about 5 years, drawing upwards of 40,000 folks. Special events throughout the weekend cater to gay and lesbian travelers throughout central Florida. Universal City Travel offers special packages (☎ 800/224-3838 for information). Carla. Also get information on the Internet by accessing **http://www.gayday.com**.

- **Walt Disney World Wine Festival.** More than 60 wineries from all over the United States participate. Events include wine tastings, seminars, food, and celebrity-chef cooking demonstrations at Disney's Yacht and Beach Club Convention Center. Call ☎ 407/827-7200 or 407/824-4321 for details.

- **Walt Disney World All-American College Orchestra and College Band.** The best collegiate musical talent in the country performs at Epcot and the Magic Kingdom throughout the summer. Call ☎ 407/824-4321 for details.

July

- **Independence Day.** Walt Disney World's Star-Spangled Spectacular brings bands, singers, dancers, and unbelievable fireworks displays to all the Disney parks, which stay open late. Call ☎ 407/824-4321 for details. Sea World also features a dazzling laser/fireworks spectacular; call ☎ 407/351-3600 for details.

- **The Silver Spurs Rodeo.** This event returns to Kissimmee every year over the July 4th weekend (see "February," above, for more information).

September

- **Night of Joy.** One weekend in September, the Magic Kingdom hosts a festival of contemporary Christian music featuring top artists. This is a very popular event;

obtain tickets early. Each year performers make a personal appearance at Long's Christian Bookstore in nearby College Park, about 20 minutes north of Disney. Admission to the concert is about $25 to $30 per night. Exclusive use of Magic Kingdom attractions is included. Call ☎ **407/824-4321** for details about the concert. For information about the free appearance at Long's, call ☎ **407/422-0293.**

October

✪ **Magic Basketball.** Penny Hardaway and his teammates continue to perform Magic long after Shaquille O'Neal opted to go Hollywood with the Los Angeles Lakers. The Magic does battle against visiting teams between October and April at the Orlando Arena, 600 W. Amelia St. Ticket prices range from about $13 to $50. There are usually a few tickets, usually single seats, available the day before games involving lesser-known NBA challengers. Call ☎ **407/896-2442** for details, 407/839-3900 for tickets.

✪ **Halloween Horror Nights.** Universal Studios Florida transforms its studios and attractions for several weeks before and after Halloween—with haunted attractions, live bands, a psychopath's maze, special shows, and hundreds of ghouls and goblins roaming the studio streets. The studio essentially closes at dusk, reopening in a new macabre form a few hours later. Special admission is charged. Call ☎ **407/ 363-8000** for details.

✪ **Walt Disney World Oldsmobile Golf Classic.** Top PGA tour players compete for a total purse of $1 million at WDW golf courses in October's major golf event. Transplanted local golf phenom Tiger Woods is usually among the players. Daily ticket prices range from $8 to $15. The event is preceded by the world's largest golf tournament, the admission-free Oldsmobile Scramble. Call ☎ **407/824-4321** for details.

• **Walt Disney World Village Boat Show.** Central Florida's largest in-the-water boat show, featuring the best of new watercraft. At the Village Marketplace, over a 3-day weekend early in the month. Call ☎ **407/824-4321** for details.

November

• **Mum Festival.** November's month-long flower festival at Cypress Gardens features millions of mums, their colorful flowers displayed in beds, "blooming" gazebos, poodle baskets, and bonsais. Call ☎ **941/324-2111** for details.

✪ **The Walt Disney World Festival of the Masters.** One of the largest art shows in the South takes place at Disney's Village Marketplace for 3 days, including the second weekend in November. The exhibition features top artists, photographers, and craftspeople—winners of juried shows throughout the country. Free admission. Call ☎ **407/824-4321** for details.

• **Walt Disney World Doll and Teddy Bear Convention.** The top doll and teddy-bear designers from around the world travel to WDW for this major November event. Call ☎ **407/824-4321** for details.

✪ **Jolly Holidays Dinner Shows.** From late November to mid-December these all-you-can-eat events are offered at the Contemporary Resort's Fantasia Ballroom. A cast of more than 100 Disney characters, singers, and dancers performs in an old-fashioned Christmas extravaganza. Call ☎ **407/W-DISNEY** (934-7639) for details and ticket prices.

• **Poinsettia Festival.** A spectacular floral showcase of more than 40,000 red, white, and pink poinsettia blooms (including topiary reindeer) highlight this flower festival from late November to mid-January at Cypress Gardens. This is actually one of the best ways to view the park. Call ☎ **941/324-2111** for details.

December

- **Burger King Classic Half-Marathon and Hooter's 5K Run.** This annual race, early in December, takes place in downtown Orlando, beginning at Church Street Market, 200 S. Orange Ave. It begins at 8am. Anyone can participate. An entry fee is charged. The event kicks off the Citrus Bowl season. Call ☎ 407/423-2476 for information.

- ✪ **Christmas at Walt Disney World.** During the Walt Disney World Christmas festivities, Main Street is lavishly decked out with lights and holly, and visitors are greeted by carolers. An 80-foot tree is illuminated by thousands of colored lights. Epcot and MGM Studios also offer special embellishments and entertainment throughout the holiday season, as do all Disney resorts. Some holiday highlights include **Mickey's Very Merry Christmas Party,** an after-dark ticketed event. The admission price is $25. This takes place weekends at the Magic Kingdom with a traditional Christmas parade and a breathtaking fireworks display; the admission price includes free cookies and cocoa and a souvenir photo. The best part? Short lines to the rides. **The Candlelight Procession** at Epcot features hundreds of candle-holding carolers, a celebrity narrator telling the Christmas story, and a 450-voice choir. Call ☎ **407/824-4321** for details about all of the above, **407/ W-DISNEY** (934-7639) to inquire about hotel/events packages. **The Osborne Family Christmas Lights** came to Disney–MGM in 1995 when the Arkansas family ran into trouble with local authorities who claimed their multimillion-light display was too much of a spectacle and interfered with air traffic. In a twinkle, Disney moved the whole thing to central Florida.

- **Christmas at Sea World.** Sea World features a special Shamu show and a luau show called *Christmas in Hawaii.* The 400-foot sky tower is lit like a Christmas tree nightly. Call ☎ **407/351-3600** for details.

- **Walt Disney World New Year's Eve Celebration.** For one night the Magic Kingdom is open until 2am for a massive fireworks exhibition. Other New Year's festivities in the WDW parks include a big bash at Pleasure Island featuring music headliners, a special *Hoop-Dee-Doo Musical Revue* show, and guest performances by well-known musical groups at Disney–MGM Studios and Epcot. Call ☎ **407/ 824-4321** for details.

- ✪ **The Citrus Bowl Parade.** On an annually selected date in late December, the parade features lavish floats and high-school bands for a nationally televised parade. Reserved seats in the bleachers are $12. Call ☎ **407/423-2476** for details.

- **CompUSA Florida Citrus Bowl New Year's.** The official New Year's Eve celebration of the CompUSA Florida Citrus Bowl takes place at Sea World. Events include headliner concerts, a laser and fireworks spectacular, a countdown to midnight, and special shows throughout the park. Admission is charged. Call ☎ **407/423-2476** for details.

4 Tips for Travelers with Special Needs

FOR PEOPLE IN RECOVERY   Those friends of Bill W. and members of other 12-step programs can call the **Central Florida Intergroup of Alcoholics Anonymous** (☎ **407/521-0012**). This is the local AA hot line and is manned with volunteers 24 hours a day. Please be considerate, however, and don't call at three in the morning just for tourist information. They can provide information, including directions, to meetings in Orange and Seminole counties, as well as those in tourist areas. They can also provide numbers for other local 12-step programs such as

Narcotics Anonymous, Al-Anon, and Overeaters Anonymous, groups which also have information hot lines, but generally don't operate 24 hours.

Those looking to party away from the sometimes alcohol-drenched tourist areas can have an alcohol-free night at **Club Soda,** 6341 N. Orange Blossom Trail, about 35 miles from the heart of tourist central near the intersection of Clarcona–Ocoee Road and Orange Blossom Trail. For information call ☎ **407/523-1556.** Sunday and Tuesday are karaoke nights. Live music with a house band on Wednesday. DJ and dance on the weekends.

FOR TRAVELERS WITH DISABILITIES   There is no reason that those with disabilities can't get full enjoyment out of the theme parks—that is, with a little advance planning. Every hotel and motel is required by law to have a special room or rooms equipped for wheelchairs. A few, including **Best Western Buena Vista Suites** (☎ **407/239-8588**), **Embassy Suites** (☎ **407/239-1144**), and **Sleep Inn** (☎ **407/ 396-1600**), have wheel-in showers. Make your special needs known when making reservations.

All public buses in Orlando have a hydraulic lift and restraining belts for wheelchairs, and they serve Universal Studios, Sea World, and the shopping areas and downtown Orlando. When staying at Disney you can get a shuttle bus from your hotel that will also accommodate wheelchairs.

Most attractions at the various theme parks, especially newer ones, are designed to be accessible to a wide variety of people. People with wheelchairs, and their parties, are often given preferential treatment so they can avoid long lines.

The assistance that is available is outlined by each major park in a brochure, and all the parks offer some parking as close as possible to the park entrance for those with disabilities. Let the booth attendant know your needs so you will be directed to the appropriate spot. Wheelchair rentals are available at most major attractions, but you will probably be most comfortable with your chair from home. Keep in mind, however, wheelchairs wider than 24.5 inches may be difficult to navigate through some attractions. If you need to rent a special wheelchair van, call **Wheelers Inc.** (☎ **407/826-0616**) or **Vantage Mini Vans** (☎ **407/521-8002**).

Call the **Florida Governor's Alliance,** 345 S. Magnolia Dr., Suite D-11, Tallahassee, FL 32301 (☎ **904/487-2223** or 904/487-2222 TTD), for a free copy of *The Florida Planning Companion for People with Disabilities.* It offers valuable information on accessibility at tourist facilities throughout the state.

Walt Disney World does everything possible to facilitate disabled guests. Its many services are detailed in the *Guidebook for Guests with Disabilities.* To obtain a copy prior to your visit, write Guest Letters, P.O. Box 10040, Lake Buena Vista, FL 32830-0040, or call ☎ **407/824-4321.** Also call that number for answers to any questions regarding special needs. Some examples of Disney services:

- Almost all Disney resorts have rooms for those with disabilities.
- Braille directories are located inside the Magic Kingdom in front of the Main Street train station and in a gazebo in front of the Crystal Palace restaurant, and complimentary guided-tour audiocassette tapes and recorders are available at Guest Services to assist visually impaired guests.
- All three parks have special parking lots.
- Personal translator units are available to amplify the audio at selected Epcot attractions (inquire at Earth Station).
- Wheelchairs can be rented at all of the Disney parks.

For information about Telecommunications Devices for the Deaf (TDDs), call ☎ 407/827-5141.

At Universal Studios: Disabled guests should go to Guest Services located just inside the main entrance for a *Disabled Guest Guidebook,* a Telecommunications Device for the Deaf (TDD), or other special assistance. Wheelchairs are for rent. Universal also provides audio descriptions on cassette for visually impaired guests and has sign-language guides and scripts for all its shows (advance notice is required; ☎ 407/363-8000 for details).

At Sea World: The park has a guide for guests with disabilities, although most of its attractions are easily accessible to those in wheelchairs. Sea World provides a braille guide for the visually impaired. It also provides a very brief synopsis of shows for the hearing impaired. For information call ☎ 407/351-2600.

Some nationwide resources: Mobility International USA, P.O. Box 10767, Eugene, OR 97440 (☎ 541/343-1284), offers accessibility information and has many interesting travel programs for the disabled. Membership ($25 a year) includes a quarterly newsletter called *Over the Rainbow.* Help (accessibility information and more) is also available from the **Society for the Advancement of Travel for the Handicapped** (SATH), 347 Fifth Ave., Suite 610, New York, NY 10016 (☎ 212/447-7284). The latter charges $5 to send requested information.

Accessible Journeys (☎ 800/TINGLES or 610/521-0339) and **Flying Wheels Travel** (☎ 800/535-6790 or 507/451-5005) offer tours for people with physical disabilities. Accessible Journeys can also provide nurse/companions to travelers. **Guided Tour Inc.** (☎ 215/782-1370) has tours for people with physical or mental disabilities, the visually impaired, and the elderly.

Recommended books: A publisher called **Twin Peaks Press,** Box 129, Vancouver, WA 98666 (☎ 360/694-2462), specializes in books for people with disabilities. Write for their *Disability Bookshop Catalog,* enclosing $5.

Amtrak (☎ 800/USA-RAIL) provides redcap service, wheelchair assistance, and special seats with 72 hours' notice. Travelers with disabilities are also entitled to a discount of 15% off the lowest available adult coach fare. Children with disabilities ages 2 to 15 can also get a 50% discount on already discounted one-way disabled adult fares. Documentation from a doctor or an ID card proving your disability is required. Amtrak also provides wheelchair-accessible sleeping accommodations on long-distance trains, and service dogs are permissible and travel free of charge. For a free booklet called *Amtrak's America,* which has a chapter detailing services for passengers with disabilities, call ☎ 800/USA-RAIL or write to Amtrak Distribution Center, P.O. Box 7717, Itasca, IL 60143.

Greyhound (☎ 800/752-4841) allows a traveler with disabilities to travel with a companion for a single fare and, if you call 48 hours in advance, they will arrange help along the way.

FOR SENIORS Always carry some form of photo ID so that you can take advantage of discounts wherever they're offered. And it never hurts to ask.

If you haven't already done so, consider joining the **American Association of Retired Persons** (AARP) (☎ 202/434-2277). Annual membership costs $8 per person or per couple. You must be at least 50 to join. Membership entitles you to many discounts. Write to Purchase Privilege Program, AARP Fulfillment, 601 E St. NW, Washington, DC 20049, to receive a free list of hotels, motels, and car-rental firms nationwide that offer discounts to AARP members.

Elderhostel is a national organization that offers low-priced educational programs for people over 55 (your spouse can be any age; a companion must be at least 50). Programs are generally a week long, and prices average about $335 per person, including room, board, and classes. For information on programs in Florida, call or write Elderhostel Headquarters, 75 Federal St., Boston, MA 02110-1941

A Fairy-Tale Wedding

Fly down the aisle on Aladdin's magic carpet? Pull up in a glass coach pulled by six white horses? Have Mickey and Minnie greet guests at the reception? Take the plunge, literally and figuratively, on the Twilight Zone Tower of Terror?

If you've always dreamed of meeting Prince Charming and then having a fairy-tale wedding, the folks at Disney are happy to oblige—for a price. Recognizing that Disney World is a popular honeymoon destination, Disney in 1995 cut out the middle man and officially went into the wedding business. The first step was building a multimillion-dollar, nondenominational chapel in the middle of the Seven Seas Lagoon. The next step was letting the world know the Disney wedding chapel was open for business. The first nuptials were televised live on Lifetime television. (Construction was still in progress at the chapel, so the bride and groom wore white hard hats.) About 1,700 couples were married that first year, and now thousands of couples mix matrimony with Disney magic at the pavilion, which resembles a Victorian summer house.

An intimate gathering for two is about $2,000. The *average* Disney wedding costs $19,000 and is attended by 100 people (Prince Charming not included). People from as far away as the Netherlands have traveled to Orlando for sometimes unusual celebrations to recognize their lifetime commitment to one another. One couple had every guest wear Mickey Mouse ears to the ceremony. Another exchanged Donald and Daisy caps instead of wedding rings. A third walked out of the church to *"Zip-a-dee-doo-dah,"* and one blushing bride topped her veil with Mickey's famous ears. Those are just the examples Disney is willing to promote.

Certainly with the only limits being imagination and money there have been wackier weddings. From rented coachmen to topiaries in the shape of Pluto, Disney serves up whichever Disney reference or character the couple desires, even if it is Goofy.

For further details on Disney weddings (and honeymoons, of course), call ☎ **407/828-3400**.

(☎ **617/426-7788**) and ask for a free U.S. catalog. Or call the Florida office at ☎ **813/864-8312**.

Amtrak (☎ **800/USA-RAIL**) offers a 15% discount off the lowest available coach fare (with certain travel restrictions) to people 62 or over.

Greyhound also offers discounted fares for senior citizens. Call your local Greyhound office for details.

FOR FAMILIES   No city in the world is more geared to family travel than Orlando. In addition to its theme parks, recreational facilities provide abundant opportunities for family fun. Every restaurant in town has a low-priced children's menu, and many hotels maintain children's activity centers (see details in chapter 5). Keep an eye opened for coupons. Many local restaurants, especially those in tourist areas, offer great discounts that are yours for the clipping. *Central Florida Family* magazine and *Black Family Today* both highlight family-friendly—often free—festivals and events in the Orlando area.

Disney–MGM Studios and Universal Studios offer parent-swap programs in which parents with children can switch off watching the young ones while the other parents ride. In both parks, ask attendants at the specific attraction what needs to be done.

Here are a few general suggestions to make traveling with kids easier:

Packing Although your home may be toddler-proof, hotel accommodations are not. Bring blank plugs to cover outlets and whatever else is necessary. Locals can spot tourists by their bright red, just-toasted glow; heed this reminder for parents and children: *Don't forget the sunscreen.*

Accommodations Children under 12, and in many cases even older, stay free in their parents' rooms in most hotels. Look for establishments that have pools and other recreational facilities. If you don't want to rent a car and aren't staying at Disney, International Drive is the place to be. Public buses run frequently, hotels often offer family discounts, and some provide free shuttle service to the homes of the Mouse, the Whale, and King Kong.

Ground Rules Set up ground rules before leaving home about issues such as bedtime and spending money on souvenirs.

At the Parks All park maps explain height restrictions or rides that may unsettle young children. Do yourself and your kids a favor by knowing these restrictions before you get in line. These rules are not bent, no matter how much your child may cry.

Take a Break The Disney parks, Universal Studios, and Sea World all have stylized play areas offering parents and kids a rest. Schedule time to take advantage of these facilities. Since most of these kid zones include toys involving water and all the parks have major water-related attractions, you'd be smart to pack a change of clothes for the kids. Rent a locker and store the spare duds until you need them. Even in summer months the Florida humidity may keep you feeling soggy all day.

Snack Times When dreaming of your vacation, you probably don't envision hours spent standing in lines and waiting and waiting. It helps to store some lightweight snacks in an easy-to-carry backpack, especially if traveling with small children. This may save you some headaches and will certainly save some money.

Bring Your Own? Unless you are unusually attached to your stroller or it is specially designed for triplets, it's better to use one provided by the park in order to avoid hauling yours to and from the car and on and off the trams, trains, or monorails.

FOR GAY & LESBIAN TRAVELERS The popularity of Orlando with gay and lesbian travelers has been highlighted as the traditional June 6 celebration at Disney World known as "Gay Day" has expanded into a "Gay Weekend," including events at Universal Studios and Sea World. In 1997, Universal City Travel first offered a **"Gay Weekend"** tour package including tickets to Universal Studios, Sea World, and Church Street Station. ("Gay Day," unofficially held at Walt Disney World since the early 1990s, has drawn as many as 40,000 folks. On that day park-goers are supposed to wear red to signify their support of the gay and lesbian community.)

For information on tour packages offered by Universal City Travel, call ☎ **800/ 224-3838.** You can also get information on the Internet by accessing **http:// www.gayday.com**.

For information about events for that weekend, or throughout the year, contact **Gay & Lesbian Community Services of Central Florida** by writing 714 E. Colonial Dr., Orlando, FL 32804, or by calling ☎ **407/425-4527.** Ask for a welcome packet. This will include the latest issue of the *Triangle,* a monthly newspaper dedicated to gay and lesbian issues, plus a calendar of events pertaining to the gay and lesbian community. This is not a tourist-specific packet, but contains valuable information. Check out the advertisement for nightclubs focused on a gay and lesbian crowd. For information on the *Triangle* specifically—for example, where it can be picked up in tourist areas—call ☎ **407/849-0099.**

Kid-Friendly Tours

Sea World lives up to its reputation for making education fun with a variety of tours. One of the newest—and most interesting—is the **Polar Expedition Guided Tour.** This hour-long tour provides kids with a chance to visit with Sea World's new stars, Klondike and Snow. It also offers a behind-the-scenes look at penguins. This tour is suitable for children of all ages. It's booked on a first-come, first-serve basis, so make reservations for one of the four daily outings upon entering the park. Go to the Guided Tour Information desk. With the price of admission, the cost is $5 for adults, $4 for children. Tours are offered at 9:30am, 10:30am, 2pm, and 3pm. For more information call ☎ 407/351-2600.

At Walt Disney World, half-day **Disney Day Camp** excursions are for children ages 7 to 10. From exploring special effects at Disney–MGM to experiencing the wonders of China at Epcot, these provide a good opportunity for kids to interact with their peers while providing parents with a little time alone. Disney offers two programs each day, the first from 8am to noon, the second from 1:30 to 5pm. The cost is $75 per child; a box lunch is provided for an additional charge. Theme park admission is not required to take part. For information call ☎ 407/939-8687. Advance registration is required. Tours are included in some comprehensive Disney packages.

Orlando is a Southern town, but same-sex dancing is acceptable at most of the clubs at WDW's Pleasure Island, especially the large, crowded Mannequins. (Really, who can tell who is dancing with whom most of the time?) Many of Universal's City Walk establishments are similarly gender blind. The tenor of crowds can change, depending on what tour is in town, so respect your own intuition.

Same-sex dancing is not expressly forbidden at Church Street Station, but the biggest dance hall is a country honky-tonk frequented by some real, local cowboys, and we *are* in Dixieland. I've never heard of anyone being asked to leave for dancing, but the crowd probably won't make for your most comfortable two-step. (Lots of line dancing is done, though.)

There are a few exclusively gay or lesbian bars and clubs in Orlando, and they're described in chapter 10.

5 Getting There

BY PLANE

THE MAJOR AIRLINES   Delta (☎ 800/221-1212) has the most flights—over 25%—into Orlando International Airport. It offers service from 200 cities and has a Fantastic Flyer program for kids. Delta Express offers direct service from 14 cities and also has the Fantastic Flyer program for kids. Other carriers include **Air Jamaica** (☎ 800/523-5585), **America West** (☎ 800/235-9292), **American** (☎ 800/433-7300), **American Trans Air** (☎ 800/293-6194), **British Airways** (☎ 800/247-9297), **Continental** (☎ 800/231-0856), **Midway** (☎ 800/446-4392), **Northwest** (☎ 800/225-2525), **SunJet** (☎ 800/4SUNJET), **Transbrasil** (☎ 800/872-3153), **TWA** (☎ 800/221-2000), **United** (☎ 800/241-6522), **US Airways** (☎ 800/428-4322), and **Virgin Atlantic** (☎ 800/862-8621).

FINDING THE BEST AIRFARE   Here are some tips for discovering the lowest airfares:

- Since advance-purchase fares are almost always the lowest available, it's a good idea to book your flight as far in advance as possible. Advance-purchase fares can be as much as 75% lower than fares booked at the last minute!
- The more flexible you can be about your travel dates and length of stay, the more money you're likely to save.
- Visit a large travel agency to investigate all options. Sometimes a good agent knows about fares you won't find on your own.
- Check newspaper ads (especially in the travel sections of high-circulation papers like the Sunday *New York Times* Travel section) for announcements of short-term promotional fares.
- Fly at off times (for instance, at night) when planes are less likely to be full.

ORLANDO'S AIRPORT   Serving over 22 million passengers each year, **Orlando International Airport** (☎ **407/825-2001**) is a thoroughly modern and user-friendly facility with restaurants, shops, a 450-room on-premises Hyatt Regency Hotel, and centrally located information kiosks. All major car-rental companies are located at or near the airport; see "Getting Around" in chapter 4 for more information on rentals.

The airport is 25 miles from Walt Disney World. **Mears Transportation Group** (☎ **407/423-5566**) shuttle vans ply the route from the airport (board outside baggage claim) to all Disney resorts and official hotels as well as most other area properties. Their comfortable, air-conditioned vehicles operate around the clock, departing every 15 to 25 minutes in either direction. Rates vary with your destination. Round trip cost for adults is $21 between the airport and downtown Orlando or International Drive, $25 for Walt Disney World/Lake Buena Vista or Kissimmee/Hwy. 192. Children ages 4 to 11 pay $14 to downtown and $17 to WDW. Children 3 and under ride free.

Note: It's always a good idea when you make your reservations to ask about transportation options between the airport and your hotel, or, if you're planning to rent a car, ask for driving directions from the airport.

BY CAR

Orlando is 436 miles from Atlanta, 1,312 miles from Boston, 1,120 miles from Chicago, 1,009 miles from Cleveland, 1,170 miles from Dallas, 1,114 miles from Detroit, 1,105 miles from New York City, and 1,261 miles from Toronto.

From Atlanta, take I-75 south to the Florida Turnpike to I-4 west.

From points northeast, take I-95 south to I-4 west.

From Chicago, take I-65 south to Nashville and then I-24 south to I-75 south to the Florida Turnpike to I-4 west.

From Cleveland, take I-77 south to Columbia, South Carolina, and then I-26 east to I-95 south to I-4 west.

From Dallas, take I-20 east to I-49 south to I-10 east to I-75 south to the Florida Turnpike to I-4 west.

From Detroit, take I-75 south to the Florida Turnpike to I-4 west.

From Toronto, take Canadian Route 401 south to Queen Elizabeth Way south to I-90 (New York State Thruway) east to I-87 (New York State Thruway) south to I-95 over the George Washington Bridge, and continue south on I-95 to I-4 west.

AAA (☎ **800/222-4357**) and some other automobile-club members can call local offices for maps and optimum driving directions.

Mickey & Bugs Battle on the High Seas

Can the Disney magic float? Michael Eisner and friends try to extend their reach all the way out to sea as the first Disney-owned and -operated cruise ships, the *Disney Magic* and *Disney Wonder,* take their maiden voyages in 1998. Seven-day cruise packages include 3 or 4 days afloat with the rest of the week divided among the land-locked properties. The average cost for a family of four is expected to be about $4,500. Cruises depart from Port Canaveral, about an hour by car from Orlando. Although Disney reported that reservations were coming in months before the maiden voyages, space will likely be available. Each ship will hold up to 1,760 passengers. These cruises will attempt to create the theme-park magic on water, complete with character visits and entertainment with the Disney touch. For information call ☎ 407/566-3500.

Premier Cruise Lines (the "Big Red Boat"), previously the official Disney cruise line, continues to offer 3- and 4-night luxury ocean cruises to the Bahamas (Nassau and Port Lucaya) in conjunction with 3- or 4-day Orlando theme-park vacations. Cruises depart from and return to Port Canaveral, 45 minutes from Walt Disney World. You can add the island segment before or after your stay in Orlando. The major change with Disney making its splash is a greater focus by Premier on other Orlando-area attractions with better deals likely to be available for those interested in visiting Universal, Sea World, and other non-Disney area attractions. Looney Tunes characters (Bugs Bunny, Tweety, Daffy Duck) are your on-board hosts. Package prices include all meals on-board ship, an Alamo rental car with unlimited mileage for 7 days, round-trip airfare to/from Orlando, and admission to varied attractions. Rates depend on stateroom and hotel category and the season you're traveling. At this writing, 7-night packages with a New York departure start at about $899 per person, based on double occupancy; $589 for children under 9. Call ☎ 800/327-7113 for details.

All ships are equipped with swimming pools, Jacuzzis, health clubs, jogging tracks, movie theaters, beauty salons, casinos, bar/lounges, video-game arcades, shops, and nightclubs.

BY TRAIN

Amtrak trains (☎ 800/USA-RAIL) pull into stations at 1400 Sligh Blvd., between Columbia and Miller streets in downtown Orlando (about 23 miles from Walt Disney World), and 111 Dakin Ave., at Thurman Street in Kissimmee (about 15 miles from Walt Disney World).

From the Orlando station, you can catch **LYNX** bus no. 50, which departs weekdays at least once an hour between 6:45am and 8:45pm (weekends, take bus no. 7 or 11 from the stop at the corner of Orange and Columbia avenues, 2 blocks away). All trips involve a transfer at the downtown bus station—not too much of a hassle because the bus will usually be right there when you arrive. This connecting bus (no. 8) makes stops about every 1 1/2 blocks along International Drive, culminating at Sea World, where you can get a taxi (about $28) to Walt Disney World–area hotels. For further details about bus transportation from the Orlando Amtrak station, call ☎ 407/841-8240. A taxi from the Orlando Amtrak station to Walt Disney World–area hotels is about $42.

From the Kissimmee Amtrak station, a taxi (about $28 to WDW-area hotels) is your only option.

FARES As with airline fares, you can sometimes get discounts if you book far in advance. There may be some restrictions on travel dates for discounted fares, mostly around very busy holiday times. Amtrak also offers money-saving packages—including hotel accommodations (some at WDW resorts), car rentals, tours, and more—with your train fare (☎ 800/321-8684).

AMTRAK'S AUTO TRAIN Amtrak's Auto Train offers the convenience of having a car in Florida without driving it there. The Auto Train begins in Lorton, Virginia—about a 4-hour drive from New York, 2 hours from Philadelphia—and ends up at Sanford, Florida, about 23 miles northeast of Orlando. Once again, reserve early for the lowest fares. The Auto Train departs Lorton and Sanford at 4:30pm daily, arriving at its destination at 9am the next morning. *Note:* You have to arrive 1 or 2 hours before departure time so they can board your car. Call ☎ **800/USA-RAIL** for details.

BY BUS

Greyhound buses connect the entire country with Orlando. They pull into a terminal at 555 N. Magruder Blvd. (John Young Parkway), between West Colonial Drive and Winter Garden Road, a few miles west of downtown Orlando (☎ **407/292-3422**), or in Kissimmee at 16 N. Orlando Ave., between Emmett and Mabbette streets, about 14 miles from Walt Disney World (☎ **407/847-3911**). There is van transport from the Kissimmee terminal to most area hotels and motels. From Orlando, you can call for a Mears shuttle van (☎ **407/423-5566**), which will cost $12 to $13 one way to a Walt Disney World–area hotel, $8 for children ages 4 to 11, free for those under 4 (round-trip fares are less). For the return trip, call from your hotel 24 hours in advance. A taxi to Walt Disney World–area hotels will cost about $40. Greyhound's fare structure tends to be complex, but the good news is that when you call to make a reservation, the agent will always give you the lowest-fare options. Once again, advance-purchase fares booked 3 to 21 days prior to travel represent vast savings. Check your phone book for a local Greyhound listing or call ☎ **800/231-2222**.

6 Packages

Frankly, the number and diversity of package tours to Orlando are staggering. But significant savings are available for those willing to do the research. Best bet: Stop at a sizable travel agency and pick up brochures from several companies. Pore over them at home, comparing offerings to find the optimum package for your trip. Also obtain the *Walt Disney World Vacations* brochure (see details at the beginning of this chapter), which lists the company's own packages. Try to find a package that meets rather than exceeds your needs; there's no sense in paying for elements you won't use. Also, read over the advantages accruing to Disney resort guests in chapter 5; some packages list as selling points services that are automatically available to every Walt Disney World guest.

Since 1996, Universal Studios has offered its own packages through **Universal City Travel Company** (☎ **800/224-3838**). These packages highlight Universal Studios and offer special VIP access to the park and rides, and discounts to other parks. Universal City Travel also offers trips that include stays at beach hotels before or after the theme-park trips. These excursions are billed as "an alternative resort experience."

Examples of airline-run packages are the **Delta Dream Vacations,** in several price ranges, which include round-trip air transport; accommodations (including state and hotel-room tax and baggage gratuities); an air-conditioned intermediate rental car with unlimited mileage or round-trip airport transfer; a "Magic Passport" that provides unlimited admission to all Walt Disney World parks for the length of your stay; one breakfast (which can be a character breakfast); and entry into a selected theme park 1 hour before regular opening time. In packages utilizing Walt Disney World Resorts, you get all the advantages accruing to guests at these properties (see chapter 5 for details). At this writing, 3-night midweek packages begin at $369 to $409 per person (based on double occupancy and New York departure; range reflects season). If you put all of those components together on your own, the cost would be much, much higher. In fact, a Delta Dream Vacation can cost less than airfare alone from certain cities. Delta also has Orlando packages for which WDW tickets and resorts are optional. For details, call ☎ **800/872-7786.**

Additional airline and tour-operator sources for airfare-inclusive packages include **US Airways Vacations** (☎ 800/455-0123), **American Airlines Fly Away Vacations** (☎ 800/321-2121), **American Express Vacations** (☎ 800/241-1700), **Travel Impressions** (☎ 800/941-2639), and **Kingdom Tours** (☎ 800/872-8857).

For Foreign Visitors 3

This chapter will provide some specifics about getting to Orlando as economically as possible from overseas, plus some helpful information about how things are done in the United States—from mailing a postcard to making a phone call.

1 Preparing for Your Trip

VISITOR INFORMATION IN THE UNITED KINGDOM

There is an **Orlando Tourism Office** in London. For information from that office, write to 18–24 Westbourne Grove, London, England, W25RH (☎ **44/171-243-8072;** fax 44/171-243-8487). You can also e-mail that office at **106211.1754@compuserve.com**.

ENTRY REQUIREMENTS

DOCUMENT REGULATIONS   Canadian citizens may enter the United States without visas; they need only proof of residence.

Citizens of the United Kingdom, New Zealand, Japan, and most other western European countries traveling on valid passports may not need a visa for fewer than 90 days of holiday or business travel to the United States, provided that they hold a round-trip or return ticket and enter the United States on an airline or cruise line that participates in the visa waiver program.

(Note that citizens of these visa-exempt countries who first enter the United States may then visit Mexico, Canada, Bermuda, and/or the Caribbean islands and then reenter the States, by any mode of transportation, without needing a visa. Further information is available from any U.S. embassy or consulate. See "Fast Facts: For the Foreign Traveler," below.)

Citizens of countries other than those stipulated above, including citizens of Australia, must have two documents: a valid **passport,** with an expiration date at least 6 months later than the scheduled end of the visit to the United States; and a **tourist visa,** available without charge from the nearest U.S. consulate. To obtain a visa, the traveler must submit a completed application form (either in person or by mail) with a 1¹/₂-inch square photo and demonstrate binding ties to a residence abroad.

Usually you can obtain a visa at once or within 24 hours, but it may take longer during the summer rush from June to August. If you cannot go in person, contact the nearest U.S. embassy or consulate for directions on applying by mail. Your travel agent or airline office may also be able to provide you with visa applications and instructions. The U.S. consulate or embassy that issues your visa will determine whether you will be issued a multiple- or single-entry visa and any restrictions regarding the length of your stay.

MEDICAL REQUIREMENTS   No inoculations are needed to enter the United States unless you are coming from, or have stopped over in, areas known to be suffering from epidemics, particularly cholera or yellow fever.

If you have a disease requiring treatment with medications containing narcotics or drugs requiring a syringe, carry a valid signed prescription from your physician to allay any suspicions that you are smuggling drugs.

CUSTOMS REQUIREMENTS   Every adult visitor may bring in free of duty: 1 liter of wine or hard liquor; 200 cigarettes or 100 cigars (but no cigars from Cuba) or 3 pounds of smoking tobacco; and $100 worth of gifts. These exemptions are offered to travelers who spend at least 72 hours in the United States and who have not claimed them within the preceding 6 months. It is altogether forbidden to bring into the country foodstuffs (particularly cheese, fruit, cooked meats, and canned goods) and plants (vegetables, seeds, tropical plants, and so on). Foreign tourists may bring in or take out up to $10,000 in U.S. or foreign currency with no formalities; larger sums must be declared to Customs upon entering or leaving.

INSURANCE

There is no national health-care system in the United States. Because the cost of medical care is extremely high, we strongly advise every traveler to secure health coverage before setting out.

You may want to take out a comprehensive travel policy that covers (for a relatively low premium) sickness or injury costs (medical, surgical, and hospital); loss or theft of your baggage; trip-cancellation costs; guarantee of bail in case you are arrested; and costs of accident, repatriation, or death. Such packages (for example, "Europe Assistance" in Europe) are sold by automobile clubs at attractive rates, as well as by insurance companies and travel agencies.

Walk-in medical clinics are available, with a visit usually costing under $50, not including prescriptions. **Centra-Care,** operated by locally run Florida Hospital, is a reputable medical facility with more than a dozen locations throughout the Orlando area. For information and the nearest location, call ☎ 407/660-8118.

MONEY

CURRENCY & EXCHANGE   The U.S. monetary system has a decimal base: one American **dollar ($1)** = 100 **cents (100¢).**

Dollar bills commonly come in $1 ("a buck"), $5, $10, $20, $50, and $100 denominations (the last two are not welcome when paying for small purchases and are not accepted in taxis). There are also $2 bills (seldom encountered).

There are six denominations of coins: 1¢ (one cent or "a penny"), 5¢ (five cents or "a nickel"), 10¢ (ten cents or "a dime"), 25¢ (twenty-five cents or "a quarter"), 50¢ (fifty cents or "a half dollar"), and the rare $1 piece.

The exchange bureaus so common in Europe are rare even at airports in the United States, and nonexistent outside major cities. Try to avoid having to change foreign money, or traveler's checks denominated other than in U.S. dollars, at a small-town bank, or even a branch in a big city.

You can exchange foreign currency at **Guest Services** windows in all three Disney parks, or at **City Hall** in the Magic Kingdom and **Earth Station** at Epcot. Currency can also be exchanged at Walt Disney World resorts and at the **Sun Bank** just across

---

Walt Disney World Services for International Visitors

Walt Disney World, which welcomes thousands of foreign visitors each year, has numerous services designed to meet their needs. Unless otherwise indicated, call ☎ **407/W-DISNEY** (934-7639) for details. Services include:

- A special phone number (☎ **407/824-7900**) to speak with someone in French or Spanish (other languages are sometimes available as well).
- Personal translator units (in French, German, and Spanish) to translate narrations at some shows and attractions.
- Detailed guidebooks to the three major parks in Spanish, French, German, Portuguese, and Japanese (available at any guest relations location).
- Currency exchange (see above).
- World Key Terminals at Epcot that offer basic park information and assistance with dining reservations in Spanish.
- Resort phones equipped with software that expedites international calls by allowing guests to dial direct to foreign destinations.

---

from the Village Marketplace. There are also exchange services at the Orlando International Airport.

TRAVELER'S CHECKS   Traveler's checks denominated in U.S. dollars are readily accepted at most hotels, motels, restaurants, and large stores, though they're much less convenient than using cash or a credit card. But the best place to change traveler's checks is at a bank. Do not bring traveler's checks denominated in other currencies.

CREDIT CARDS   Most major credit cards are widely accepted: Visa (BarclayCard in Britain), MasterCard (EuroCard in Europe, Access in Britain, Chargex in Canada), American Express, Diners Club, Discover, and Carte Blanche. You can save yourself trouble by using plastic rather than cash or traveler's checks in most hotels, motels, restaurants, and retail stores. American Express, MasterCard, and Visa are accepted for admission to the Disney Parks and all restaurants therein. They are also accepted at the other major parks, Sea World, and Universal. You must have a credit card to rent a car. It can also be used as proof of identity (often carrying more weight than a passport), or as a "cash card," enabling you to draw money from banks that accept them.

SAFETY

While the Walt Disney World/Orlando area in general—and the theme parks in particular—are extremely safe, there are some general precautions you can take to minimize your chances of being the victim of crime.

GENERAL SAFETY   U.S. urban areas tend to be less safe than those in Europe or Japan. Visitors should always stay alert. This is particularly true of large U.S. cities. It is wise to ask the local tourist office if you're in doubt about which neighborhoods are safe. Avoid deserted areas, especially at night. Don't go into any city park at night unless there is an event that attracts crowds. Avoid carrying valuables with you on the street, and don't display expensive cameras or electronic equipment.

Remember also that hotels are open to the public, and in a large hotel, security may not be able to screen everyone entering. Always lock your room door—don't assume that once inside your hotel you are automatically safe and no longer need to be aware of your surroundings.

DRIVING

Speed Limits   Obey all posted speed limits. On city highways it is usually 55 or 65 miles per hour. In some rural areas it goes up to 70 miles per hour. In residential areas, 35 miles per hour is generally safe. The corridor between the attractions and downtown Orlando is rumored to be one of the most heavily ticketed stretches of road in the United States.

Seat Belts   Seat belts for all passengers are required by Florida law. Children under 3 must ride strapped in a car seat and police will issue tickets to parents who do not put their children in restraints while driving. Rental-car agencies will provide car seats, some for free.

Air Bag Safety   Children, in or out of car seats, should ride only in the back seats of cars that are equipped with air bags. Air bags have been linked to several deaths involving children in the United States. Air bags are a standard feature on most new-model cars.

Drinking & Driving   Law enforcement frowns on drunk drivers and in Florida the rules are strict and strictly enforced. If you are planning to drink alcohol, especially after an exhausting day in the park, designate a sober driver or find an alternative means of transportation. Some nightclubs provide free soft drinks to designated drivers. It doesn't hurt to ask.

Defensive Driving   Drive with extra care in tourist-heavy areas where cars slowing down unexpectedly to read road signs and making sudden turns are not the exception but the rule. (People often come nearly to a stop on the highway while attempting to decipher the Disney signs.) Assume all other drivers have no idea where they are going—which is often not too far from the truth—and you should do just fine.

Lights On   Law requires that drivers put their lights on during rainstorms. These are, at least, a daily occurrence during the summer months.

If You Get Lost   You may have to be content to simply turn around and reenter the highway by accessing the on-ramp near where you just got off. Downtown Orlando is the exception to this rule, but signage has been improved to help direct tourists and visitors from the suburbs. Avoid pulling over to ask directions from people on the street; instead, stop at a convenience store and ask the clerk, who should be able to help with basic directions.

Safety While Driving   Question your rental agency about personal safety, or ask for a brochure of traveler safety tips when you pick up your car. Obtain from the agency written directions, or a map with the route marked in red, showing how to get to your destination. And, if possible, arrive and depart during daylight hours.

Recently, more and more crime has involved cars and drivers. If you drive off a highway into a doubtful neighborhood, leave the area as quickly as possible. If you have an accident, even on the highway, stay in your car with the doors locked until you assess the situation or until the police arrive. If you are bumped from behind on the street or are involved in a minor accident with no injuries and the situation appears to be suspicious, motion to the other driver to follow you. *Never* get out of your car in such situations. Go directly to the nearest police precinct, well-lighted service station, or all-night store.

If you see someone on the road who indicates a need for help, *do not* stop. Take note of the location, drive on to a well-lighted area, and telephone the police by dialing ☎ 911.

Park in well-lighted, well-traveled areas if possible. Always keep your car doors locked, whether attended or unattended. Look around you before you get out of your car, and never leave any packages or valuables in sight. If someone attempts to rob you or steal your car, *do not* try to resist the thief/carjacker—report the incident to the police department immediately.

2 Getting To & Around the U.S.

Travelers from overseas can take advantage of the **APEX (Advance Purchase Excursion) fares** offered by all the major U.S. and European carriers.

British Airways (☎ **0345/222-111** from within the U.K.) offers direct flights from London to Miami and Orlando, as does **Virgin Atlantic** (☎ **0129/374-774** from within the U.K.). You might also try **Continental** (☎ **0293/776-446**).

Canadian readers might book flights with **Air Canada** (☎ **800/361-8620**), which offers service from Toronto and Montréal to Miami and Tampa. Other airlines that fly to Florida from Canada include **US Airways** (☎ **800/428-4322**); **Delta** (☎ **800/361-6770**); **TWA** (☎ **800/892-4141**); **American** (☎ **800/624-6262**); and **Northwest** (☎ **800/225-2525**).

Some large American airlines (for example, TWA, American Airlines, Northwest, United, and Delta) offer travelers on their transatlantic or transpacific flights special discount tickets under the name **Visit USA,** allowing travel between any U.S. destinations at minimum rates. They are not on sale in the United States, and must therefore be purchased before you leave your foreign point of departure. This system is the best, easiest, and fastest way to see the United States at low cost. You should obtain information well in advance from your travel agent or the office of the airline concerned, since the conditions attached to these discount tickets can be changed without advance notice.

The visitor arriving by air, no matter what the port of entry, should cultivate patience and resignation before setting foot on U.S. soil. Getting through Immigration Control may take as long as 2 hours on some days. Add the time it takes to clear Customs, and you'll see that you should make very generous allowance for delay in planning connections between international and domestic flights—an average of 2 to 3 hours, at least.

In contrast, travelers arriving by car or by rail from Canada will find border-crossing formalities streamlined to the vanishing point. And air travelers from Canada, Bermuda, and some places in the Caribbean can sometimes go through Customs and Immigration at the point of departure, which is much quicker and less painful.

GETTING AROUND THE ORLANDO AREA Though I give some tips on train and bus passes below, you're going to need a car to get around unless you are committed to staying at Disney. It's really only possible to rely on public transportation in the United States in a few urban areas with comprehensive mass transit systems—and Orlando is not among them.

Renting a Car To rent a car, you really need a major credit card, and a valid driver's license is required (sometimes a hefty cash deposit can be used instead of a credit card). You also must be at least 25 years old. Some companies do rent to younger people but add a daily surcharge. Be sure to return your car with the same amount of gas you started out with; rental companies charge excessive prices for gasoline. All the major car-rental companies are represented in Florida (see "Getting Around" in chapter 4 for a list).

Renting a Motor Home The following companies rent mobile homes, and all have outlets in Orlando: **Cruise America,** 613 E. Colonial Dr., Orlando, 32804 (☎ **800/ 327-7799** or 407/273-5020); **Florida RV World,** 4260 U.S. 92 E., Plant City, 33566 (☎ **800/330-6171**); **Giant Recreation World,** 13906 W. Colonial Dr., Winter Garden, 34787 (☎ **407/656-6444**).

Traveling by Train International visitors can buy a **USA Railpass,** good for 15 or 30 days of unlimited travel on Amtrak trains. The pass is available through many foreign travel agents. You can buy passes for a specific region, for example the Southwest or Southeast, or for the entire United States. Prices in 1997 for a pass to travel the entire country were as follows: a 15-day pass costs $230 off-peak (Jan–May), $375 peak (June–Dec.); a 30-day pass costs $350 off-peak, $480 peak.

With a foreign passport, you can also buy passes at some Amtrak offices in the United States, including locations in San Francisco, Los Angeles, Chicago, New York, Miami, Boston, and Washington, D.C. Reservations are generally required and should be made for each part of your trip as early as possible.

Visitors should be aware of the limitations of long-distance rail travel in the United States. With a few notable exceptions (for instance, the Northeast Corridor line between Boston and Washington, D.C.), service is rarely up to European standards: Delays are common, routes are limited and often infrequently served, and fares are rarely significantly lower than discount airfares. Thus, cross-country train travel should be approached with caution.

Traveling by Bus Bus travel in the United States can be both slow and uncomfortable, so this option is not for everyone. Although short hops between cities are often the most economical form of public transit, at this writing bus passes are priced slightly higher than similar train passes. Greyhound, the sole nationwide bus line, offers an Ameripass for unlimited travel for 7 days ($179), 15 days ($289), and 30 days ($399).

For further information about travel to Florida, see "Getting There," in chapter 2.

FAST FACTS: For the Foreign Traveler

Automobile Organizations Auto clubs will supply maps, suggested routes, guidebooks, accident and bail-bond insurance, and emergency road service. The major auto club in the United States, with 983 offices nationwide, is the **American Automobile Association** (AAA). Members of some foreign auto clubs have reciprocal arrangements with AAA and enjoy its services at no charge. If you belong to an auto club, inquire about AAA reciprocity before you leave. AAA can provide you with an **International Driving Permit** validating your foreign license. You may be able to join AAA even if you are not a member of a reciprocal club. To inquire, call ☎ **800/JOIN-AAA.** In addition, some automobile-rental agencies now provide these services, so you should inquire about their availability when you rent your car.

Business Hours Banks are open weekdays from 9am to 3 or 4pm, although there's 24-hour access to the automatic teller machines (ATMs) at most banks and other outlets. Some branch offices in Florida are open until noon on Saturday. Generally, offices are open weekdays from 9am to 5pm. Stores are open 6 days a week, with many open on Sunday, too; department stores usually stay open until 9pm at least 1 day a week.

Climate See "When to Go," in chapter 2.

Currency & Exchange   See "Money" in "Preparing for Your Trip," earlier in this chapter.

Drinking Laws   See "Liquor Laws" in "Fast Facts," in chapter 4.

Electricity   The United States uses 110 to 120 volts, 60 cycles, compared to 220 to 240 volts, 50 cycles, as in most of Europe. In addition to a 100-volt converter, small appliances of non-American manufacture, such as hair dryers or shavers, will require a plug adapter, with two flat, parallel pins.

Embassies and Consulates   All embassies are located in Washington, D.C.; some consulates are located in major cities, and most nations have a mission to the United Nations in New York City. Foreign visitors can obtain telephone numbers for their embassies and consulates by calling "Information" in Washington, D.C. (☎ 202/ 555-1212).

   The Canadian consulate closest to Orlando is at 200 S. Biscayne Blvd., Suite 1600, Miami, FL 33131 (☎ 305/579-1600). There's a British consulate located at 1001 S. Bayshore Dr., Miami, FL 33131 (☎ 305/374-1522); for emergency situations, there is an office in Orlando at the Sun Bank Tower, Suite 2110, 200 S. Orange Ave. (☎ 407/426-7855).

Emergencies   Call ☎ 911 to report a fire, call the police, or get an ambulance. This call is free from all public telephones.

Gasoline (Petrol)   One U.S. gallon equals 3.75 liters, while 1.2 U.S. gallons equal one Imperial gallon. You'll notice there are several grades (and price levels) of gasoline available at most gas stations. And you'll also notice that their names change from company to company. The unleaded ones with the highest octane are the most expensive (most rental cars take the least expensive, "regular" unleaded) and leaded gas is the least expensive, but only older cars can take this, so check if you're not sure.

Holidays   On the following legal national holidays, banks, government offices, post offices, and many stores, restaurants, and museums are closed: January 1 (New Year's Day); third Monday in January (Martin Luther King, Jr. Day); third Monday in February (Presidents' Day, Washington's Birthday); last Monday in May (Memorial Day); July 4 (Independence Day); first Monday in September (Labor Day); second Monday in October (Columbus Day); November 11 (Veteran's Day/ Armistice Day); fourth Thursday in November (Thanksgiving Day); and December 25 (Christmas). The Tuesday following the first Monday in November is Election Day and is a legal holiday in presidential-election years; the next presidential election is in 2000.

Languages   Major hotels may have multilingual employees. Unless your language is very obscure, they can usually supply a translator on request. Especially in southern Florida and, increasingly, in central Florida, many people are fluent in Spanish. Establishments catering to tourists make a special effort to have bilingual speakers on staff.

Legal Aid   The foreign tourist will probably never become involved with the American legal system. If you are stopped for a minor infraction, such as speeding or some other traffic violation, never attempt to pay the fine directly to a police officer; you may wind up arrested on the much more serious charge of attempted bribery. Pay fines by mail, or directly into the hands of the clerk of the court. If accused of a more serious offense, it's wise to say and do nothing before consulting a lawyer. Under U.S. law, an arrested person is allowed one telephone call to a party of his or her choice. Call your embassy or consulate.

Mail　If you want your mail to follow you on your vacation and you aren't sure of your address, your mail can be sent to you, in your name, c/o General Delivery at the main post office of the city or region where you expect to be. The addressee must pick it up in person and produce proof of identity (driver's license, credit card, passport, etc.).

Mailboxes　Mailboxes are blue with a red-and-white stripe and carry the inscription "U.S. Mail." Make sure you see this inscription. Overnight delivery companies also often have drop-off boxes along the road. Don't forget to add the five-figure postal code, or ZIP code, after the two-letter abbreviation of the state to which the mail is addressed (CA for California, FL for Florida, NY for New York, and so on).

Within the United States, it costs 20¢ to mail a standard-size postcard and 32¢ to send an oversize postcard (larger than 4½ by 6 inches, or 10.8 by 15.4 centimeters). Letters that weigh up to 1 ounce (that's about five pages, 8-by-11-inch paper) cost 32¢, plus 23¢ for each additional ounce. A standard postcard to Mexico costs 30¢, a half-ounce letter 35¢; a postcard to Canada costs 30¢, a 1-ounce letter 40¢. A postcard to Europe, Australia, New Zealand, the Far East, South America, or elsewhere costs 40¢, while a letter is 60¢ for each half-ounce.

Newspapers & Magazines　National newspapers include the *New York Times*, *USA Today*, and the *Wall Street Journal*. National news weeklies include *Newsweek*, *Time*, and *U.S. News & World Report*. All over Florida, you'll be able to purchase the *Miami Herald*, one of the most highly respected dailies in the country. The local newspaper is the *Orlando Sentinel*.

Many **Walgreen** and **Eckerd's** drugstores in areas catering to tourists also carry newspapers from the United Kingdom.

Radio & Television　Six coast-to-coast networks—ABC, CBS, NBC, Fox, PBS (the Public Broadcasting System), and CNN (Cable News Network), play a major part in American life; two newer, smaller networks (the Paramount and WB networks) are also available in most major television markets. In Orlando, viewers have a choice of all these. Options on your hotel TV set may be limited, though.

You'll also find a wide choice of local radio stations, each broadcasting particular kinds of talk shows and/or music—classical, country, jazz, pop, gospel—punctuated by news broadcasts and frequent commercials. Most central Florida cable networks also carry at least two Spanish-language stations and there are numerous Spanish-language radio stations, mostly on the AM dial.

Safety　See "Safety" in "Preparing for Your Trip," earlier in this chapter.

Taxes　In the United States, there is no VAT (Value-Added Tax) or other indirect tax at a national level. Every state, and each city in it, has the right to levy its own local tax on all purchases, including hotel and restaurant checks, airline tickets, and so on. In Florida, sales tax is 6%. Hotel tax in Orlando and Kissimmee (which includes sales tax) is 11%.

Telephone, Telegraph, and Fax　Pay phones can be found in most restaurants, hotels, gas stations, and stores. Local calls in the United States usually cost 25¢.

Most long-distance and international calls can be dialed directly from any phone. For direct overseas calls, dial 011 first, then the country code (Australia, 61; Republic of Ireland, 353; New Zealand, 64; United Kingdom, 44) followed by the city code, and then the number you wish to call. To place a call to Canada, the Caribbean, or another U.S. state, dial 1 followed by the area code and the seven-digit number.

Generally, hotel surcharges on long-distance and local calls are astronomical. You are usually better off using a public pay telephone. Hotels sometimes even charge a fee if you use your own telephone credit card or call a toll-free number (with an 800 or 888 area code), so ask about surcharges before you dial.

For "collect" (reversed-charge) calls and for "person-to-person" calls, dial 0 (zero, *not* the letter "O") followed by the area code and number you want; an operator will then come on the line, and you should specify that you are calling collect, or person-to-person, or both. If your operator-assisted call is international, ask for the overseas operator.

Prepaid **calling cards,** which generally provide a fair per-minute rate—probably lower than that charged by your hotel—are becoming increasingly popular. Calling cards are sold in many convenience stores and drugstores and can generally be purchased in $5 or $10 increments.

For local directory assistance ("Information"), dial ☎ 411; for long-distance information in Canada or the United States, dial 1, then the appropriate area code and ☎ 555-1212.

Like the telephone system, **telegraph** and **telex** services are provided by private corporations like ITT, MCI, and above all, Western Union, the most important. You can bring your telegram into the nearest **Western Union** office (there are hundreds across the country) or dictate it over the phone (a toll-free call, ☎ **800/ 325-6000**). You can also telegraph money, or have it telegraphed to you, very quickly over the Western Union system.

It's also easy to send a **fax.** Most hotels have fax service. If yours doesn't, small copy shops found in most neighborhoods provide fax service. **Kinko's** is a prominent local printing chain that also provides fax service. They are listed in the White Pages of the telephone directory. Faxes are sent for a small fee—usually around $2 per page. If you make arrangements, some places will also receive faxes for you and call you when anything arrives.

Time   The United States is divided into four time zones (six, if Alaska and Hawaii are included). From east to west, these are: eastern standard time (EST), central standard time (CST), mountain standard time (MST), Pacific standard time (PST), Alaska standard time (AST), and Hawaii standard time (HST). Orlando, like most of Florida, is on eastern standard time, which is 8 hours behind Greenwich Mean Time. When it is noon in Orlando, it's 11am in New Orleans (CST), 10am in Salt Lake City (MST), 9am in Los Angeles (PST), 8am in Anchorage (AST), and 7am in Honolulu (HST).

Daylight saving time is in effect from the first Sunday in April through 2am on the last Sunday in October except in Arizona, Hawaii, part of Indiana, and Puerto Rico. Daylight saving time moves the clock 1 hour ahead of standard time.

Tipping   Service in the United States tends to be good, but it is rarely included in the price of anything. The amount you should tip does depend on the service you have received. Good service warrants the following tips: Bartenders (do tip them here), 15%; bellhops, at least $2 to $5 depending on the amount of luggage they carry for you; cab drivers, 15%; checkroom attendants, $1 per garment (unless there is a charge, then no tip); hairdressers, 15% to 20%; parking valets, $1; redcaps (in airports), at least $1 per piece; restaurants and nightclubs, 15%.

Toilets   Foreign visitors often complain that public toilets are hard to find in most U.S. cities. True, there are none on the streets, but the visitor can usually find one in a bar, restaurant, hotel, museum, department store, or service station—and it will probably be clean. In particular, Mobil service stations have made, and kept, a public pledge to provide spic-and-span bathrooms, most decorated with homey touches. Within the theme parks, rest rooms will be clearly marked on the park maps.

THE AMERICAN SYSTEM OF MEASUREMENTS

Length

1 inch (in.)			=	2.54cm			
1 foot (ft.)	=	12 in.	=	30.48cm	=	.305m	
1 yard (yd.)	=	3 ft.			=	.915m	
1 mile (mi.)	=	5,280 ft.					= 1.609km

To convert miles to kilometers, multiply the number of miles by 1.61 (example, 50 mi. × 1.61 = 80.5km). Note that this conversion can be used to convert speeds from miles per hour (mph) to kilometers per hour (kmph).

To convert kilometers to miles, multiply the number of kilometers by .62 (example, 25km × .62 = 15.5 mi.). Note that this same conversion can be used to convert speeds from kilometers per hour to miles per hour.

Capacity

1 fluid ounce (fl. oz.)			=	.03 liter		
1 pint (pt.)	=	16 fl. oz.	=	.47 liter		
1 quart (qt.)	=	2 pints	=	.94 liter		
1 gallon (gal.)	=	4 quarts	=	3.79 liters	=	.83 Imperial gal.

To convert U.S. gallons to liters, multiply the number of gallons by 3.79 (example, 12 U.S. gal. × 3.79 = 45.58 liters).

To convert liters to U.S. gallons, multiply the number of liters by .26 (example, 50 liters × .26 = 13 U.S. gal.).

To convert U.S. gallons to Imperial gallons, multiply the number of U.S. gallons by .83 (example, 12 U.S. gal. × .83 = 9.96 Imperial gal.).

To convert Imperial gallons to U.S. gallons, multiply the number of Imperial gallons by 1.2 (example, 8 Imperial gal. × 1.2 = 9.6 U.S. gal.).

Weight

1 ounce (oz.)			=	28.35g			
1 pound (lb.)	=	16 oz.	=	453.6g	=	.45 kg	
1 ton	=	2,000 lb.			=	907kg	= .91 metric ton

To convert pounds to kilograms, multiply the number of pounds by .45 (example, 90 lb. × .45 = 40.5kg).

To convert kilograms to pounds, multiply the number of kilos by 2.2 (example, 75kg × 2.2 = 165 lb.).

Area

1 acre			=	.41ha		
1 square mile (sq. mi.)	=	640 acres	=	2.59ha	=	2.6 sq. km

To convert acres to hectares, multiply the number of acres by .41 (example, 40 acres × .41 = 16.4ha).

To convert hectares to acres, multiply the number of hectares by 2.47 (example, 20ha × 2.47 = 49.4 acres).

To convert square miles to square kilometers, multiply the number of square miles by 2.6 (example, 80 sq. mi. × 2.6 = 208 sq. km).

To convert square kilometers to square miles, multiply the number of square kilometers by .39 (example, 150 sq. km × .39 = 58.5 sq. mi.).

Temperature

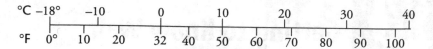

To convert degrees Fahrenheit to degrees Celsius, subtract 32 from °F, multiply by 5, then divide by 9 (example, 85°F − 32 × $^5/_9$ = 29.4°C).

To convert degrees Celsius to degrees Fahrenheit, multiply °C by 9, divide by 5, and add 32 (example, 20°C × $^9/_5$ + 32 = 68°F).

4

Getting to Know Walt Disney World & Orlando

There was a time when visitors seldom ventured beyond Disney World. When the Mouse moved to Orlando in 1971, there was good reason. If you weren't into watching citrus grow, there wasn't a whole heck of a lot to do in Orlando outside of Walt Disney World.

Oh, but how success breeds competition. Not only has Disney expanded, to include four major parks, but has also over the years added water parks, miniature golf, and nightclubs. But as Disney has expanded, so have the entertainment opportunities beyond.

Plan to spend at least part of your vacation exploring the rest of Orlando, or at least the fast-growing Universal Studios. Because of major renovations, even places you've seen before, such as Sea World or downtown Orlando, are worth another look.

If you do travel, many area hotels offer transportation to the airport and city attractions.

1 Orientation

VISITOR INFORMATION

Contact the **Orlando/Orange County Convention & Visitors Bureau,** 8723 International Dr., Suite 101, Orlando, FL 32819 (☎ 407/363-5871). They can answer all your questions and will be happy to send you maps, brochures (including the informative *Official Visitors Guide,* the *Official Attractions Guide,* the *Official Accommodations Guide,* and the *African-American Visitors Guide*), and the "Magicard," good for discounts of 10% to 50% on accommodations, attractions, car rentals, and more. Discount tickets to attractions other than Disney parks are sold on the premises, and the multilingual staff can also make dining reservations and hotel referrals. The bureau is open daily, except Christmas, from 8am to 8pm.

For general information about Walt Disney World—and a copy of the informative *Walt Disney World Vacations*—write or call the **Walt Disney World Co.,** Box 10000, Lake Buena Vista, FL 32830-1000 (☎ 407/934-7639).

If you're driving, you can stop at the **Disney/AAA Travel Center** in Ocala, Florida, at the intersection of I-75 (exit 68) and Fla. 200, about 90 miles north of Orlando (☎ 904/854-0770). Here you can purchase tickets and Mickey ears, get help planning your

The Orlando Area/Walt Disney World Area

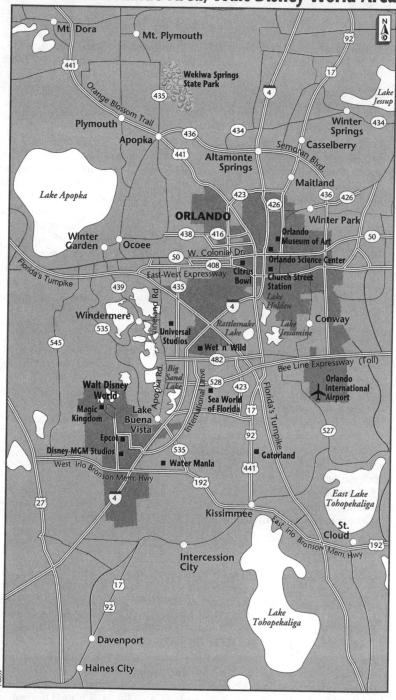

park itinerary, and make hotel reservations. Hours are 9am to 6pm; until 7pm June through August.

Also contact the **Kissimmee–St. Cloud Convention & Visitors Bureau,** 1925 E. Irlo Bronson Memorial Hwy. (P.O. Box 422007), Kissimmee, FL 34742-2007 (☎ **800/327-9159** or 407/847-5000). They'll send maps, brochures, discount coupon books, and the *Kissimmee–St. Cloud Vacation Guide,* which details the area's accommodations and attractions.

ON-LINE RESOURCES

If you have Internet access, you can visit Walt Disney World's own web site at **http://www.disneyworld.com**, which has extensive, entertaining, and regularly updated information, including a live-action look from video cameras perched throughout the various parks. (This is mostly long-distance shots of tourists walking about, but is still a chance to see those blue Orlando skies and dream ahead to vacation time.) There are dozens of web pages devoted to Disney, especially Disney trivia. But one is a very informative newsgroup on Usenet called **rec.arts.disney**.

Information about Universal Studios can be found at **http://www.usf.com** and Sea World information is available at **http://4adventure.com**. Both sites offer maps and a basic description of rides, shows, and ticket information. The city newspaper, the *Orlando Sentinel,* also produces *Orlando Sentinel Online* at **http://www.oso@aol.com**. Once there, click into "Theme Park Central" for a variety of information and updates on what is going on at local attractions.

ONCE YOU REACH ORLANDO

And at the Orlando International Airport, arriving passengers can stroll over to **Greetings from Walt Disney World Resort,** a shop and information center on the third floor in the main lobby just behind the Northwest counter. This facility sells WDW park tickets, makes dinner-show and hotel reservations at Disney properties, and provides brochures and assistance. Open daily from 6am to 9pm.

Upon entering WDW grounds, you can tune your radio to 1030 AM when you're approaching the Magic Kingdom, or 850 AM when approaching Epcot. Tune to 1200 AM when departing from the Magic Kingdom, or 910 AM when departing Epcot. TVs in all Disney resorts and official Disney hotels also have park information stations.

Nearly all hotel lobbies have a rack containing brochures for various area attractions. If this guidebook doesn't convince you of which places to hit, these pamphlets might help you make up your mind. The brochures also often include discount coupons.

CITY LAYOUT

Orlando's major artery is **I-4,** which runs diagonally across the state from Tampa to Daytona Beach. Exits from I-4 take you to Walt Disney World, Sea World, International Drive, U.S. 192, Kissimmee, Lake Buena Vista, Church Street Station, downtown Orlando, and Winter Park. Most of the exits are well marked, although you should know that the exit to Universal Studios takes you past the entrance and around the block before you go in. (Watch carefully for the signs.) The **Florida Turnpike** crosses I-4 and links up with I-75 to the north. **U.S. 192,** a major east–west artery, stretches from Kissimmee (along a major motel strip) to U.S. 27, crossing I-4 near the Walt Disney World entrance road. Farther north, a toll road called the **Bee Line Expressway** (Fla. 528) goes east from I-4 past Orlando International Airport to Cape Canaveral. The **East–West Expressway** (also known as Fla. 408) is a toll road that might be helpful in bypassing surface traffic outside of the main tourist areas.

Walt Disney World property is bounded roughly by I-4 and Fla. 535 to the east (the latter also north), World Drive (the entrance road) to the west, and U.S. 192 to the south. Epcot Center Drive (Hwy. 536/the south end of International Drive) and Buena Vista Drive cut across the complex in a more or less east-west direction; the two roads cross at Bonnet Creek Parkway. In spite of excellent highways and explicit signage, it is relatively easy to get lost. Again, pay close attention and drive carefully because chances are everyone else is lost too. *Note:* The Disney parks are actually much closer to Kissimmee than to downtown Orlando.

NEIGHBORHOODS IN BRIEF

Walt Disney World   A city unto itself, WDW sprawls over more than 26,000 acres containing theme parks, resorts, hotels, shops, restaurants, and recreational facilities galore. Copious details below.

Lake Buena Vista   This area centers on a hotel village/marketplace owned and operated by Walt Disney World on the eastern edge of Disney property. However, while Disney owns all the real estate, many of the hotels, and some shops and res taurants here, are independently owned. Lake Buena Vista is a charming area of manicured lawns and verdant thoroughfares with traffic islands shaded by towering oak trees.

Celebration   Imagine living in a Disney world? Disney tries to re-create its squeaky-clean, completely controlled magic in this town, the first residential area ever to receive the special Disney touch. Located on 4,900 acres in northwest Osceola County, Celebration will eventually have about 8,000 residents living in Disney-designed homes and attending a Disney-run school. The homes go for around $193,000. Celebration's downtown is, however, designed for the tourist trade, being architecturally interesting with some first-rate shops and restaurants.

Kissimmee   South of the Disney parks, Kissimmee centers on U.S. 192/Irlo Bronson Memorial Highway—a somewhat tacky strip, as archetypical of American cities as Main Street. U.S. 192 is lined with budget motels, lesser attractions—like Gatorland—and every fast-food restaurant you can name.

International Drive (Fla. 536)   Can you say tourist mecca? This area extends 7 to 10 miles north of the Disney parks between Fla. 535 and the Florida Turnpike. From bungee jumping to ice-skating and dozens of theme restaurants and T-shirt shops, this is *the* tourist strip in central Florida. It contains numerous hotels, restaurants, shopping centers, and the Orange County Convention Center, and it offers easy access to Sea World and Universal Studios. *Note:* Locally, this road is always referred to as **I-Drive.**

Downtown Orlando   Reached via I-4 East, this burgeoning Sunbelt metropolis is 17 miles northeast of Walt Disney World. It includes the entertainment/shopping complex Church Street Station and the Orlando Science Center, a recently completed multimillion-dollar complex, which is the largest in the Southeast. Dozens of clubs, shops, and restaurants are located in the heart of the city, one of the fastest-growing in the country. Dozens of antiques shops line "Antique Row" on Orange Avenue near Lake Ivanhoe. The new Lymmo bus system, which begins operating in late 1997, is a free downtown shuttle that makes getting around the heart of the city a breeze.

Winter Park   Just north of downtown Orlando, Winter Park is the place many of central Florida's old-money families call home. As the name implies, it began as a haven for Yankees traveling away from the cold. Today, it's home to Park Avenue, a collection of upscale shops and restaurants along an original cobblestoned street that is frequented by local ladies who lunch. With the main attractions being shopping, dining, and several small museums, Winter Park is definitely a grown-up diversion.

2   Getting Around

In a city that thrives on its visitor attractions, you won't find it difficult to get around. If you are traveling outside of the tourist areas, avoid traveling during peak rush-hour times—7 to 9am and 4 to 6pm—so you don't get caught in the daily traffic jams. Signage problems in the downtown area have been corrected through brightly colored signs that have a definite Disney influence. Nearly all hotels offer transport to and from theme parks and other tourist destinations. It's not difficult getting places, but it can be expensive.

THE DISNEY TRANSPORTATION NETWORK   If you plan to stay at a Disney resort and visit mostly Disney parks and attractions, there's a very thorough free-transportation network throughout the complex.

Disney resorts and official hotels offer unlimited—and efficient—complimentary transportation via bus, monorail, ferry, and water taxi to all three parks from 2 hours prior to opening until 2 hours after closing; also to Disney Village Marketplace, Typhoon Lagoon, River Country, Blizzard Beach, Pleasure Island, Fort Wilderness, and other Disney resorts. Disney properties offer transportation to other area attractions as well, though you have to pay.

There are a few advantages to using this on-property transportation system: It's free, providing a big savings on car rental, insurance, and gas. You don't have to pay for parking ($5 per day in Walt Disney World). You avoid long waits in traffic coming into the parking lots. And if your party wants to split up, you can easily board transport to different areas.

The disadvantages? You are at the mercy of Disney's schedule and you often have to take a ferry to catch a bus to get the monorail to go to the hotel. The system makes a complete route, but not necessarily an easy one. You also have to wait as each bus makes multiple stops, loading and unloading a large number of passengers. Schedules, too, often entail long waits for some of these connections.

BY CAR

To rent or not to rent? First decide exactly how you envision your vacation. If you will happily stay immersed in everything Disney, or you are staying on International Drive, you'll do just as well without your own wheels. A car, however, may drastically cut the commuter time between the parks and hotels not directly on the monorail routes.

But, in general, if you will spend all your time at Disney, there's no sense renting a car that will sit in the parking lot between trips to the airport.

But if you're on an extended stay—more than a week—you will probably want to rent a car for at least a day or two to explore beyond tourist areas. (Yes, there is something beyond the tourist areas.) Discover downtown Orlando, visit museums, the Space Coast, or just hang out for a day at the beach. The tourist areas of Orlando are kind of like Las Vegas: You just can't spend too much time in that world of bright lights and make-believe without needing a good dose of reality. Too much time immersed in all things WDW and you find a new, darker meaning to "It's A Small World."

If you're staying at a Disney property, the question to ask when deciding whether to rent a car is how, exactly, do you get to the major parks? If the Magic Kingdom is accessible by taking a bus, switching to the monorail, and then catching a ferry, you may want to opt for a car.

Another thing to consider is where to pick up the rental. If possible, contract with an agency that operates at or near your hotel. This will help to save time—and headaches. Dropping a car off with an airport-based rental service often means riding a shuttle to a lot off-site. That means turning in the car will eat up much of your final day. That is especially true during the holidays or peak season when lots of other folks will be doing the same thing. *Somebody* is renting the miles and miles of rental cars stored in the lots visible from the freeway.

All major rental companies are represented in Orlando and maintain desks at the airport. Many major car-rental agencies provide discount coupons in publications targeted at tourists. When planning your trip, and poring over all those brochures, keep an eye out for discounts on car rentals. You may also want to ask your travel agent if he or she has a recommendation or whether a discount is included in any available packages. Also, it never hurts to ask if there is a special available.

I was quoted the lowest rates by **Value Rent-A-Car** (☎ 800/GO-VALUE), which also turned out to offer excellent service and 24-hour pickup and return. Some other handy phone numbers: **Alamo** (☎ 800/327-9633), **Avis** (☎ 800/331-1212), **Budget** (☎ 800/527-0700), **Dollar** (☎ 800/800-4000), **Hertz** (☎ 800/654-3131), and **Thrifty** (☎ 800/367-2277).

BY BUS

Mears Transportation Group (☎ 407/423-5566) operates buses to all major attractions, including Cypress Gardens, Kennedy Space Center, Universal Studios, Sea World, Busch Gardens (in Tampa), and Church Street Station, among others. Call for details.

BY TAXI

Taxis line up in front of major hotels, and at smaller properties the front desk will be happy to call you a cab. Or call **Yellow Cab** (☎ 407/699-9999). The charge is $2.75 for the first mile, $1.50 per mile thereafter.

FAST FACTS: Walt Disney World & Orlando

Ambulances   See "Emergencies," below.

Baby-sitters   Most Orlando hotels offer baby-sitting services, and several Disney properties have marvelous child-care facilities with counselor-supervised activity programs on the premises. Disney properties use KinderCare sitters (☎ 407/827-5444), so you can be sure they've been very carefully checked out. If you're not staying at a Disney accommodation, you can call them on your own. Rates for in-room service are: $9 per hour for one child, $10 per hour for two children, $11 per hour for three children, $14 per hour for four children. There is a 4-hour minimum, the first half hour of which is travel time for the sitter. Twenty-four-hour advance notice is required.

Car Rentals   See "Getting Around," above.

Climate   See "When to Go," in chapter 2.

Convention Center   The Orange County Convention/Civic Center is located at 9800 International Dr. (☎ 407/345-9800).

Crime   See "Safety," below.

Doctors and Dentists   Your best bet is to inquire at your hotel desk. Disney has first-aid centers in all three major parks. There's also a very good 24-hour service in the area called **HouseMed** (☎ 407/396-1195). HouseMed doctors—who can dispense medication—make "house calls" to all area hotels. HouseMed also operates the Medi-Clinic, a walk-in medical facility (not for emergencies) at the intersection of I-4 and Hwy. 192, open daily from 8am to 9pm (same phone). Call for directions from your hotel. See also "Hospitals" and "Pharmacies," below.

To find a dentist, call **Dental Referral Service** (☎ 800/917-6453). They can tell you the nearest dentist who meets your needs. Phones are manned from 5:30am to 6pm daily. Check the yellow pages for 24-hour emergency services.

Emergencies   Dial ☎ 911 to contact the police or fire department or to call an ambulance.

Florist   Floral and fruit arrangements can be delivered anywhere on Walt Disney World Resort property by calling ☎ 407/827-3505 between 8am and 8pm.

Hospitals   Sand Lake Hospital, 9400 Turkey Lake Rd., is about 2 miles south of Sand Lake Road (☎ 407/351-8550). From the WDW area, take I-4 east to exit 29, turn left at the exit onto Sand Lake Road, and make a left on Turkey Lake Road. The hospital is 2 miles up on your right.

Walk-in medical clinics are available, with a visit usually costing under $50. Prescriptions are extra. Centra-Care, operated by locally run Florida Hospital, is a reputable medical facility with more than a dozen locations throughout the Orlando area. For information, and the nearest location, call ☎ 407/660-8118.

Kennels   All of the major theme parks offer animal-boarding facilities at reasonable fees. At Walt Disney World, there are kennels at Fort Wilderness, Epcot, the Magic Kingdom, and Disney–MGM Studios. Sea World and Universal also offer kennels where you can leave your animals during the day. If you're traveling with a pet, don't leave it in the car—even with a window cracked—while you enjoy the park. Many pets have perished this way in the hot Florida sun.

Kosher Food   It can be arranged at restaurants at Disney parks and resorts with 24 hours' advance notice. Call ☎ 407/WDW-DINE (939-3463).

Liquor Laws   Minimum drinking age is 21. No liquor is served in the Magic Kingdom at Walt Disney World; however, drinks are available at the other parks.

Lockers   You can rent lockers at all of the Disney parks and at Universal Studios and Sea World. Many other attractions, such as miniature golf courses or water parks, also offer this service. The cost is usually 50¢ or a dollar for the day. Inquire at Guest Relations.

Lost Children   Every theme park has a designated spot for parents to meet up with lost children (or lost spouses). Find out where it is when you enter any park and instruct your children to ask park personnel to take them there if they are lost. Point out what park personnel look like. Young children should have name tags.

Newspapers and Magazines   The *Orlando Sentinel* is the major local newspaper, but you can also purchase papers of major cities (most notably, the *New York Times*) in most hotel gift shops. The Friday edition of the *Sentinel* includes extensive entertainment and dining listings.

Many Eckerd's and Walgreen drugstores in tourist areas also carry Spanish-language dailies. *Downtown Orlando Monthly* covers events downtown. The

Orlando Weekly is a free, alternative paper that has significant entertainment listings.

Pharmacies   Walgreen Drug Store, 1003 W. Vine St. (Hwy. 192), just east of Bermuda Avenue (☎ 407/847-5252), operates a 24-hour pharmacy. They can deliver to hotels for a charge ($10 from 7am to 5pm, $15 at all other times).

Photography   Two-hour film processing is available at all three major Disney parks. Look for the Photo Express sign. You can also buy film and rent or buy 35mm, disc, and video cameras in all three parks.

Post Office   The main post office in Lake Buena Vista is at 12541 Fla. 535, near TGI Friday's in the Crossroads Shopping Center (☎ 407/828-2606). It's open Monday through Friday from 9am to 4pm, Saturday from 9am to noon.

Safety   Whenever you're traveling in an unfamiliar city, stay alert. Be aware of your immediate surroundings. It's a good idea to keep your valuables in a safety-deposit box (inquire at the front desk), though some hotels nowadays are equipped with in-room safes. Do keep a close eye on your valuables when you're in a public place—restaurant, theater, even airport terminal. And don't leave valuables in your car, even in the trunk.

If you are renting a car, read carefully the safety instructions that the rental company provides. Never stop for any reason in an unpopulated area, and remember that children should never ride in the front seat of a car equipped with air bags.

Taxes   Hotel tax in Orlando and Kissimmee is 11%, which includes a state sales tax (6%) that is also charged on all goods except most grocery store items and medicines.

Time   Call ☎ 407/646-3131 for the correct time and temperature.

Tourist Information   See "Orientation," earlier in this chapter.

Weather   Call ☎ 407/851-7510 for a weather recording. Also look for the weather channel on the local cable carrier, Time Warner Cable. Most hotels carry basic cable. The *Orlando Sentinel* also includes a daily forecast.

5

Accommodations

You'll find a wealth of hotel options in the Walt Disney World area. Beautifully landscaped multifacility resorts are the rule, but there's something to suit every taste and pocketbook. And, of course, you should reserve as far in advance as possible. . . the minute you've decided on the dates of your trip.

HOW TO CHOOSE A HOTEL & SAVE MONEY

Many people assume that motels outside the Disney parks will cost you less than staying on WDW premises, but that isn't always the case.

If you don't have a car, be sure to note the price of hotel shuttle buses to and from Walt Disney World parks. Compute these charges—which can be as high as $12 per person per day—in determining hotel price value. Or, if you drive your own car, don't forget to count parking fees. All Disney-owned properties and Disney "official" hotels offer complimentary transportation to and from WDW parks (see details on this, and other advantages of staying at Disney properties, below).

In or out of Walt Disney World, if you book your hotel as part of a package (see chapter 2 for details), you'll likely enjoy big savings.

Many people don't know that you can bargain with the reservations clerk when booking a hotel. The reason: An unoccupied room nets a hotel zero dollars, and any reasonable offer is better than that. Of course, this works only if you book upon arrival, preferably late in the afternoon when the desk knows there will be empty rooms. It will also work better outside of Walt Disney World.

Another money-saving tip: Reserving via toll-free numbers at chain hotels sometimes puts you into the running for lower rates than reserving at individual properties. And ask about special discounts for students, government employees, senior citizens, military, AAA, and/or corporate clients.

In some hotel listings below, I've mentioned **concierge levels.** In these "hotels within a hotel," guests enjoy a luxurious private lounge (usually with spectacular views) that is the setting for complimentary continental breakfasts, hot and cold hors d'oeuvres at cocktail hour, and late-night cordials and pastries. Rooms are usually on high floors and room decor is upgraded. Guests are cosseted with special services (private registration and checkout, a personal concierge, nightly bed turndown) and amenities (upgraded toiletries, bathroom scales, terry robes, hair dryers). Ask for specifics when you reserve. Concierge levels are especially attractive to businesspeople traveling on their own.

Also mentioned under "Facilities" in some cases are **counselor-supervised child-care/activity centers.** Very popular in Orlando, these are marvelous, creatively run facilities where kids enjoy Disney movies, video games, arts and crafts, storytelling, puppet shows, indoor and outdoor activities, and much more. Some centers provide meals and/or have beds where a child can go to sleep while you're out on the town. Check individual hotel listings for these facilities and call to find out exactly what is offered.

RESERVATION SERVICES

Many of the Kissimmee hotels listed below in "Best Bets" can be booked by calling the **Kissimmee–St. Cloud Convention & Visitors Bureau** at ☎ **800/333-KISS.**

Also consider using the services of an Orlando-based organization called **Check-In** (☎ **800/237-1033** or 941/756-4880; fax 941/739-2703). A central booking agency, it has listings for hundreds of condos, resorts, hotels, villas, and luxurious private homes in all price ranges. A minimum stay of 3 nights is required. Check-In doesn't accept credit cards, but it does take personal checks. There's no fee for the service.

You can also get information on Disney hotels on the Internet at **http:// www.disneyworld.com.**

HOW TO USE THIS CHAPTER

The hotels listed below are first divided by location, and then by price category alphabetically within a given district. All of the properties I've selected offer easy access to the Walt Disney World parks and other nearby major attractions.

Hotels listed in the **inexpensive** category are those charging $80 or less for a double room (don't blame me, I didn't invent inflation). Properties with $80 to $150 rooms make up the **moderate** category, $150 to $200 I've listed as **expensive,** and anything above that ranks as **very expensive.** Any extras included in the rates (for example, breakfast or other meals) are listed for each property. Categories are approximate because hotel rates do vary considerably, depending on whether you visit in peak or off-seasons.

1 Best Bets

- **Best for Families:** All of the Disney properties cater to families, with special menus for kids and character meals, video-game arcades, free transport to the parks, and many, many recreational facilities. Camping at woodsy Fort Wilderness (☎ **407/W-DISNEY** [934-7639] or 407/824-2900) makes for a special family experience. Bunk beds and a geyser going off in the lobby? What more could kids ask for? Keep in mind the Wilderness Lodge (☎ **407/W-DISNEY** [934-7639] or 407/824-3200).
- **Best Moderately Priced Hotels:** Disney's Dixie Landings (☎ **407/W-DISNEY** [934-7639] or 407/934-6000) and Port Orleans Resort (☎ **407/W-DISNEY** [934-7639] or 407/934-5000), offering magnificently landscaped grounds and extensive facilities, are worthy of much higher prices.
- **Best Inexpensive Hotels:** That's easy: Disney's All-Star Music Resort (☎ **407/ W-DISNEY** [934-7639] or 407/939-6000) and All-Star Sports Resort (☎ **407/ W-DISNEY** [934-7639] or 407/939-5000). You can't beat 'em with a stick. Mount Vernon Inn in Winter Park offers old-fashioned Southern hospitality without airs at a low price (☎ **407/647-1166**).

- **Best Budget Motel:** Rock-bottom rates are offered at the Motel 6 on 5731 W. Irlo Bronson Memorial Hwy. (U.S. 192; ☎ 800/4-MOTEL-6 or 407/396-6333). Prices begin at just $25.99 for two, and children under 17 stay free. If you can't get in here, there's another Motel 6 close by. Both are well run and perfectly safe.
- **Best for Business Travelers:** Marriott's Orlando World Center (☎ 800/621-0638 or 407/239-4200) offers full concierge service, 24-hour room service, fine restaurants and spacious lounges, and an extensive array of business services, not to mention golf, tennis, and other recreational facilities should you find time to relax.
- **Best for a Romantic Getaway:** The 1,500-acre grounds of the Hyatt Regency Grand Cypress (☎ 800/233-1234 or 407/239-1234) are a veritable botanic garden surrounding a swan-filled lake. Couples enjoy stunning accommodations, great service, first-rate restaurants, and every imaginable facility. Also consider the luxurious lodgings—with fireplaces and whirlpool tubs—at the adjoining Villas of Grand Cypress (☎ 800/835-7377 or 407/239-4700).
- **Best Location:** Disney's Grand Floridian Beach Resort (☎ 407/W-DISNEY [934-7639] or 407/824-3000), Polynesian Resort (☎ 407/W-DISNEY [934-7639] or 407/824-2000), or Contemporary Resort (☎ 407/W-DISNEY [934-7639] or 407/824-1000)—all are right on the monorail to whisk you straight to the parks for early opening.
- **Best Service:** The elegant Peabody Orlando (☎ 800/PEABODY or 407/352-4000) offers 24-hour concierge and room service, nightly bed turndown, and other attentive pampering.
- **Best Pools:** All of the Walt Disney World resorts have terrific swimming pools— generally Olympic-size and often with themes. The pool at the Caribbean Beach Resort (☎ 407/W-DISNEY [934-7639] or 407/934-3400), for instance, replicates a Caribbean fort with stone walls and cannons; it also has a water slide. Outside the Disney complex, the Hyatt Regency Grand Cypress (☎ 800/233-1234 or 407/239-1234) also has a notable pool: A half-acre lagoonlike affair, it flows through rock grottos, is spanned by a rope bridge, and has 12 waterfalls and two steep water slides.
- **Best Health Club:** The Walt Disney World Dolphin (☎ 800/227-1500 or 407/934-4000) has a fully equipped Body By Jake club complete with a weight room overlooking a lake. It contains a full complement of Polaris, Lifestep, Lifecycle, and Liferower equipment; offers aerobics classes throughout the day, personal training, massage, and body wraps; and includes saunas and a large whirlpool.

2 The Perks of Staying with Mickey

Described below are the 15 Disney-owned properties (hotels, resorts, villas, wilderness homes, and campsites) and 9 privately owned properties designated as "official" hotels. All are within the Walt Disney World complex.

In addition to location (they all offer close proximity to the parks), there are a number of advantages to staying at a Disney property or official hotel, especially the former. The following are included at all Disney resorts and official hotels:

- Unlimited complimentary transportation via bus, monorail, ferry, and water taxi to and from all three Disney World parks from 2 hours prior to opening until 2 hours after closing. Unlimited complimentary transport is also provided to and from Disney Village Marketplace, Typhoon Lagoon, River Country, Blizzard Beach, Pleasure Island, Fort Wilderness, and other Disney resorts. Three properties—the Polynesian, Contemporary, and Grand Floridian—are stops on the monorail. This free transport can save a lot of money you'd otherwise have to spend on a rental car or expensive hotel shuttle buses. It also means you're guaranteed admission to all parks, even during peak times when parking lots sometimes fill up.

- Free parking at WDW parking lots (other visitors pay $5 a day).
- Reduced-price children's menus in almost all restaurants.
- Character breakfasts and/or dinners at many restaurants.
- TVs equipped with the Disney channel and Walt Disney World information stations.
- A guest-services desk where you can purchase tickets to all WDW theme parks and attractions and obtain general information.
- Use of—and in some cases, complimentary transport to—the five Disney-owned golf courses and preferred tee times (these can be booked up to 30 days in advance).
- Access to most recreational facilities at other Disney resorts.
- Mears airport shuttle service.

Additional perks at Disney-owned hotels, resorts, villas, and campgrounds—as well as at the Walt Disney World Swan and Dolphin, but not at other official hotels—include the following:

- Charge privileges at restaurants and shops throughout Walt Disney World.
- Early admission, prior to public opening, to the Magic Kingdom, Epcot, and Disney–MGM on specific days (except at the Dolphin).
- On-premises National Car Rental desk.

WALT DISNEY WORLD CENTRAL RESERVATIONS OFFICE

To reserve a room at Disney hotels, resorts, and villas; official hotels; or Fort Wilderness homes and campsites, contact **Central Reservations Operations,** P.O. Box 10000, Lake Buena Vista, FL 32830-1000 (☎ **407/W-DISNEY** [934-7639]), open Monday through Friday from 8am to 10pm, Saturday and Sunday from 9am to 6pm. Have your dates and credit card ready when you call.

CRO can recommend accommodations that will suit your specific needs as to price, location (perhaps you wish to be closest to Epcot, Magic Kingdom, or Disney–MGM Studios), and facilities such as counselor-supervised child-care centers, a pool large enough for lap swimming, a state-of-the-art health club, on-premises golf or tennis (or other recreational facilities), a kitchen, and so on.

Be sure to inquire about Disney's numerous package plans, which include meals, tickets, recreation, and other features. The right package plan can save you money and time (more of your vacation is planned in advance), and a comprehensive plan is helpful in computing the cost of your vacation in advance.

CRO can also give you information about various park ticket options and make dinner-show reservations for you at the *Hoop-Dee-Doo Musical Revue* or the *Polynesian Luau Dinner Show* when you book your room.

OTHER SOURCES FOR PACKAGES

In addition to the CRO, there are other sources for packages utilizing Disney resorts. These include **Delta Dream Vacations** (☎ 800/872-7786), **US Airways Vacations** (☎ 800/455-0123), **American Airlines Fly Away Vacations** (☎ 800/321-2121), **American Express Vacations** (☎ 800/241-1700), **Travel Impressions** (☎ 800/ 941-2639), and **Kingdom Tours** (☎ 800/872-8857). Best bet: Stop at a sizable travel agency and pick up brochures from all of the above (and others). Pore over them at home, comparing offerings to find the optimum package for your trip.

COMING SOON

Down the pike is the deluxe 1,000-room **Disney's Mediterranean Resort,** which will occupy a prime monorail location on the Seven Seas Lagoon. Its architecture and landscaping will "capture the romance of the sunny resorts of the Greek Islands."

3 Disney Resorts & Official Hotels

DISNEY RESORTS
VERY EXPENSIVE

✪ Disney's Beach Club Resort

1800 Epcot Resorts Blvd. (off Buena Vista Dr.; P.O. Box 10000), Lake Buena Vista, FL 32830-1000. ☎ **407/W-DISNEY** (934-7639) or 407/934-8000. Fax 407/354-1866. 584 rms, 17 suites. A/C MINIBAR TV TEL. $225–$295 double, depending on view and season. Additional person $15 extra. Children 17 and under stay free in parents' room. AE, MC, V. Free self- and valet parking.

From its palm-fringed entranceway and manicured gardens to its plush, sun-dappled lobby, the Beach Club resembles a luxurious Victorian Cape Cod resort. A big plus here, especially for families, is Stormalong Bay, a vast free-form swimming pool/water park that sprawls over 3 acres between the Yacht and Beach clubs and flows into a lake; it includes a 150-foot serpentine water slide. So posh is the Beach Club—and so extensive are its sports facilities—that you might consider it for an upscale resort vacation even without the draw of Disney parks nearby. In a similar category are its sister property, the Yacht Club, and the Grand Floridian (see below). Charming rooms—some with balconies—are furnished in bleached woods, decorated in beachy hues, and equipped with ceiling fans, extra phones in the bath, and safes.

Dining/Entertainment: The very elegant Ariel's is open for seafood dinners nightly. Ideal for family dining is the Cape May Café, serving character breakfasts and authentic New England clambake buffet dinners. Other facilities here serve drinks, wines by the glass, light fare, and ice-cream specialties.

Services: 24-hour room service, guest-services desk, complimentary daily newspaper, baby-sitting, boat transport to MGM theme park.

Facilities: Large swimming pool, Jacuzzi, quarter-mile sand beach, boat rentals, fishing, two tennis courts, state-of-the-art health club, volleyball/croquet/bocci ball courts, 2-mile jogging trail, coin-op washers/dryers, unisex hair salon, shops, business center, video-game arcade, Sandcastle Club (a counselor-supervised children's activity center).

✪ Disney's BoardWalk

2101 N. Epcot Resorts Blvd. (off Buena Vista Dr.; P.O. Box 10000), Lake Buena Vista, FL 32830-1000. ☎ **407/W-DISNEY** (934-7639) or 407/939-5100 (407/939-6200 for villas). Fax 407/354-1866. 358 rms, 20 suites, 532 villas. A/C TV TEL. $225–$350 double; $380–$450 concierge level; $540–$1,525 suites. Villas: $210–$250 studios; $285–$310 one-bedrooms; $385–$405 two-bedrooms; $780 grand villas. Range depends on view and season. Extra person $15. Children under 18 stay free in parents' room. AE, MC, V. Free self- and valet parking.

The BoardWalk—occupying 45 acres along the shores of Lake Crescent—takes its theme from the plush mid-Atlantic Victorian seaside resorts of the 1920s and 1930s. A large deck with rocking chairs overlooks a village green and the lake beyond, and the stunning 70-foot lobby has a working fireplace. Two- to five-story buildings with shingled rooftops and awnings surround private courtyards and New England–style flower gardens. There is even a quarter-mile boardwalk lined with shops and restaurants that doubles as a setting for performers and vendors (of cotton candy and the like). Extensive nightlife options here make this a good choice for singles and couples. Accommodations, done up in quaint B&B style, are just gorgeous; yours might have a brass or four-poster bed. All are equipped with safes and irons and ironing boards. Hair dryers and refrigerators are available. Villas, though a tad pricey, may be a deal for large families or groups since some offer kitchenettes or full kitchens and washers/dryers (a few even have whirlpools). The resort is within walking distance of Epcot and the Yacht and Beach clubs.

Dining/Entertainment: Ranged along the boardwalk promenade to provide scenic water views, dining facilities include the upscale Flying Fish Café for steak and seafood; Spoodle's—a casual Mediterranean market–themed eatery serving Greek, Spanish, and Italian fare at all meals; the Big River Grille and Brewing Works (featuring handcrafted beers and ales); a bakery; and an espresso shop. Lots to do here at night. A 10-piece orchestra plays music from the 1940s through Top 40s at the Atlantic Dance, a 1920s-style dance hall. Jellyrolls, a sing-along bar, features dueling pianos. And a sports bar airs nonstop worldwide athletic events, hosts radio interviews with sports notables, and has the latest interactive sporting and virtual-reality games on hand. There are also several cocktail lounges and a carousel-themed pool bar.

Services: Concierge, 24-hour room service, guest-services desk, complimentary daily newspaper, baby-sitting, boat transport (to MGM, Epcot, and Epcot resorts).

Facilities: Large swimming pool with roller coaster–themed water slide, two additional secluded pools, kiddie pool, whirlpool, two tennis courts, croquet, bike rental, 2-mile jogging path, playground, convention center, full business center, shops, extensively equipped health club, two video-game arcades, Community Hall (for games, crafts, and recreational-equipment rentals), Harbour Club (a counselor-supervised child-care activity center).

Disney's Contemporary Resort

4600 N. World Dr. (P.O. Box 10000), Lake Buena Vista, FL 32830-1000. ☎ **407/W-DISNEY** (934-7639) or 407/824-1000. Fax 407/354-1866. 1,041 rms, 80 suites. A/C TV TEL. $195–$240 double; $220–$280 concierge level. Extra person $15. Children under 17 stay free in parents' room. AE, MC, V. Free self- and valet parking.

When it opened in 1971, the Contemporary's aesthetic was cutting-edge. Today its dramatic angular planes, free-form furnishings, and abstract paintings appear, rather charmingly, retro-modern. Centering on a sleek, 15-story A-frame tower, the property comprises 26 acres bounded by a natural lake and the Disney-made Seven Seas Lagoon. Kids are thrilled that the monorail whizzes right through the hotel, and they also enjoy on-premises character meals. Rooms with art-deco furnishings (bleached woods with ebony accents) are decorated in neutral hues with splashes of color and cheerful Matisse prints on the walls. Amenities include safes and two phones. The 14th floor of the tower is the concierge level.

Dining/Entertainment: The magnificent 15th-floor California Grill (details in chapter 6) provides panoramic vistas of the Magic Kingdom. Other options here include the Concourse Steakhouse, the garden-themed Contemporary Café (for character breakfasts and prime-rib buffet dinners), and several other spots for drinks and light fare.

In the Words of Walt Disney

My operations are based on experience, thoughtful observation, and warm fellowship with my neighbors at home and around the world.

Walt Disney World Accommodations

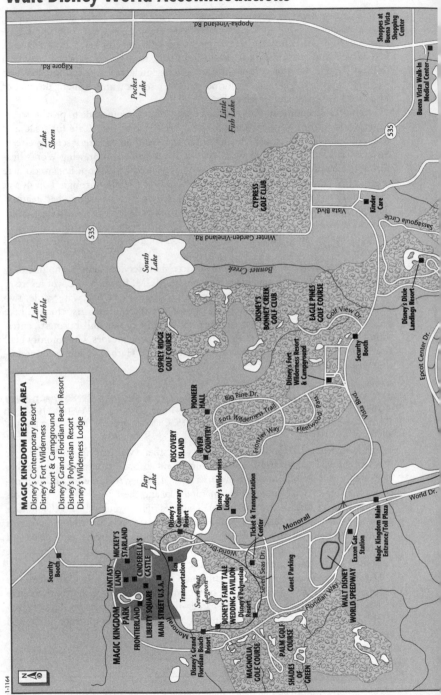

MAGIC KINGDOM RESORT AREA
Disney's Contemporary Resort
Disney's Fort Wilderness
   Resort & Campground
Disney's Grand Floridian Beach Resort
Disney's Polynesian Resort
Disney's Wilderness Lodge

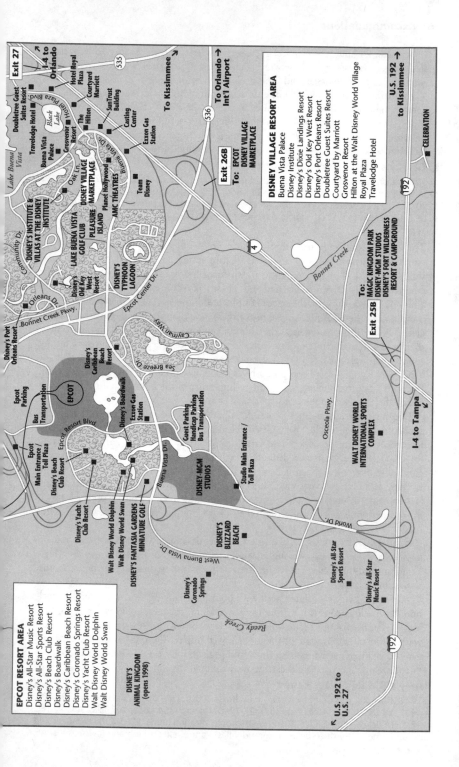

EPCOT RESORT AREA

Disney's All-Star Music Resort
Disney's All-Star Sports Resort
Disney's Beach Club Resort
Disney's Boardwalk
Disney's Caribbean Beach Resort
Disney's Coronado Springs Resort
Disney's Yacht Club Resort
Walt Disney World Dolphin
Walt Disney World Swan

DISNEY VILLAGE RESORT AREA

Buena Vista Palace
Disney Institute
Disney's Dixie Landings Resort
Disney's Old Key West Resort
Disney's Port Orleans Resort
Doubletree Guest Suites Resort
Courtyard by Marriott
Grosvenor Resort
Hilton at the Walt Disney World Village
Royal Plaza
Travelodge Hotel

Exit 27

← I-4 to Orlando

To Orlando Int'l Airport →

U.S. 192 → to Kissimmee

To Kissimmee

Exit 26B
To: EPCOT
DISNEY VILLAGE MARKETPLACE

Exit 25B
To:
MAGIC KINGDOM PARK
DISNEY-MGM STUDIOS
DISNEY'S FORT WILDERNESS
RESORT & CAMPGROUND

I-4 to Tampa

CELEBRATION

DISNEY'S
ANIMAL KINGDOM
(opens 1998)

Disney's All-Star
Sports Resort

Disney's All-Star
Music Resort

Disney's
Coronado
Springs

DISNEY'S BLIZZARD BEACH

DISNEY'S FANTASIA GARDENS
MINIATURE GOLF

Walt Disney World Dolphin
Walt Disney World Swan

Disney's Yacht
Club Resort

Disney's Beach
Club Resort

Epcot
Main Entrance /
Toll Plaza

Epcot
Parking

Bus
Transportation

EPCOT

Disney's Boardwalk

Exxon Gas
Station

Epcot Resort Blvd

Guest Parking
Handicap Parking
Bus Transportation

Studio Main Entrance /
Toll Plaza

DISNEY-MGM STUDIOS

Disney's Caribbean
Beach Resort

WALT DISNEY WORLD
INTERNATIONAL SPORTS
COMPLEX

Osceola Pkwy.

World Dr.

West Buena Vista Dr.

Buena Vista Dr.

Reedy Creek

Bonnet Creek

Sea Breeze Dr.

Cayman Way

Epcot Center Dr.

Bonnet Creek Pkwy.

Orleans Dr.

Disney's Port
Orleans Resort

Disney's Old
Key West
Resort

DISNEY'S
TYPHOON
LAGOON

LAKE BUENA VISTA
GOLF CLUB

DISNEY'S INSTITUTE &
VILLAS AT THE DISNEY
INSTITUTE

DISNEY VILLAGE
MARKETPLACE

PLEASURE
ISLAND

AMC THEATRES

Planet Hollywood

Team
Disney

Community Dr.

Oak Ln.

Buena Vista Dr.

Grosvenor
Resort

Buena Vista
Palace

Travelodge Hotel

Doubletree Guest
Suites Resort

The Hilton

SunTrust
Building

Casting
Center

Exxon Gas
Station

Courtyard
Marriott

Hotel Royal
Plaza

Black
Lake

Lake Buena
Vista

← U.S. 192 to
U.S. 27

535

536

4

192

192

Services: 24-hour room service, guest-services desk, daily newspaper delivery, baby-sitting, boat transport (to Discovery Island, Fort Wilderness, and River Country), monorail to the Polynesian and Grand Floridian resorts.

Facilities: Two swimming pools, kiddie pool, white-sand beach with volleyball court, shuffleboard, boat rentals, unisex hair salon, six tennis courts (lessons available), shops, American Express desk, coin-op washers/dryers, full business center, extensive health club, sauna/massage/tanning rooms, video-game arcade, the Mouseketeer Clubhouse (a counselor-supervised child-care/activity center).

✪ Disney's Grand Floridian Beach Resort

4401 Floridian Way (P.O. Box 10000), Lake Buena Vista, FL 32830-1000. ☎ **407/W-DISNEY** (934-7639) or 407/824-3000. Fax 407/354-1866. 899 rms, 34 suites. A/C MINIBAR TV TEL. $290–$365 double, depending on view and season; $450–$490 concierge floors; $580–$1,810 suite. Extra person $15. Children under 18 stay free in parents' room. AE, MC, V. Free self- and valet parking.

The Grand Floridian is magnificent from the moment you step into its opulent five-story lobby (complete with a Chinese Chippendale aviary) under triple-domed stained-glass skylights. Here, amid plush furnishings and potted palms, a pianist entertains during afternoon tea, and an orchestra plays big-band music every evening. This could be a romantic choice for couples and honeymooners (there's even a wedding pavilion here). And if you're into fitness, you'll appreciate the first-rate health club. Though this resort houses a notable convention center and a full business center, they're in a separate building and won't inconvenience independent travelers. Sunny rooms—with private balconies or verandas overlooking formal gardens, the pool, or a 200-acre lagoon—have two-poster beds made up with lovely floral-chintz spreads. In-room amenities include safes and ceiling fans; in the bath, you'll find an extra phone, hair dryer, and terry robe.

Dining/Entertainment: Victoria & Albert's, Orlando's finest restaurant, is described in chapter 6. The lovely Grand Floridian Café, overlooking formal gardens, features Southern specialties. The exposition-themed 1900 Park Fare is the setting for character breakfasts and dinners. Flagler's offers northern Italian fare. At the gazebolike Narcoossee's, grilled meats and seafood are prepared in an exhibition kitchen. Intimate and very Victorian, Mizner's Lounge features an international selection of ports, brandies, and appetizers. The Garden View Lounge off the lobby is the setting for ultraelegant afternoon teas. Other options include the Gasparilla Grill (open 24 hours) and a pool bar.

Services: 24-hour room service, guest-services desk, nightly turndown, complimentary daily newspaper, baby-sitting, on-premises monorail, boat transport to the Magic Kingdom and the Polynesian Resort, free trolley transport around the hotel grounds, shoe shine, massage.

Facilities: Large swimming pool with poolside changing area, kiddie pool, whirlpool, two tennis courts, boat rentals, waterskiing, croquet, volleyball, playground, jogging trails, fishing excursions, white-sand beach, unisex hair salon, coin-op washers/dryers, shops, state-of-the-art spa, wedding pavilion, video-game arcade, organized children's activities in summer and peak seasons, the Mouseketeer Clubhouse (a counselor-supervised child-care activity center).

Disney's Old Key West Resort

1510 N. Cove Rd. (off Community Dr.; P.O. Box 10000), Lake Buena Vista, FL 32830-1000. ☎ **407/W-DISNEY** (934-7639) or 407/827-7700. Fax 407/354-1866. 709 villas. A/C TV TEL. $195–$215 deluxe rooms; $265–$290 one-bedroom vacation home; $365–$385 two-bedroom vacation home; $780 three-bedroom grand villas. Range reflects high and low seasons. AE, MC, V. Free parking.

The Disney Institute: The Mouse Grows Up

President Clinton has his annual invitation-only Renaissance Weekends, where family fun means lectures on philosophy between games of touch football. The masses have the Disney Institute, where families can expand their minds in classes ranging from gourmet cooking to how to be a lounge singer. It's definitely not for children under 10.

Opened during 1996, the Disney Institute fell far short of the projected intellectually interested throngs. People continue to come to the Mouse for mindless entertainment where the biggest brainteaser is reading the park map. (Isn't that what vacations are for?) There was even a rumor that park employees were being pulled from their jobs so important speakers weren't talking to empty seats.

But the Institute goes on, although there is a greater focus on convention business than individual families.

Like Peter Pan, it may fly if Disney continues to think happy thoughts and believe. The idea is interesting enough. People custom-design an education-entertainment (edu-tainment?) package in this anxiety-free learning environment where guests are always the teachers' pets and there are no grades.

Guest artists and speakers such as Marshall Brickman, Chris Columbus, Siskel and Ebert, Randy Newman, and Morton Gould are the type of instructors to expect during various Entertainment Arts programs.

Other areas of study will include Sports and Fitness, Lifestyles, Story Arts, Culinary Arts, Design, The Environment, and Architecture. Choices are almost limitless. You might opt for golf or tennis clinics, study animation, indulge in an array of luxurious spa treatments, learn topiary gardening, canoe local waterways, trace your family roots, create puppets, go out on bird-watching expeditions, or try rock climbing. Guests are encouraged to participate in a variety of different programs during their stay.

The Institute—designed to resemble a small town with a village green and architecture suggestive of barns, mills, and country houses—sprawls over 265 acres of lakes, streams, and woodlands. Its resort-style public areas and accommodations (bungalows and one- and two-bedroom townhouses) are gorgeous. An elegant, on-premises restaurant called Seasons—each of its four dining rooms representing a season of the year—features nightly changing menus and cuisines. Other facilities include an 18-hole/par-72 championship golf course, four tennis courts, golf/tennis pro shops, six swimming pools, five whirlpools, a kiddie pool, bike rental/bike trails, three sand volleyball courts, a softball/multipurpose sports field, a rock-climbing wall, boat rentals, a state-of-the-art sports and fitness center, spa services/facilities, two playgrounds, a 3.4-mile jogging course, free washers/dryers, a shop, and BBQ grills/picnic tables. Nightly performances and recitals take place in a 1,150-seat open-air amphitheater and a 250-seat performance center, and films are screened weeknights in a 450-seat state-of-the-art movie theater. A counselor-supervised youth center offers a full roster of daytime programs and activities for children ages 10 and up, as well as activities for teens.

The Institute, at 1960 N. Magnolia Way, is adjacent to the Disney Village Marketplace. Based on double occupancy, 3-night packages range from $582 to $916, 4-night packages $690 to $1,135, and 7-night packages $1,208 to $1,986. The pricing structure is complex. Rates include all the above listed advantages of staying at a Disney property. For further information on programs and rates, call ☎ **800/4-WONDER** (496-6337) or 407/827-4800.

An understated theme (at least by Disney standards) makes the Old Key West a good choice for those seeking a quieter environment. Architecturally mirroring Key West at the turn of the century, this is a "vacation ownership" (time-share) property. However, you can rent accommodations here when they're not in use by owners. The 156-acre complex is beautifully landscaped. Most accommodations are gorgeous home-away-from-home residences with living rooms (equipped with large-screen TVs and VCRs, smaller sets and extra phones in the bedroom), fully equipped kitchens, furnished patios (offering water, woodland, or fairway views; the property overlooks the Buena Vista Golf Course), and laundry rooms. Many units contain whirlpool tubs in the master suite, and grand villas have stereo systems.

Dining/Entertainment: The Key West–themed Olivia's Cafe, overlooking a canal, serves all meals. There are a few other spots for drinks and light fare.

Services: Guest-services desk, baby-sitting, ferry service to Disney Village Marketplace and Pleasure Island, free bus transport around the grounds and to nearby grocery stores.

Facilities: Two tennis courts, basketball court, white-sand play area, four swimming pools, whirlpool, kiddie pool, bicycle rental, boat rental, playground, extensive health club, sauna, shuffleboard, horseshoes, volleyball, complimentary use of washers/dryers, general store, video-game arcade, video library. The Community Hall, a recreation center, shows Disney movies nightly and offers various activities.

Disney's Polynesian Resort

1600 Seven Seas Dr. (P.O. Box 10000), Lake Buena Vista, FL 32830-1000. ☎ **407/W-DISNEY** (934-7639) or 407/824-2000. Fax 407/354-1866. 841 rms, 12 suites. A/C TV TEL. $260–$315 double, depending on view and season; $335–$395 concierge floors; $385–$1,100 suite. Extra person $15. Children under 18 stay free in parents' room. AE, MC, V. Free self- and valet parking.

Just below the Magic Kingdom, the 25-acre Polynesian Resort is fronted by lush tropical foliage, waterfalls, and koi ponds. Inside, its skylit lobby is a virtual rain forest of tropical plantings—gorgeous by day, but rather depressingly lit in the evenings. A private, white-sand beach—dotted with canvas cabanas, hammocks, and large swings—looks out on a 200-acre lagoon, and waterfalls, grottoes, and a water slide enhance an immense swimming pool. Large, beautiful rooms—most with balconies or patios—have canopied beds, bamboo and rattan furnishings, and walls hung with Gauguin prints. If you're willing to spend the money, this is a great choice for kids, who will enjoy the extensive Polynesian theme and child-pleasing eateries.

Dining/Entertainment: O'Hana Feast is the setting for character breakfasts and all-you-can-eat island dinners featuring open-pit rock-grilled specialties. Luau Cove hosts Mickey's Tropical Luau and the Polynesian Luau Dinner Show. There are several other restaurants and bars, including a 24-hour ice-cream parlor.

Services: Room service, guest-services desk, complimentary daily newspaper, baby-sitting, on-premises monorail, boat transport (to the Magic Kingdom and the Grand Floridian Beach Resort, Discovery Island, Fort Wilderness, and River Country).

Facilities: Two swimming pools, kiddie pool, boat rental, waterskiing, volleyball, playground, 1¹/₂-mile jogging trail, fishing excursions, coin-op washers/dryers, shops, video-game arcade, the Neverland Club (a counselor-supervised evening activity center for children).

Disney's Yacht Club Resort

1700 Epcot Resorts Blvd. (off Buena Vista Dr.; P.O. Box 10000), Lake Buena Vista, FL 32830-1000. ☎ **407/W-DISNEY** (934-7639) or 407/934-7000. Fax 407/354-1866. 630 rms, 12 suites. A/C MINIBAR TV TEL. $225–$295 double, depending on view and season; $360–$405 concierge level. Extra person $15. Children under 18 stay free in parents' room. AE, MC, V. Free self- and valet parking.

Though first-time visitors to Orlando—who generally spend all their time in the parks—don't require extensive recreational facilities, return visitors will appreciate the extensive sports and entertainment options here. This stunning resort—its main five-story, oyster-gray, clapboard building evocative of a turn-of-the-century New England yacht club—shares a 25-acre lake, facilities, and gorgeous landscaping with the adjacent Beach Club (described above). The nautical theme carries over to very inviting rooms, decorated in snappy blue and white, with brass sconces, ship lights, and vintage maps on the walls. French doors open onto porches or balconies. Amenities include ceiling fans, extra phones in the baths, and safes. The fifth floor is a concierge level, which will especially appeal to business travelers.

Dining/Entertainment: The plush, pine-paneled Yachtsman Steakhouse grills select cuts of steak, chops, and fresh seafood over oak and hickory. The Yacht Club Galley, a comfortable family restaurant, serves American regional fare. Crew's Cup Lounge airs sporting events and offers light fare and frosted mugs of international ales and beers. And the cozy Ale and Compass Lounge, a lobby bar with a working fireplace, features specialty coffees and cocktails.

Services: 24-hour room service, guest-services desk, complimentary daily newspaper, baby-sitting, boat transport to MGM theme park, tram and boat transport to Epcot.

Facilities: Yacht Club facilities are identical to those of the Beach Club (see above).

EXPENSIVE

◐ Disney's Wilderness Lodge

901 Timberline Dr. (on the southwest shore of Bay Lake, just east of the Magic Kingdom; P.O. Box 10000), Lake Buena Vista, FL 32830-1000. ☎ **407/W-DISNEY** (934-7639) or 407/824-3200. Fax 407/354-1866. 697 rms, 25 junior suites, 6 suites. A/C TV TEL. $159–$215 double, depending on view and season; $270–$290 junior suite; $580–$625 suite. Extra person $15. Children under 18 stay free in parents' room. AE, MC, V. Free self- and valet parking.

This is one of my favorite Disney resorts, and one I think will appeal to adults as much as it does to kids. Its main dining room, Artist Point, could provide the setting for a romantic dinner. Reminiscent of rustic turn-of-the-century national park lodges, this 56-acre resort is surrounded by towering oak and pine forests. Its imposing lobby centers on a massive stone fireplace embedded with replicas of ancient Yellowstone fossils. A geothermal spring flows from the lobby into Silver Creek, which itself empties into beautiful 340-acre Bay Lake. Outside, "volcanic" meadow landscaping is punctuated by bubbling craters, a babbling brook, a cascading waterfall, and a spewing geyser. Five-minute geyser shows take place in the meadow periodically throughout the day, and nightly electric water pageants can be viewed from the shores of Bay Lake. There's a lakefront sand beach, and an immense, serpentine swimming pool is seemingly excavated out of the rocks.

Guest rooms—with patios or balconies overlooking lake, woodland, or meadow scenery—are furnished in Mission style and adorned with tribal friezes and landscape paintings of the Northwest. In-room safes are a plus.

Dining/Entertainment: The stunning, lodgelike Artist Point is described in chapter 6. The rustic, western-themed Whispering Canyon Cafe serves up hearty, all-you-can-eat family-style meals in iron skillets. There are additional venues for drinks and light fare.

Services: Room service, guest-services desk, baby-sitting, boat transport to Magic Kingdom and Contemporary Resort, bus transport to MGM, Epcot, and other park areas.

Facilities: Immense swimming pool (see above), kiddie pool with water slide, lakefront sand beach, spa pools, boat rentals, bicycle rental, 2-mile jogging/bike trail with exercise stations, video-game arcade, gift shop, Cub's Den (a counselor-supervised activity center for children ages 4 to 12).

MODERATE

✪ Disney's Caribbean Beach Resort

900 Cayman Way (off Buena Vista Dr.; P.O. Box 10000), Lake Buena Vista, FL 32830-1000. ☎ **407/W-DISNEY** (934-7639) or 407/934-3400. Fax 407/354-1866. 2,112 rms. A/C MINIBAR TV TEL. $95–$129 double. Extra person $12. Children under 17 stay free in parents' room. AE, MC, V. Free parking.

Though facilities here aren't as extensive as those at some other Disney resorts, the Caribbean Beach offers especially good value for families. Extensively themed, it occupies 200 lush, palm-fringed tropical acres, with accommodations in five distinct Caribbean "villages" grouped around a large, duck-filled lake. The main swimming pool here replicates a Spanish-style Caribbean fort, complete with water slide, kiddie pool, and whirlpool. There are other pools as well as lakefront white-sand beaches in each village, and a 1.4-mile promenade—popular for jogging—circles the lake. An arched wooden bridge leads to Parrot Cay Island, where there's a short nature trail, an aviary of tropical birds, and a picnic area. Rooms are charming, with pineapple-motif oak furnishings and exquisite floral-print chintz bedspreads. Amenities include coffeemakers and ceiling fans; refrigerators are available at $5 per night. All rooms have verandas, many of them overlooking the lake.

Dining/Entertainment: Facilities include a festive food court, the nautically themed Captain's Tavern for American fare, and a pool bar.

Services: Room service (pizza only), guest-services desk, baby-sitting, complimentary shuttle around the grounds.

Facilities: Seven swimming pools including one Caribbean-themed pool, video-game arcade, shops, boat rentals, bicycle rental, coin-op washers/dryers, playgrounds.

Disney's Coronado Springs Resort

1000 Buena Vista Dr., near All-Star Resorts and Blizzard Beach, Lake Buena Vista, FL 32830. ☎ **407/W-DISNEY** (934-7639), 407/934-6632, or 407/824-1000. Fax 407/828-5392. 1,923 rms, 44 suites (95 rms specifically designed for handicapped accessibility). A/C MINIBAR TV TEL. The rates, not set at press time, are expected to be comparable to those at the Caribbean Beach Resort. Extra person $12. Children under 17 stay free in parents' room. AE, MC, V. Free parking.

Everything here is themed on the American Southwest, with lots of muted pastels, sculptured wolves, and cacti. Its four- and five-story haciendalike buildings have terra-cotta tile roofs and palm-shaded courtyards, and the property itself also houses a major 95,000-square-foot convention center and the largest ballroom in the Southeast.

Dining/Entertainment: There is a 420-seat food court, called the Pepper Market, to satisfy the munchies with a variety of fast food. Francisco's is a sit-down 220-seat Mexican restaurant where the emphasis is on fine dining. You won't find a triple-decker burrito here, but rather superbly prepared native dishes such as corn tamales in a spicy green sauce.

Services: Room service from 6am to 11pm, nightly turndown, lounge, transportation to all WDW parks.

Facilities: White-sand beach, beach volleyball, boat rentals, four large swimming pools, kiddie pool, arcade, complimentary parking, boutiques, shops, access to golf course, voice-mail system, spa, coin-op laundry.

Disney's Dixie Landings Resort

1251 Dixie Dr. (off Bonnet Creek Pkwy.; P.O. Box 10000), Lake Buena Vista, FL 32830-1000. ☎ **407/W-DISNEY** (934-7639) or 407/934-6000. Fax 407/934-5777. 2,048 rms. A/C TV TEL. $95–$129 for up to 4 in a room. AE, MC, V. Free parking.

Low rates, extensive child-oriented facilities, and a food court make Dixie Landings popular with families, though adults traveling alone might prefer a more sedate setting. Nestled on the banks of the "mighty Sassagoula River" and dotted with bayous, it shares its 325-acre site with the Port Orleans Resort (described below). It includes Ol' Man Island, a woodsy, $3^1/_2$-acre recreation area containing an immense rustic-themed swimming pool with waterfalls cascading from a broken bridge and a water slide, a playground, children's wading pool, whirlpool, and fishin' hole (buy bait and rent poles, and angle for catfish and bass). Accommodation areas, themed after the Louisiana countryside, are divided into "parishes," with rooms housed in stately colonnaded plantation homes or rural Cajun-style dwellings. The former, fronted by brick courtyards and manicured lawns, are elegantly decorated in Federalist blue and gold, with brass-trimmed maple furnishings. Cajun rooms, on the other hand, are set amid bayous and stands of towering pine; they feature bed frames made of bent branches, patchwork quilts, and calico-print drapes.

Dining/Entertainment: Boatwright's Dining Hall, housed in a replica of an 1800s boat-building factory, serves American/Cajun fare at breakfast and dinner. The Cotton Co-op lounge airs Monday-night football games and offers entertainment (singers and comedians) Tuesday through Saturday nights. A food court and pool bar round out the facilities.

Services: Room service (pizza only), guest-services desk, baby-sitting, boat transport (to Port Orleans, Village Marketplace, and Pleasure Island).

Facilities: Six large swimming pools including one pool with water slide, coin-op washers/dryers, video-game arcade, bicycle rental, boat rentals, 1.7-mile riverfront jogging/biking path, Fulton's General Store.

✪ Disney's Port Orleans Resort

2201 Orleans Dr. (off Bonnet Creek Pkwy.; P.O. Box 10000), Lake Buena Vista, FL 32830-1000. ☎ 407/W-DISNEY (934-7639) or 407/934-5000. Fax 407/934-5353. 1,008 rms. A/C TV TEL. Regular rate, $124–$139; holiday rate, $134–$149 for up to 4 in a room. AE, MC, V. Free parking.

This beautiful resort, themed after turn-of-the-century New Orleans, shares a site on the banks of the Sassagoula with Dixie Landings, described above. Its identical room rates and comparable facilities make it, also, a good bet for families. Pastel-hued accommodation buildings, with shuttered windows and lacy wrought-iron balconies, are fronted by lovely flower gardens opening onto fountained courtyards. Pretty cherry-wood furnishings, swagged draperies, and walls hung with botanical prints and family photographs make for pretty room interiors. And landscaping throughout the property is a delight, with stately oaks, formal boxwood hedges, azaleas, and fragrant jasmine.

Dining/Entertainment: Bonfamille's Café is open for breakfast and dinner, the latter featuring Creole specialties. Scat Cat's Club, a cocktail lounge off the lobby, airs Monday-night football and features family-oriented live entertainment. A food court and pool bar round out the facilities.

Services: Room service (pizza only), guest-services desk, baby-sitting, boat transport (to Dixie Landings, Village Marketplace, and Pleasure Island).

Facilities: The larger-than-Olympic–size Doubloon Lagoon swimming pool is surmounted by an enormous water slide. Whirlpool, kiddie pool, coin-op washers/dryers, video-game arcade, bicycle rental, boat rentals, 1.7-mile riverfront jogging path, shops.

INEXPENSIVE

✪ Disney's All-Star Music Resort

1801 W. Buena Vista Dr. (at World Dr. and Osceola Pkwy.; P.O. Box 10000), Lake Buena Vista, FL 32830-1000. ☎ 407/W-DISNEY (934-7639) or 407/939-6000. Fax 407/354-1866.

1,920 rms. A/C TV TEL. $69–$79 double. Extra person $8. Children under 18 stay free in parents' room. AE, MC, V. Free parking.

Though the unbeatable combination of rock-bottom rates and extensive facilities at Disney's All-Star Music and Sports resorts (see below) is very attractive to families, there is one caveat: Rooms are small (a mere 260 sq. ft.). They're ideal for single adults or couples traveling with one child; larger families had best be into togetherness. Nestled among pristine pine forests, this Disney property is part of a 246-acre complex that also includes the adjacent All-Star Sports Resort (see below). Its 10 buildings are musically themed around country, jazz, rock, calypso, or Broadway show tunes. The calypso building, for instance, has a palm-fringed roof frieze and balconies adorned with tropical birds and musical notes, while a convoy of 18-wheelers travels around the country building, which is adorned with fiddles and banjos. Oversized "icons" in public areas—such as three-story cowboy boots or a walk-through jukebox—are lit by neon and fiber optics at night. Rooms are attractive, with musically themed bedspreads, paintings, and wallpaper borders. In-room safes are a plus.

Dining/Entertainment: There's a cheerful food court and adjoining bar.

Services: Room service (pizza only), guest-services desk, baby-sitting.

Facilities: Two vast swimming pools, kiddie pool, playground, coin-op washers/dryers, large retail shop, video-game arcade.

Disney's All-Star Sports Resort

1701 W. Buena Vista Dr. (at World Dr. and Osceola Pkwy.; P.O. Box 10000), Lake Buena Vista, FL 32830-1000. ☎ **407/W-DISNEY** (934-7639) or 407/939-5000. Fax 407/354-1866. 1,920 rms. A/C TV TEL. $79–$89 double. Extra person $8. Children under 18 stay free in parents' room. AE, MC, V. Free parking.

Adjacent to and sharing facilities with the above-listed All-Star Music Resort, this 82-acre property has an elaborate sports theme, with rooms housed in buildings designed around football, baseball, basketball, tennis, and surfing motifs. For instance, the turquoise surf buildings have waves along their rooflines, surfboards mounted on exterior walls, and pink fish swimming along balcony railings. Immense public-area "icons" here include tennis-ball–can stairways and four-story football helmets and whistles. Cheerful rooms feature sports-action–motif bedspreads, paintings, and wallpaper borders; in-room safes are among your amenities. As noted above, however, rooms here are small.

Dining/Entertainment: There's a brightly decorated food court with an adjoining bar.

Services: Room service (pizza only), guest-services desk, baby-sitting.

Facilities: Two vast swimming pools (one surfing themed with two 38-foot shark fins, the other shaped like a baseball diamond with an "outfield" sundeck), kiddie pool, playground, coin-op washers/dryers, shop, video-game arcade.

A DISNEY CAMPGROUND

Disney's Fort Wilderness Resort and Campground

3520 N. Fort Wilderness Trail (P.O. Box 10000), Lake Buena Vista, FL 32830-1000. ☎ **407/ W-DISNEY** (934-7639) or 407/824-2900. Fax 407/354-1866. 784 campsites, 408 wilderness homes. AC TV TEL (homes only). $35–$54 campsite, depending on season, location, number of people, size, and extent of hookup; $180–$215 wilderness home. AE, MC, V. Free self-parking.

This woodsy 780-acre camping resort—shaded by towering pines and cypress trees and crossed by fish-filled streams, lakes, and canals—makes an ideal venue for family vacations. Though it is a tad less central than other Disney properties, its abundance of on-premises facilities more than compensates. Secluded **campsites** offer

110/220-volt outlets, barbecue grills, picnic tables, and children's play areas. There are also **wilderness homes**—rustic, one-bedroom cabins with piney interiors that accommodate up to six people. These have cozy living rooms with Murphy beds, fully equipped eat-in kitchens, picnic tables, and barbecue grills. Guests here enjoy extensive recreational facilities ranging from a riding stable to a nightly campfire program hosted by Chip 'n' Dale.

Dining/Entertainment: The rustic, log-beamed Trails End offers buffet meals, and the cozy Crockett's Tavern features Texas fare. During summer, guests enjoy a dazzling electrical water pageant from the beach, nightly at 9:45pm. And the rambunctious *Hoop-Dee-Doo Musical Revue* takes place nightly in Pioneer Hall.

Services: Guest-services desk, baby-sitting, boat transport (to Discovery Island, the Magic Kingdom, and the Contemporary Resort).

Facilities: Comfort station in each campground area (with rest rooms, private showers, ice machines, phones, and laundry rooms), two large swimming pools, white-sand beach, horseback riding (trail rides, pony rides), petting farm, fishing, three sand volleyball courts, ball fields, tetherball, shuffleboard, bike rentals, boat rentals, 1.5-mile nature trail, 2.3-mile jogging path, two tennis courts, two 18-hole championship golf courses, shops, kennel, two video-game arcades.

LAKE BUENA VISTA/OFFICIAL HOTELS

These properties, designated "official" Walt Disney World hotels, are located on and around Hotel Plaza Boulevard. Guests at the below-listed hotels enjoy many privileges (see section 2 of this chapter). And the location is a big plus—close to the Disney parks and within walking distance of Disney Village Marketplace and Crossroads shops and restaurants, as well as Pleasure Island nightlife.

Note: In addition to the addresses and toll-free phone numbers provided in each listing below, you can also make reservations at any of these official hotels through the Central Reservations Office, P.O. Box 10000, Lake Buena Vista, FL 32830-1000 (☎ 407/W-DISNEY [934-7639]).

EXPENSIVE

Buena Vista Palace

1900 Buena Vista Dr., just north of Hotel Plaza Blvd. (P.O. Box 22206), Lake Buena Vista, FL 32830. ☎ **800/327-2990** or 407/827-2727. Fax 407/827-6034. 887 rms, 127 suites. A/C MINIBAR TV TEL. $145–$235 double; $219–$250 Crown Level double; $245–$290 one-bedroom suite; $390–$455 two-bedroom suite. Range reflects view and season. Extra person $15. Children under 18 stay free in parents' room. AE, CB, DC, DISC, MC, V. Free self-parking; valet parking $7 per night.

This 27-acre waterfront resort offers boating, tennis, and other recreational facilities. Additionally, it pampers guests at a European-style spa and houses a first-rate restaurant. Accommodations—most with lake-view balconies or patios—are appealingly decorated and equipped with cable TVs (with Spectravision movie options), safes, bedroom and bath phones, and ceiling fans. There are also luxurious, residential-style one- and two-bedroom suites with living and dining rooms and a 10th-floor concierge level.

Dining/Entertainment: Arthur's 27 (perched on the 27th floor) offers haute-cuisine dinners and panoramic park views, as well as live jazz, piano-bar entertainment, and dancing in an adjoining lounge. In the Outback Restaurant (complete with a three-story indoor waterfall), an Australian storyteller entertains during dinner (steak and seafood are featured). Character breakfasts take place in the Watercress Cafe. Several other venues for dining and drinking include the Laughing Kookaburra Good Time Bar, which offers a selection of 99 beers and hosts happy-hour buffets and live bands for dancing nightly.

Services: 24-hour room service, guest-services desk (sells tickets and arranges transportation to all nearby attractions), complimentary newspaper for Crown Level, baby-sitting, shoe shine/repair.

Facilities: Two large swimming pools, whirlpool, kiddie pool, three tennis courts, boat rentals, 2- and 3-mile jogging paths, sand volleyball court, bike rental, playground, full business center, shops, coin-op washers/dryers, video-game arcade, Kids Stuff (a counselor-supervised child-care program). The spa offers massage, herbal wraps, a fully equipped health club, a sauna, whirlpools, a unisex beauty salon, and more.

Hilton at Walt Disney World Village

1751 Hotel Plaza Blvd. (just east of Buena Vista Dr.), Lake Buena Vista, FL 32830. ☎ **800/ 782-4414** or 407/827-4000. Fax 407/827-3890. 787 rms, 27 suites. A/C MINIBAR TV TEL. $150–$260 double, depending on season. Tower rooms $40 additional. Extra person $20. Children of any age stay free in parents' room. Inquire about weekend rates. AE, CB, DC, DISC, JCB, MC, V. Free self-parking; valet parking $8 per night.

Okay, you want to enjoy all the privileges of a Disney resort, but a relentless theme isn't your thing. This property offers traditional Hilton panache. Heralded by a palm-fringed, circular driveway leading up to an imposing waterfall and fountain, it occupies 23 beautifully landscaped acres including two large lakes. Accommodations—done up in soft earth tones with floral-print bedspreads—are equipped with cable TVs (with HBO and Spectravision movie options), coffeemakers, and phones with voice-mail and computer jacks. The 9th and 10th floors comprise The Towers, a concierge level.

Dining/Entertainment: Choices include Finn's Grill, a Key West–themed steak and seafood restaurant; Benihana Japanese Steakhouse (for teppanyaki dining and nightly entertainment, including karaoke); and a cheerful coffee shop. John T's Plantation Bar offers nightly entertainment for dancing. Kids love the Old-Fashioned Soda Shoppe for pizzas, burgers, and ice-cream sundaes; it even has video games. And a cedar gazebo is the scene of frequent live poolside entertainment.

Services: Concierge (sells tickets and arranges transport to all other nearby attractions/airport), 24-hour room service, baby-sitting.

Facilities: Two very large swimming pools, whirlpool, children's spray pool, two tennis courts, boat rental, volleyball, water volleyball, badminton, playground, unisex beauty salon, business center, fully equipped health club, sauna, shops, coin-op washers/dryers, video-game arcade, Vacation Station Kids Hotel (a counselor-supervised child-care center).

MODERATE

✪ Courtyard by Marriott

1805 Hotel Plaza Blvd. (between Lake Buena Vista Dr. and Apopka–Vineland Rd./Fla. 535), Lake Buena Vista, FL 32830. ☎ **800/223-9930** or 407/828-8888. Fax 407/827-4623. 321 rms, 2 suites. A/C TV TEL. $89–$149 double, depending on view and season. AE, CB, DC, DISC, JCB, MC, V. Free parking.

Courtyard is a moderately priced link in the Marriott chain, with lower prices achieved via limited services. But don't envision a spartan, no-frills atmosphere. This property was recently renovated to the tune of $4.5 million, and it's looking great. Attractive rooms—most with balconies—have in-room safes, coffeemakers, and cable TVs (with HBO, pay-movie options, and Nintendo); refrigerators are available on request. A full-service restaurant serves American fare at all meals and provides room service. There's also a lobby cocktail lounge, a poolside bar (in season), and an on-premises deli featuring pizza and frozen yogurt. The guest-services desk sells tickets and arranges transport to all nearby attractions. Other facilities include two swimming pools, a whirlpool, a kiddie pool, boat rental at nearby Disney Village Marina, a playground, an exercise room, shops, coin-op washers/dryers, and a video-game arcade.

Doubletree Guest Suites Resort

2305 Hotel Plaza Blvd. (just west of Apopka–Vineland Rd./Fla. 535), Lake Buena Vista, FL 32830. ☎ 800/222-TREE (8733) or 407/934-1000. Fax 407/934-1011. 229 suites. A/C TV TEL. $139–$235 for up to 6 people in a one-bedroom suite; $275–$475 two-bedroom suite. Extra person $20. Children under 18 stay free in parents' room. Range depends on view and season. AE, CB, DC, DISC, JCB, MC, V. Free self-parking.

Entered via a cheerful skylit atrium lobby with an aviary of tropical birds and theme-park murals, this seven-story, all-suite hotel is a great choice for families. Children have their own check-in desk, where they receive a free gift. Large one-bedroom suites—which can sleep up to six—are delightfully decorated and include full living rooms, dining areas, and separate bedrooms. Among your in-room amenities are a wet bar, refrigerator, coffeemaker, microwave oven, remote-control cable TVs (with pay-movie options) in the living room and bedroom, a smaller black-and-white TV in the bath, two phones, and a hair dryer.

Dining/Entertainment: The festive Streamers serves buffet and à la carte breakfasts and dinners featuring American fare with Southwestern specialties. A bar lounge adjoins, as does a theater where kids can watch Disney movies while Mom and Dad linger over coffee. Another bar serves the pool.

Services: Room service, guest-services desk (sells tickets and arranges transport to all nearby attractions), baby-sitting, free shuttle to WDW parks.

Facilities: Large swimming pool, whirlpool, kiddie pool with fountain, two tennis courts, golf courses nearby, boat rental at nearby Disney Village Marina, jogging path, volleyball, playground, exercise room, shops (including a grocery), coin-op washers/dryers, video-game arcade, kids' theater.

Grosvenor Resort

1850 Hotel Plaza Blvd. (just east of Buena Vista Dr.), Lake Buena Vista, FL 32830. ☎ 800/624-4109 or 407/828-4444. Fax 407/828-8192. 626 rms, 7 suites. A/C TV TEL. $99–$175 for up to 4 people, depending on view and season. AE, CB, DC, DISC, JCB, MC, V. Free self-parking; valet parking $6 per night.

In the moderately priced category, the Grosvenor is a comfortable choice with a British Colonial theme and a few unique entertainment options. Occupying 13 lushly landscaped lakeside acres, it centers on a 19-story, peach stucco building fronted by towering palms. Rooms are nicely decorated in an attractive resort motif and equipped with remote-control cable TVs with VCRs (movie tapes can be rented), coffeemakers, safes, and minibars (stocked on request); refrigerators can be rented.

Dining/Entertainment: The Baskervilles Restaurant—with a Sherlock Holmes museum on the premises—hosts a Saturday-night mystery dinner-theater and buffet breakfasts and dinners, some with Disney characters. Also here: Moriarty's Pub (offering live entertainment in high season), a 24-hour food court, a pool bar, and a lounge where sporting events are aired on a large-screen TV.

Services: Room service, guest-services desk (sells tickets and arranges transport to all nearby attractions), free daily newspaper, baby-sitting.

Facilities: Two swimming pools, whirlpool, kiddie pool, exercise room, two tennis courts, boat rental, playground, lawn games, coin-op washers/dryers, shops, video-game arcade.

Royal Plaza

1905 Hotel Plaza Blvd. (between Buena Vista Dr. and Apopka–Vineland Rd./Fla. 535), Lake Buena Vista, FL 32830. ☎ **800/248-7890** or 407/828-2828. Fax 407/827-6338. 373 rms, 21 suites. A/C MINIBAR TV TEL. $89–$149 for up to 5 people in a room; $139–$179 executive king; $119–$159 concierge level; $550 signature suite. Range reflects view and season. AE, CB, DC, DISC, JCB, MC, V. Free self- and valet parking.

The Royal Plaza recently completed a multimillion-dollar renovation and upgrade, including the refurbishment of all accommodations and public areas. Spiffy new rooms—decorated in soft resort hues with bleached oak furnishings—are equipped with VCRs (movies can be rented), safes, coffeemakers, and hair dryers. Pool-view rooms have patios or balconies, and both executive kings and concierge-level rooms contain Jacuzzis (the former also offer full living rooms). Most unique are a pair of suites decorated, respectively, by Burt Reynolds and Barbara Mandrell, who supplied family photographs, platinum records/acting awards, and other personal memorabilia.

Dining/Entertainment: Plaza Diner is a full-service family restaurant specializing in American foods such as burgers and meat loaf. Intermission, a sports bar with a handful of big-screen televisions, offers a chance to catch that big game—whether hockey, basketball, baseball, or football. A pool bar is set up during the busy season.

Services: Room service, guest-services desk (sells tickets and arranges transport to all nearby attractions), baby-sitting, foreign-currency exchange.

Facilities: Large L-shaped swimming pool, whirlpool, four tennis courts, boat rental, sauna, coin-op washers/dryers, shops, video-game arcade.

Travelodge Hotel

2000 Hotel Plaza Blvd. (between Buena Vista Dr. and Apopka–Vineland Rd./Fla. 535), Lake Buena Vista, FL 32830. ☎ **800/348-3765** or 407/828-2424. Fax 407/828-8933. 321 rms, 4 suites. A/C MINIBAR TV TEL. $99–$169 for up to 4 people, depending on room size and season. Inquire about packages. AE, DC, DISC, MC, V. Free parking.

This 12-acre lakefront property is spiffy and immaculate, with rooms and public areas more upscale than you might expect at a Travelodge. Rates are also higher than the Travelodge norm but represent good value for your money. The reason: This is the company's flagship hotel. Designed to resemble a Barbados plantation manor house, it has a Caribbean resort ambiance enhanced by tropical foliage and bright, floral-print fabrics and carpeting. Rooms are particularly inviting, with light bleached-wood furnishings and lovely framed botanical prints and floral friezes. Furnished balconies overlook Lake Buena Vista. Amenities include cable TVs (with Spectravision movie options and Nintendo), coffeemakers, safes, and hair dryers. Free local phone calls are a plus.

Dining/Entertainment: Traders, with a wall of windows facing a wooded area, is open for breakfast and steak and seafood dinners. On the 18th floor, Toppers offers magnificent views of Lake Buena Vista, as well as dancing, music videos, pool tables, and dartboards; it's a great vantage point for watching nightly laser shows and fireworks. There's also a cocktail bar and a casual self-service eatery.

Services: Room service, guest-services desk (sells tickets and arranges transport to all nearby attractions), free newspaper weekdays, baby-sitting.

Facilities: Large swimming pool, sundeck, kiddie pool, boat rental, playground, coin-op washers/dryers, shops, video-game arcade, conference rooms.

THE DOLPHIN & THE SWAN

The Dolphin and the Swan, both within walking distance of Epcot, occupy some kind of middle ground between Disney properties and official hotels. They offer

---

🚸 Family-Friendly Hotels

Disney Hostelries & Official Hotels *(see p. 52–68)* These offer many advantages for kids, including proximity to Walt Disney World parks, complimentary transportation between the hotel and the parks, and reduced-price children's menus and Disney character appearances in hotel restaurants. Extensive facilities might include lakefront beaches, boating, waterskiing, bike rentals, playgrounds, video-game arcades, swimming pools with waterfalls and slides, and/or organized children's activities.

Disney's Fort Wilderness Resort and Campground *(see p. 62)* All of the above and more is offered here, including nightly campfire programs with Chip 'n' Dale, trail rides, pony rides, and a petting farm. . . and you get to go camping.

Residence Inns *(see p. 70, 74, 82)* Not only do they have swimming pools, children's playgrounds, and other recreational facilities, but also accommodations with fully equipped kitchens—a potential money-saver for families. Rates include breakfast. The Lake Cecile hostelry has on-premises barbecue grills and picnic tables and offers fishing, bumper rides, jet skiing, and waterskiing on a scenic lake.

Holiday Inn Sunspree Resort Lake Buena Vista *(see p. 72)* This Holiday Inn has a special check-in desk for kids and on-premises mascots to welcome them. Rooms are equipped with kitchenettes, and there are themed "kidsuites" available. Kids under 12 eat free in their own restaurant, where movies and cartoons are shown. Numerous organized children's activities are free.

The **Holiday Inn Hotel & Suites** *(see p. 73)* offers children's facilities identical to Sunspree Resort.

---

almost all the perks of Disney-owned properties, such as advance reservations at WDW restaurants and shows, including Epcot establishments, via the hotel concierge. Both are also distinctive for Michael Graves's fantastical architectural style, which people tend to adore or detest.

Walt Disney World Dolphin

1500 Epcot Resorts Blvd. (off Buena Vista Dr.; P.O. Box 22653), Lake Buena Vista, FL 32830-2653. ☎ **800/227-1500** or 407/934-4000. Fax 407/934-4884. 1,373 rms, 136 suites. A/C MINIBAR TV TEL. $210–$295 double, depending on view and season; $330–$410 Dolphin Towers floors; $475–$2,890 suite. Extra person $15. Up to 2 children under 18 stay free in parents' room. Inquire about packages. AE, CB, DC, DISC, JCB, MC, V. Free self-parking; valet parking $6.

Though distinctive architecture is its keynote, sports enthusiasts will also appreciate this resort's extensive health club, boat rentals, and tennis facilities. Designed by whimsical architect Michael Graves, the property centers on a 27-story pyramid with two 11-story wings crowned by 56-foot twin dolphin sculptures. Graves dubs his more-Disneyesque-than-Disney creations "entertainment architecture." Close to a dozen cascading fountains on the property range from a seven-dolphin extravaganza at the entrance to waters rushing across rock-faced grottoes in a fiber-optic "starlit" foyer. A free-form rock-sculpted grotto pool—with waterfalls, a water slide, rope bridge, and three secluded whirlpools—sprawls over 2 acres between the Dolphin and the adjoining Swan. Both properties also share a white, sandy beach on Crescent Lake.

There are thousands of works of art in public areas. In the rooms, walls are hung with art prints (Picasso, Matisse, and others), and painted wood furnishings are stenciled with palm trees and pineapples. Amenities include pay movies, desk and bedside phones, safes, coffeemakers, hair dryers, and irons/ironing boards. The Dolphin Towers comprise a 77-room concierge level.

Dining/Entertainment: The elegant Sum Chows serves haute-cuisine pan-Asian dinners. Juan and Only's Bar & Jail offers moderately priced Tex-Mex fare. Harry's Safari Bar & Grille, highlighting steak and seafood, is open for dinner nightly and Sunday character-brunch buffets (details in chapter 6). Other venues are the delightful fish-themed Coral Cafe for American fare, an ice-cream/malt shop, a 24-hour cafeteria, Copa Banana, (with a DJ spinning tunes for nightly dancing plus karaoke), a lobby lounge, and a poolside bar.

Services: Concierge, 24-hour room service, guest-services desk (sells tickets and arranges transport to all nearby attractions), baby-sitting, water launch transport to Epcot and Disney–MGM Studios, Japanese tour desk.

Facilities: See also facilities at the Swan, below. Water volleyball, boat rentals, four hard-surface night-lit tennis courts, tennis pro shop, fully equipped Body by Jake health club, two beach volleyball courts, miniature golf, 3-mile jogging trail, coin-op washers/dryers, unisex hair salon, shops, full business center, Delta Airlines desk, large video-game arcade, Camp Dolphin (a counselor-supervised children's activity center, open daily).

Walt Disney World Swan

1200 Epcot Resorts Blvd. (off Buena Vista Dr.; P.O. Box 22786), Lake Buena Vista, FL 32830-2786. ☎ **800/248-SWAN** (7926), 800/228-3000, or 407/934-3000. (*Note:* You may get a lower rate by reserving through the second toll-free number for Westin hotels). Fax 407/934-4499. 702 rms, 56 suites. A/C MINIBAR TV TEL. $280–$410 double, depending on view and season; $340–$370 concierge floors; $290–$1,750 suite. Extra person $25. Children under 18 stay free in parents' room. Inquire about packages. AE, CB, DC, DISC, JCB, MC, V. Free self-parking; valet parking $8.

Operated by Westin Hotels & Resorts, this 12-story hotel—its rooftop flanked by 45-foot swan statues and seashell fountains—is adjacent to, and shares a white-sand lakeside beach and facilities with, the above-mentioned Dolphin. The hotels are connected by a canopied walkway. Here Michael Graves has created a festive interior replete with swan fountains, sea horse–motif chandeliers, hallway walls painted with beach scenes, and striped room doors evocative of cabanas. Luxurious accommodations, decorated in cheerful pastels, have furnishings stenciled with parrots and pineapples, swan- and palm-tree–motif lamps, and, like the Dolphin, walls hung with fine-art prints. In-room amenities include pay movies, desk and bedside phones, and safes. King-bedded rooms have pullout sleeper sofas. The 11th and 12th floors comprise the Royal Beach Club, a concierge level.

Dining/Entertainment: Serving dinner only, the casually elegant Italian-*moderne* Palio has large windows overlooking scenic canals. Strolling musicians entertain while you dine. The delightful Garden Grove Café serves steaks and prime rib, and in the morning, a traditional Japanese breakfast is an option. A few other venues include Kimono's, which serves a wide selection of sushi and becomes a karaoke bar after 8:30pm.

Services: Concierge, 24-hour room service, guest-services desk, complimentary daily newspaper, nightly turndown on request, baby-sitting, complimentary water launch to Epcot and Disney–MGM Studios.

Facilities: See also facilities at the Dolphin, above. Olympic-size lap pool, children's wading pool, fully equipped health club, full business center, children's playground, shops, video-game arcade.

4 Other Lake Buena Vista–Area Hotels

All of the below-listed hotels are within a few minutes' drive of WDW parks.

VERY EXPENSIVE

✪ Hyatt Regency Grand Cypress

1 Grand Cypress Blvd. (off Fla. 535), Orlando, FL 32836. ☎ **800/233-1234** or 407/239-1234; fax 407/239-3800. For villas ☎ 800/835-7377 or 407/239-4700; fax 407/239-7219. 676 rms, 74 suites, 146 villas. A/C MINIBAR TV TEL. $185–$310 for up to 5 people in a room; $305–$410 Regency Club; $190–$1,400 one- to four-bedroom villas. Range reflects room size, view, and season. AE, CB, DC, DISC, JCB, MC, V. Free self-parking; valet parking $8 per night.

This dazzling, multifacility resort is in a class by itself. Of all Orlando properties, it's the most alluring for a romantic getaway. Also appealing are its fabulous sports and recreational facilities: a half-acre swimming pool spanned by a rope bridge and flowing through rock grottoes (with 12 waterfalls and two steep water slides), three whirlpools, a white-sand beach, 12 tennis courts, a 45-hole/par-72 Jack Nicklaus–designed golf course, a 9-hole pitch-and-putt golf course, a highly acclaimed equestrian center offering lessons and trail rides, complimentary bicycles, and boat rentals, among others. Tropical plantings in the atrium lobby comprise a small rain forest, with stone-bedded streams and live birds in brass cages. And the grounds (comprising 1,500 acres) are dotted with babbling brooks, flower beds, and rock gardens ablaze with bougainvillea and hibiscus. Sailboats and swans glide serenely on 21-acre Lake Windsong. Accommodations are deluxe, decorated in bright tropical hues with wicker furnishings. Amenities include pay-movie options, safes, and, in the bath, hair dryers, robes, scales, and fine toiletries. Two floors comprise the Regency Club, a concierge level. Especially gorgeous are the Mediterranean-style **Villas of Grand Cypress,** all with patios, kitchens, living rooms, and dining rooms; some have working fireplaces and whirlpool baths.

Dining/Entertainment: Hemingway's and the Black Swan are reviewed in chapter 6. At the plush La Coquina, serving "New World" cuisine (it's like continental with international influences), a harpist entertains at dinner and Sunday brunches are exquisite. Other venues include the White Horse Saloon for prime-rib dinners and country music; Trellises, a bar/lounge where a jazz ensemble entertains in the evenings; the lovely, lake-view Cascade, serving American fare at all meals plus Japanese breakfasts; and several poolside and snack bars. The Rock Hyatt Club, adjoining the video-game arcade, offers movies, music, and games for teens 13 to 17.

Services: Concierge (sells tickets to WDW parks and other nearby attractions), 24-hour room service, baby-sitting, free transportation around the grounds, hourly shuttle between the hotel and all WDW parks (round-trip fare is $6 per person), Mears airport shuttle.

Facilities: Golf and tennis instruction/pro shops (the golf school here has been called one of the finest in the country), 45-acre Audubon nature walk, 4.7-mile jogging path, racquetball/volleyball/shuffleboard courts, playground, car rental, unisex beauty salon, full business center, state-of-the-art health club, shops, helicopter landing pad, video-game arcade, counselor-supervised child-care center/Camp Hyatt activity center.

EXPENSIVE

Marriott's Orlando World Center

8701 World Center Dr. (on Fla. 536 between I-4 and Fla. 535), Orlando, FL 32821. ☎ **800/ 621-0638** or 407/239-4200. Fax 407/238-8777. 1,503 rms, 85 suites. A/C MINIBAR TV TEL.

$179–$239 for up to 5 people in a room (range reflects season); pool-view rooms $10 additional per night (14-day advance-purchase rates $144–$179, subject to availability); $265–$2,400 suite. AE, CB, DC, DISC, JCB, MC, V. Free self-parking; valet parking $10 per night.

Providing the only viable competition for the above-mentioned Hyatt, this sprawling 230-acre multifacility resort, just 2 miles from WDW parks, is a top convention venue that also offers numerous recreational facilities for the tourist. These include three swimming pools (one larger than Olympic size with slides and waterfalls), eight tennis courts, and an 18-hole/par-71 Joe Lee–designed championship golf course. A grand, palm-lined driveway, flanked by rolling golf greens, leads to the main building—a massive, 27-story tower fronted by flower beds and fountains. It houses spacious guest rooms, cheerfully decorated in pastel hues with bamboo and rattan furnishings. All have patios or balconies, and in-room amenities include extensive pay-movie options, irons and ironing boards, safes, and hair dryers in the bathroom. Step outside the tower and you'll find magnificently landscaped grounds punctuated by rock gardens, shaded groves of pines and magnolias, and cascading waterfalls; swans and ducks inhabit over a dozen lakes and lagoons spanned by graceful, arched bridges.

Dining/Entertainment: Two of the Marriott's premier restaurants, Tuscany and the Mikado Japanese Steak House, are reviewed in chapter 6. JW's Steakhouse serves sun-dappled breakfasts and lunches on a screened balcony and cozy dinners in a rustic pine interior. Allie's American Grille is a rather elegant family restaurant. And several smaller eateries and bars include the plush Pagoda Lounge for nightly piano-bar entertainment and Champion's, a first-rate sports bar.

Services: Concierge, 24-hour room service, Mears transportation/sightseeing desk (sells tickets to all nearby attractions, including WDW parks; also provides transport, by reservation, to WDW, other attractions, and the airport), complimentary newspaper weekdays, baby-sitting, shoe shine, 1-hour film developing. Round-trip fare to WDW parks is $5 per day, free for children under 12.

Facilities: Golf and tennis pro shops/instruction, 18-hole miniature golf course, two volleyball courts, four whirlpools, large kiddie pool, car rental, unisex beauty salon, extensive business center, state-of-the-art health club, coin-op washers/dryers, shops, video-game arcade, Lollipop Lounge (a counselor-supervised child-care/activities center). Inquire as well about organized children's activities—games, movies, nature walks, and more.

Residence Inn by Marriott

8800 Meadow Creek Dr. (just off Fla. 535 between Fla. 536 and I-4), Orlando, FL 32821. ☎ **800/331-3131** or 407/239-7700. Fax 407/239-7605. 688 suites. A/C TV TEL. $159–$189 one-bedroom suite (for up to 4 people); $179–$219 two-bedroom suite (for up to 6 people). Range reflects season. Rates include full breakfast. AE, CB, DC, JCB, MC, V. Free self-parking.

This delightful, all-suite hostelry occupies 50 acres, alternating wooded grounds with neatly manicured lawns, duck-filled ponds, fountains, and flower beds. Guests here enjoy a serene environment that offers the seclusion and safety of a private community (you have to drive through a security gate to enter). They can also avail themselves of the extensive facilities at the adjoining Marriott's Orlando World Center (see details above), with room-charge privileges. Tastefully decorated accommodations—with fully equipped eat-in kitchens, private balconies or patios, and large living rooms—are equipped with Spectravision movie options and VCRs (movies can be rented), two phones (kitchen and bedroom), ceiling fans, and safes. Two-bedroom units have two baths.

Dining/Entertainment: A full breakfast is available in the gatehouse each morning, a Pizza Hut is on the premises, and local restaurants deliver food.

Services: Guest-services desk (sells tickets and provides transport to all nearby theme parks and attractions; round-trip to WDW parks is $6), complimentary daily newspaper, baby-sitting, next-day film developing, free food-shopping service, Mears airport shuttle.

Facilities: Three large swimming pools, two whirlpools, sports court (basketball, badminton, volleyball, paddle tennis, shuffleboard), tennis court, playground, coin-op washers/dryers, shops, two video-game arcades.

Summerfield Suites Lake Buena Vista

8751 Suiteside Dr. (off Apopka–Vineland Rd./Fla. 535), Lake Buena Vista, FL 32836. ☎ **800/833-4353** or 407/238-0777. Fax 407/238-0778. 150 suites. A/C TV TEL. $169–$209 one-bedroom suite (for up to 4 people); $199–$249 two-bedroom suite (for up to 8 people). Range reflects season. Rates include continental breakfast. AE, CB, DC, DISC, JCB, MC, V. Free parking.

This all-suite property, offering free transport to and from the nearby Disney parks, is an excellent choice for families—notable for its friendliness and immaculate accommodations. Spacious, residential-style suites—in buildings surrounding a palm-fringed brick courtyard with umbrellaed tables, fountains, and gazebos—have fully equipped eat-in kitchens, comfortable living rooms, and a bath for each bedroom. Amenities include bedroom and kitchen phones (with two lines), cable TVs in each bedroom and the living room (with HBO and pay-movie options), VCRs (movies can be rented), and irons and ironing boards.

Dining/Entertainment: Guests enjoy continental breakfast in the pleasant dining room or at umbrellaed tables in the courtyard; omelets and waffles may be purchased. An on-premises lobby deli (which sells light fare and liquor) also serves the pool area. Many local restaurants deliver to the hotel.

Services: Room service, guest-services desk (sells tickets to WDW parks and other nearby attractions, many of them discounted), $35 shuttle to airport/nearby attractions, free daily newspaper, baby-sitting, complimentary grocery shopping.

Facilities: Large swimming pool, whirlpool, kiddie pool, car rental, full business services, exercise room, coin-op washers/dryers, shops, video-game arcade.

Vistana Resort

8800 Vistana Center Dr. (off Fla. 535, between I-4 and Fla. 536), Orlando, FL 32821. ☎ **800/877-8787** or 407/239-3100. Fax 407/239-3062. 1,028 two-bedroom villas. A/C TV TEL. $175–$275 for up to 6 to 8 people. Range reflects season. Inquire about packages and weekly rates. AE, CB, DC, DISC, MC, V. Free self-parking.

This deluxe resort pampers guests with attentive service and a host of recreational facilities. It lies on 135 beautifully landscaped acres encompassing shimmering lakes (home to ducks and black swans) and cascading waterfalls. There are 6 swimming pools (one of them an immense, free-form affair with a rock waterfall, water volleyball, and water slide), 7 outdoor whirlpools (some secluded), 13 tennis courts, and a full health club and recreation center (offering sauna, steam room, tanning salon, and massage).

Accommodations—stunning two-bedroom, two-bath villas—are decorated in beautiful tropical pastels, with bleached wood, wicker, and bamboo furnishings. All offer full living rooms (with convertible sofas and cable TVs equipped with VCRs), full dining areas (often there's a second dining setup on the patio), fully equipped kitchens, washers and dryers, and patios or balconies (some screened, many overlooking scenic waterways). Some master-bedroom baths have whirlpool tubs, and there are ceiling fans in many rooms.

Dining/Entertainment: Open for all meals, the gardenlike Flamingo Cafe & Lounge—with seating at canvas-umbrellaed tables and windows overlooking a weeping willow–shaded pond—specializes in steak, seafood, and pasta; kids love the Flamingo's create-your-own-sundae bar. There's also a casual spot called Zimmie's and a poolside bar.

Services: Two guest-services desks provide concergelike assistance, sell tickets (many of them discounted), and arrange transportation to/from all nearby attractions. Transportation to/from Disney parks is free. Baby-sitting, grocery shopping (you can have your room prestocked with food on request).

Facilities: Five children's wading pools, an 18-hole/par-38 miniature golf course, basketball/sand volleyball/shuffleboard courts, tennis pro shop/instruction, bicycle rental, raft rental, children's playgrounds, game library, outdoor barbecue grills, $1^1/2$-mile/12-station jogging path, general store (includes movie-rental library), three video-game arcades. A comprehensive daily activities schedule for adults and children features nature walks, casino nights, Ping-Pong tournaments, arts and crafts, barbecues, karaoke, and much, much more.

MODERATE

✪ Holiday Inn Sunspree Resort Lake Buena Vista

13351 Fla. 535 (between Fla. 536 and I-4), Lake Buena Vista, FL 32821. ☎ **800/FON-MAXX** or 407/239-4500. Fax 407/239-7713. 507 rms. A/C TV TEL. $89–$129 for up to 4 people, depending on season. AE, CB, DC, DISC, JCB, MC, V. Free parking.

About a mile from the Disney parks, this Holiday Inn offers the chain's "no surprises" dependability, while catering to children in a big way. Kids "check in" at their own pint-size desk; receive a free fun bag containing a video-game token coupon, a lollipop, and a small gift; and get a personal welcome from animated raccoon mascots, Max and Maxine. Camp Holiday activities—magic shows, clowns, sing-alongs, arts and crafts, and much more—are available at a minimal charge for kids ages 2 to 12. And parents can arrange (by reservation) for Max to come tuck a child into bed. Pretty rooms have kitchenettes with refrigerators, microwave ovens, and coffeemakers. And if you're renting a second room for the children, "kidsuites" here—themed as igloos, space capsules, Noah's Ark, and others—sleep up to three. Amenities include VCRs (tapes can be rented), hair dryers, and safes.

Dining/Entertainment: Maxine's serves all meals, including steak and seafood dinners. Max's Funtime Parlor offers nightly Bingo and karaoke; it also airs sporting events on a large-screen TV. Kids 12 and under eat all meals free, either in a hotel restaurant with parents or in Kid's Kottage, a cheerful facility where movies and cartoons are shown and dinner includes a make-your-own sundae bar.

Services: Room service, guest-services desk (sells tickets to all nearby attractions, including WDW parks), free scheduled transport to WDW parks (there's a charge for transport to other nearby attractions).

Facilities: Large swimming pool, two whirlpools, kiddie pool, playground, fitness center, coin-op washers/dryers, shops, car rental, video arcade, Camp Holiday (a counselor-supervised child-care/activity center for ages 2 to 12).

Wyndham Garden Hotel

8688 Palm Pkwy. (between Fla. 535 and I-4), Lake Buena Vista, FL 32830. ☎ **800/WYNDHAM** or 407/239-8500. Fax 407/239-8591. 164 rms, 3 suites. A/C TV TEL. $74–$149 double, depending on season; $125–$150 suites. Extra person $10. Children under 18 stay free in parents' room. AE, CB, DC, DISC, MC, V. Free self-parking.

This property's location—on a pleasant, tree-lined street and overlooking a lake out back—is a big plus. The Crossroads Shopping Center and Walt Disney World Village put dozens of shops, services, and restaurants within easy walking distance. And to compete with nearby "official" hotels, the Wyndham Garden offers free shuttle transport to and from Disney parks. A recent massive renovation gave public areas a fresh new look, and rooms have been redecorated with bleached pine furnishings and cheerful resort-themed prints. They're equipped with cable TVs (with pay movies, a tourism-information station, and Nintendo), hair dryers, irons and ironing boards, and coffeemakers; some have convertible sofas.

Dining/Entertainment: The Garden Café, serving American fare at breakfast and dinner, has an outdoor poolside seating area and an adjoining bar/lounge.

Services: Room service, Universal Studios and Sea World guest-services desk (sells tickets, many of them discounted, and arranges transport to all nearby attractions), complimentary shuttle to/from Disney parks, complimentary daily newspaper, babysitting.

Facilities: Nice-size swimming pool and whirlpool, coin-op washers/dryers, exercise room, business center, small video-game arcade.

INEXPENSIVE

✪ Comfort Inn

8442 Palm Pkwy. (between Fla. 535 and I-4), Lake Buena Vista, FL 32830. ☎ **800/999-7300** or 407/239-7300. Fax 407/239-7740. 640 rms. A/C TV TEL. $39–$69 for up to 4 people, depending on season. AE, CB, DC, DISC, MC, V. Free parking.

This is an ideally located, large, and attractively landscaped property with two small man-made lakes amid expanses of manicured lawn and lush greenery. And it offers free transport to WDW parks, which are just 2 miles away. In-room safes are among the amenities in immaculate guest rooms. The Boardwalk Buffet serves reasonably priced buffet meals at breakfast and dinner; kids under 12 eat free. A bar/lounge adjoins. And complimentary tea and coffee are served in the lobby every afternoon. The guest-services desk sells tickets (most of them discounted) and provides transport to all nearby theme parks, dinner shows, and the airport. On-premises facilities include two swimming pools, coin-op washers/dryers, a gift shop, and a video-game arcade. Pets are permitted.

5 On U.S. 192/Kissimmee

This very American stretch of highway dotted with fast-food eateries isn't what you'd call scenic, but it does contain many inexpensive hotels within 1 to 8 miles of WDW parks.

MODERATE

✪ Holiday Inn Hotel & Suites

5678 Irlo Bronson Hwy. (U.S. 192; between I-4 and Poinciana Blvd.), Kissimmee, FL 34746. ☎ **800/FON-KIDS** or 407/396-4488. Fax 407/396-1296. 504 rms, 55 suites, 55 "kidsuites." A/C TV TEL. $75–$105 for up to 4 people; one-bedroom suites with kitchenettes $99–$195. Range reflects season. Inquire about packages. AE, CB, DC, DISC, JCB, MC, V. Free parking.

Just 3 miles from the entrance to the Magic Kingdom, this attractively landscaped, 23-acre property offers identical facilities to the Holiday Inn Sunspree Resort Lake Buena Vista (described earlier), including its own Camp Holiday and all the kid-pleasing features (here the welcoming mascots are Holiday and Holly Hound). There's even a small merry-go-round in the lobby. Accommodations are in two-story, motel-style buildings enclosing courtyard swimming pools. Pets are permitted. In 1996, the hotel began offering "kidsuites" especially designed for children, with kid-sized furniture and individual beds (including some bunk beds). These suites have private themed playrooms/bedrooms with separate areas for parents. Varieties include Old West fort, polar igloo, and Noah's ark.

Dining/Entertainment: The Vineyard Cafe serves breakfast and dinner, the latter featuring steak and seafood. There's also a food court and a pool bar proffering frozen tropical drinks. Kids 12 and under eat all meals free, either in a hotel restaurant with parents or in the Gingerbread House, a cheerful facility where movies and cartoons are shown on a large-screen TV and dinner includes a make-your-own sundae bar.

Services: Room service, guest-services desk (sells tickets to all nearby attractions, including WDW parks), baby-sitting, free scheduled transport to WDW parks (there's a charge for transport to other nearby attractions), Mears airport shuttle.

Facilities: Two Olympic-size swimming pools, two whirlpools, kiddie pool, playground, two tennis courts, sand volleyball, basketball court, coin-op washers/dryers, shops, two video-game arcades, Camp Holiday (a counselor-supervised child-care/activity center for ages 3 to 12).

Residence Inn by Marriott on Lake Cecile

4786 W. Irlo Bronson Memorial Hwy. (between Fla. 535 and Siesta Lago Dr.), Kissimmee, FL 34746. ☎ **800/468-3027** or 407/396-2056. Fax 407/396-2909. 159 suites. A/C TV TEL. Studios, $69–$129 for up to 4 people; bilevel penthouses, $189 for up to 6 people. Rates include extended continental breakfast. AE, CB, DC, DISC, JCB, MC, V. Free parking.

Beautiful landscaping on the banks of 223-acre Lake Cecile—and home-away-from-home accommodations—set this Residence Inn apart from neighboring properties. Tastefully decorated suites offer fully equipped eat-in kitchens and comfortable living-room areas. All but studio doubles have wood-burning fireplaces (logs are available), and cathedral-ceiling penthouses contain full baths upstairs and down. Many suites have balconies overlooking the lake. Amenities include cable TVs (VCRs are available on request) and safes.

Dining/Entertainment: The lovely gatehouse lounge off the lobby, with comfy sofas facing a working fireplace, is the setting for an extended continental breakfast each morning. An alfresco bar serves light fare and drinks poolside on a canopied wooden deck. Local restaurants deliver food (there are menus in each room).

Services: Guest-services desk (sells tickets—most of them discounted—and provides transport to all nearby theme parks and attractions; round-trip to WDW parks is $5), complimentary daily newspaper, free food-shopping service.

Facilities: Small swimming pool, whirlpool, sports court (basketball, volleyball, badminton, paddle tennis), playground, coin-op washers/dryers, picnic tables, barbecue grills. Lake activities include fishing, jet skiing, bumper rides, and waterskiing.

INEXPENSIVE

Colonial Motor Lodge

1815 W. Vine St. (U.S. 192, between Bermuda and Thacker aves.), Kissimmee, FL 34741. ☎ **800/325-4348** or 407/847-6121. Fax 407/847-0728. 83 rms, 40 apts. A/C TV TEL. $22.95–$50 for up to 4 people; $49.95–$89.95 two-bedroom apt for up to 6 people. Range reflects season. Rates include continental breakfast. AE, DC, DISC, MC, V. Free parking.

This well-run motor lodge has a pleasantly furnished lobby where there's a complimentary continental breakfast each morning. There are both standard motel rooms and two-bedroom apartments (with living rooms and fully equipped eat-in kitchens) that represent a good choice for families. On-premises facilities include two junior Olympic-size swimming pools and a kiddie pool. Adjacent to the Colonial are an IHOP and a shopping center. Guest services sells tickets to all Disney parks and nearby attractions (some of them discounted) and offers paid transportation to and from them and the airport. Round-trip transport to WDW parks is $12.

Kissimmee Area Accommodations

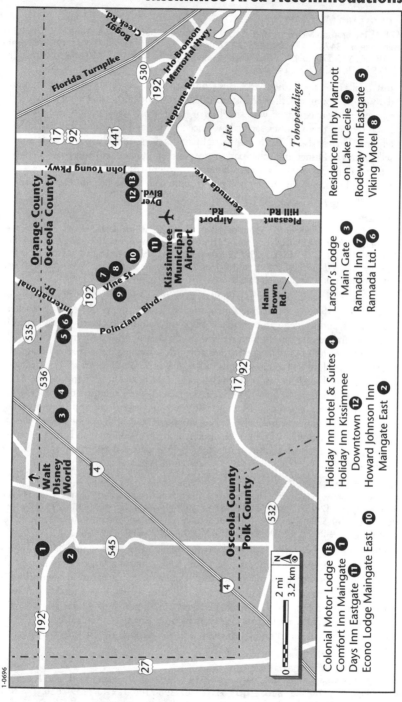

Colonial Motor Lodge ⑬
Comfort Inn Maingate ①
Days Inn Eastgate ⑪
Econo Lodge Maingate East ⑩

Holiday Inn Hotel & Suites ④
Holiday Inn Kissimmee Downtown ⑫
Howard Johnson Inn Maingate East ②

Larson's Lodge Main Gate ③
Ramada Inn ⑦
Ramada Ltd. ⑥

Residence Inn by Marriott on Lake Cecile ⑨
Rodeway Inn Eastgate ⑤
Viking Motel ⑧

Comfort Inn Maingate

7571 W. Irlo Bronson Memorial Hwy. (U.S. 192, between Reedy Creek Blvd. and Sherbeth Rd.), Kissimmee, FL 34747. ☎ 800/221-2222 or 407/396-7500. Fax 407/396-7497. 281 rms. A/C TV TEL. $38–$70 double, depending on season; garden rooms, $6–$10 additional. AE, CB, DC, DISC, JCB, MC, V. Free parking.

Just 1 mile from the Disney parks, this Comfort Inn houses clean, spiffy-looking standard motel accommodations. Most upscale are the garden rooms, facing a lawn with a gazebo; they're equipped with small refrigerators, coffeemakers, and hair dryers. A restaurant on the premises serves low-priced meals, and a comfortable bar/lounge adjoins. There's also a Waffle House right across the street. The guest-services desk sells tickets to Disney and other parks (most of them discounted) and provides transport to all nearby attractions and the airport; round-trip to WDW parks costs $7. Facilities include a swimming pool, playground, coin-op washers/dryers, and video-game arcade.

Days Inn

4104 and 4125 W. Irlo Bronson Memorial Hwy. (U.S. 192, at Hoagland Blvd. N.), Kissimmee, FL 34741. ☎ 800/DAYS-INN, 800/647-0010, or 407/846-4714. Fax 407/932-2699. 194 rms, 32 efficiency units. A/C TV TEL. $29–$59 for up to 4 people, depending on season; $37–$63 efficiency unit; $55–$75 Jacuzzi room (for 1 or 2 people). Rates may be higher during major events. Rates include continental breakfast. AE, CB, DC, DISC, MC, V. Free parking.

Offering good value for your hotel dollar, these two Days Inn properties—on either side of U.S. 192—share facilities, including two swimming pools, coin-op washers and dryers, and a video-game arcade. A big plus: Round-trip fare to WDW parks is free. Several restaurants (which deliver food), a large shopping mall with a 12-theater movie house, and a supermarket are in close walking distance. Rooms at both locations are clean and attractive standard motel units. Best bets are efficiencies with fully equipped kitchenettes at the 4104 location. On the other hand, at the 4125 location you can ask for a room with a large Jacuzzi, a refrigerator, and a microwave oven. All accommodations offer free HBO, pay-movie options, and in-room safes, and both locations serve free coffee, juice, and doughnuts in their lobbies each morning. Guest services at 4104 sells tickets (many of them discounted) and arranges transport to all nearby attractions, including WDW parks. Airport transfers can be arranged.

Days Inn Eastgate

5245 W. Irlo Bronson Memorial Hwy. (U.S. 192, between Poinciana and Polynesian Isle blvds.), Kissimmee, FL 34746. ☎ 800/423-3864 or 407/396-7700. Fax 407/396-0293. 200 rms. A/C TV TEL. $40–$79 for up to 4 people, depending on view and season. Rates may be higher during major events. AE, CB, DC, DISC, JCB, MC, V. Free parking.

The Days Inn Eastgate's U-shaped configuration of two-story pink stucco buildings forms an attractively landscaped courtyard around a large swimming pool. Families will appreciate picnic tables and a children's play area on the lawn. Rooms are nicely decorated. Lucille's Cafe serves buffet breakfasts. Other facilities include a video-game room, coin-op washers/dryers, and a gift shop. Guest services sells tickets to all WDW parks and nearby attractions (many of them discounted) and offers transportation to and from them and the airport. Round-trip transport to WDW parks is $7.

Econo Lodge Maingate East

4311 W. Irlo Bronson Memorial Hwy. (U.S. 192, between Hoagland Blvd. and Fla. 535), Kissimmee, FL 34746. ☎ 800/ENJOY-FL or 407/396-7100. Fax 407/239-2636. 173 rms. A/C TV TEL. $29–$79 for up to 4 people, depending on season. AE, CB, DC, DISC, JCB, MC, V. Free parking.

Ever spent a sleepless night at a motel (the word does derive from "motorist" and "hotel") because of traffic noise? It won't happen here. At this attractively landscaped Econo Lodge, accommodations are set well back from the highway in rustic two- and three-story buildings with cedar balconies and roofing. Well-maintained rooms are equipped with safes, and small refrigerators can be rented. A pool bar serves light fare, including full breakfasts and lunches at umbrellaed tables under towering live oaks. The guest-services desk sells tickets (most of them discounted) and provides transport to all nearby attractions and the airport. Scheduled round-trip transport to and from WDW parks is free. On-premises facilities include a large swimming pool, kiddie pool, volleyball, shuffleboard, horseshoes, coin-op washers/dryers, picnic tables, barbecue grills, and a video-game arcade. This is one of six area hotels under the same ownership, all of which can be booked via the above toll-free number.

Holiday Inn Kissimmee Downtown

2009 W. Vine St. (U.S. 192 at Thacker Ave.), Kissimmee, FL 34741. ☎ **800/624-5905** or 407/846-2713. Fax 407/846-8695. 200 rms. A/C TV TEL. $38–$99 for up to 4 people, depending on season; add $15 for an efficiency unit with a kitchenette. Children under 19 stay free in parents' room. AE, CB, DC, DISC, MC, V. Free parking.

Just 8 miles from Walt Disney World, this Holiday Inn gives you a few more facilities than you might expect in its price range. It offers immaculate motel rooms, as well as efficiency units with living room areas and fully equipped kitchens. Pets are permitted. A steak house serves all meals and provides room service, and its adjoining bar/lounge features karaoke nights. The guest-services desk sells tickets (many of them discounted) to all nearby theme parks and can arrange transportation to and from other nearby attractions and the airport. Round-trip to WDW parks is $10. Facilities include two swimming pools (one very large), a kiddie pool, a whirlpool, a sundeck, a playground, a tennis court, a gift shop, coin-op washers/dryers, a restaurant, a picnic area, and a video-game arcade.

Howard Johnson Inn—Maingate East

6051 W. Irlo Bronson Memorial Hwy. (U.S. 192, just east of I-4), Kissimmee, FL 34747. ☎ **800/288-4678** or 407/396-1748. Fax 407/649-8642. 567 rms, 9 family suites. A/C TV TEL. $60–$80 for up to 4 people; $90–$100 family suite, depending on season. Children under 19 stay free in parents' room. Add $10 for an efficiency unit with a kitchenette. Inquire about packages. AE, CB, DC, DISC, JCB, MC, V. Free self-parking.

Several factors make this Howard Johnson's property a worthwhile choice. Just 2 miles from the Magic Kingdom—and offering free transport to and from the Disney parks—it maintains a special guest-services phone number (☎ **800/TOUR-FLA**) that you can call in advance of your trip to arrange to purchase attraction tickets, paid transportation, car rental, and other vacation needs. Accommodations here are nicely decorated with quilted bedspreads and beach-themed paintings on the walls; amenities include cable TVs (with pay-movie options and Nintendo) and safes. Efficiency units have fully equipped kitchenettes with small refrigerators, two-burner stoves, and sinks. And family suites have both full kitchens and living rooms with convertible sofas.

Facilities include a medium-size swimming pool, whirlpool, kiddie pool, children's playground, coin-op washers/dryers, video-game arcade, and pool table. Adjoining the property is a large water park called Watermania and an IHOP where kids under 12 with an adult eat free. On the premises, a pool bar serves light fare and drinks, and coffee and tea are served each morning in the lobby. Guest services sells tickets to all Disney parks and nearby attractions (some of them discounted) and offers transportation to and from them and the airport. Free transportation to WDW parks is also available.

✪ Larson's Lodge Main Gate

6075 W. Irlo Bronson Memorial Hwy. (U.S. 192, just east of I-4), Kissimmee, FL 34747. ☎ **800/ 327-9074** or 407/396-6100. Fax 407/396-6965. 128 rms. A/C TV TEL. $39–$79 double, depending on season; add $15 for an efficiency unit with a kitchenette. Extra person $8. Children under 19 stay free in parents' room. Inquire about packages. AE, CB, DC, DISC, MC, V. Free parking.

With its large, on-premises water park (Watermania), playground, poolside picnic tables, barbecue grills, and cheerful on-site Shoney's restaurant, Larson's Lodge is a good choice for families. Accommodations are equipped with VCRs (movies can be rented), small refrigerators, microwave ovens, and safes. There are also efficiency units with fully equipped kitchenettes. A supermarket is just a few minutes away by car.

The guest-services desk sells tickets to all nearby theme parks (many of them discounted), and can arrange transport to other nearby attractions and the airport. Round-trip to WDW parks is $8. On-premises facilities include a large heated swimming pool and whirlpool, shops, coin-op washers/dryers, and a video-game arcade. Guests enjoy a free newspaper and coffee in the lobby each morning and free tennis at the above-mentioned Holiday Inn Kissimmee Downtown. Pets are permitted.

Ramada Inn

4559 W. Irlo Bronson Memorial Hwy. (U.S. 192, between Siesta Lago Dr. and Bass Rd./Old Vineland Rd.), Kissimmee, FL 34746. ☎ **800/544-5712** or 407/396-1212. Fax 407/396-7926. 114 rms. A/C TV TEL. $23.95–$44.95 for up to 4 people, depending on season; $6 per night additional for efficiency unit. AE, DC, DISC, MC, V. Free self-parking.

This Ramada offers standard motel rooms; refrigerators are available on request for $6 a night. Efficiency units offer two-burner stoves, extra sinks, and small refrigerators (no eating or cooking utensils are provided). Facilities include coin-op washers/ dryers, a swimming pool, children's playground, and picnic tables. The 1950s-style Hollywood Diner—which has an adjoining bar/lounge—serves American fare at all meals. Shuttle service to WDW parks is available for $9 per person, round-trip. Pets are accepted ($6 per night).

Ramada Ltd.

5055 W. Irlo Bronson Memorial Hwy. (U.S. 192, between Poinciana Blvd. and Fla. 535), Kissimmee, FL 34746. ☎ **800/446-5669** or 407/396-2212. Fax 407/396-0253. 107 rms. A/C TV TEL. $29.95–$55.95 for up to 4 people, depending on season. Rates include continental breakfast. AE, DC, DISC, MC, V. Free self-parking.

Less than 4 miles from Walt Disney World parks, this Ramada houses its rooms in a three-story stucco building. Refrigerators are available on request for $6 a night. Facilities include a swimming pool, game room, and coin-op washers/dryers. Continental breakfast is served in the lobby each morning. Shuttle service to WDW parks is available for $9 per person, round-trip. Pets are accepted ($6 per night).

Viking Motel

4539 W. Irlo Bronson Memorial Hwy. (U.S. 192, between Fla. 535 and Hoagland Blvd. N.), Kissimmee, FL 34746. ☎ **800/396-8860** or 407/396-8860. Fax 407/396-2088. 49 rms. A/C TV TEL. $27–$75 double, depending on season. Extra person $5. Add $10 for kitchenette units. AE, DISC, MC, V. Free self-parking.

Kids love this family-owned property housed in a fantasy castle, with towers topped by little Viking ships. Owners Bert and Christine Langenstroer are from Germany, and they've prettified their motel's Alpine-style balconies with neat flower boxes. Immaculate rooms have peach stucco walls hung with old-fashioned lithograph portraits in oval frames and kitschy landscape paintings. All are equipped with cable TVs (with HBO), safes, and Magic Fingers bed massagers. Some units have refrigerators, and a few offer fully equipped kitchenettes and cozy breakfast nooks.

On-premises facilities include coin-op washers/dryers, a shuffleboard court, a Viking-themed playground and sandbox, and a small free-form swimming pool with outdoor tables under thatched umbrellas and barbecue grills on the sundeck. A miniature golf course is next door. Transportation is available to WDW parks (round-trip fare is $8 per person), other area attractions, and the airport. The Viking is 6 miles from the Magic Kingdom.

6 On International Drive

Hotels and resorts listed here are 7 to 10 miles north of the Walt Disney World parks (a quick freeway trip on I-4) and close to Universal Studios and Sea World. Though you won't get away from rambunctious kids anywhere in this town, International Drive properties do tend to be more adult-oriented.

Note: There's a moderately priced Courtyard by Marriott (see description of a similar property under "Lake Buena Vista/Official Hotels," above) at 8600 Austrian Court (off International Drive), Orlando, FL 32819 (☎ **800/321-2211** or 407/351-2244; fax 407/351-1933).

VERY EXPENSIVE

✪ Peabody Orlando

9801 International Dr. (between the Bee Line Expressway and Sand Lake Rd.), Orlando, FL 32819. ☎ **800/PEABODY** or 407/352-4000. Fax 407/351-0073. 834 rms, 57 suites. A/C MINIBAR TV TEL. $240–$300 for up to 3 people; $300 for Peabody Club; $450–$1,350 suite. Children under 18 stay free in parents' room; seniors 50 and over pay $95. Inquire about packages and holiday/summer discounts. AE, CB, DC, DISC, JCB, MC, V. Free self-parking; valet parking $7 per night.

This deluxe, 27-story resort (one of Florida's finest) has some especially famous avian residents. Every morning at 11am, five fluffy ducks proudly parade along a red carpet to the beat of John Philip Sousa's *King Cotton* march, their journey culminating at a marble fountain in the lobby where they splash about all day. The hallmark of the Peabody is an ambiance of sophistication not found elsewhere in Orlando, and this aura extends to its top-rated restaurants. Luxurious rooms have handsome bamboo and bleached-wood furnishings and walls hung with quality artworks. Amenities include two phones, cable TVs with Spectravision and laser-disc movie setups (there's a vast video library), and in the bath, cosmetic lights, fine European toiletries, a hair dryer, and a small TV. The concierge-level Peabody Club occupies the top three floors. *Seniors:* Do note the over-50 price above—compensation for wrinkles indeed.

Dining/Entertainment: Dux, the Peabody's elegant signature restaurant; Capriccio, for sophisticated Italian fare; and the casual 24-hour B-Line Diner are detailed in chapter 6. Combos play jazz, blues, and show tunes in the atrium Lobby Bar nightly. The lobby itself is the weekday setting for exquisite afternoon English teas. Sporting events are aired in the cozy, duck-themed Mallards Lounge. And alfresco jazz concerts take place on the fourth-floor recreation level in the spring and fall.

Services: Concierge 7am to 11pm, 24-hour room service, nightly bed turndown on request, free daily newspaper, baby-sitting, transport between the hotel and all WDW parks throughout the day (unlimited daily round-trips cost $6), Mears transportation/sightseeing desk (sells tickets to all nearby attractions, including WDW parks and dinner shows; also provides transport, by reservation, to attractions and the airport).

Facilities: Olympic-length swimming pool, outdoor whirlpool, kiddie pool, four tennis courts, golf privileges at four nearby courses, 7-mile jogging path, car rental,

Delta Airlines desk, full-service unisex salon, business center, state-of-the-art health club, shops, video-game arcade.

EXPENSIVE
Summerfield Suites

8480 International Dr. (between the Bee Line Expressway and Sand Lake Rd.), Orlando, FL 32819. ☎ **800/830-4964** or 407/352-2400. Fax 407/238-0778. 146 suites. A/C TV TEL. $169–$209 one-bedroom suite (for up to 4 people); $189–$269 two-bedroom suite (for up to 8 people). Range reflects room size and season. Rates include continental breakfast. AE, CB, DC, DISC, MC, V. Free parking.

This delightful hotel—with potted palms on open-air balconies creating a welcoming resort ambiance—is built around a nicely landscaped central courtyard. Like its sister property in Lake Buena Vista (see above), it's notably friendly and well run. Spacious, neat-as-a-pin, residential-style suites, very attractively decorated, contain fully equipped eat-in kitchens, comfortable living rooms, and large dressing areas. All offer irons and ironing boards, phones in each bedroom and the kitchen, and satellite TVs (with HBO and pay-movie options) in each bedroom and the living room (the latter with a VCR; rent movies downstairs).

Dining/Entertainment: An extensive continental buffet breakfast is served in a charming dining room (waffles and omelets can be purchased), and the cozy lobby bar is a popular gathering place in the evening. Local restaurants deliver food to the premises.

Services: Concierge/tour desk (sells tickets to WDW parks and other nearby attractions), dry cleaning, laundry service, secretarial service, daily newspaper delivery, transport between the hotel and all WDW parks (round-trip fare is $7), shuttle available to the airport and nearby attractions, complimentary grocery shopping, complimentary refreshments in lobby.

Facilities: Nice-size swimming pool, whirlpool, kiddie pool, car rental, business services, exercise room, coin-op washers/dryers, 24-hour shop, video-game arcade.

MODERATE
✪ Orlando Marriott

8001 International Dr. (at Sand Lake Rd.), Orlando, FL 32819. ☎ **800/421-8001** or 407/351-2420. Fax 407/345-5611. 1,064 rms, 16 suites. A/C TV TEL. $79–$139 double, depending on view and season; $110–$300 suite. Extra person $10. Children under 18 stay free in parents' room. AE, DC, DISC, MC, V. Free self-parking.

The grounds at this verdant, 48-acre property—varying neatly manicured lawns and flower beds with fern gullies, lush tropical foliage, and serene lagoons—provide a feeling of resort seclusion that's all the more appealing because you're actually in the heart of a busy area, with proximity to many great restaurants. And rates are very reasonable in light of the facilities you'll enjoy here. Accommodations, housed in pale-pink stucco bilevel villas, are attractively decorated in resort mode; half have balconies or patios, and about a fifth contain full kitchens. All offer safes and TVs with pay-movie stations; many are also equipped with hair dryers, electric shoe-shine machines, and irons/ironing boards.

Dining/Entertainment: The Chelsea Cafe serves American fare at all meals. A club called Illusions features a DJ spinning Top 40 tunes, as well as blackjack, a pool table, and darts. Other choices are Pizza Hut, Kentucky Fried Chicken, and Taco Bell, plus a cozy lobby bar and several poolside bars.

Services: Room service, guest-services desk (sells tickets, many of them discounted, and arranges transportation to/from WDW parks and all other nearby attractions),

International Drive Area Accommodations & Dining

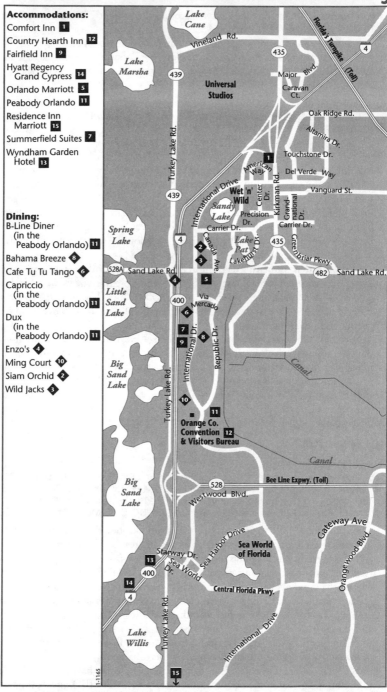

Accommodations:
Comfort Inn **1**
Country Hearth Inn **12**
Fairfield Inn **9**
Hyatt Regency
 Grand Cypress **14**
Orlando Marriott **5**
Peabody Orlando **11**
Residence Inn
 Marriott **15**
Summerfield Suites **7**
Wyndham Garden
 Hotel **13**

Dining:
B-Line Diner
 (in the
 Peabody Orlando) **11**
Bahama Breeze **8**
Cafe Tu Tu Tango **6**
Capriccio
 (in the
 Peabody Orlando) **11**
Dux
 (in the
 Peabody Orlando) **11**
Enzo's **4**
Ming Court **10**
Siam Orchid **2**
Wild Jacks **3**

baby-sitting, 24-hour free tram service around the property, Mears airport shuttle. Round-trip fare to WDW parks is $8.

Facilities: Three swimming pools (one quite large), two kiddie pools, whirlpool, four tennis courts, sand volleyball court, playground, business center, exercise room, 1.4-mile jogging trail, coin-op washers/dryers, car rental, unisex hair salon, shops, two video-game arcades.

✪ Residence Inn by Marriott

7975 Canada Ave. (just off Sand Lake Rd., a block east of International Dr.), Orlando, FL 32819. ☎ **800/227-3978** or 407/345-0117. Fax 407/352-2689. 176 suites. A/C TV TEL. $115 studio (up to 4 people); $125 studio double (up to 4 people); $175 bilevel penthouse (up to 8 people). Rates include extended continental breakfast. AE, DC, DISC, MC, V. Free parking.

Marriott's Residence Inns were designed to offer home-away-from-home comfort for traveling businesspeople, but the concept also works well for families. Accommodation buildings are surrounded by well-tended lawns, shrubbery, and beds of geraniums, and handsomely decorated suites offer full eat-in kitchens and comfortable living-room areas. All but studio doubles have wood-burning fireplaces, and two-bedroom penthouses have full baths upstairs and down. Amenities include irons and ironing boards and safes.

Dining/Entertainment: The comfortably furnished gatehouse is the setting for an extended continental breakfast daily, and complimentary beer, wine, and hors d'oeuvres Monday through Thursday from 5:30 to 7pm. If you're traveling alone, it's easy to meet people in this congenial setting. Local restaurants deliver food (there are menus in each room).

Services: Guest-services desk (sells tickets—most of them discounted—and provides transport to all nearby theme parks and attractions), complimentary daily newspaper, free food-shopping service (microwave dinners are sold in the lobby), Mears airport shuttle. Round-trip fare to WDW parks is $10.

Facilities: Large swimming pool, whirlpool, basketball court, sand volleyball court, free use of nearby health club, coin-op washers/dryers, food/sundries shop, picnic tables, barbecue grills.

INEXPENSIVE

Country Hearth Inn

9861 International Dr. (between Bee Line Expressway and Sand Lake Rd.), Orlando, FL 32819. ☎ **800/447-1890** or 407/352-0008. Fax 407/352-5449. 150 rms. A/C TV TEL. $59–$139 double, depending on view and season. Extra person $10. Children under 18 stay free in parents' room. Rates include continental breakfast. AE, CB, DC, DISC, MC, V. Free self-parking.

Though it doesn't offer much in the way of resort facilities, the Country Hearth Inn's low rates, great location, and very pretty rooms and restaurant—not to mention wine-and-cheese receptions for guests several times a week—make this an appealing choice. Centered on a white-trimmed pale-peach octagonal building crowned by a windowed cupola, the inn evokes 19th-century Florida—the leisurely era of riverboat travel and gracious plantations. Ceiling fans whir slowly over verandas and balconies furnished with wicker rocking chairs, and a charmingly landscaped courtyard with neat lawns and flower beds encompasses a large free-form swimming pool backed by verdant woodlands and a wide canal. Charming guest rooms, furnished in handsome maple or mahogany pieces, are adorned with floral friezes and 19th-century folk art. French doors open onto patios, balconies, or courtyards, and baths have art-nouveau lighting fixtures. In-room amenities include cable TVs (with HBO and Spectravision movie options), coffeemakers, phones with modem jacks, wood-bladed chandelier ceiling fans, safes, and small refrigerators. Larger deluxe rooms offer sleeper sofas, microwave ovens, and hair dryers.

Dining/Entertainment: The elegant Country Parlor, in the balustraded Victorian lobby, serves moderately priced American fare at all meals; a pianist entertains at Sunday champagne brunches. Equally turn-of-the-century in decor is the Front Porch Lounge; a popular gathering spot for locals, it features happy-hour buffets weekdays from 5:30 to 7pm.

Services: Room service, guest-services desk (sells tickets, many of them discounted, and arranges transport to all nearby attractions, including WDW parks), baby-sitting, Mears airport shuttle. Round-trip fare to WDW parks costs $10.

Fairfield Inn by Marriott

8342 Jamaican Court (off International Dr., between the Bee Line Expressway and Sand Lake Rd.), Orlando, FL 32819. ☎ **800/228-2800** or 407/363-1944. Fax 407/363-1944. 134 rms. A/C TV TEL. $35–$70 for up to 4 people. Range reflects season. Rates include continental breakfast. AE, CB, DC, DISC, JCB, MC, V. Free parking.

I love this property's quiet and safe location in a secluded area off International Drive. It nestles in Jamaican Court, a neatly landscaped complex of hotels and restaurants (that means a number of eateries are within walking distance). The rooms are spiffy-looking, and phones are equipped with 25-foot cords and modem jacks. Daily newspapers and local calls are free, as is the continental breakfast served in the lobby each morning.

The guest-services desk sells tickets to Universal Studios, Wet 'n' Wild, and Sea World (most of them discounted) and can arrange transport to all nearby theme parks and attractions and the airport; round-trip fare to WDW parks is $10. A small swimming pool and video-game room are on the premises; the lobby has a microwave oven for guest use and supplies coffee, tea, and hot chocolate 24 hours.

7 At the Airport

Hyatt Regency Orlando International Airport

9300 Airport Blvd., Orlando, FL 32827. ☎ **800/233-1234** or 407/825-1234. Fax 407/856-1672. 446 rms, 23 suites. A/C TV TEL. $205 double; $225–$450 suite. Extra person $25. Children under 18 stay free in parents' room. AE, CB, DC, DISC, JCB, MC, V. Self-parking $8; valet parking $11.

If you have to catch an early-morning flight out of Orlando, treat yourself to a night at this gorgeous multifacility hotel right in the airport's main terminal. It's luxurious from the moment you set foot in the plush, 40,000-square-foot palm court atrium lobby. Large, resort-style rooms—off balconies bordered by planters of bougainvillea or philodendrons—are attractively decorated and equipped with large desks, three phones (desk, bedside, and bath), cable TVs (with Spectravision movie, tourism-information, and flight arrival/departure channels), full-size ironing boards/irons, and hair dryers. Rooms are soundproof, so you don't hear planes taking off and landing.

Dining/Entertainment: The elegant Hemisphere Restaurant serves sophisticated American fare at lunch and northern Italian specialties at dinner; a pianist entertains weekend nights. McCoy's Bar & Grill centers on a display kitchen with an oak-burning pizza oven. You can also avail yourself of all the airport eateries, including a food court.

Services: 24-hour concierge/room service, shoe shine, car rental, baby-sitting, full business center, currency exchange.

Facilities: Airport shopping mall, airline desks, unisex hair salon, swimming pool, sundeck, fully equipped health club, travel agency, business center, game rooms, and shopping arcade.

8 Beyond Disney Into Orlando

MODERATE

The Courtyard at Lake Lucerne

211 N. Lucerne Circle E., Orlando, FL 32801. ☎ **800/444-5289** or 407/648-5188. Fax 407/246-1368. 1 rm, 23 suites. A/C TV TEL. $69 double; $96–$165 suites. Rates include continental breakfast. AE, DC, MC, V. Free self-parking. Take Orange Ave. south, immediately following City Hall (domed building with fountains and glass sculpture) turn left onto Anderson. After two lights, at Delaney Ave., turn right. Take first right onto Lucerne Circle N. Be aware of one-way streets. Follow brown, "historic inn" signs.

Orlando literally grew around this B&B standing incongruously amid a tangle of interstate ramps. Each unit in the three distinct buildings that make up the property was designed by a different artist or decorator. Rich Victorian colors and fabrics dominate the Norment–Perry, the city's oldest home (1883). With wide porches and ceiling fans, the I. W. Phillips House (1916) creates an antebellum splendor that never actually flourished this far south. Adventurous? Book the Art Deco Honeymoon Suite in the Wellborn (1940), a wacky 1950s retrospective in red, black, and white.

Although most visitors probably won't notice, small patches of peeling paint in the lobby indicate a need for more consistent maintenance.

Suites at the Phillips overlook a shared courtyard insulated from the urban hum by old-growth trees. A fountain's gentle trickle is the only sound while strolling the brick walkways. The solitude isn't as complete in the front rooms of Norment–Perry. Traffic sounds there are minimal, but audible.

Since opening in 1986, the Courtyard has served mostly business VIPs and locals on weekend getaways. With few amenities, it's a place for simple, private pleasures.

Request a claw-foot tub, lingering in a long, peaceful soak before enjoying the downtown nightlife blocks away. Downtown's most famous entertainment district, Church Street Station, is less than six blocks north. Overall downtown has an ever-growing and lively nightlife with dozens of clubs and restaurants along Orange Avenue. Walk or take a cab to begin the night, but the urban setting makes riding home the safest choice.

Services: The staff fulfills most duties of a hotel concierge. Nightly turndown, coffee and refreshments in lobby, complimentary chilled wine with check-in.

Facilities: Suites in the Wellborn include minikitchens with refrigerators, microwaves, and coffeemakers. The Courtyard's two honeymoon suites have double whirlpool tubs. Others have claw-foot tubs and sun rooms. The single room has a basic shower and closet-sized toilet.

Best Western Mount Vernon Inn

110 S. Orlando Ave., Winter Park, FL 32789 ☎ **407/647-1166.** Fax 407/647-8011. 147 rms. A/C TV TEL. $72–$82 single, $78–$88 double; manager special from Mar until Christmas, $51.50 double. AE, MC, V. Free self-parking. The Inn is located on U.S. Rte. 17–92 between Fairbanks Ave. and Lee Rd., across from Houston's steak house.

This is one of the best bargains in town, a place where old-money families know their guests will get comfortable accommodations at a reasonable price. Look for lots of late-model Caddies in the parking lot. There are some nice views available overlooking the pool, and about a block away across the street is a city park the kiddies will love. But, overall, there is nothing too fancy about the Mount Vernon. It is, however, centrally located between the beaches and the theme parks and very close to downtown Winter Park and downtown Orlando.

Dining/Entertainment: The Red Fox Lounge features nightly entertainment that's generally along the lines of a guy with a hair weave and a synthesizer. Unless that sounds really hip to you, it's better to venture to downtown Winter Park or Orlando for entertainment.

The Coach Dining room is open for breakfast and lunch from 6:30am to 2pm. The food is plentiful and filling, but this is a place you eat to be sated, not necessarily satisfied. There are many fine restaurants nearby. One tip: If you make reservations significantly in advance, save yourself a late-night check-in headache by calling before you leave home to make sure you are still on the books.

Services: The friendly desk is glad to answer questions, but from there you are pretty much on your own. What do you expect for $72?

Facilities: Pool.

The Harley of Orlando

151 E. Washington St., Orlando, FL 32801. ☎ **800/321-2323** or 407/841-3220. Fax 407/849-1839. 264 rms. A/C TV TEL. $95–$150 single or double. AE, MC, V. Free self-parking. Take I-4 to the Anderson St. exit. Turn left on Rosalind. The hotel entrance is located on the left, directly across from the entrance to Lake Eola Park.

Just 15 minutes from the Orlando International Airport and about 25 minutes from the attractions, the Harley of Orlando is an urban alternative to the Disney resorts. Request a balcony room so you can overlook Lake Eola Park, one of the most beautiful spots in the city. The carpet in this five-story structure is a little threadbare in places, and the pictures of Leona Helmsley, the Queen of Mean, are gone from the elevators, but the rooms, done in dark colors, are comfortable and clean.

Dining/Entertainment: The Cafe on the Park Restaurant does a competent job on standards such as prime rib. The Sunday brunch, which is buffet-style, is well worth the price. The Monkey Bar Lounge, done up in gilded chrome and leather, isn't the hippest place in town, but the drinks pack a punch and you don't have to drive to get home. The Church Street Station entertainment complex and the nightclubs and restaurants of downtown are just a short walk away. (Or catch a ride on the free city bus, Lymmo, which picks up passengers just up the block.)

Services: Room service, nonsmoking rooms, complimentary morning paper (Monday through Friday), free parking.

Facilities: Pool, sundeck, underground parking garage.

Radisson Place Hotel Orlando

60 S. Ivanhoe Blvd., Orlando, FL 32804. ☎ **800/333-3333** or 407/425-4455. Fax 407/425-7440. 340 rms and 27 suites. A/C TV TEL. $104–$129. AE, DISC, MC, V. Take I-4 to Princeton St. (Exit 43). Turn right at the bottom of the ramp. Turn left on Orange Ave. Go through the light, bearing to the right around the landscaping and the miniature Statue of Liberty; the hotel is on the left.

The 15-story Radisson Place Hotel, built in 1985, is really geared more toward the business traveler than the family-leisure crowd, but located right off I-4, just blocks from downtown and 15 minutes from the airport, it's also a good bet for families. The kids—and adults—might be tempted to play on the escalators rising for two floors in the sun-filled atrium and lobby. But this place has a relatively stuffy air, with all that gleaming brass, marble, and oversized ferns. The rooms are tastefully appointed with solid bedspreads and carpets. The views of downtown Orlando from the upper floors are impressive, and the suites are a cut above what you will find for the price elsewhere. It is located just across from Lake Ivanhoe, which has a series of exercise stations and a well-lit path for walking or jogging. There is even a small park for the kids less than a mile away. Minibars are available in most rooms, and some rooms are specifically designed to meet the needs of the handicapped.

Dining/Entertainment: 'Lando Sam's Restaurant offers American cuisine in a casual, colorful setting with a piano player tinkling the ivories on a dark-wood baby grand. The decor is heavy on the shiny brass and ferns. The food isn't anything you wouldn't expect at any run-of-the-mill hotel eatery. The same goes for 'Lando Sam's Lounge. There are daily breakfast and luncheon buffets in the restaurant that are, if nothing else, solid values for the price. Your best bet, however: Ask for a list of restaurants in nearby downtown; there are a few choice eateries within walking distance (if under a mile or so is walking distance). Try Brian's, just down the street, a non-retro diner with great breakfast food and coffee.

Services: Concierge, room service (including late-night room service), valet parking, transportation desk to arrange for taxi or limo service, attraction ticket information available. (Also, right next door is the Greater Orlando Chamber of Commerce, which has plenty of brochures on area attractions in the lobby.)

Facilities: Outdoor swimming pool, Jacuzzi, sundeck, two outdoor tennis courts, well-equipped health club, boutique.

Twin Towers and Convention Center

5780 Major Blvd., Orlando, FL 32819. ☎ **800/327-2110** or 407/351-1000. Fax 407/363-0106. 742 rms, 19 suites. A/C TV TEL. Summer $119–145 double depending on the season; $375–$900 suite year-round. AE, DC, DISC, MC, V. Located directly across from the main gate of Universal Studios.

From your balcony you can watch the palms waving at Universal's entrance and the bungee jumpers in the parking lot next door waving on their way down. The Twin Towers was originally built in the 1970s as a convention hotel, but after a major face-lift in the 1980s, owners realized the families would be flocking to Universal right across the street. This location offers the convenience of still being in the midst of things without the congestion of International Drive proper, and you're just minutes from WDW without being engulfed by the Mouse and the associated higher prices. The hotel still attracts a lot of convention business, but those facilities are in a building separate from the rooms. Aside from occasionally being trapped in the elevator with a herd of human Elk, you hardly notice. Just a side note: That red building on the property that looks like an old-fashioned schoolhouse is just that—the Little Red School House, a public school run in cooperation with the local school district for the children of Twin Towers employees.

Dining/Entertainment: The Palm Court Restaurant serves three meals a day and the Everglades Lounge has frequent entertainment and a big-screen TV. Although Palm Court does an adequate job, there are plenty of other dining options nearby. Most, like the Hard Rock Cafe, are comparable in price but more interesting. The lounge acts are best left alone, although the big-screen TV offers a great respite for sports fans who need a break from quality time with the family.

Services: Room service, baby-sitting, children's program, laundry.

Facilities: Deli, pool, whirlpool, sauna, exercise room, playground, game room.

Dining 6

Orlando has fast become the theme-restaurant capital of the Planet (Hollywood, anyone?). From souped-up cars to supermodels to superheroes, every genre is represented. But there are still some restaurants where the focus is not only the decor but the delicacies.

Since most visitors spend the majority of their time in the Walt Disney World area, I've focused on the best dining choices there. Also listed are some worthwhile restaurants beyond the realm. These "local" eateries often benefit from the high concentration of culinary talent brought to central Florida by the attractions.

Parents will be pleased to note that most mid-priced restaurants offer a children's menu. Many offer kiddie distractions like something to color or a maze to complete. (At the Fireworks Factory at Disney's Pleasure Island, anyone can color on the butcher-block paper.)

If you go to a place catering to children, expect the noise level to rise. Kids don't take a vacation from screaming, howling, and tantrums. That's the bad news, Coy.

The good news is the higher the average cost of an entree, the less likely you are to find little people. If you're looking for a quiet meal, head for the fancier restaurants further from Disney parks, on International Drive or on into Orlando. Or patronize the more expensive park offerings. If those howling youngsters belong to you, take advantage of the many in-hotel baby-sitting services for one night while you go out alone.

If kids really get your goat, by all means steer clear of any dining establishment that features "characters." (See also listings for dinner shows in chapter 10.)

Listings are divided by the following price categories: **very expensive** (the average main course at dinner is more than $25), **expensive** ($20 to $25), **moderate** ($10 to $20), and **inexpensive** (under $10). Keep in mind that the above categories refer to dinner prices, and some very expensive restaurants offer affordable lunches and/or cheaper early-bird dinners. Also, I'm going by the assumption that you're not stinting when you order. Some restaurants, for instance, have main courses ranging from $12 to $20. In most cases, you can dine for less if you order carefully. Especially noteworthy restaurants and those that offer especially good value are marked with a star.

For additional information on-line about area restaurants, use the Keyword: Orlando on America Online to visit **Digital City**

Orlando. From there, click on "Entertainment" and you'll find a complete listing of, among other things, Orlando restaurants, A to Z.

1 Best Bets

- **Best for Kids:** Kids adore the meals with Disney characters offered at almost all Walt Disney World resorts and elsewhere in the WDW complex (details below). Don't forget the jungle-themed **RainForest Cafe** (☎ 407/827-8500), at Disney Village Marketplace, where monkey business is encouraged.
- **Best Spot for a Romantic Dinner:** The elegant candlelit **Dux** at the Peabody Orlando (☎ 407/345-4550) combines a warmly inviting ambiance with great food.
- **Best Spot for a Business Lunch:** Generally, **Hemingway's,** an upscale, Key West–style restaurant at the Hyatt Regency Grand Cypress (☎ 407/239-1234), is kid-free, and its intimate dining areas are perfect for business lunches.
- **Best Spot for a Celebration:** There is no better place than the festive **Bubble Room** (☎ 407/628-3331), located in Maitland, just north of downtown.
- **Best Decor: Victoria & Albert's** takes the prize, with its plush Louis XIII–style furnishings, brocaded walls, and central dome. (☎ 407/WDW-DINE [939-3463]).
- **Best View: Artist Point** (☎ 407/WDW-DINE [939-3463]). This carefully crafted resort restaurant offers the illusion that you're dining in a rustically elegant, turn-of-the-century national-park lodge. Large windows overlook a lake and a waterfall. Weather permitting, there's also terrace seating.
- **Best Wine List:** "Sip" for yourself why **Maison et Jardin** (☎ 407/862-4410) in Altamonte Springs was recently honored by *Wine Spectator* magazine for its outstanding wine cellar.
- **Best Value:** At **Romano's Macaroni Grill** (☎ 407/239-6676), the ambiance and the northern Italian cuisine are first rate and prices are low, low, low.
- **Best American Cuisine:** Meat loaf and mashed potatoes that would make mama proud at **B-Line Diner,** in the Peabody Orlando hotel (☎ 407/345-4460).
- **Best Chinese Cuisine: Ming Court** (☎ 407/351-9988) features delicacies from all regions of China.
- **Best California Cuisine:** Waterfalls and animal sounds can't drown out the flood of flavorful dishes at the **RainForest Cafe** (☎ 407/827-8500).
- **Best Barbecue:** You can follow your nose to **Bubbaloo's Bodacious BBQ** (☎ 407/295-1212) by catching a whiff of the tangy hickory smoke. It tastes as good as it smells.
- **Best Italian Cuisine:** I'd pick the northern Italian fare at the charming **Capriccio,** in the Peabody Orlando (☎ 407/352-4000), and also the sedate and elegant **Tuscany** at Marriott's Orlando World Center (☎ 407/239-4200).
- **Best Seafood:** The 19th-century–style clambake buffet at the **Cape May Café** at Disney's Beach Club Resort (☎ 407/WDW-DINE [939-3463]) is a feast—seafood stews, clams, mussels, lobster, and more cooked in a rockweed steamer pit.
- **Best Tapas: Cafe Tu Tu Tango** (☎ 407/248-2222) takes the tapas concept international with items ranging from Cajun egg rolls to Thai salad.
- **Best Steak House:** At the **Yachtsman Steakhouse** at Disney's Yacht Club Resort (☎ 407/WDW-DINE [939-3463]), aged prime steaks, chops, and seafood are grilled over oak and hickory.
- **Best Late-Night Dining:** The trendy **B-Line Diner** (☎ 407/345-4460) at the Peabody Orlando is open around the clock for eclectic fare ranging from filet mignon to a falafel sandwich.

- **Best Character Breakfast:** At the revolving **Garden Grill** (☎ 407/WDW-DINE [939-3463]), in the Land Pavilion at Epcot, diners enjoy hearty family-style fare, a just-folks country-style theme, and interesting changes of scenery as the restaurant circles through environments ranging from prairie to rain forest; all this and Minnie and Mickey, too.
- **Best Outdoor Dining:** The terrace at **Artist Point** (☎ 407/WDW-DINE [939-3463]), the premier restaurant at Disney's Wilderness Lodge, overlooks a lake, waterfall, and scenery evocative of America's national parks.
- **Best People-Watching:** It can only be **Planet Hollywood** (☎ 407/827-7827)!
- **Best Afternoon Tea:** The **Garden View Lounge** (☎ 407/WDW-DINE [939-3463]) at Disney's Grand Floridian Beach Resort—a plush venue with potted palms and a wall of Palladian windows overlooking formal gardens—serves full afternoon teas from 3 to 6pm daily; a pianist entertains while you dine on tea, sandwiches, crumpets, and scones with Devonshire cream. The cost is $27 for two. The **Peabody Orlando** (☎ 407/345-4550) hosts similar afternoon teas on weekdays from 3 to 4:30pm in its gorgeous skylit atrium lobby. Frolicking in a nearby fountain while you sip your Earl Grey are the Peabody's five resident ducks. The cost is $8.95 per person.
- **Best Brunch:** It's a tie: **Capriccio** at the Peabody Orlando (☎ 407/352-4000) and **La Coquina** at the Hyatt Regency Grand Cypress (☎ 407/239-1234), both of which offer lavish buffets of first-rate fare with free-flowing champagne.

2 Restaurants by Cuisine

AMERICAN

B-Line Diner (International Drive, *M*)

Baby Cakes (downtown Orlando, *M*)

The Bubble Room (Maitland, *M*)

50's Prime Time Cafe (Disney–MGM Studios, *M*)

Hollywood Brown Derby (Disney–MGM Studios, *E*)

King Stefan's Banquet Hall (Magic Kingdom, *E*)

Liberty Tree Tavern (Magic Kingdom, *E*)

Plaza Restaurant (Magic Kingdom, *IE*)

Sci-Fi Dine-In Theater Restaurant (Disney–MGM Studios, *M*)

White Wolf Cafe (Downtown Orlando, *M*)

AMERICAN/CONTINENTAL

Black Swan (Lake Buena Vista, *VE*)

AMERICAN REGIONAL

Fireworks Factory (Pleasure Island, *M*)

Planet Hollywood (Pleasure Island, *M*)

Victoria & Albert's (Lake Buena Vista, *VE*)

BARBECUE

Bubbaloo's Bodacious BBQ (Winter Park, *IE*)

Wild Jacks (International Drive, *M*)

BRITISH

Rose & Crown (Epcot, *M*)

CALIFORNIA

California Grill (Lake Buena Vista, *E*)

Pebbles (Lake Buena Vista, *M*)

RainForest Cafe (Disney Village, *M*)

CANADIAN

Le Cellier (Epcot, *M*)

Key to Abbreviations: *E*=Expensive; *I*=Inexpensive; *M*=Moderate; *VE*=Very Expensive;

CARIBBEAN

Bahama Breeze (International Drive, *M*)

CHARACTER BREAKFASTS & DINNERS

Artist Point (*E*)
Cape May Café (*E*)
Chef Mickey's (Breakfast *E*, Dinner *M*)
Garden Grill (Breakfast *E*, Lunch and Dinner *M*)
Café (*E*)
King Stefan's Banquet Hall (*E*)
Liberty Tree Tavern (*M*)
Mickey's Tropical Luau (*M*)
Minnie's Menehune (*E*)
1900 Park Fare (Breakfast *E*)
Soundstage Restaurant (*E*)
Watercress Café (*M*)

CHINESE

Lotus Blossom Café (Epcot, *IE*)
Ming Court (International Drive, *M*)
Nine Dragons (Epcot, *M*)

CONTINENTAL/INTERNATIONAL

Dux (International Drive, *VE*)

CUBAN

Rolando's (Casselberry, *IE*)

FOOD COURT

Sunshine Season Food Fair (Epcot, *IE*)

FRENCH

Au Petit Café (Epcot, *M*)
Bistro de Paris (Epcot, *E*)
Chefs de France (Epcot, *E*)
Maison et Jardin (Maitland, *E*)

GERMAN

Biergarten (Epcot, *M*)
Sommerfest (Epcot, *IE*)

ITALIAN

Capriccio (International Drive, *M*)
Enzo's (International Drive, *IE*)
L'Originale Alfredo di Roma (Epcot, *E*)
Portobello Yacht Club (Pleasure Island, *M*)

Romano's Macaroni Grill (Lake Buena Vista, *IE*)
Tony's Town Square Restaurant (Magic Kingdom, *E*)
Tuscany (Lake Buena Vista, *E*)

JAPANESE

Mikado Japanese Steak House (Lake Buena Vista, *E*)
Mitsukoshi Restaurant (Epcot, *E*)
Yakitori House (Epcot, *IE*)

MEXICAN

Cantina de San Angel (Epcot, *IE*)
San Angel Inn (Epcot, *M*)

MOROCCAN

Marrakesh (Epcot, *M*)

NEW ORLEANS

Boatwright's Dining Hall (Lake Buena Vista, *IE*)
Bonfamille's Cafe (Lake Buena Vista, *IE*)

NORWEGIAN

Akershus (Epcot, *M*)
Kringla Bakeri og Kafe (Epcot, *IE*)

PACIFIC RIM

'Ohana (Lake Buena Vista, *M*)

SEAFOOD/STEAKS/CHOPS

Ariel's (Lake Buena Vista, *E*)
Artist Point (Lake Buena Vista, *M*)
Cape May Café (Lake Buena Vista, *IE*)
Coral Reef (Epcot, *M*)
Fulton's Crab House (Pleasure Island, *E*)
Hemingway's (Lake Buena Vista, *E*)
Yachtsman Steakhouse (Lake Buena Vista, *E*)

TAPAS

Cafe Tu Tu Tango (International Drive, *M*)
Spoodles (Lake Buena Vista, *M*)

THAI

Siam Orchid (International Drive, *M*)

VIETNAMESE

Little Saigon (Orlando, *IE*)

3 In Walt Disney World

The following listings encompass restaurants in Epcot, Magic Kingdom, Disney–MGM Studios, and Disney Village.

AT EPCOT

Though an ethnic meal at one of the World Showcase pavilions is a traditional part of the Epcot experience, I find many of the below-listed establishments just a tad pricey for the value received. Unless money is no object, you might want to consider the numerous lower-priced walk-in places at each national pavilion and throughout the park that don't require reservations (for details, check the *Epcot Guidemap* that you get upon entering the park). Or go at lunch, when entree prices are lower. Almost all of the establishments listed below serve lunch and dinner daily (hours vary with park hours), and, unless otherwise noted, they offer children's meals for $3.99.

Note: Since the clientele at even the fanciest Epcot World Showcase restaurants are coming directly from the parks, you don't have to dress up for dinner.

EXPENSIVE

✪ Bistro de Paris

France Pavilion, World Showcase. ☎ 407/WDW-DINE (939-3463). Priority seating. Main courses $20.50–$26.95. AE, MC, V. Daily 4pm to 1 hr. before park closes. FRENCH.

The Bistro de Paris, upstairs from Chefs de France and serving dinner only, offers similar fare in a more serene country-French setting. Also under the auspices of famous chefs Bocuse, Vergé, and LeNôtre, it's rather elegant, with seating in burgundy tufted-leather banquettes, French windows, candlelit white-linen–cloth tables, and art-nouveau lighting fixtures. Highlights here include Bocuse's duck foie gras salad appetizer with fresh greens and artichoke hearts, and Vergé's classic bouillabaisse served with garlic sauce and croutons. Another notable entree: Bocuse's roasted red snapper wrapped in thin-sliced potato crust and served on a bed of sautéed spinach with red-wine lobster sauce. Stay with Bocuse for dessert; his crème brûlée is unbeatable.

Chefs de France

France Pavilion, World Showcase. ☎ 407/WDW-DINE (939-3463). Priority seating. Main courses $8.95–$14.95 at lunch, $15.95–$24.25 at dinner. AE, MC, V. Daily 11am to 1 hr. before park closes. FRENCH.

Chefs de France is under the auspices of a world-famous culinary triumvirate—Paul Bocuse, Roger Vergé, and Gaston LeNôtre. Its art-nouveau/fin-de-siècle interior is agleam with mirrors and brass candelabra chandeliers, etched-glass and brass dividers create intimate dining areas, and tables are elegantly appointed. To start off, I recommend the seafood cream soup with crab dumplings (as featured by Vergé at Moulin de Mougins). Main courses at dinner include a superb broiled salmon in sorrel cream sauce *à la façon de Bocuse* (it's served with ratatouille and new potatoes) and Vergé's sautéed beef tenderloin with raisins and brandy sauce. And the dessert of choice is LeNôtre's superb soufflé Grand-Marnier. The distinguished chefs also composed the restaurant's wine list, any item of which can be purchased at Au Palais du Vin, a wine shop in the pavilion.

L'Originale Alfredo di Roma Ristorante

Italy Pavilion, World Showcase. ☎ 407/WDW-DINE (939-3463). Priority seating. Main courses $7.25–$15.95 at lunch, $9.25–$24.75 at dinner; fixed-price dinner $15.75 (served from 4:30–6pm). AE, MC, V. Daily 11am to 1 hr. before park closes. ITALIAN.

How to Arrange Priority Seating at WDW Restaurants

Priority seating is similar to a reservation. It means that you get the next table available when you arrive at a restaurant, but a table is not kept empty pending your arrival. You can arrange priority seating up to 60 days in advance at almost all full-service Magic Kingdom, Epcot, Disney–MGM Studios, resort, and Disney Village restaurants—as well as character meals and shows throughout the complex—by calling **407/WDW-DINE** (939-3463). Nighttime shows can actually be booked as far in advance as you wish.

Since this priority-seating phone number was instituted in 1994, it has become much more difficult to obtain a table by just showing up. So I strongly advise you to avoid disappointment by calling ahead.

However, if you don't reserve in advance, you can take your chances reserving in the parks themselves:

- **At Epcot:** Make reservations at the Worldkey interactive terminals at Guest Relations in Innoventions East, at Worldkey Information Service Satellites located on the main concourse to World Showcase and at Germany in World Showcase, or at the restaurants themselves.
- **At the Magic Kingdom:** Reserve at the restaurants themselves.
- **At Disney–MGM Studios:** Make reservations at the Hollywood Junction Station on Sunset Boulevard or at the restaurants themselves.

You might also keep these restaurant facts in mind:

- All park restaurants have nonsmoking interiors; you can smoke on patios and terraces.
- Magic Kingdom restaurants serve no alcoholic beverages, but liquor is available at Epcot and Disney–MGM eateries and elsewhere in the WDW complex.
- All sit-down restaurants in Walt Disney World take American Express, MasterCard, Visa, and the Disney Card.
- Guests at Disney resorts and official properties can make restaurant reservations through guest services or concierge desks.
- All WDW restaurants offer low-priced children's menus.

Patterned after Alfredo De Lelio's celebrated establishment in Rome, L'Originale Alfredo di Roma Ristorante evokes a seaside Roman palazzo with beautiful *trompe-l'oeil* frescoes of 16th-century patrician villas inspired by Veronese. The theatricality of an exhibition kitchen, charming Italian waiters, and exuberant strolling musicians creates a festive ambiance. If you want a quieter setting, ask for a seat on the veranda. De Lelio invented fettuccine Alfredo—and it remains an excellent choice here. Other recommendables are garlicky linguine al pesto and veal scaloppine served with roasted potatoes and vegetables. And there's a sublime tiramisu for dessert. A special vegetarian menu (with excellent grilled veggies, among other items) is available, and the list of Italian wines is extensive. On your way in or out, note the entrance-room walls; they're covered with photographs of celebrity diners in Rome, most notably Douglas Fairbanks and Mary Pickford, who discovered Alfredo's on their honeymoon and told *tout* Hollywood. A great deal here is a three-course early-bird dinner.

Mitsukoshi Restaurant

Japan Pavilion, World Showcase. ☎ **407/WDW-DINE** (939-3463). Priority seating for teppanyaki; reservations not accepted at the tempura counter. Teppanyaki main courses: $9.25–$16.50 at lunch, $14.75–$25.95 at dinner; fixed-price menu $39.50 for 2 at lunch, $59.90 for

2 at dinner; tempura $9.25—$11.95 at lunch, $14.75—$22.75 at dinner. AE, MC, V. Daily 11am to 1 hr. before park closes. JAPANESE.

The Mitsukoshi Restaurant centers on a teppanyaki steak house where diners sit at grill tables and white-hatted chefs rapidly dice, slice, stir-fry, and propel cooked food onto your plate with amazing dexterity. Kids especially love watching the chef wield his cleaver and utensils. Since you share a table with strangers, teppanyaki makes for a convivial dining experience. An elaborate dinner for two (of which an abbreviated version is available at lunch) includes a shrimp appetizer, salad with ginger dressing, soup (ask for the *miroshiru*—soybean soup with tofu and mushrooms), grilled fresh vegetables with udon noodles, succulent morsels of grilled beef tenderloin and lobster, steamed rice, choice of dessert (perhaps chestnut cake), and green tea. And even à la carte entrees include plenty of extras. Kirin beer, plum wine, and sake are among your beverage options, along with specialty drinks (some of them nonalcoholic, for kids) such as *tachibana* (light rum, orange curaçao, and mandarin orange juice).

Adjoining the teppanyaki rooms is a U-shaped tempura counter where you can eat shrimp, scallops, chicken, and fresh vegetables that have been lightly battered and deep-fried. Some sushi and sashimi items are served here as well. No reservations required for counter seating.

MODERATE
Akershus

Norway Pavilion, World Showcase. ☎ **407/WDW-DINE** (939-3463). Priority seating. Lunch buffet $11.95 for adults, $4.50 for children ages 4–9, age 3 and under free; dinner buffet $17.95 for adults, $7.50 for children. There are also non-smorgasbord children's meals for $4. AE, MC, V. Daily 11am to 1 hr. before park closes. NORWEGIAN.

Akershus re-creates a 14th-century castle fortress that stands in Oslo's harbor. Its pristine white-stone interior, with lofty beamed ceilings and leaded glass windows, features intimate dining niches divided by Gothic archways. Soft lighting emanates from gas lamps, candelabra chandeliers, and flickering sconces. The meal is an immense smorgasbord of traditional *småvarmt* (hot) and *koldtbord* (cold) dishes— smoked pork with honey mustard, strips of venison in cream sauce, gravlax in mustard sauce, smoked mackerel, Norwegian tomato herring, an array of Norwegian breads and cheeses, stuffed pork loin, potato salad, red cabbage, boiled red potatoes, eggs Nordique, and much more. Norwegian beer and aquavit complement a list of French and California wines. And do consider the Lillehammer brandy for an after-dinner drink. Desserts, such as a "veiled maiden"—an applesauce and whipped cream concoction—are à la carte.

Au Petit Café

France Pavilion, World Showcase. ☎ **407/WDW-DINE** (939-3463). Reservations not accepted. Main courses $7.75–$15.50. AE, MC, V. Daily 11am to 1 hr. before park closes. FRENCH.

Light fare is available throughout the day at Au Petit Café, a sidewalk bistro adjacent to Chefs de France on an awninged terrace overlooking the lagoon. It's a great venue for watching IllumiNations. Traditional cafe fare is featured—ham-and-cheese–filled croissants, crepes, quiche Lorraine, salade niçoise, and a few heartier entrees such as chicken baked in puff pastry with port-wine cream sauce and brochette of prawns with rice and basil butter.

Biergarten

Germany Pavilion, World Showcase. ☎ **407/WDW-DINE** (939-3463). Priority seating. Lunch buffet $9.95, dinner buffet $14.50. AE, MC, V. Daily 11am to 1 hr. before park closes. GERMAN.

Lit by street lamps, the Biergarten simulates a Bavarian village courtyard at Oktoberfest with autumnal trees, a working water wheel, and geranium-filled flower boxes adorning Tudor-style houses. Waiters are in lederhosen, waitresses in peasant dresses, and entertainment is provided by oom-pah bands, singers, dancers, and a strolling accordionist. Musical shows take place five to seven times a day (depending on the season). Guests are encouraged to dance as the band strikes up polkas and waltzes, and to sing along with yodelers and folk singers. All-you-can-eat buffet meals featuring traditional fare (sauerbraten, herring salad, red cabbage, spaetzle with gravy, roasted potatoes, sauerkraut with ham and spicy sausage, pork with fruit, roast chicken, salads) are offered at lunch and dinner. Beverages and desserts are extra. Wash it all down with a stein of Beck's or a glass of liebfraumilch.

Coral Reef

Living Seas Pavilion, Future World. ☎ 407/WDW-DINE (939-3463). Priority seating. Main courses $12.25–$19.75 at lunch, $12.25–$23.75 at dinner—more for lobster or a clambake combination. AE, MC, V. Daily 11am to 1 hr. before park closes. SEAFOOD.

Dine under the sea at the enchanting Coral Reef, where tables ring a 5.6-million–gallon aquarium inhabited by more than 4,000 denizens of the deep. Strains of Debussy's *La Mer* and Handel's *Water Music* playing softly in the background help set the tone. This is the most notable restaurant in the front section of Epcot. Tiered seating—much of it in semicircular booths—ensures everyone a good view, and diners are given "fish-identifier" sheets with labeled pictures so they can put names to the species swimming by. The menu features (what else?) seafood—creamy lobster bisque, sautéed mahi-mahi in lemon-caper butter, and shrimp satay served atop red-pepper pasta. There are also some steak and chicken dishes. For dessert, choose frangelico-laced white-chocolate mousse cake served on crème anglaise and crowned with dark chocolate Mickey ears. Coral Reef features premium wines by the glass and matches nightly entrees with selected labels.

Le Cellier

Canadian Pavilion, World Showcase. ☎ 407/WDW-DINE (939-3463). Reservations not accepted. Main courses $7.50–$9.95 at lunch, $9.95–$15.95 at dinner. AE, MC, V. Daily 11am to 1 hr. before park closes. CANADIAN.

This self-service buffet—for which no reservations are accepted or required—is a good choice for families. Located in the Victorian Hotel du Canada, with its French Gothic facade and steeply pitched copper roofs, **Le Cellier** has a castlelike ambiance with seating in tapestried chairs under vaulted stone arches, and amber light emanating from black wrought-iron sconces. Regional dishes include cheddar-cheese soup, carved pemeal bacon (a pork loin with a light cornmeal crust), a French-Canadian pork-and-potato–filled pie called *tourtière,* chicken and meatball stew, maple-syrup pie, and Canadian beers. *Note:* The kid's meal of macaroni and cheese might even tempt adults.

✪ Marrakesh

Morocco Pavilion, World Showcase. ☎ 407/WDW-DINE (939-3463). Priority seating. Main courses $9.95–$15.95 at lunch, $13.75–$19.95 at dinner; Moroccan diffa $29.95 for 2 at lunch, $49.95 for 2 at dinner. AE, MC, V. 11am to 1 hr. before park closes. MOROCCAN.

The palatial Marrakesh—with its hand-set mosaic tile work, latticed teak shutters, and intricate cut-brass chandeliers suspended from a ceiling painted with elaborate Moorish motifs—represents 12 centuries of Arabic design. Exquisitely carved faux-ivory archways frame the central dining area, where belly dancers perform to *oud, kanoun,* and *darbuka* music. Of all Epcot restaurants, this exotic venue best typifies the international-experience spirit of the park. The Moroccan *diffa* (traditional feast) that lets you sample a variety of dishes is recommended. At dinner it includes a hearty saffron-seasoned *harira* soup flavored with onions, tomatoes, lentils, and lamb; beef *brewats* (minced beef seasoned with coriander, ginger, cinnamon, and saffron, rolled

Epcot Dining

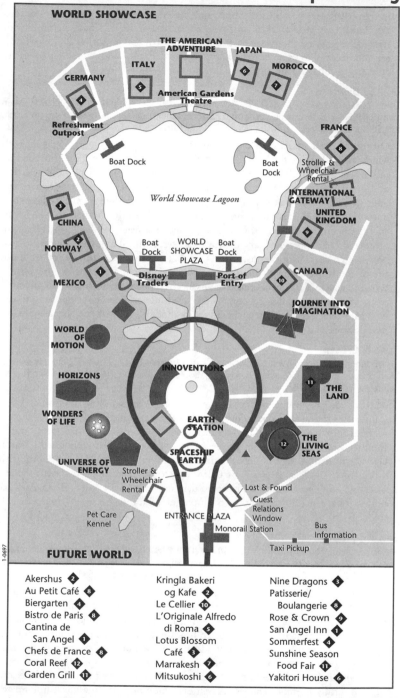

WORLD SHOWCASE

THE AMERICAN ADVENTURE

JAPAN
⑥

MOROCCO
⑦

ITALY
⑤

GERMANY
④

American Gardens Theatre

FRANCE
⑧

Refreshment Outpost

Boat Dock

Boat Dock

Stroller & Wheelchair Rental

World Showcase Lagoon

INTERNATIONAL GATEWAY

CHINA
③

UNITED KINGDOM
⑨

NORWAY
②

Boat Dock

WORLD SHOWCASE PLAZA

Boat Dock

CANADA

MEXICO
①

Disney Traders

Port of Entry

⑩

JOURNEY INTO IMAGINATION

WORLD OF MOTION

INNOVENTIONS

THE LAND
⑪

HORIZONS

WONDERS OF LIFE

EARTH STATION

THE LIVING SEAS
⑫

UNIVERSE OF ENERGY

SPACESHIP EARTH

Stroller & Wheelchair Rental

Lost & Found

Guest Relations Window

Pet Care Kennel

ENTRANCE PLAZA

Monorail Station

Bus Information

Taxi Pickup

FUTURE WORLD

Akershus ②
Au Petit Café ⑧
Biergarten ④
Bistro de Paris ⑧
Cantina de San Angel ①
Chefs de France ⑧
Coral Reef ⑫
Garden Grill ⑪

Kringla Bakeri og Kafe ②
Le Cellier ⑩
L'Originale Alfredo di Roma ⑤
Lotus Blossom Café ③
Marrakesh ⑦
Mitsukoshi ⑥

Nine Dragons ③
Patisserie/ Boulangerie ⑧
Rose & Crown ⑨
San Angel Inn ①
Sommerfest ④
Sunshine Season Food Fair ⑪
Yakitori House ⑥

1-0697

in thin pastry layers, and fried); roast lamb served with almond- and raisin-studded rice; braised tagine of chicken with green olives and preserved lemon; couscous with seasonal vegetables; Moroccan pastries; and mint tea. Combination appetizer plates are another way to experience culinary diversity. French and Moroccan wines are available to complement your meal.

✪ Nine Dragons

China Pavilion, World Showcase. ☎ **407/WDW-DINE** (939-3463). Priority seating. Main courses $9.50–$18.50 at lunch, $10.50–$23.75 at dinner; fixed-price meal $11.50 at lunch, $39.50 (for 2) at dinner. AE, MC, V. Daily 11am to 1 hr. before park closes. CHINESE.

One of the most attractive of the World Showcase restaurants, Nine Dragons, with windows overlooking the lagoon, has intricately carved rosewood paneling and furnishings and a beautiful dragon-motif ceiling. Begin your meal here with a selection of dim sum such as honey-glazed spareribs, delicious shrimp toast, pan-fried dumplings (pot stickers) stuffed with pork and vegetables, and ginger-nuanced steamed dumplings stuffed with pork, shrimp, and water chestnuts. Main dishes highlight cooking from four regions of China—**Mandarin** Great Wall duck shredded with green and red peppers and served with pancakes; from **Shanghai,** a saucy stir-fried boneless chicken with onions, carrots, and green peas; **Cantonese** tender sliced sirloin and broccoli stir-fried in oyster sauce; and **Szechuan** deep-fried shrimp ambrosia in a Mao Tai liqueur-spiked fruit sauce. You can order Chinese or California wines with your meal, but I especially love fresh melon juice, either alone or mixed with rum or vodka. For dessert, there's red-bean ice cream with fried banana or Chinese pastries.

Rose & Crown

United Kingdom Pavilion, World Showcase. ☎ **407/WDW-DINE** (939-3463). Priority seating. Main courses $9.25–$11.75 at lunch, $12.25–$20.75 at dinner. AE, MC, V. Daily 11am to 1 hr. before park closes. BRITISH.

The Rose & Crown, entered via a cozy pub, evokes Victorian England with dark oak wainscoting, beamed Tudor ceilings, and English and Scottish folk music. It also offers outdoor seating at tables overlooking the lagoon—a good place to watch IllumiNations. Dinner here might be an appetizer of smoked salmon with Stilton cheese, prime rib with Yorkshire pudding, and a sherry trifle. Wash it all down with a pint of Irish lager, Bass ale, or Guinness stout. Traditional tea, with scones, pastries, and finger sandwiches, is served daily at 3:30pm; the cost is $9.95. Another option is bar fare (sausage rolls, Cornish pasties, a Stilton cheese and fruit plate), all under $4.50.

San Angel Inn

Mexico Pavilion, World Showcase. ☎ **407/WDW-DINE** (939-3463). Priority seating. Main courses $9.75–$15.75 at lunch, $13.25–$23.25 at dinner; special vegetarian main courses from $7.25–$11.75. AE, MC, V. Daily 11am to 1 hr. before park closes. MEXICAN.

The setting for the San Angel Inn is a hacienda courtyard amid dense jungle foliage in the shadow of a crumbling Yucatán pyramid. It is nighttime: Tables are candlelit (even at lunch), and lighting is very low. The Popocatepetl volcano erupts in the distance, spewing molten lava, and you can hear the sounds of faraway birds. Thunder, lightning, and swiftly moving clouds add a dramatic note, but the overall ambiance is soothing. The fare is authentic and prepared from scratch. Order an appetizer of *queso fundido* (melted cheese with Mexican pork sausage, served with homemade corn or flour tortillas). Among entrees, specialties include *mole poblano* (chicken simmered with more than 20 spices and a hint of chocolate) and *filete ranchero* (grilled tenderloin of beef served over corn tortillas with sauce ranchero, poblano pepper strips,

Monterey Jack cheese, onions, and refried beans). Combination platters are available at both meals. There's chocolate Kahlúa mousse pie for dessert, and drink options include Dos Equis beer and margaritas.

INEXPENSIVE

Cantina de San Angel

Mexico Pavilion, World Showcase. ☎ 407/827-8570. Reservations not accepted. Entrees start at $6.50. Children's meal $3.18. AE, MC, V. Daily 11am to 1 hr. before park closes. MEXICAN.

Cantina de San Angel, a cafeteria with outdoor seating at umbrellaed tables overlooking the lagoon, offers affordable tacos, burritos, and combination plates, along with frozen margaritas.

Kringla Bakeri og Kafe

Norway Pavilion, World Showcase. ☎ 407/560-5179. Reservations not accepted. Most entree prices around $6.50. AE, MC, V. Daily 11am to 1 hr. before park closes. NORWEGIAN.

The informal facility in the Norway pavilion is Kringla Bakeri og Kafe, offering covered outdoor seating and inexpensive light fare. The menu includes such items as open-faced sandwiches like smoked salmon stuffed with hard-boiled egg, cheese and fruit platters, waffles sprinkled with powdered sugar, and fresh-baked Norwegian pastries.

Lotus Blossom Café

China Pavilion, World Showcase. ☎407/827-5678. Reservations not accepted. Most entrees around $6; children's meal $2.70. AE, MC, V. Daily 11am to 1 hr. before park closes. CHINESE.

If you wish to opt for lighter fare—egg rolls, pork-fried rice, and entrees such as stir-fried chicken and vegetables served over noodles—try the open-air Lotus Blossom Café, a pleasant (and inexpensive) self-service outlet. There are cooking demonstrations near the entrance several times a day.

Sommerfest

Germany Pavilion, World Showcase. ☎ 407/WDW-DINE (939-3463). Reservations not accepted. All items under $5. AE, MC, V. Daily 11am to 1 hr. before park closes. GERMAN.

At Sommerfest—a cafeteria with indoor seating backed by a mural of German castles and countryside and courtyard tables overlooking a fountain—you can purchase bratwurst sandwiches with sauerkraut, goulash soup, and desserts such as apple strudel.

Sunshine Season Food Fair

Land Pavilion, Future World. ☎ 407/WDW-DINE (939-3463). Reservations not accepted. Prices start at $5.95. AE, MC, V. Daily 11am to 1 hr. before park closes. FOOD COURT.

Located on the lower level of the Land Pavilion, the Sunshine Season Food Fair is a good choice for family dining. Vendors proffer an array of low-priced items— barbecued chicken and ribs, homemade soups and fresh salads, immense cinnamon rolls, fresh fruit, pastas, stuffed baked potatoes, sandwiches, oven-fresh cakes and pastries, ice cream, and more. Colorful umbrellaed tables under a skylit tent-top ring a splashing fountain, and hot-air balloons add to the festive decor.

Yakitori House

Japan Pavilion, World Showcase. ☎ 407/WDW-DINE (939-3463). Reservations not accepted. All items under $7; children's meal $2.69. AE, MC, V. Daily 11am to 1 hr. before park closes. JAPANESE.

Housed in a replica of the 16th-century Katsura Imperial Villa in Kyoto is Yakitori House, a bamboo-roofed cafeteria serving shrimp tempura over noodles, chicken yakitori, and other Japanese snack-fare items. Umbrellaed tables on a terrace overlooking a rock waterfall are a plus.

IN THE MAGIC KINGDOM

In addition to the four places mentioned below, there are plenty of fast-food outlets located throughout the park. I find a quiet sit-down meal an essential respite from theme-park hullabaloo.

EXPENSIVE
King Stefan's Banquet Hall

Cinderella Castle. ☎ 407/WDW-DINE (939-3463). Priority seating. Main courses $10.95–$16.75 at lunch, $17.50–$25.75 at dinner. AE, MC, V. Open 11am to park closing. AMERICAN.

King Stefan's Banquet Hall has a Gothic interior with leaded-glass windows and heraldic banners suspended from a vaulted ceiling. The only anachronistic note: Background music is from Disney movies. The menu features hearty cuts of beef such as prime rib and grilled sirloin served with fresh sautéed vegetables and soup. And while you're piling on cholesterol, might as well opt for an appetizer of almond-breaded brie served with wild-lingonberry relish. Less caloric entrees include grilled swordfish and a vegetarian plate. There's berry and apple cobbler topped with vanilla ice cream for dessert. *Note:* Cinderella often greets guests in the downstairs entrance hall. King Stefan's also hosts a daily character breakfast; see details below.

MODERATE
Liberty Tree Tavern

Liberty Square. ☎ 407/WDW-DINE (939-3463). Priority seating. Main courses $9.75–$14.25 at lunch; dinners here are all-you-can-eat character meals (discussed in Section 7 of this chapter). AE, MC, V. Open 11am to park closing. AMERICAN.

The Liberty Tree Tavern replicates an 18th-century pub, with peg-plank oak floors, displays of pewterware in oak hutches, and a vast brick fireplace hung with copper pots in its entranceway. Background music is appropriate to the period, and even the windows have panes of hand-pressed glass, a detail typical of Disney thoroughness. Entrees range from New England pot roast braised in burgundy and served with mashed potatoes and vegetables to a traditional roast turkey dinner with all the trimmings. Precede these with a bowl of creamy New England clam chowder. There's apple crisp topped with vanilla ice cream for dessert. I prefer the food here to King Stefan's, and this restaurant is also more likely to be able to seat large parties.

Tony's Town Square Restaurant

Main St. ☎ 407/WDW-DINE (939-3463). Priority seating. Main courses $2.75–$7.75 at breakfast, $7.75–$15.25 at lunch, $16.25–$22.75 at dinner. AE, MC, V. Daily 8:30am to park closing. ITALIAN.

Inspired by *Lady and the Tramp,* Tony's Town Square Restaurant is Victorian plush, with rich cherry-wood beams and paneling, a central fountain, cut-glass mirrors, and globe lighting fixtures. Walls are hung with original cels from the movie. There's additional seating in a sunny, plant-filled solarium. Tony's opens early for breakfast (you can eat here while waiting for the other lands to open); menu items range from Lady- and the Tramp-shaped waffles to French toast tossed in cinnamon sugar and served with warm maple or fruit syrup. The rest of the day, the fare is Italian, featuring appetizers such as a five-cheese vegetable pizza and fried calamari with marinara sauce. The lunch menu lists a variety of pastas, calzones, subs, and salads, while at dinner your options range from garlicky sautéed shrimp and seasonal vegetables over linguine in a light cream sauce to a 12-ounce strip steak/sautéed lobster combination, also served with linguine in garlic cream sauce.

😊 Family-Friendly Restaurants

Keep in mind that almost all Walt Disney World restaurants offer very inexpensive kids' meals (usually $4), as do most restaurants in this very child-oriented town. Theming that appeals to youngsters and place mats with puzzles and pictures to color are also the norm. Of course, all the character meals described in this chapter delight the kids. Some other notables:

Sci-Fi Dine-In Theater Restaurant *(see p. 102)*   A drive-in movie theater at Disney–MGM Studios where you dine in actual convertible cars, eyes glued to a movie screen.

50's Prime Time Cafe *(see p. 102)*   Also at Disney–MGM Studios, this highly themed restaurant re-creates the world of 1950s sitcoms, with TV sets airing old shows visible from every table. Homey food, such as meat loaf and mashed potatoes, is also of that era.

Mickey's Tropical Luau *(see p. 121)*   Not just a meal but a Polynesian floor show featuring Minnie, Mickey, Pluto, and Goofy along with a cast of South Sea Islanders. At Disney's Polynesian Resort in Luau Cove. Character breakfasts here, too.

Cape May Café Clambake Buffet *(see p. 111)*   This old-fashioned nightly clambake at Disney's Beach Club Resort is fun for the whole family.

'Ohana *(see p. 110)*   Centering on an 18-foot fire-pit grill, 'Ohana, at Disney's Polynesian Resort, is a sumptuous island feast enhanced by storytellers, hula-hoop contests, and lots of audience participation.

Hoop-Dee-Doo Musical Revue *(see p. 206)*   I've never met anyone who didn't have a great time at this whoopin' and hollerin' country-music dinner show in Fort Wilderness's Pioneer Hall. A less expensive variation on the same theme is the **Diamond Horseshoe Saloon Revue** in the Magic Kingdom's Frontierland *(see p. 138)*.

RainForest Cafe *(see p. 99)*   Monkeys screech in the background, waterfalls drop near your table, you sit atop zebra or rhinoceros legs. Perfect for kids.

Planet Hollywood *(see p. 104)*   Kids love all the action and excitement—a fiber-optic ceiling, video walls, hundreds of movie costumes and props on display, and the elusive possibility that they'll actually see someone famous. Long waits in line to get in, however.

INEXPENSIVE

Plaza Restaurant
Main St. ☎ **407/WDW-DINE** (939-3463). Priority seating. Sandwiches, burgers, and salads $7.75–$10.75. AE, MC, V. Open 11am to park closing. AMERICAN.

Near the end of Main Street, to your right as you enter the park, is the pretty Plaza Restaurant, with an art-nouveau interior. It serves burgers, salads, and sandwiches (tuna and Swiss on whole wheat, a Reuben, hot roast-beef double-deckers) that you can wash down with a vanilla, chocolate, or strawberry shake. Or skip the shake and leave room for a hot-fudge sundae. There's waiter service.

AT DISNEY–MGM STUDIOS

There are more than a dozen places to eat in this Hollywood theme park, with movie-lot monikers like the Studio Commissary and Starring Rolls Bakery. The three listed below are my favorites.

Other Walt Disney World Dining

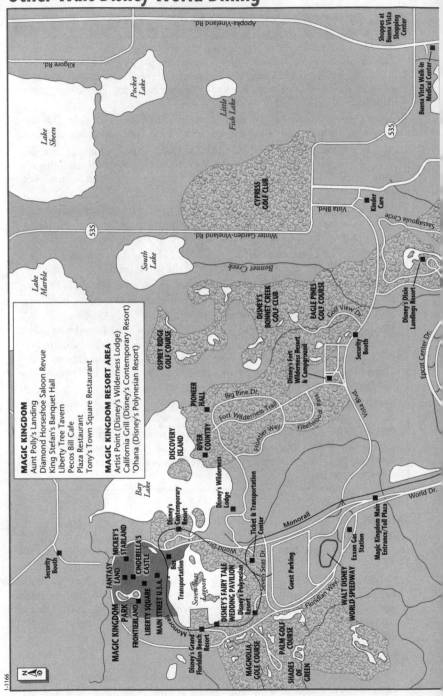

MAGIC KINGDOM
Aunt Polly's Landing
Diamond Horseshoe Saloon Revue
King Stefan's Banquet Hall
Liberty Tree Tavern
Pecos Bill Cafe
Plaza Restaurant
Tony's Town Square Restaurant

MAGIC KINGDOM RESORT AREA
Artist Point (Disney's Wilderness Lodge)
California Grill (Disney's Contemporary Resort)
'Ohana (Disney's Polynesian Resort)

1-1166

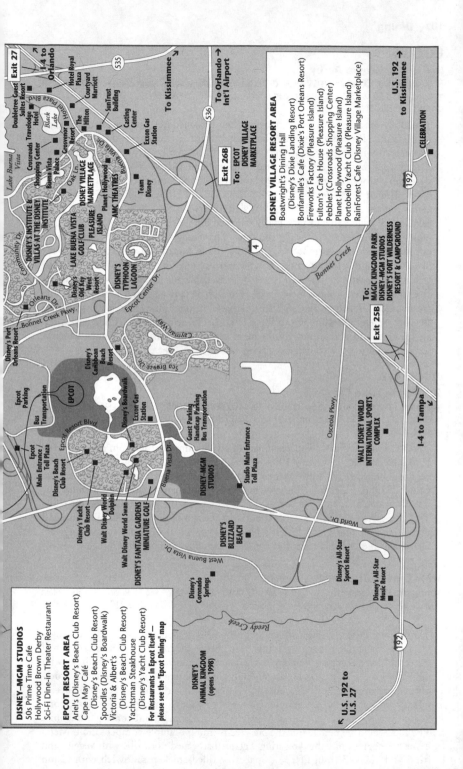

DISNEY-MGM STUDIOS
50s Prime Time Cafe
Hollywood Brown Derby
Sci-Fi Dine-in Theater Restaurant

EPCOT RESORT AREA
Ariel's (Disney's Beach Club Resort)
Cape May Café
   (Disney's Beach Club Resort)
Spoodles (Disney's Boardwalk)
Victoria & Albert's
   (Disney's Beach Club Resort)
Yachtsman Steakhouse
   (Disney's Yacht Club Resort)
For Restaurants in Epcot itself —
please see the "Epcot Dining" map

DISNEY VILLAGE RESORT AREA
Boatwright's Dining Hall
   (Disney's Dixie Landing Resort)
Bonfamille's Cafe (Dixie's Port Orleans Resort)
Fireworks Factory (Pleasure Island)
Fulton's Crab House (Pleasure Island)
Pebbles (Crossroads Shopping Center)
Planet Hollywood (Pleasure Island)
Portobello Yacht Club (Pleasure Island)
RainForest Cafe (Disney Village Marketplace)

101

EXPENSIVE

Hollywood Brown Derby

Hollywood Blvd. ☎ **407/WDW-DINE** (939-3463). Priority seating. Main courses $8.95–$16.50 at lunch, $16.50–$23.75 at dinner; early-bird dinner $15.75. AE, MC, V. Open 11am to park closing. AMERICAN.

The Hollywood Brown Derby, modeled after the famed Los Angeles celebrity haunt where Louella Parsons and Hedda Hopper held court, evokes its one-time West Coast counterpart with interior palm trees, roomy semicircular leather booths, and derby-shaded sconces. Mahogany wainscoted walls are hung with 1,600 caricatures of major stars who patronized the California restaurant—everyone from Bette Davis to Sammy Davis. Brown Derby legend abounds: It was at this Hollywood shrine that Clark Gable proposed to Carole Lombard, Wallace Beery poured ketchup over his sponge cake, and Lucille Ball and Jack Haley chucked dinner rolls at each other across the tables! A pianist entertains while you dine. The Derby's signature dish is the Cobb salad, invented by owner Bob Cobb in the 1930s, but, frankly, I don't love it; it's like a salad run through a blender. Dinner entrees come with a choice of soup or salad (select the champagne-nuanced oyster brie, available à la carte at lunch). Go on to an entree of baked grouper meunière, served atop pasta in a light, lemony white-wine cream sauce. Grapefruit cake with cream-cheese frosting is the Derby's signature dessert, but I prefer the white-chocolate cheesecake. There's a full bar, California wines are featured, and after-dinner drinks are a specialty. The early-bird dinner, which is served from 4 to 5:30pm daily, is a good value.

MODERATE

50's Prime Time Cafe

Near the Indiana Jones Stunt Spectacular. ☎ **407/WDW-DINE** (939-3463). Priority seating. Main courses $9.95–$17.50 at lunch, $11.95–$20.25 at dinner. AE, MC, V. Open 11am to park closing. AMERICAN.

The 50's Prime Time Cafe places diners in a 1950s time warp/sitcom psychodrama. Eating areas look like homey 1950s kitchens, wherein black-and-white TV sets air clips of shows like "My Little Margie" and "Topper." The wait staff greets diners like family ("Hi Sis, I'll go tell Mom you're home"), and may threaten you with no dessert if you don't eat your veggies, or tell on you for resting your elbows on the table. The food—meat loaf with mashed potatoes, Granny's pot roast, Dad's chili, and such—isn't all that great, but the place is so much fun, you'll love it anyway. Desserts include banana splits and S'mores. The adjacent Tune-In Lounge serves inexpensive light fare.

Sci-Fi Dine-In Theater Restaurant

Across from the Monster Sound Show. ☎ **407/WDW-DINE** (939-3463). Priority seating. Main courses $7.95—$12.95 at lunch, $9.50–$22.75 at dinner. AE, MC, V. Open 11am to park closing. AMERICAN.

The Sci-Fi Dine-In Theater Restaurant replicates an archetypical 1950s Los Angeles drive-in movie emporium. Diners are ensconced in flashy, chrome-trimmed convertible cars (complete with fins and whitewalls) under a twinkling, starlit sky with the Hollywood hills as a backdrop. Friendly carhops bring your food order and complimentary popcorn. While you eat, you can watch the movie screen, where a mix of zany newsreels (for example, *News of the Future*) is interspersed with cartoons, horror-movie clips (*Frankenstein Meets the Space Monster*), and coming attractions. The food could be better, but the creative theming is ample compensation. Menu items have names like the Towering Terror (barbecued pork ribs with veggies and fries) and Plucked from Deepest Space (a grilled-chicken sandwich with Cajun remoulade sauce and fries). Finish up with the Cheesecake That Ate New York. Though the restaurant basically appeals to kids (whose menu items are all under $4), beverages include wine and beer (there's a full bar), as well as milkshakes. Your bill is presented as a speeding ticket.

WALT DISNEY WORLD VILLAGE/PLEASURE ISLAND

Located about 2¹/₂ miles from Epcot off Buena Vista Drive, Walt Disney World Village is a very pleasant complex of cedar-shingled shops and restaurants overlooking a scenic lagoon. Pleasure Island, a nighttime entertainment center, adjoins.

Note: You don't have to pay the entrance fee to Pleasure Island to dine at any of its restaurants. Coming soon to Walt Disney World Village, Orlando's most exciting culinary coup ever: Wolfgang Puck's Café.

EXPENSIVE

Fulton's Crab House

Aboard the riverboat docked at Pleasure Island. ☎ **407/934-BOAT.** Reservations not accepted. Main courses $14.95–$50, with most in the $20 range. AE, MC, V. Daily 4pm–midnight; light fare served 11:30am–2am. Free self-parking; valet parking $5. SEAFOOD.

Fulton's is housed aboard a replica of a 19th-century Mississippi riverboat that is permanently moored on the shores of Lake Buena Vista. Its interior is enhanced by authentic nautical artifacts, marine-themed early-American lithographs, fishing paraphernalia, and maps. Ceilings are whimsically adorned with hand-painted constellations, crabs, and fish. There is a deck for outdoor dining, and the casual Stone Crab Lounge serves light fare (garlicky steamed clams, oyster-bar selections, peel-and-eat shrimp, cold cracked crab with mustard sauce, and the like). Chef Ron Pollack's daily-changing menus will feature the freshest market specialties. A meal here might begin with an appetizer of roasted Pacific oysters topped with sourdough crumbs, smoked bacon, and arugula butter. Among entrees, specialties will include a cioppino loaded with seafood in a zesty herbed tomato broth and a clambake consisting of Maine lobster, clams, mussels, red potatoes, and corn. All fish and seafood dishes can be prepared to your specifications—charcoal grilled, pan roasted, blackened, sautéed, or steamed Asian style. If you don't care for seafood, you might opt for filet mignon with roasted mushrooms and potatoes whipped with fresh corn. Save room for a dessert of milk-chocolate crème brûlée. The carefully crafted wine list will change seasonally and offer a good number of by-the-glass selections. Fulton's is also a character-breakfast venue.

MODERATE

Fireworks Factory

1630 Lake Buena Vista Dr., Pleasure Island. ☎ **407/934-8989.** Reservations recommended. Main courses $6.95–$12.95 at lunch, $13.95–$25 at dinner. AE, MC, V. Daily 11:30am–11:30pm (dinner served from 4pm); light fare and drinks served until 2am. Free self-parking; valet parking $5. AMERICAN REGIONAL.

According to Disney legend, Captain Merriweather Adam Pleasure, the mythological 19th-century ship merchant and adventurer who developed Pleasure Island, manufactured fireworks as a hobby and staged dazzling spectaculars every July 4th. Pleasure was lost at sea in 1839, but his former corrugated-tin warehouse survives in the form of this "explosively" exuberant casual restaurant. The Factory has exposed-brick walls hung with neon signs and vintage advertisements for fireworks, and missile fireworks are prominently displayed. You can eat downstairs, enjoy the lively scene from a balcony level, or sit outdoors on a patio overlooking Lake Buena Vista. This is a good choice for family dining.

Lunch or dinner, you might start off with an appetizer sampler (spicy chicken wings, shrimp quesadillas, and apple-wood–smoked baby back ribs). Dinner entrees range from Cajun shrimp pasta to oak-roasted salmon served with roasted tomato/corn relish and angel-hair sweet potatoes. And at lunch you might opt for a mesquite-smoked barbecued-beef sandwich. For dessert: a giant Toll House cookie served warm, topped with vanilla ice cream and hot fudge. In addition to "explosive" specialty drinks (try a 21 Rum Salute) and wines, the Fireworks Factory offers more than 45 varieties of domestic and imported beer, ale, and stout, including microbrewery selections.

Planet Hollywood

1506 E. Buena Vista Dr., Pleasure Island. ☎ **407/827-7827.** Reservations not accepted. Main courses $7.50–$18.95 (most under $13). AE, DC, MC, V. Daily 11am–2am. AMERICAN REGIONAL.

Planet Hollywood crashed into the local theme-park system with a stellar 1994 lavish opening-night party hosted by Schwarzenegger, Stallone, Willis, and Moore. The excitement they generated has started to dim and the once hours-long lines have thinned. A fiber-optic ceiling creates a planetarium effect, and a veritable show-business museum displays more than 300 items ranging from Peter O'Toole's *Lawrence of Arabia* costume to the front end of the bus from the movie *Speed* (it's suspended from the ceiling!). Previews of soon-to-be-released movies and video montages from films and TV are aired while you dine.

The big surprise amid all the special effects is that the food is pretty good. You can opt to nosh on appetizers—hickory-smoked buffalo wings, pot stickers, or nachos. There are also burgers, sandwiches, salads, pizzas, pastas, and platters of grilled steak, ribs, or pork chops. Beverages run the gamut from chocolate malts to exotic specialty drinks with movie-inspired names like "Beetle Juice" and "Die Harder." Try Arnold's mother's apple strudel topped with nutmeg ice cream or the Ebony and Ivory brownie for dessert.

Portobello Yacht Club

1650 Lake Buena Vista Dr., Pleasure Island. ☎ **407/934-8888.** Reservations not accepted (arrive early to avoid a wait). Main courses $6.95–$9.95 at lunch, $12.95–$22.95 at dinner; pizzas $6.95–$8.95. AE, MC, V. Daily 11:30am–midnight (dinner served from 4pm). Free self-parking; valet parking $5. NORTHERN ITALIAN.

Occupying a Bermuda-style gabled house, the Yacht Club is nautically themed, its interior, though casual, evoking a luxury cruise ship. Walls are plastered with photographs of racing yachts, navigational charts, and yachting flags, and shelves are lined with racing trophies. From the lively, mahogany-paneled bar, you can watch oak-fired pizzas being prepared in an exhibition kitchen. Multipaned windows overlook Lake Buena Vista, as do tables on awninged patios.

Those oak-fired pizzas have crisply thin crusts and toppings such as *quattro formaggi*—mozzarella, Romano, Gorgonzola, and provolone—with sun-dried tomatoes. At dinner, you might select a main course of charcoal-grilled half chicken marinated in olive oil, garlic, and fresh rosemary and served with garlicky oven-roasted mashed potatoes and seasonal vegetables. Or choose a pasta dish such as penne with plum tomatoes, Italian bacon, garlic, and fresh basil. There's an extensive list of Italian and California wines. A dessert of *crema brucciotto* (white-chocolate custard with a caramelized sugar glaze) is recommended.

RainForest Cafe

In the Disney Village Marketplace, 1800 E. Buena Vista Dr., Lake Buena Vista. ☎ **407/827-8500.** Reservations not accepted. Main courses $5.50– $17.95. AE, DISC, MC, V. Sun–Thurs 10:30am–11pm; Fri–Sat 10:30am–midnight. CALIFORNIAN.

With its lush interiors, calls of the wild, and unique anim[...]
ing of the RainForest Cafe in the summer of 1996 was[...]
waits were long during those early days as people line[...]
like Rasta Pasta—bow-tie noodles mixed with spinach, roa[...]
and Parmesan cheese, the whole dish smothered in a garlic-pes[...]
the restaurant, which aspires to be both a restaurant and educationa[...]
star of the show. A $3-million makeover transformed this former Chef Micke[...]
a tropical paradise. Kids, especially, love the junglelike setting. This is, after all, on[...]
place where monkey business is encouraged. But, as with Planet Hollywood, attention to preparation is not overshadowed by the production. Not only a fun place to
visit, this is a good place to eat. There is an extensive menu, including a reduced-price
menu for children. Top off your meal with Coconut Bread Pudding with dried apri-
cots; the lavish garnish of whipped cream, toasted coconut, and chocolate shaving is
almost as good as the dessert itself. A fairly good selection of beer and wine is served.

The back of this eco-friendly establishment is filled with disclaimers explaining
how the fish were *not* caught in a net, the beef is *only* from countries that don't destroy their rain forests, and pesticides and chemicals are *strictly* taboo.

Spoodles

On the Disney Boardwalk, Lake Buena Vista. ☎ **407/939-3463.** Reservations not accepted.
Main courses $10–$22. AE, MC, V. Daily 7am–10pm. TAPAS/MEDITERRANEAN.

The soft, pale colors and clapboard buildings of Disney's Boardwalk leading to this,
one of WDW's newest restaurants, evoke the easy living of summer vacations on the
coast. The food at Spoodles, however, is not for those with a pastel palette. This is
true Mediterranean cuisine.

Chef David Reynoso has added spice to the traditional Spanish tapas. The barbecued Moroccan beef skewers with raisins, toasted almonds, and couscous are drenched
in a hot, tangy sauce. The artichoke ravioli with garlic, cherry tomatoes, and arugula
is a vegetarian delight. Those with heartier appetites—or those not inclined to share—
can try the "Tapas Grande," such as potato-crusted salmon simmered with
wild mushrooms in veal broth with truffle oil. Disney has gone to great lengths to
provide an impressive wine menu, so be sure to indulge. (Their efforts have caught
the attention of national wine magazines.) Tableside sangria presentations, where the
fruit-laced libation is sliced and spiked before your eyes, also add something special
to the evening. There is a kid's menu featuring "you make it, we bake it" pizzas.
During the height of the summer tourist season, Spoodles can get crowded and the
wait can be long, so it may not be the best option for famished families coming
straight from the parks. It is, however, a nice, relaxed option for grown-ups.

4 Lake Buena Vista Area

This section is largely composed of notable restaurants at Disney resorts and other
area accommodations. Since most of these are gorgeous properties, they're fun to visit.
Before or after your meal, take a stroll around the grounds and public areas.

VERY EXPENSIVE

Black Swan

In the Hyatt Regency Grand Cypress Resort, 1 N. Jacaranda (off FL 535). ☎ **407/239-1999.**
Reservations recommended. Main courses $25–$34. AE, CB, DC, DISC, JCB, MC, V. Daily 6–
10pm. Free self-parking. AMERICAN/CONTINENTAL.

Overlooking the magnificent emerald fairways of this posh resort's golf course, the
Black Swan has a lodgelike, split-level interior with a big working fireplace and a

amed knotty-pine cathedral ceiling. Large, pine-framed windows overlook the
ole, and that verdant view is echoed within by lovely floral arrangements and
ters of greenery. Golfers make up the majority of the clientele. It's not unusual
re to see someone rise up excitedly from a table and demonstrate how he eagled
he 17th and birdied the 18th hole to win a match. Barring that, dinner entertainment consists of a pianist at a white baby grand.

A meal here might begin with an appetizer of grilled marinated portobello mushroom nestled on a bed of wilted arugula and topped with a trilogy of wild mushrooms
and Asiago cheese gratinée. A main dish of roast rack of lamb (thick, juicy slices
grilled in an herbed honey-Dijon crust) comes with mashed potatoes and rosemary
jus. Another, corn-tortilla–crusted breast of chicken, is served with black beans and
roasted corn relish and cilantro chili fettuccine. A warm, crisp apple tart on caramel
sauce topped with honey-vanilla ice cream and whipped cream might provide a fitting finale. The Black Swan has an extensive wine list with many dessert libations
(cognacs, ports, etc.).

✪ Victoria & Albert's

In Disney's Grand Floridian Beach Resort, 4401 Floridian Way. ☎ 407/WDW-DINE (939-
3463). Fax 407/824-2458. Reservations required. Jackets required for men. Prix-fixe meal $80
per person, $30 additional for Royal Wine Pairing. AE, MC, V. Two dinner seatings daily, 5:45–
6:30pm and 9–9:45pm. Free self-parking and validated valet parking. AMERICAN REGIONAL.

It's not often that I'd ever describe a dining experience as flawless, but Victoria &
Albert's, the World's most elite restaurant (Walt Disney World, that is), managed to
win that adjective from me. Its intimate dining room is plush; diners sink into leather-
upholstered Louis XIII–style chairs at exquisitely appointed tables lit by silver-shaded
Victorian lamps. A maid and butler provide deft and gracious service, and a harpist
plays softly while you dine.

Dinner, a seven-course affair, is described in a personalized menu sealed with a gold
wax insignia. The fare changes nightly. You might begin with an hors d'oeuvre of
Florida lobster tail with aioli. A more formal appetizer is the vermouth-poached
jumbo sea scallops served in a crisp rice-noodle basket on shallot-chive sauce with
garnishes of caviar and Chinese tat soi leaves; a shot of peppered vodka adds piquancy
to a velvety plum-tomato bisque sprinkled with smoked bacon and lightly topped
with pesto cream sauce. For an entree, you could select a fan of pink juicy sautéed
Peking duck breast slices with wild rice and crabapple chutney. A salad of esoteric
greens in an orange sherry vinaigrette clears the palate for the next course—English
Stilton served with pine-nut bread, port wine, and a pear poached in burgundy,
cognac, and cinnamon sugar. The conclusion: I would suggest a sumptuous
hazelnut-and-Frangelico soufflé, followed by coffee and chocolate truffles. This is a
highly nuanced cuisine to be slowly savored. There is, of course, an extensive
recherché wine list. I suggest you opt for the Royal Wine Pairing, which provides an
appropriate wine with each course and lets you sample a variety of selections from
the restaurant's distinguished cellars.

EXPENSIVE

✪ Ariel's

In Disney's Beach Club Resort, 1800 Epcot Resorts Blvd. ☎ 407/WDW-DINE (939-3463). Priority seating. Main courses mostly $17.95–$24. AE, MC, V. Daily 6–10pm. Free self- and valet
parking. SEAFOOD.

Named for the *Little Mermaid* character, this exquisite restaurant overlooking
Stormalong Bay is awash in sea-foam green, peach, and coral. A prismed 2,000-
gallon coral-reef tank is filled with tropical fish, walls are hung with oil paintings of

Sitting at the Chef's Table: The Best Seat in the (Walt Disney) World

There's a special dining option at Victoria & Albert's. Reserve the **Chef's Table** here, and dine in a charming alcove hung with copper pots and dried flower wreaths at an elegantly appointed candlelit table. . . right in the heart of the kitchen! You'll sip champagne with chef Scott Hunnell while discussing your food preferences for the seven- to nine-course menu he'll be creating especially for you. There's a cooking seminar element to this experience; diners get to tour the kitchen and observe the artistry of highly skilled chefs at work. The Chef's Table can accommodate up to six people a night. It's a leisurely affair, lasting 3 or 4 hours. The price is $115 without wine, $160 per person including five wines (I strongly recommend the latter). Let me further whet your appetite: There's a surprise during dinner, but I can't tell you what it is or it won't be one. Chef's Table is immensely popular. Reserve far in advance (even months ahead) by calling **407/WDW-DINE** (939-3463) or 407/824-1089.

scenes from the movie, and whimsical fish mobiles and glass bubbles dangle from a vaulted ceiling. You'll feel like you're dining in an underwater kingdom.

Appetizers (which supplement a complimentary smoked clam dip) include scrumptious New England silver-dollar crab cakes served with a spicy tartar sauce. Or start off with a Cajun-style shellfish gumbo replete with chunks of shrimp, lobster, and smoky andouille sausage. For your entree, a traditional Spanish *paella*—an array of fresh lobster, scallops, mussels, calamari, and shrimp inside a ring of saffron rice— is highly recommended. A few nonseafood options are offered as well, among them USDA choice New York strip steak grilled over a hickory and oak fire. Desserts include a rich Chambord raspberry chocolate cake, and an extensive award-winning wine list indicates which selections best complement your entree. A children's menu lists items like chicken nuggets and spaghetti with meat sauce in the $4-to-$6 range.

✪ California Grill

At Disney's Contemporary Resort, 4600 N. World Dr. ☎ **407/WDW-DINE** (939-3463) for reservations, or 407/824-1576. Fax 407/824-3611. Reservations recommended. Main courses $14.75–$27.50. AE, MC, V. Daily 5:30–10pm. Lounge open noon–midnight. CALIFORNIAN.

You might see Disney CEO Michael Eisner dining here with fellow corporate honchos; it's one of his favorite WDW dining rooms. High above the Magic Kingdom (on the Contemporary Resort's 15th floor), this stunning, California-style restaurant offers scenic views of the park and lagoon below. A zig-zaggy Wolfgang Puckish interior incorporates art-deco elements (a cove ceiling, curved pear-wood walls, vivid splashes of color, polished black granite surfaces), but the central focus is a dramatic exhibition kitchen with a hearthlike wood-burning oven and rotisserie. Gorgeous flower arrangements and cornucopialike displays of fruits and vegetables are further embellishments.

Chef Clifford Pleau's menus change seasonally. A sushi sampler makes a good beginning here, as does ravioli filled with goat cheese, shiitake mushrooms, and sun-dried tomatoes. And whole-wheat–crusted pizzas might comprise a light entree. Heartier choices include braised lamb shank (with wild chanterelle risotto and orange-nuanced bread topping) or grilled pork tenderloin served atop polenta with crimini mushrooms and a garnish of crispy fried sage. For dessert, it's hard to surpass the butterscotch crème brûlée with almond biscotti. If you like a close-up view of chefs at work, ask to sit at the kitchen counter. There's a good selection of California wines to complement your meal. And light fare (sushi, quesadillas, spring rolls) is available at the plush adjoining bar lounge.

✪ Hemingway's

In the Hyatt Regency Grand Cypress, 1 Grand Cypress Blvd. (off Fla. 535). ☎ **407/239-1234.** Reservations recommended. Main courses $7.50–$19.75 at lunch, $20–$28 at dinner. AE, CB, DC, DISC, JCB, MC, V. Tues–Sat 11:30am–2:30pm; daily 6–10:30pm. Free self- and validated valet parking. SEAFOOD.

Fronted by a waterfall that cascades into stone-bedded streams, Hemingway's evokes Key West and honors its most famous denizen; walls are hung with sepia photographs of "Papa" and his fishing and hunting trophies. This casually elegant (and generally child-free) restaurant is a good choice for romantic dinners. In a warren of intimate dining areas under a high, weathered-pine ceiling, elegantly appointed tables are lit by gleaming brass hurricane lamps. Weather permitting, you can sit on a screened wooden deck near the waterfall.

Ask not for whom the bell tolls but rather for an appetizer of deep-fried baby squid and grilled eggplant in garlicky herb-seasoned tomato coulis. Follow up with an entree of golden brown beer-battered coconut shrimp; it's served with roasted potatoes, a colorful array of al dente vegetables, and orange marmalade-horseradish sauce. Also recommended are the deliciously light, moist, and fluffy crab cakes; ask for Cajun tartar sauce with them. For dessert, key lime pie appropriately reaches its apogee here. The lunch menu offers similar fare, along with paella, sandwiches, and salads. In the adjoining Hurricane Lounge—a most congenial setting with a beautiful oak bar— specialties include a variety of island rums and the Papa Doble, a potent tropical rum and fruit libation invented by Hemingway himself (legend has it he once drank 16 of them at one sitting!).

Mikado Japanese Steak House

In Marriott's Orlando World Center, 8701 World Center Dr. (off Fla. 536). ☎ **407/238-8664.** Reservations recommended. Main courses $12.95–$28.95. AE, CB, DC, DISC, JCB, MC, V. Daily 6–10pm. Free self- and validated valet parking. JAPANESE.

This gorgeous, 230-acre resort houses a beautiful teppanyaki restaurant. Its serene interior, with intimate seating areas created by shoji screens, has windows overlooking rock gardens, reflecting pools, and a palm-fringed pond. Japanese music helps set the tone. Plan to arrive early and enjoy a cocktail at sunset on the wooden deck overlooking the swimming pool.

Meals here are teppanyaki style—which means you're seated with other patrons at a grill-topped table. For businesspeople dining alone, the socializing that happens naturally here can be a plus. A highly trained chef wheels a cart full of raw food to the table and with dazzling dexterity trims, chops, sautés, and flips it onto your waiting plate. Appetizer selections include softshell crab, smoked salmon, cucumber sushi, and assorted tempura vegetables and shrimp. Entrees—offering various combinations of steak and seafood—come with a complimentary hors d'oeuvre of grilled shrimp or scallops, soup (select the tastier miso), salad, steamed rice (yummy fried rice is available for an additional $2.25), an array of stir-fried vegetables, and green tea. A decanter of warm sake is recommended, and green tea or ginger ice cream makes a refreshing dessert. Low-priced meals are available for children.

✪ Tuscany

In Marriott's Orlando World Center, 8701 World Center Dr. (off Fla. 536). ☎ **407/239-4200.** Reservations recommended. Main courses $15–$27. AE, CB, DC, DISC, JCB, MC, V. Daily 6–10pm. Free self-parking; valet parking available. TUSCAN.

The showplace restaurant of a luxury resort, Tuscany has rich cherry- and mahogany-paneled walls hung with gilt-framed Michelangelo prints. White-linen–cloth tables are set with fresh flowers, and diners are comfortably ensconced in roomy tapestried armchairs, booths, and Regency chairs. Soft lighting and opera music complete the ambiance.

A pasta appetizer is a good way to begin your meal here—most notably, the gnocchi served with Gorgonzola sauce and a garnish of diced plum tomatoes. Impressive entrees—such as rack of lamb in a light demiglace sauce with roasted eggplant purée, white beans, potato croquette, and haricots verts—are aesthetically presented on large, white platters. Herbed focaccia bread served with light, garlicky goat cheese accompanies your meal. An extensive European/California wine list includes many by-the-glass selections. Desserts change nightly; I recently enjoyed an exquisite, thin-sliced apple tart served atop crème anglaise and garnished with fresh berries.

Yachtsman Steakhouse

In Disney's Yacht Club Resort, 1700 Epcot Resorts Blvd. ☎ **407/WDW-DINE** (939-3463). Priority seating. Main courses $20–$29. AE, MC, V. Daily 5:30–10pm. Free self- and valet parking. STEAK/CHOPS/SEAFOOD.

The Yacht Club, a gorgeous resort inspired by New England's grand turn-of-the-century summer mansions, houses a fittingly elegant signature restaurant. Lacquered knotty-pine beams, paneling, and plank flooring create a warm, woody feel that is enhanced by burgundy leather-upholstered oak chairs. USDA grain-fed beef—hand selected to ensure top marbling for natural juices and tenderness—is aged, cured, cut, and ground on the premises. You can see these prime cuts on display in a glass-enclosed beef-aging room, and an exhibition kitchen provides a tantalizing glimpse of sizzling steaks, chops, and seafood being grilled over oak and hickory.

You might begin your meal here with an appetizer of garlicky escargots marinated in dry vermouth and served en crôute with rich burgundy sauce. Beef entrees—such as succulent filet mignon, prime rib of beef au jus, or an 18-ounce Kansas City strip steak served on the bone (it's a cattle-drive tradition)—are served with baked potato, a board of fresh-baked bread, and a choice of béarnaise or bordelaise sauce. Side dishes, such as a skillet of fresh mushrooms sautéed in cognac and creamed spinach, are noteworthy. Other dishes run the gamut from lamb chops with apple mint butter and rosemary gin sauce to crisp-grilled chicken in apricot brandy sauce. And for the truly intrepid, there's a brownie fudge sundae for dessert. An extensive wine list is available, and a children's menu offers full meals for $3.75 to $6.50.

MODERATE

Artist Point

In Disney's Wilderness Lodge, 901 W. Timberline Dr. ☎ **407/WDW-DINE** (939-3463). Priority seating. Main courses $17–$26. AE, MC, V. Daily 5:30–10pm. Free self- and valet parking. STEAK AND SEAFOOD/GAME SPECIALTIES.

This stunning resort restaurant centers on western-theme murals inspired by Rocky Mountain School artists Albert Bierstadt and Thomas Moran (they do deviate a bit, however—look for the hidden Mickeys). The illusion that you're dining in a rustically elegant, turn-of-the-century national-park lodge is enhanced by large windows overlooking a lake and waterfall. Weather permitting, there's also terrace seating.

The menu changes seasonally. On a recent visit, I enjoyed a Northwest salmon sampler appetizer (smoked pepperlachs, cured gravlax, and pan-seared salmon served with onion/pepper/caper relish). And entrees ranged from a 16-ounce grilled porterhouse steak (served with red-skin potatoes, fire-roasted onions, garlic, and mushrooms) to grilled maple-glazed king salmon served with roasted vegetables, roasted apples, and couscous studded with morsels of sun-dried cherries, pignoli nuts, and smoked onion. Game specials and Pacific Northwestern wines are featured. Desserts—such as chocolate-silk bread pudding topped with vanilla ice cream and chocolate sauce—are immense (consider sharing) and delicious.

'Ohana

At Disney's Polynesian Resort, 1600 Seven Seas Dr. ☎ **407/WDW-DINE** (939-3463). Priority seating. Buffet $19.75 for adults, $13 for children ages 12–16, $8 for ages 4–11, under 4 free. AE, MC, V. Daily 5–10pm. PACIFIC RIM.

You'll be welcomed here with warm island hospitality by a server who addresses you as "cousin." 'Ohana means "family" in Hawaiian, and you're about to enjoy a convivial meal with the extended clan. The setting is South Seas exotic, with thatched roofing and tapa-cloth tenting overhead, carved Polynesian columns, and an open kitchen centering on a wood-burning, 18-foot fire-pit grill. There's lots going on at all times. The blowing of a conch shell summons a storyteller, coconut races take place down the central aisle, couples get up and dance to island music, and people celebrating birthdays participate in hula hoop contests as everyone sings "Happy Birthday" to them in Hawaiian. Kids especially love all the hoopla, but if you're looking for an intimate venue, this isn't it.

Soon after you're seated, a lazy Susan arrives laden with steamed dumplings in soy/ sesame oil, Napa cabbage slaw with honey mustard, black-bean and corn relish, and several tangy sauces. And course succeeds course in rapid succession (ask your waiter to slow the pace if it's too fast). The feast includes salad; fresh-baked herbed focaccia bread; grilled chicken, smoky pork sausage, marinated turkey breast, mesquite-seasoned beef, teriyaki ribs, and jumbo shrimp; stir-fried noodles and vegetables; fresh pineapple with caramel sauce; soft drinks; and coffee. Passion-fruit crème brûlée is extra, but worth it. A full bar offers tropical drinks, including nonalcoholic ones for kids.

Pebbles

12551 Fla. 535, in the Crossroads Shopping Center, Lake Buena Vista. ☎ **407/827-1111**. Reservations not accepted. Sandwiches and salads $4.95–$8.50; main courses mostly $7.95–$15.95. AE, CB, DC, DISC, MC, V. Sun–Thurs 11am–11pm, Fri–Sat 11am–midnight. Free self-parking. Pebbles also has a location in downtown Orlando. CALIFORNIAN.

Pebbles is one of Orlando's most popular restaurants, especially with a young yuppie crowd. The multilevel dining room centers on a sunken bar under a cross-beamed skylit ceiling, and though it's a large space, white wooden shutters and windowed enclosures create a warren of intimate dining areas. Lush tropical greenery, fountains, and canvas tenting contribute to the garden-party ambiance. During the day, sunshine streams in; at night, flickering hurricane lamps provide romantic lighting.

The same menu is offered throughout the day, supplemented by specials. Start off with a "lite bite" of creamy baked chèvre served atop chunky tomato sauce with hot garlic bread. Pebbles offers the option of a casual meal—perhaps a cheddar burger on toasted brioche, honey-roasted spareribs, or a Caesar salad tossed with grilled chicken. Or you can select a more serious entree such as tender leg of smoked duck that has been rubbed with fennel, glazed with triple sec, and slow roasted to sear in flavorful juices. Dessert of choice: the gold brick sundae—a scoop of vanilla ice cream encased in a candylike chocolate/almond shell and served atop caramel sauce with fresh strawberries. There's a full bar, and many premium wines are offered by the glass.

INEXPENSIVE

Boatwright's Dining Hall

In Disney's Dixie Landings Resort, 1251 Dixie Dr. (off Bonnet Creek Pkwy.). ☎ 407/ WDW-DINE (939-3463). Priority seating. Breakfast items $5.25–$7.25; main courses $10.50– $17.95; sandwiches $6.95. AE, MC, V. Daily 7am–10pm. Free self-parking. NEW ORLEANS.

Boatwright's is themed to look like an 1800s boat-building factory, complete with the wooden hull of a Louisiana fishing boat suspended from its lofty beamed ceiling. An uncommonly pretty factory, it has oak-plank floors and two large working brick fireplaces. Kids will enjoy the wooden toolboxes on every table; each contains a salt shaker that doubles as a level, a wood-clamp sugar dispenser, a pepper-grinder-cum-ruler, a jar of unmatched utensils, shop rags (to be used as napkins), and a little metal pail of crayons.

Cajun breakfasts offer intriguing possibilities. French toast here is made with sourdough—sweet potato baguette tossed in rich egg custard, deep-fried, and coated with cinnamon sugar. Another option: a pan of sautéed crawfish, mushrooms, green onions, and tomatoes in mustard cream sauce (served with home-style potatoes topped with two eggs, and an oven-fresh buttermilk biscuit). Start with deep-fried bacon-wrapped oysters and scallops, then follow with an entree of rich bouillabaisse redolent of oaken cognac or a medley of blackened seafood served over brown-buttered pasta in creamy garlic sauce. For dessert, there's homemade fruit cobbler topped with vanilla ice cream and smothered in whipped cream.

Bonfamille's Cafe

In Disney's Port Orleans Resort, 2201 Orleans Dr. (off Bonnet Creek Pkwy.). ☎ 407/ WDW-DINE (939-3463). Priority seating. Breakfast items $4.25–$6.95; main courses mostly $8.25–$14.95; salads and po'boy sandwiches $6.95. AE, MC, V. Daily 7–11:30am and 5–10pm. Free self-parking. NEW ORLEANS.

Named for a character in *The Aristocats,* the charming Bonfamille's is patterned after a fountained French Quarter courtyard. Exposed-brick walls are hung with paintings of New Orleans, big baskets of flowering plants are suspended from beams overhead, and Dixieland jazz plays softly in the background. During breakfast it's light and sunny; in the evening, candle lamps provide soft lighting.

Louisiana-style breakfasts range from fresh, hot beignets and café au lait to a skillet of crawfish and andouille sausage topped with zesty Creole sauce and melted sharp cheddar. The latter is served with home-style fried potatoes topped with eggs and a hot buttermilk biscuit. A typical dinner here: an appetizer of chicken wings tossed in spicy Louisiana hot sauce served with celery and blue-cheese dip, followed by grilled Atlantic salmon (served with spicy pecan butter, rice, and sautéed vegetables), and a dessert of Bourbon Street pudding with strawberry and caramel bourbon sauces. After dinner, families can head over to the hotel's Scat Cats Lounge, where entertainment—sing-alongs and live music with lots of audience participation—is featured most nights.

✪ Cape May Café

In Disney's Beach Club Resort, 1800 Epcot Resorts Blvd. ☎ 407/WDW-DINE (939-3463). Priority seating. Adults $19.95, ages 7–10 $9.50, ages 3–6 $4.50, under 3 free. Lobster is additional. AE, MC, V. Daily 5:30–9:30pm. Free self- and valet parking. SEAFOOD.

A hearty, 19th-century–style New England clambake buffet is featured nightly at this charming peach and sea-foam–green restaurant, where sand sculptures, paintings of turn-of-the-century beach scenes, croquet mallets, and furled striped beach umbrellas evoke an upscale seaside resort. Diners sit in oversized chairs at birch-wood tables, and large towel napkins are provided. Aromatic chowder, steamed clams and mussels, corn on the cob, chicken, lobster, and red-skin potatoes are cooked up in a crackling rockweed steamer pit that serves as the restaurant's centerpiece. And these traditional clambake offerings are supplemented by dozens of salads (pasta, seafood, fruit, vegetables), hot entrees (barbecued ribs, smoked sausage, pasta dishes), and a wide array of oven-fresh breads and desserts. There's also a full bar.

✪ Romano's Macaroni Grill

12148 Apopka–Vineland Rd. (just north of C.R. 535/Palm Pkwy.). ☎ **407/239-6676.** Fax 407/ 239-6718 for priority seating. Main courses $4.95–$8.25 at lunch, $6.95–$15.95 at dinner (most under $10). AE, CB, DC, DISC, MC, V. Sun–Thurs 11am–10pm, Fri–Sat 11am–11pm. Free self-parking. NORTHERN ITALIAN.

Though friends had raved about the Macaroni Grill, I didn't really expect much from a chain restaurant. Upon entering, I was favorably impressed by its cheerful interior, with arched stone walls, shuttered windows, colorful murals of Venice, and lights festively strung overhead. A welcoming glow emanated from the exhibition kitchen where white-hatted chefs were tending an oak-burning pizza oven, and foodstuffs, Chianti, flowers, and desserts were aesthetically arrayed on counters.

But the big surprise was the food. Everything was made from the freshest ingredients, and the quality of cuisine would have been notable at three times the price. The thin-crusted pizzas—such as the Mediterranean topped with fresh tomato sauce, shrimp, and feta and mozzarella cheeses—were scrumptious, as was a dish of bow-tie pasta tossed with grilled chicken, pancetta, and red and green onions in Asiago cream sauce. Equally good: an entree of sautéed chicken with mushrooms, artichoke hearts, capers, and pancetta in lemon butter; it came with spaghettini. There were fresh-baked breads, as well—focaccia and *ciabatta* (a crusty, country loaf) for sopping up sauces or dipping in extra-virgin olive oil. And desserts—especially an apple custard torte with hazelnut crust and caramel topping—kept to the same lofty standard. There's a full bar, premium wines are sold by the glass, and a children's menu offers an entree and beverage for just $3.25. Bravo Romano!

5 International Drive Area

Some of the best area restaurants are along International Drive, within about 10 minutes of Walt Disney World parks by car.

VERY EXPENSIVE

✪ Dux

In the Peabody Orlando, 9801 International Dr. ☎ **407/345-4550.** Reservations recommended. Main courses $19–$45. AE, CB, DC, DISC, JCB, MC, V. Mon–Thurs 6–10pm, Fri and Sat 6–11pm. Free self- and validated valet parking. INTERNATIONAL.

Named for the hotel's signature ducks that parade ceremoniously into the lobby each morning to Sousa's *King Cotton* march, this is one of central Florida's most highly acclaimed restaurants. And since the Peabody is the headquarters hotel for nearby Universal Studios, you're likely to see a celebrity or two among the diners. Upholstered bamboo chairs and cushioned banquettes provide seating at candlelit tables set with flowers and beautiful ceramic show plates. A lavish dessert display table with a floral centerpiece serves as a visual focus, and the textured gold walls are hung with ornately framed mirrors and watercolors representing 72 ducks!

The menu varies seasonally. At a recent dinner, appetizer selections included a unique version of pot stickers—stuffed with portobello mushrooms, scallions, and creamed goat cheese and garnished with Asiago twigs. An entree of Sonoma lamb chops glazed with Hunan barbecue sauce was accompanied by roasted Chinese mushrooms and green onions, with a small "treasure packet" of Pacific rice concealed under the lamb. Also listed that night: grilled Florida black grouper marinated in fearless (read *hot*) West Indian spices and served with a plantain-yam mash and tropical chutney. Desserts included a sublime hazelnut meringue napoleon topped with homemade frangelico ice cream and a dusting of Brazilian cocoa. Dux has an extensive, award-winning wine list.

MODERATE
B-Line Diner
In the Peabody Orlando, 9801 International Dr. ☎ **407/345-4460**. Reservations not accepted. Main courses $2.75–$8.50 at breakfast, $6.50–$10.95 at lunch, $5.95–$29 (most under $15) at dinner. AE, CB, DC, DISC, JCB, MC, V. Daily 24 hours. Free self- and validated valet parking. AMERICAN.

This popular local diner is of the nouvelle art-deco genre, which is to say that it's an idealized version of America's ubiquitous roadside establishments. Its interior is agleam with chrome edging that adorns everything from a cove ceiling to peach Formica tables, and the jukebox is stocked with oldies tunes. Gorgeous flower arrangements add upscale panache. Though the B-Line is a sophisticated venue, kids get their own low-priced menu, a duck-theme coloring/activities book, and crayons; they can also enjoy ice-cream sundaes for dessert here.

The seasonally varying menu offers haute versions of diner food such as a superior chicken pot pie, pan-seared pork (with grilled apples, sun-dried cherry stuffing, and brandy honey sauce), or a ham-and-cheese sandwich on a baguette. Other items—such as a falafel sandwich on pita bread with mint yogurt sauce—bear no relation to traditional diner fare. Portions are hearty. A glass display case up front is filled with scrumptious fresh-baked desserts: everything from coffee and chocolate eclairs to white-chocolate/Grand Marnier mousse cake. There's a full bar.

✪ Bahama Breeze
8849 International Dr., Orlando. ☎ **407/248-2499**. Reservations not accepted. Main courses $6.95–$14.95; sandwiches and salads $5.95–$6.95. AE, MC, V. Sun–Thurs 4pm–1am, Fri–Sat 4pm–2am. CARIBBEAN.

Traditional Caribbean foods are used to create unusual items such as "fish in a bag"— strips of mahi-mahi in a parchment pillow flavored with carrots, sweet peppers, mushrooms, celery, and spices. Moist and tasty. Also try the paella, a rice dish brimming with shrimp, fish, mussels, chicken, and chunks of sausage. The coconut curry chicken is a light-tasting treat—sautéed chunks of chicken sprinkled with fresh coconut. For dessert try the piña-colada bread pudding, a cube of custard bread in a sweet coconut sauce, or the tart key lime pie. Created by Orlando-based Darden Restaurants, the same folks who brought you Red Lobster and Olive Garden, this Bahama Breeze is essentially a test kitchen for what may soon be a national chain. Unlike Darden's other creations, which serve solid but not necessarily savory offerings, Bahama Breeze is a unique dining experience that challenges the taste buds. You can even watch your entrees being prepared in the open kitchen. The drink menu includes over 50 beers, and the expected collection of fruity, pseudo-exotic drinks, such as the Very, Berry Daiquiri. Happy-hour prices are featured round-the-clock.

✪ Cafe Tu Tu Tango
8625 International Dr. (just west of the Mercado). ☎ **407/248-2222**. Fax 407/352-3690. AE, DISC, MC, V. Tapas (small plates) $3.75–$7.95. Sun–Thurs 11:30am–11pm, Fri and Sat 11:30am–1am. Free self- and valet parking. INTERNATIONAL/TAPAS.

Though one might question the need for yet one more theme experience outside the parks, this zany restaurant is a welcome respite from Orlando's predictable "chain gang." For one thing, there's an ongoing performance-art experience taking place while you dine: One evening, an elegantly dressed couple might tango past your table. Another time, a belly dancer might perform, or a magician might do a few tricks tableside. In addition, there are always artists in a studio area creating pottery, paintings, and jewelry.

Tu Tu's colorful ambiance is a lot of fun, but its food is the real draw. The larger your party, the more dishes you can sample; two full plates will sate most appetites. My favorites include Cajun egg rolls (filled with blackened chicken, corn, and cheddar and goat cheeses, served with chunky tomato salsa and Creole mustard) and pepper-crusted, seared tuna sashimi with crispy rice noodles and cold spinach in a sesame-soy vinaigrette. International wines can be ordered by the glass or bottle. Great desserts here, too—such as creamy almond/amaretto flan and rich guava cheesecake with strawberry sauce.

Capriccio

In the Peabody Orlando, 9801 International Dr. ☎ 407/352-4000. Reservations recommended. Main courses mostly $12–$22 (with most pizza and pasta dishes priced below $14); Sun champagne brunch buffet $24.95 for adults, $12.95 for children 4–12, under 4 free. AE, CB, DC, DISC, JCB, MC, V. Tues–Sun 6–11pm; Sun brunch 11am–2:30pm. Free self- and validated valet parking. ITALIAN.

Capriccio's striking Italian *moderne* interior features a gleaming black-and-white checkerboard marble-tile floor and black Italian marble tables elegantly appointed with Tuscan-look Villeroy & Boch show plates. An exhibition kitchen occupying an entire wall showcases chefs tending mesquite-burning pizza ovens and grills.

Seasonally changing menus bring verve and imagination to traditional Italian cookery. On a recent visit, I enjoyed an appetizer of fried calamari served with three *aiolis* (garlicky Basque mayonnaises) flavored, respectively, with sun-dried tomato, basil, and saffron. Also scrumptious: a pasta dish of *bucatini* tossed with chunks of mesquite-grilled chicken and mushrooms in a slightly garlicky herbed white-wine/pesto sauce and finished with tomato concasse. And an entree of pan-seared tuna with braised fennel and radicchio was served with lentil flan and a buttery citrus sauce. The kitchen also turns out fabulous pizzas, and oven-fresh breads are accompanied by herb-infused extra-virgin olive oil; dip and exult. But save room for Capriccio's desserts, which include the definitive *zuppa inglese*. An extensive, award-winning wine list is available. *Note:* Capriccio also serves a great champagne Sunday brunch.

✪ Ming Court

9188 International Dr. (between Sand Lake Rd. and the Bee Line Expressway). ☎ 407/351-9988. Reservations recommended. Dim sum mostly $1.95–$2.50; main courses $4.50–$7.95 at lunch, $12.50–$19.95 at dinner. AE, CB, DC, DISC, JCB, MC, V. Daily 11am–2:30pm and 4:30pm–midnight. Free self-parking. CHINESE.

At this Chinese restaurant, the clientele includes more local food cognoscenti than tourists. Ming Court is fronted by a serpentine "cloud wall," crowned by engraved sea-green Chinese tiles (it's a celestial symbol; you dine above the clouds here, like the gods). The newly renovated candlelit interior is stunningly decorated in soft earth tones. Glass-walled terrace rooms overlook lotus ponds filled with colorful koi, and a plant-filled area under a lofty skylight ceiling evokes a starlit Ming Dynasty courtyard. A musician plays classical Chinese music on a *zheng* (a long zither) at dinner.

The innovative menu offers specialties from diverse regions of China and often features fresh Florida seafood. Begin by ordering a variety of appetizers such as wok-charred Mandarin pot stickers, crispy wontons stuffed with vegetables and cream cheese, and wok-smoked shiitake mushrooms topped with sautéed scallions. Entrees will open up new culinary vistas to even the most sophisticated diners. Lightly battered, deep-fried chicken breast is served with a delicate lemon-tangerine sauce. Szechuan charcoal-grilled filet mignon is topped with a toasted onion/garlic/chili sauce and served with stir-fried julienne vegetables. And crispy, stir-fried jumbo Szechuan shrimp is enhanced by a light fresh-tomato sauce nuanced with sake. At lunch, you can order dim-sum items in addition to other menu offerings. There's an extensive wine list, and, as a concession to Western palates, Ming Court features sumptuous desserts such as a moist cake layered with Mandarin oranges, key lime, and fresh whipped cream in orange-vanilla sauce. Dress is upscale, but casual.

Siam Orchid

7575 Republic Dr. (between Sand Lake Rd. and Carrier Dr.). ☎ **407/351-0821.** Reservations recommended. Main courses $10.25–$18.95. AE, DC, DISC, MC, V. Daily 5–11pm. Free self-parking. THAI.

Patterned after a palace in northern Thailand, Siam Orchid centers on a platform used to display wood carvings of angels and musicians representing figures from the *Ramayana,* an ancient Hindu epic poem. The split-level dining room, with lofty knotty-pine cathedral ceilings on either side, seats diners in cushioned booths and banquettes, and bamboo chairs at white-linen–cloth tables, some of them overlooking a lake. For intimate dining, request a *khun toke*—a private carved-teak enclosure that is the Thai answer to Japanese tatami rooms.

Owners Tim and Krissnee Martsching grow many necessary ingredients—fresh chilies, mint, cilantro, lemongrass, and wild lime—in their own garden, and their fare is authentic and delicious. Begin with *tom kha gai* (a savory chicken-and-mushroom soup) and continue with shared appetizers such as *satay* (grilled skewers of pork or chicken, marinated in coconut cream and mild curry, served with hot peanut sauce) and *tod man* (crispy fried chicken patties flavored with lemongrass, basil, and wild lime leaf). Not to be missed (share an order) is an entree of *pad Thai* (soft rice noodles tossed with ground pork, fresh minced garlic, shrimp, crab claws, crabmeat, crushed peanuts, and bean sprouts in a tangy-sweet sauce). Curries—such as the royal Thai, replete with chunks of chicken, potato, and onion in a yellow curry sauce—are also a specialty. There's a full bar, and beverage choices include sake, plum wine, and Thai beers. Homemade coconut ice cream topped with crushed peanuts makes a refreshing dessert.

Wild Jacks

7364 International Dr. (between Sand Lake Rd. and Carrier Dr.). ☎ **407/352-4407.** Fax 407/352-1899. Reservations not accepted. AE, CB, DC, DISC, JCB, MC, V. Main courses $9.45–$17.95. Daily 4:30–11pm. Free self-parking. Wild Jacks also has locations in Altamonte Springs and Kissimmee. STEAKS AND BARBECUE.

This upscale but exuberantly western steak-and-barbecue restaurant has a whimsical decor, including neon beer signs, mounted buffalo heads, and a longhorn steer poised to jump from a giant horseshoe above the copper bar. Soft lighting emanates from massive, wrought-iron wagon-wheel chandeliers, as well as antlered and steer-head-motif fixtures. There's an exhibition kitchen with an open-pit grill. Diners are seated at tables covered with checkered plastic cloths. And the music is country.

Appetizers here are first rate: skewers of tangy barbecued shrimp served over Texas rice (it's studded with corn kernels and red and green peppers), miniature tacos filled with smoked chicken and cheeses, and spicy potato skins topped with melted cheese, chunks of chicken, pico de gallo, sour cream, and guacamole. The best entree choice is the smoked brisket barbecue, served with salad, warm molasses bread and honey, and your choice of two side dishes—take the jalapeño mashed potatoes and grilled corn on the cob. Steaks and prime rib are other options, along with two new pasta dishes. For dessert, there's peach cobbler topped with vanilla ice cream sprinkled with cinnamon. The bar has an iced-beer well.

INEXPENSIVE
Enzo's

7600 Dr. Phillips Blvd., Suite 12, in the Marketplace Shopping Center (off Sand Lake Rd., just west of I-4). ☎ **407/351-1187.** Reservations not accepted. Panini $4.75–$5.95; main courses $4.50–$6.95 at lunch, $8.50–$12.75 at dinner. AE, CB, DC, DISC, MC, V. Mon–Thurs 11:30am–10pm, Fri–Sat 11:30am–11pm. Free self-parking. ITALIAN.

Upon entering this charming little restaurant and Italian charcuterie, you'll walk past display cases filled with antipasti, deli meats, pàtés, and cheeses, and shelves stocked with homemade pastas and other fancy foodstuffs. And if that's not enough to whet your appetite, you'll also glimpse chefs tending a pizza oven in an exhibition kitchen. The dining area is cheerful and inviting, with glossy pine-plank floors, peach walls hung with fine-art prints, and tables covered with butcher paper (crayons are provided). Italian music (most of it operatic arias) enhances the atmosphere. Enzo's is a casual kind of place that's very popular locally.

Pretty much the same menu is available throughout the day. Families troop in for pizzas—either the traditional American kind or Napoli pies with more sophisticated toppings and crisp, delicate crusts. Until 4:30pm, you can also opt for *panini* (sandwiches on crusty Italian bread), with fillings such as Italian sausage, grilled onions, and peppers; they're served with potato salad. A more serious dinner might begin with an appetizer of paper-thin slices of Norwegian salmon and onion served with extra-virgin olive oil, capers, lemon, and red peppers. Homemade pastas include fat *bucatini* tossed with mushrooms, fresh-grated Parmesan, prosciutto, bacon, and peas in a robust sauce. And Enzo's most fabulous entree is *pollo alla cecco* (roasted breast of free-range chicken with rosemary potatoes and an Italian version of ratatouille). Beer and wine are available. For dessert try *zuccotto* (Italian sponge cake soaked in Grand Marnier, layered with fresh fruit and crème anglaise, and topped with chocolate shavings). In busy seasons, arrive off-hours to avoid a wait.

6 Orlando & Beyond

Visitors wanting a break from themed eating can enjoy some of the local favorites, like great barbecue and authentic Cuban cuisine. There is epicurean life outside of Disney.

For further Orlando eateries, check out the Church Street Station listing in chapter 10. All directions assume you are coming from the WDW, International Drive area.

EXPENSIVE
Maison et Jardin

430 Wymore Rd., Altamonte Springs, 10 min. north of downtown Orlando. ☎ **407/862-4410.** Main courses $18.50–$28.50. AE, DISC, DC, MC, V. Mon–Sat 6–10pm; Sun 6–9pm; Sun brunch 11am–2pm. Free self-parking. Take I-4 East to Maitland Blvd./East Exit. Stay in the far lane, turning right at Lake Destiny Dr. At the next light, turn left onto Wymore Rd. FRENCH.

The succulent beef Wellington served here—a local special-occasion favorite—tastes even better after a diet of theme park burritos. If you're game, try the Elk Medallions sautéed and served with a raspberry sauce. For dessert, the crepes Suzette. You can order from a full bar, but what really makes Maison et Jardin worth the drive is one of the best wine cellars in the world. The restaurant was recently honored by *Wine Spectator* magazine for its outstanding selection. This is the place for lovers of good wine. (And definitely not the place for children.)

Orlando Area Accommodations & Dining

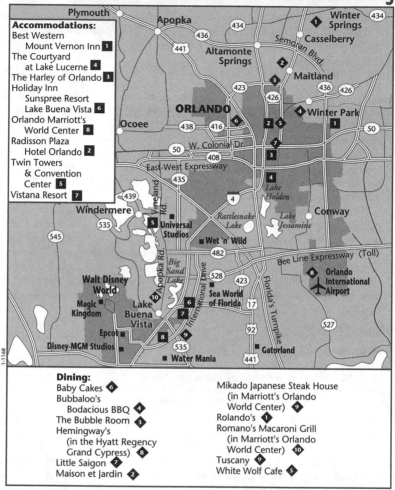

Accommodations:
Best Western
Mount Vernon Inn **1**
The Courtyard
at Lake Lucerne **4**
The Harley of Orlando **3**
Holiday Inn
Sunspree Resort
Lake Buena Vista **6**
Orlando Marriott's
World Center **8**
Radisson Plaza
Hotel Orlando **2**
Twin Towers
& Convention
Center **5**
Vistana Resort **7**

Dining:
Baby Cakes ◆**6**
Bubbaloo's
Bodacious BBQ ◆**4**
The Bubble Room ◆**3**
Hemingway's
(in the Hyatt Regency
Grand Cypress) ◆**8**
Little Saigon ◆**7**
Maison et Jardin ◆**2**

Mikado Japanese Steak House
(in Marriott's Orlando
World Center) ◆**9**
Rolando's ◆**1**
Romano's Macaroni Grill
(in Marriott's Orlando
World Center) ◆**10**
Tuscany ◆**9**
White Wolf Cafe ◆**5**

MODERATE

The Bubble Room

1351 S. Orlando Ave., Maitland (about 10 min. north of downtown Orlando). ☎ **407/ 628-3331.** Reservations recommended. Main Courses $11.95–$18.95. AE, DISC, MC, V. Daily 11:30am–4pm; Sun–Thurs 4–10pm; Fri–Sat 4–11pm. Free self-parking. Take I-4 east to Lee Rd. (Exit 45). Turn right at bottom of ramp. Turn left at Orlando Ave. (17-92). The Bubble Room is on the left, just past the railroad overpass. AMERICAN.

There is nothing subtle about the Bubble Room. You can rock in the Tunnel of Love while a toy train rolls just below the ceiling on a suspended track. Some people might find the hyped-up wait staff—also called Bubble Scouts—a little much. This *is* a place you come to celebrate. The Scouts are part of the party. Like the wacky waits, the cutesy entree names are a little over the top. But, like the decor that mixes Christmas lights with vintage movie stills, somehow it all works. At the Bubble Room everything from the portions to the staff is overwrought, which makes for high-energy fun. The prime rib, in Tarzan and Jane cuts, is a tender favorite that always includes a doggy bag. Also try the Maltese Chicken, roasted and stuffed, served with wild rice, a light gravy, and steamed vegetables. Make up for all those calories you burned trekking through the parks with a huge slab of a Bubble Room specialty, red velvet cake.

White Wolf Cafe

1829 N. Orange Ave. (about a mile from Loch Haven Park), Orlando. ☎ **407/895-9911.** Reservations not accepted. Main courses $4.25–$6.75 at lunch, $6.95–$12.95 at dinner. AE, MC, V. Mon 10am–6pm, Tues–Thurs 10am–10pm, Fri–Sat 10am–midnight. Free self-parking. Take I-4 east to Princeton St. (Exit 43). Turn right at Orange Ave. Look for striped awnings on the left. AMERICAN.

Even White Wolf's often clueless and notoriously slow servers can't overshadow the first-rate food. No mass-producing theme machine for tourists, this restaurant's meals emerge fresh from a tiny, deli-style kitchen. With rough-cut marble tables, a furry mascot panting near the door, and an eclectic, handwritten menu, it seems like you're eating in the crowded, funky, and slightly pretentious downtown loft of friends.

For lunch share the meaty Caribbean chicken salad, lightly accented with tangy apricot vinaigrette. (Get extra dressing.) Three-cheese lasagna, firm pasta slathered in a lightly spiced marinara, is a dinner favorite served with a warm hunk of French bread. For an appetizer pick black-bean soup kissed with onion. Avoid the salmon lavosh.

Note these tips from regulars. Slow service rules out firm postdinner plans. Fortunately, peanut-butter-and-brownie ice cream pie, a lush sugar rush dripping with hot fudge, is the perfect reward for patience.

INEXPENSIVE

Baby Cakes

2401 Edgewater Dr., Orlando (about 5 min. from downtown, 30 min. from Disney). ☎ **407/ 872-2332.** Reservations not accepted. Main courses $6.25–$7.50. AE, MC, V. Tues–Sat noon–9pm. Free self-parking. Take I-4 east to Princeton St. (Exit 43). Turn left. Turn right at Edgewater Dr. The restaurant is about 2 blocks on the right. AMERICAN.

The name "Baby Cakes" comes from a time when this small, casual restaurant specialized in small pastries. But as business grew, so did the menu. Its sweet roots are still evident in the mandatory walk to the dessert case, where the owners make choosing between a huge slab of velvet or cheese cake quite a production. This is not a case of the tail wagging the dog. The same attention to details and mastery of the culinary arts that makes chocolate bread pudding or blueberry layer cake to die for goes into the main dishes. Try the meat loaf, loaded with garlic and onions and served with golden brown roasted potatoes. Also, for any vegetarian in the group, try Clara's Shells, large tubes of pasta stuffed with a thick blend of cheese topped with marinara sauce. Ohh, baby.

Bubbaloo's Bodacious BBQ

1471 Lee Rd., Winter Park (about 5 min. from downtown Orlando). ☎ **407/295-1212.** Reservations not accepted. Main courses $4.95–$7.95. Mon–Thurs 10am–9pm, Fri–Sat 10am–10:30pm, Sun 11am–9pm. AE, MC, V. Free self-parking. Take I-4 east to Lee Rd. (Exit 45). Follow your nose; Bubbaloo's is on the left, next to a dry-cleaning shop. BARBECUE.

You can smell the hickory smoke for blocks, the tangy scent cutting through the humid Florida air. This is, hands down, some of the best barbecue you'll find anywhere. And, if nothing else, you gotta love the name. There are other things on the menu, such as fried clams, but go for the full pork platter with a heaping helping of pork and all the fixin's. The uninitiated should stay away from the "Killer" sauce, which produces a tongue buzz lasting for hours; and taste test the mild before moving up to the hot. The beans are the perfect side dish. Only the sometimes-soggy garlic bread brings the meal down. Beer available.

In case you want to see the world.

At American Express, we're here to make your journey a smooth one. So we have over 1,700 travel service locations in over 120 countries ready to help. What else would you expect from the world's largest travel agency?

do more

AMERICAN EXPRESS

Travel

http://www.americanexpress.com/travel

In case you want to be welcomed there.

We're here to see that you're always welcomed at establishments everywhere. That's why millions of people carry the American Express® Card – for peace of mind, confidence, and security, around the world or just around the corner.

do more

Cards

In case you're running low.

We're here to help with more than 118,000 Express Cash locations around the world. In order to enroll, just call American Express before you start your vacation.

do more

Express Cash

And just in case.

We're here with American Express® Travelers Cheques and Cheques *for Two*.® They're the safest way to carry money on your vacation and the surest way to get a refund, practically anywhere, anytime.

Another way we help you...

do more ®

Travelers Cheques

Little Saigon

1106 E. Colonial Dr. (Colonial is also called Hwy. 50.), near downtown Orlando. ☎ 407/
423-8539. Reservations not accepted. Main courses under $5 at lunch, $4.95–$10.95 at din-
ner. AE, DISC, MC, V. Daily 10am–9pm. Free self-parking. Take the Colonial Dr. (Hwy. 50) exit;
head east. Located between Mills and Thorton aves. Look for the fish mural. Turn right onto
Thorton. Lot is immediately to the left. VIETNAMESE.

Few would expect to find a Little Saigon, a bustling enclave of Asian immigrants, in
the midst of Orlando. But both the community and the first-class restaurant of the
same name make their home near downtown. For an appetizer, don't miss the unfried
summer rolls, a soft wrap filled with rice, shrimp, and pork served with a delicious
peanut sauce. At $2.50 for two, you could easily make a meal of these sumptuous
rolls. But go on to sample some of the healthy, light dishes in the dozens of menu
selections. Try one of the traditional soup dishes with noodles, rice, vegetables, and
either chicken, beef, or seafood. The numbered menu is in badly translated English—
"soup serve aside"—so don't be afraid to ask your servers exactly what goes into No.
86. Little Saigon's one drawback is the scarcity of English-speaking servers, so don't
hesitate to ask for the manager. As far as being authentic, the tables are usually filled
with members of the local Vietnamese community, with the owner working the tables
like a good ole boy at the corner diner. Stay away from the weak, slightly bitter iced
tea. Stick with hot tea, soda, or some of the limited beer and wine options available.

✪ Rolando's

870 E. Fla. 436 (Semoran Blvd., between Red Bug Rd. and U.S. 17-92), in Casselberry. ☎ **407/**
767-9677. Reservations not accepted. Main courses $3.25–$4.75 at lunch, $5.75–$11.50 at
dinner. AE, DISC, MC, V. Tues–Sat 11am–10pm, Sun 1–8pm. Free self-parking. Take I-4 east to
the East–West Expressway, head east, and make a left on Fla. 436. CUBAN.

About 40 minutes from Walt Disney World, this inexpensive mom-and-pop place
serves up huge portions of authentic Cuban fare. Its two dining rooms are pleasant
but plain, with Formica tables, stucco walls hung with photographs of Cuba, and pots
of philodendrons suspended from the ceiling. Soft lighting adds a smidge of ambiance.

I recommend ordering up a bunch of appetizers to share: deep-fried ripe plantains,
papas rellenas—breaded, deep-fried balls of mashed potato stuffed with spicy *picadillos*
(garlicky ground beef cooked with onions, olives, raisins, and green peppers in a
tomato sauce)—flavorful Cuban tamales topped with picadillos, and slightly sweet
batter-fried corn fritters that are light as air. An entree of roast chicken is brushed with
crushed garlic, white-wine vinegar, cumin, and oregano, then briefly deep-fried just
before serving. Tender, shredded beef is simmered in a richly seasoned, tomato-based
sauce with potatoes, olives, peas, pimentos, onions, green peppers, and sweet red peppers. And paella is an option if you call a few hours in advance to order it. Entrees
are served with fresh-baked hot rolls, house salad, rice, and plantains or *yuca* (a chewy
root plant); take the plantains. For dessert, try the *dulce de tres leche* (a meringue-
topped yellow cake mixed with condensed milk, evaporated milk, and cream). At
lunch a hearty sandwich of hot Cuban bread stuffed with slices of ham, roast pork,
Swiss cheese, and pickles is served with black-bean soup. Beer and wine are available.

7 Only in Orlando: Dining with Disney Characters

Especially for the 10-and-under set, it's a thrill to dine in a restaurant where costumed
Disney characters show up to greet the customers, sign autographs, pose in family
photos, and interact with little kids. Make reservations as far in advance as possible
for these very popular meals. *Note:* On selected days, Disney resort guests can arrive
earlier at some of the below-listed character breakfasts.

120   **Dining**

Artist Point
At Disney's Wilderness Lodge, 901 Timberline Dr. ☎ 407/WDW-DINE (939-3463). Priority seating. Breakfast with Pocahontas and friends $13.50 adults, $8.25 children 3–11. AE, MC, V. Daily 7:30–11am.

In a rustic lodgelike dining room with a beamed ceiling supported by tree-trunk beams and large windows providing scenic lake views, Pocahontas and friends host all-you-can-eat buffet breakfasts

Cape May Café
At Disney's Beach Club Resort, 1800 Epcot Resorts Blvd. ☎ 407/WDW-DINE (939-3463). Priority seating suggested. Character buffet breakfast $13.50 adults, $8.25 children 3–11, free for children 2 and under. AE, MC, V. Daily 7:30–11am.

The Cape May Café, a delightful New England–themed dining room, serves lavish buffet character breakfasts with Admiral Goofy and his crew—Chip 'n' Dale and Pluto (exact characters may vary)—as hosts.

Chef Mickey's
At Disney's Contemporary Resort, 4600 N. World Dr. ☎ 407/WDW-DINE (939-3463). Priority seating. Character buffet breakfast $13.95 adults, $7.95 children 3–11, free for children 2 and under; character prime-rib buffet dinner $17.95 adults, $7.95 children 3–11, free for children 2 and under. AE, MC, V. Daily 7:30–11:30am and 5–9:30pm.

The whimsical Chef Mickey's is the setting for buffet character breakfasts and dinners. On hand to meet, greet, and mingle with guests are Mickey and various pals. Chef Mickey's character prime-rib buffet dinners include a make-your-own-sundae bar.

Garden Grill
In The Land Pavilion at Epcot. ☎ 407/WDW-DINE (939-3463). Priority seating. Character breakfast $14.95 adults, $7.95 children 3–11; lunch $16.95 adults, $9.95 children 3–11; dinner $19.50 adults, $9.95 children 3–11, plus theme-park admission. All meals are free for children 2 and under. AE, MC, V. Daily 8:30–11:30am, 11:30am–3:30pm, and 3:30–8pm.

This is a revolving restaurant with seating in comfortable, semicircular booths. As you dine, your table travels past desert, prairie, farmland, and rain-forest environments. There's a "momma's-in-the-kitchen" theme here: You'll be given a straw hat at the entrance, and the just-folks service staff speaks in country lingo. Hearty family-style meals are hosted by Mickey, Minnie, and Chip 'n' Dale. American breakfast and lunch choices are extensive; dinners include several entrees (roast chicken, farm-raised fish, and hickory-smoked steak), mashed potatoes, vegetables, squaw bread and biscuits, salad, beverage, and dessert.

King Stefan's Banquet Hall
In Cinderella Castle in the Magic Kingdom. ☎ 407/WDW-DINE (939-3463). Priority seating strongly recommended. Character breakfast $14.95 adults, $7.95 children 3–11, free for children 2 and under. AE, MC, V. Daily 8–10am.

This Gothic castle—the focal point of the park—serves up character-breakfast buffets daily. Hosts vary, but Cinderella always puts in an appearance. This is one of the most popular character meals in the park, so reserve far in advance. It's a great way to start your day in the Magic Kingdom.

○ Liberty Tree Tavern
In Liberty Square in the Magic Kingdom. ☎ 407/WDW-DINE (939-3463). Priority seating. Character dinner $19.50 adults, $9.95 children 3–11 plus theme-park admission, free for children 2 and under. AE, MC, V. Daily 4pm to park closing.

This Williamsburg-like 18th-century pub offers character dinners hosted by Mickey, Goofy, Pluto, Chip 'n' Dale, and Tigger (some or all of them). Meals, served family style, consist of salad, roast chicken, marinated flank steak, trail sausages, mashed potatoes, rice pilaf, vegetables, and a dessert of warm apple crisp with vanilla ice cream.

Minnie's Menehune & Mickey's Tropical Luau

At Disney's Polynesian Resort, 1600 Seven Seas Dr. ☎ **407/WDW-DINE** (939-3463). Priority seating. Character breakfast $13.50 adults, $8.25 children 3–11, free for children 2 and under; character luau dinner $30 adults, $14 children 3–11, free for children 2 and under. AE, MC, V. Daily 7:30–10:30am; luau at 4:30pm. No characters at the regular luau dinner show.

Luau Cove, an exotic open-air facility, is the setting for an island-themed character show called Mickey's Tropical Luau. It's an abbreviated version of the Polynesian Luau Dinner Show described in chapter 10, "Walt Disney World & Orlando After Dark," featuring Polynesian dancers along with Mickey, Minnie, Pluto, and Goofy. Your prix-fixe meal includes honey-roasted chicken, vegetables, glazed cinnamon bread, and an ice-cream sundae. Guests are presented with shell leis on entering.

The Polynesian also hosts Minnie's Menehune Character Breakfast in the Polynesian-themed 'Ohana (described above). Traditional breakfast foods are prepared on an 18-foot fire pit and served family-style. Minnie, Goofy, and Chip 'n' Dale appear, and there are children's parades with Polynesian musical instruments.

1900 Park Fare

At Disney's Grand Floridian Beach Resort, 4401 Floridian Way. ☎ **407/WDW-DINE** (939-3463). Priority seating. Character breakfast $15.95 adults, $9.95 children 3–11, free for children 2 and under; character dinner buffet $19.95 adults, $9.50 children 3–11, free for children 2 and under. AE, MC, V. Daily 7:30–11:30am and 5:30–9pm.

This exquisitely elegant Disney resort hosts character meals in the festive exposition-themed 1900 Park Fare. Big Bertha—a French band organ that plays pipes, drums, bells, cymbals, castanets, and xylophone—provides music. Mary Poppins, Winnie the Pooh, Goofy, Pluto, Chip 'n' Dale, and Minnie Mouse appear at the elaborate buffet breakfasts. Mickey and Minnie appear at nightly buffets featuring prime rib, stuffed pork loin, fresh fish, and more.

Soundstage Restaurant

At Disney–MGM Studios, adjacent to the Magic of Disney Animation. ☎ **407/WDW-DINE** (939-3463). Character buffet breakfast $13.95 adults, $7.95 children 3–11, free for children 2 and under; character lunch $16.95 adults, $9.95 children ages 3–11, free for children 2 and under. AE, MC, V. Daily 8:30–10:30am and 11:30am–3:30pm.

A vast buffet meal is set out in this warehouse-motif restaurant decorated with movie props and posters, and selected characters from the movies *Aladdin* and *Pocahontas* sign autographs as favorite tunes from both Disney hits play in the background.

Watercress Café

At the Buena Vista Palace, 1900 Buena Vista Dr. ☎ **407/827-2727.** Reservations not accepted. Character breakfast $12.95 adults, $6.95 children 4–12, free for children 3 and under; à la carte breakfast also available. AE, MC, V. Sun 8–10:30am.

The plant-filled Watercress Café—with large windows overlooking Lake Buena Vista—is the setting for Sunday-morning character breakfasts featuring Minnie, Goofy, and Pluto. Both à la carte and buffet meals are offered. Since reservations are not accepted, arrive early to avoid a wait.

7

On Your Mark, Get Set, Go! What to See & Do In & Around Walt Disney World

We all know what the big attraction is here—the one that put Orlando on the map. With the exception of conventioneers (and I'm sure many of them sneak off to the parks, as well), most people who come to Orlando have come to meet—or become reacquainted with—the Mouse. ·

Walt Disney World, attracting more than 13 million visitors annually, is one of the world's most popular travel destinations. All of the Disney parks make the industry's top 10 list for attendance. And why not? It provides a welcome retreat in a star-spangled, all-American fantasyland where wonderment, human progress, and old-fashioned family fun are the major themes. And these themes are presented in spectacular parades and fireworks displays, 3-D, 4-D, and 360° Circle-Vision movies, and adventure-filled journeys through time and space. Though it's not inexpensive, you'll seldom hear people complain about not getting their money's worth. Disney delivers!

The Magic Kingdom opened in 1971. Later additions include Epcot, where guests take exhilarating voyages around the world and into the future; Disney–MGM Studios, centered on "Hollywood Boulevard" and providing a thrilling behind-the-scenes look at motion-picture and TV studios; Pleasure Island, an ongoing street festival in a 6-acre complex of nightclubs and shops, featuring live concerts nightly as well as Planet Hollywood; Walt Disney World Village, a charming lakeside enclave of shops and restaurants; Typhoon Lagoon, a 56-acre water park where you can catch the world's largest man-made waves or plummet down steep water flumes; River Country, another water park; Blizzard Beach, a water park that's meant to be "a ski resort in the tropics"; and Discovery Island, an utterly delightful nature preserve and aviary. Now, there is even a miniature golf course based on the classic *Fantasia*.

After celebrating its 25th anniversary in 1996, Disney will unveil its fourth park—Animal Kingdom—in early 1998. The company's early polling tested the cost of a 1-day ticket going as high as $43, a $4.50 increase. For a 5-day park-hopper pass, prices range from $117 to $271.

1 Essentials

GETTING INFORMATION IN ADVANCE

Before leaving home, call or write the **Walt Disney World Co.,** Box 10000, Lake Buena Vista, FL 32830-1000 (☎ **407/934-7639**), for a copy of the very informative *Walt Disney World Vacations* brochure—an invaluable planning aid. When you call, also ask about special events that will be on during your stay (see also "When to Go," in chapter 2 of this book).

Once you've arrived in town, **guest services** and **concierge desks** in all area hotels—especially Disney properties and official hotels—have up-to-the-minute information about happenings in the parks. Stop by to ask questions and pick up literature, including a schedule of park hours and special events. If you have questions your hotel can't answer, call ☎ **407/824-4321.**

There are also **information locations** in each park—at City Hall in the Magic Kingdom, at Innoventions East near the WorldKey terminals in Epcot, and the Guest Services Building in Disney–MGM Studios.

If you are hooked up to the Internet, or have access to a library with Internet access, there is a World Wide Web site at **http://www.disneyworld.com**, which has extensive, entertaining, and regularly updated information, including a live-action look from video cameras perched throughout the various parks. (This is mostly long-distance shots of tourists walking about, but is still a chance to see those blue Orlando skies and dream ahead to vacation time.) There are dozens of web pages devoted to Disney, especially Disney trivia. But one is a very informative newsgroup on Usenet called **rec.arts.disney**.

The city newspaper, the *Orlando Sentinel,* also produces *Orlando Sentinel Online* at **http://www.oso@aol.com**. Once there, click on "Theme Park Central" for a variety of information and updates on what is going on at local attractions.

GETTING TO WDW BY CAR

The exits to all the Disney parks are well marked. Off of Interstate 4, exits 25, 26, and 27 lead to the Disney parks. Once inside, colorful signs will direct you to your destination. If you miss the exit marked for your specific park, don't panic. Simply get off at the next one. It may take more time, but it's safer than slashing through five lanes of traffic to make the off-ramp.

PARKING

All of the WDW lots are tightly controlled; the Disney folks have parking cars down to a science. You park where those nice young people in their yellow-striped shirts tell you to park—or else.

Visitors are also encouraged to ride the trams. Do this if you're parked in the massive Magic Kingdom lot. You can skip waiting for the trams in lots at Epcot and MGM Studios and walk on up. The parking lots are not necessarily designed for pedestrians, so watch out for those trams.

Parking generally costs $5. There are special lots at each park for travelers with disabilities (☎ **407/824-4321** for details).

Walt Disney World Parks & Attractions

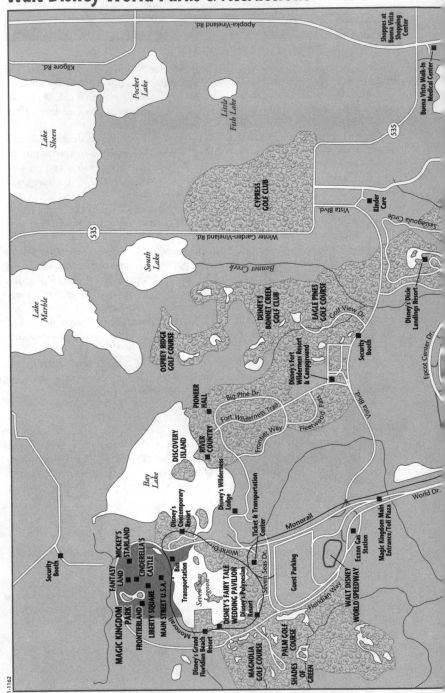

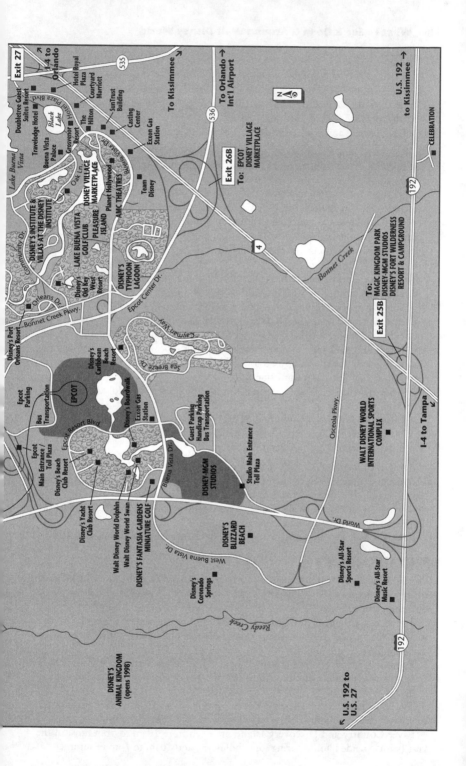

125

TICKETS

There are several ticket options. Most people get the best value from 4- and 5-day passes. All passes offer unlimited use of the WDW transportation system. The prices quoted below do *not* include sales tax, and they are, of course, subject to change.

Adult prices are paid by anyone over 10 years of age. Children's rates are for ages 3 to 9. Children 2 and under are admitted free.

- The **4-Day Value Pass** provides admission for 1 day at the Magic Kingdom, 1 day at Epcot, 1 day at Disney–MGM Studios, and 1 day at your choice of any of those three parks; you can use it on any 4 days following purchase, but you cannot visit more than one park on any given day. When it opens, Animal Kingdom will be included in your choices. Adults pay $136.74; children, $109.18.
- The **4-Day Park-Hopper Pass** provides unlimited admission to the three major parks on any 4 days; in other words, you can hop from park to park on any given day. Animal Kingdom will be included in this pass when it opens. Adults pay $152.64; children, $121.90.
- The **5-Day World-Hopper Pass** provides unlimited admission to the Magic Kingdom, Epcot, and Disney–MGM Studios on any 5 days; you can visit any combination of parks on any given day. It also includes admission to Typhoon Lagoon, River Country, Blizzard Beach, Discovery Island, and Pleasure Island for a period of 7 days beginning the first date stamped. Adults pay $207.76; children, $166.42.
- A **1-day, one-park ticket** for the Magic Kingdom, Epcot, or Disney–MGM Studios is $40.81 for adults, $32.86 for children. When it opens, Animal Kingdom will have a similar 1-day admission price.
- A **1-day ticket** to Typhoon Lagoon or Blizzard Beach is $26.45 for adults, $20.67 for children.
- A **1-day ticket** to River Country is $16.91 for adults, $13.25 for children.
- A **1-day ticket** to Discovery Island is $12.67 for adults, $6.89 for children.
- A **1-day ticket** to Pleasure Island is $19.03.

If you're staying at any Walt Disney World resort or "official" hotel (see chapter 5, "Accommodations"), you're also eligible for a money-saving **Be Our Guest Pass** priced according to length of stay. It also offers special perks.

If you plan on visiting Walt Disney World more than one time during the year, inquire about a money-saving annual pass.

Be on the lookout for special deals for Animal Kingdom when it opens in 1998.

OPERATING HOURS

Hours of operation vary somewhat throughout the year and can be influenced by special events, so it is generally a good idea to call during your visit to check opening/closing times.

The **Magic Kingdom** and **Disney–MGM Studios** are generally open from 9am to 7pm, with extended hours—sometimes as late as midnight—during major holidays and the summer months.

Epcot is generally open from 9am to 9pm, with Future World open from 9am to 9pm and World Showcase from 11am to 9pm—once again with extended holiday hours.

Typhoon Lagoon and **Blizzard Beach** are open from 10am to 5pm most of the year (with extended hours during some holidays), and 9am to 8pm in summer.

River Country and **Discovery Island** are open from 10am to 5pm most of the year (with extended hours during some holidays), and 10am to 7pm in summer.

Note: Epcot and MGM sometimes open a half hour or more before the posted time. Keep in mind, too, that Disney-resort guests enjoy early admission to all three major parks on designated days. When it opens, **Animal Kingdom** will probably have hours similar to the Magic Kingdom and Disney–MGM Studios, but be sure to check in your park brochures.

2 Making Your Visit More Enjoyable

HOW WE'VE MADE THIS CHAPTER USEFUL TO PARENTS

Before every listing in the three major parks, you'll note the "Recommended Ages" entry that tells you which age group will most enjoy every ride and attraction. Though most families will want to do everything, you may find this guideline helpful in planning your daily itinerary.

BEST TIME OF YEAR TO VISIT

There is really no "off" season for Disney, but during the winter months, usually from January through April, the park crowds are smallest, the weather coolest, and the air least humid. The summer months, when the masses throng to the park, are not only crowded but hot, hot, hot, sticky, and humid. During the cooler months, you also don't have to worry about the daily summer storms.

BEST DAYS TO VISIT

The busiest days at the Magic Kingdom and Epcot are Monday to Wednesday; at Disney–MGM Studios, they're Thursday and Friday. Surprisingly, weekends are the least busy at all parks. Sunday is generally a slow day. Major holidays, such as Christmas, Easter, and Thanksgiving are also generally slow. In peak seasons especially, arrange your visits accordingly. Crowds also tend to thin later in the day.

PLAN YOUR VISIT

How you plan your time at Walt Disney World will depend on a number of factors, including the ages of children in your party, what you've seen on previous visits, your specific interests, and whether you're traveling at a peak time or off-season (when lines are shorter and you can cram more in). Planning, however, is essential. Choose age-appropriate activities.

Nothing can spoil a day in the parks more than a child devastated because he or she can't do something promised. Before you get to the park, review this book and the suggested ages for children, especially height restrictions. The WDW staff does not bend those rules, no matter how loud your little one may wail.

Unless you're staying for considerably more than a week, you can't possibly experience all the rides, shows, and attractions here—not to mention the vast array of recreational facilities. And you'll only wear yourself to a frazzle trying. It's far better to follow a relaxed itinerary, including leisurely meals and some recreation, than to make a demanding job out of trying to see everything.

Note: Many of these suggestions are also applicable at non-Disney theme parks.

CREATE AN ITINERARY FOR EACH DAY

Read the above-mentioned *Walt Disney World Vacations* brochure and the detailed descriptions in this book and plan your visit to include all shows and attractions that pique your interest and excitement. It's a good idea to make a daily itinerary, putting these in some kind of sensible geographical sequence, so you're not zigzagging all over the place. Familiarize yourself in advance with the layout of each park.

I repeat this advice—schedule in sit-down shows, recreational activities (a boat ride or swim late in the afternoon can be wonderfully refreshing), and at least some un-hurried meals. My suggested itineraries are below.

SUGGESTED ITINERARIES

A Day in the Magic Kingdom

The key to getting the most out of your theme-park experience is going against the crowd. Do arrive with everyone else a little before opening time, having already pur-chased tickets. When the gates open, *don't* make a dash for Fantasyland, which is where everyone else will go. Start in one of the lesser realms to avoid the crowds.

While the families are still going loco over the Lion King, hightail it to Frontierland and ride Splash Mountain—another biggie—before long lines form there. There is little shade near this ride and you definitely don't want to be wait-ing there in the middle of the day. When you come off, it will still be early enough to beat the lines at another major attraction; head over to Adventureland and do Pirates of the Caribbean.

Complete whatever else interests you in Adventureland. Or eat a heavy snack, like a turkey leg from one of the vendor carts, and keep riding during lunch to take ad-vantage of shorter lunchtime lines. Have lunch while taking in the early-afternoon shows in the Diamond Horseshoe Saloon Revue show (they don't take reservations, so arrive early).

By 2:30pm (earlier in peak seasons), you should start looking for a seat along the parade route. Liberty Square is where most people settle, so look at the map and pick a spot further down the route, which winds through the park.

If you are a ride junkie, skip the parade and hit Alien Encounters and other high-volume rides while the rest of the crowd concentrates along the curb.

This an especially good idea if SpectroMagic is on during your stay. That is the parade to see. After the parade, it should be safe to venture into Fantasyland, although there is never a truly good time since it contains the heart of what most adults re-member from their first Disney visit.

If you have little kids (8 and under) in your party, start your day instead by tak-ing the WDW Railroad from Main Street to Mickey's Toontown Fair. That should provide a sufficient Mickey fix so you can work your way through Adventureland and Tomorrowland. Save Fantasyland for after lunch. Take an air-conditioned break at the Country Bear Jamboree in Frontierland.

That's a long enough day for most young children, and your best plan is to go back to your hotel for a nap or swim.

If You Can Spend Only 1 Day at Epcot

Epcot really requires at least 2 days, so this is a highlight tour. As above, arrive early, tickets in hand. If you haven't already made lunch reservations by calling ☎ 407/ **WDW-DINE** (939-3463; see chapter 6, "Dining"), make your first stop at the WorldKey terminals in Innoventions East. I suggest a 1pm lunch at the San Angel Inn Restaurant in Mexico. If you don't like Mexican food, move up one pavilion to Norway and reserve for the buffet at Akershus. You can make dinner reservations at the same time. Plan dinner for about 7pm, which will allow you time to eat and find a good viewing spot for IllumiNations (usually at 9pm, but check your schedule).

Spend no more than an hour exploring Innoventions East. Then move on to the Universe of Energy show. Continue to the Wonders of Life Pavilion, where must-sees include Body Wars, Cranium Command, and The Making of Me.

In the Words of Walt Disney

Family fun is as necessary to modern living as a kitchen refrigerator.

Part of the Disney success is our ability to create a believable world of dreams that appeals to all age groups.

And if time allows—it will depend on line waits at attractions—take in the show at Horizons before heading into World Showcase for lunch. Over lunch, check your show schedule and decide which shows to incorporate into your day.

Then walk around the lagoon, visiting highlight attractions such as Wonders of China, The American Adventure, Impressions de France, and O Canada!, allowing yourself some time for browsing and shopping. After dinner, stay on for IllumiNations.

If You Can Spend 2 Days at Epcot

Ignore the 1-day itinerary above, but do begin your day by making all necessary restaurant reservations—once again for lunch in Mexico or Norway at about 1pm. Make reservations for Day 2 at the same time.

Skip Innoventions East for now and work your way thoroughly through the Universe of Energy, Wonders of Life, Horizons, and World of Motion pavilions, keeping your lunch reservation time in mind.

After lunch, walk clockwise around the lagoon, visiting each pavilion and taking in as many shows as you like (consult your show schedule and try to keep pace as well as possible). Leave IllumiNations for your second day's visit.

Begin your second day exploring Innoventions East and proceed counterclockwise, taking in Spaceship Earth, Innoventions West, The Living Seas (its Coral Reef restaurant is a good choice for lunch), and all the other pavilions on the west side of the park. Cap off your Epcot visit with IllumiNations.

A Day at Disney–MGM Studios Theme Park

Since show times change frequently here, it's impossible to really give you a workable itinerary. Upon entering the park, if you haven't already made dining arrangements, stop at the Hollywood Brown Derby (details in chapter 6) and make reservations for lunch. Or you might want to conserve park-touring time by having a light lunch at a casual eatery and saving the Derby for a relaxing dinner.

Nutritional needs accounted for, make a beeline for the Twilight Zone Tower of Terror 2. While you're waiting in line, plan the rest of your schedule, being sure to include these not-to-be-missed attractions: the Magic of Disney Animation, the Indiana Jones Stunt Show, Jim Henson's Muppet*Vision 4D, and the Monster Sound Show.

If you have girls under 11 in your party, *The Voyage of the Little Mermaid* and *Beauty and the Beast* will probably be major priorities; for the latter shows, get in line 45 minutes prior to show time. And all kids love the parade; snag a good seat on the parade route 30 minutes ahead of time as well. Keep in mind that people tend to congregate along the route near the back of the park, so go where everyone else is not.

Time for more? Do Superstar Television, the Indiana Jones Epic Stunt Spectacular, Star Tours, Inside the Magic, and the Backstage Studio Tour. In peak seasons, stay on for fireworks.

SERVICES & FACILITIES IN THE PARKS

ATMs   Money machines are available near the entrances to all parks and usually one other place inside the park. These machines honor cards from banks using the Cirrus, Honor, and Plus systems and they are marked on the park guide map.

Baby Care   All parks have a Baby Care Center equipped with rocking chairs and selling basic supplies such as disposable diapers. Disposable diapers are also available at Guest Services. All women's rest rooms and some men's rest rooms are equipped with changing tables.

Cameras & Film   Film and Kodak disposable cameras are sold at various locations in all parks. Camcorders are available for rent in Epcot and MGM but not the Magic Kingdom.

First Aid   All parks have manned first-aid stations near the entrances.

Lost Children   Every park has a designated spot for lost children and also keeps written records of those children. In the Magic Kingdom it's usually City Hall or the Baby Care Center; in Epcot, the Earth Center or the Baby Care Center; in Disney–MGM, Guest Services. Children under 7 should have name tags.

Package Pickup   Clerks at nearly all WDW stores can arrange for large packages to be taken to the front of the park. Allow at least 3 hours for delivery.

Pets   Don't leave your pet in a parked car, even with a window cracked open. The interior of a car becomes incredibly hot baking in the Florida sun. (A dead pet will not enhance your trip.) Only service animals are permitted in the parks, but there are four kennels in the WDW complex. Those at the Transportation and Ticket Center in the Magic Kingdom and near the entrance to Fort Wilderness board animals overnight. Day accommodations are offered at kennels just outside the Entrance Plaza at Epcot and at the entrance to Disney–MGM Studios.

Stroller Rental   Strollers are available for rent near the entrances of all the parks. The cost is $6. Deposits, usually $1 or $2, may vary.

Wheelchair Rental   Both electric and regular wheelchairs are available at all the parks. A regular wheelchair costs about $6. Electric wheelchairs rent for $32 to $35. The deposit, usually only a few dollars, may vary.

FOR TRAVELERS WITH SPECIAL NEEDS

WDW does everything possible to facilitate guests with disabilities. Its many services are detailed in the **Guidebook for Guests with Disabilities.** To obtain a copy prior to your visit, write Guest Letters, P.O. Box 10040, Lake Buena Vista, FL 32830-0040, or call ☎ **407/824-4321.** Also call that number for answers to any questions regarding special needs. Some examples of Disney services: Almost all Disney resorts have rooms for those with disabilities; there are Braille directories inside the Magic Kingdom—in front of the Main Street train station and in a gazebo in front of the Crystal Palace restaurant; there are special parking lots at all three parks; complimentary guided-tour audiocassette tapes and recorders are available at Guest Services to assist visually impaired guests; personal translator units are available to amplify the audio at selected Epcot attractions (inquire at Earth Station); and wheelchairs can be rented at all of the Disney parks. For information about Telecommunications Devices for the Deaf (TDDs), call ☎ **407/827-5141.**

3 The Magic Kingdom

Centered around Cinderella's Castle—its medieval spires are Walt Disney World's most recognizable symbol, after Mickey Mouse—the Magic Kingdom occupies about 100 acres, with numerous attractions, restaurants, and shops in seven theme sections, or "lands."

A Dozen Tips So You'll Have Fewer Headaches

1. **Go Where the Crowds Aren't:** Head to the left when the rush is moving to the right. Save the major attractions for late in the day. Eat a little earlier or a little later than the rest of the crowd.

2. **Write down your car's location:** That purple minivan in the next space may not be there when you get out. Write down where your car is or do whatever is necessary to commit the location to memory. This is especially important at Epcot and MGM where lots are not as well marked as in the Magic Kingdom.

3. **Avoid Rush Hour:** I-4 is woefully over capacity, so avoid being on the roads during rush hour, from 8 to 9am and from about 4:30 to 6pm. This is especially true if you are driving toward the downtown area. But remember, the theme parks are also serviced by thousands of office workers keeping bankers hours.

4. **Don't overplan:** Face it, you aren't going to do everything in any park. Agree as a group to a list of three "must-do" activities for each day. If your children are old enough to be responsible, split and reunite at an agreed-upon time.

5. **Pace Yourself:** It's not unusual to see people literally running across the parking lot to the trams. Relax, the park isn't going anywhere. Once inside, stagger long lines with air-conditioned shows or even breaks on a bench in the shade.

6. **Make Dining Reservations:** If a sit-down dinner is important, make sure to get priority-seating reservations either before your visit or when you enter the park.

7. **Set a Spending Limit:** Kids should know they have a set amount to spend on take-home trinkets. So should Mom and Dad. Set a budget, building in a small contingency fund for emergencies.

8. **Take a Break:** If you are staying at a WDW property, spend the late afternoon napping or unwinding. Return to parks for a few more attractions and the closing shows.

9. **Dress Comfortably:** This may seem like a no-brainer, but judging by the limping, blistered crowds, some don't understand they will be walking—a lot. This is not the place to break in those way-cool clogs. Comfortable walking shoes are a must.

10. **Sunscreen, Sunscreen, Sunscreen:** Locals spot tourists by their painful bright-red glow. The Florida sun can bake, even in the shade and even in the cooler months. A bad first-day burn can ruin the whole trip. Protect yourself and your kids.

11. **Travel Light:** Don't carry large amounts of cash. The Pirates of the Caribbean aren't the only thieves in WDW. There are ATM machines in all the parks if you begin to run short of cash.

12. **Get a Little Goofy:** Relax, put on those Mickey Mouse ears, eat that extra piece of fudge, even sing along at the shows. Don't worry about what the staff thinks; they've seen just about everything. Everyone else is on vacation, too.

The Magic Kingdom

MAIN STREET, U.S.A.:
Main Street Cinema ③
Main Street Vehicles ②
Walt Disney World Railroad ①

ADVENTURELAND:
Jungle Cruise ④
Pirates of the Caribbean ⑤
Swiss Family Treehouse ⑦
Tropical Serenade with the
   Enchanted Tiki Birds ⑥

FRONTIERLAND:
Big Thunder Mountain
   Railroad ⑭
Country Bear Jamboree ⑧
The Diamond Horseshoe
   Saloon Revue ⑩
Frontierland Shootin'
   Arcade ⑨
Splash Mountain ⑫
Tom Sawyer Island ⑪
Walt Disney World Railroad ⑬

LIBERTY SQUARE:
The Hall of Presidents ⑯
The Haunted Mansion ⑱
Liberty Square Riverboat ⑮
Mike Fink Keelboats ⑰

FANTASYLAND:
Castle Forecourt Stage ⑲
Cinderella's Castle ⑳
Cinderella's Golden
   Carousel ㉑

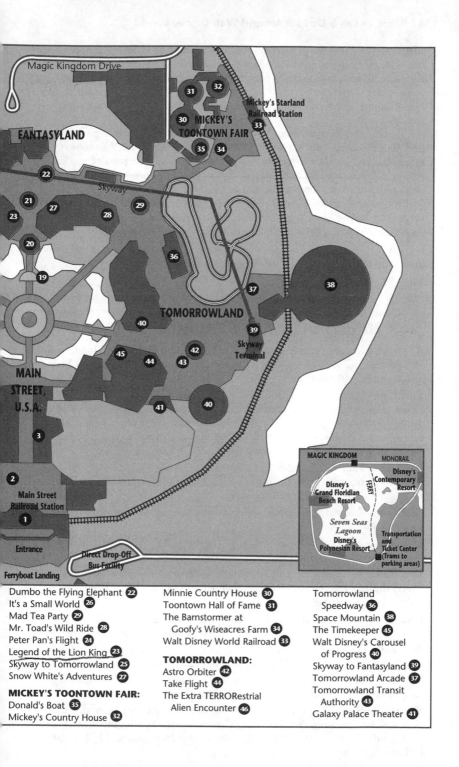

Magic Kingdom Drive

Mickey's Starland Railroad Station

MICKEY'S TOONTOWN FAIR

FANTASYLAND

Skyway

TOMORROWLAND

Skyway Terminal

MAIN STREET, U.S.A.

Main Street Railroad Station

Entrance

Ferryboat Landing

Direct Drop-Off Bus Facility

MAGIC KINGDOM — MONORAIL

Disney's Contemporary Resort

Disney's Grand Floridian Beach Resort

FERRY

Seven Seas Lagoon

Disney's Polynesian Resort

Transportation and Ticket Center (Trams to parking areas)

Dumbo the Flying Elephant **22**
It's a Small World **26**
Mad Tea Party **29**
Mr. Toad's Wild Ride **28**
Peter Pan's Flight **24**
Legend of the Lion King **23**
Skyway to Tomorrowland **25**
Snow White's Adventures **27**

MICKEY'S TOONTOWN FAIR:
Donald's Boat **35**
Mickey's Country House **32**

Minnie Country House **30**
Toontown Hall of Fame **31**
The Barnstormer at
    Goofy's Wiseacres Farm **34**
Walt Disney World Railroad **33**

TOMORROWLAND:
Astro Orbiter **42**
Take Flight **44**
The Extra TERRORestrial
    Alien Encounter **46**

Tomorrowland
    Speedway **36**
Space Mountain **38**
The Timekeeper **45**
Walt Disney's Carousel
    of Progress **40**
Skyway to Fantasyland **39**
Tomorrowland Arcade **37**
Tomorrowland Transit
    Authority **43**
Galaxy Palace Theater **41**

ARRIVING   From the parking lot, you have to take a short monorail or ferry ride to the Magic Kingdom entrance. During peak attendance times, arrive at the Magic Kingdom no later than an hour prior to opening time to avoid long lines at these conveyances. Sections of the parking lot are named for Disney characters (Goofy, Pluto, Minnie, and so on), and aisles are numbered. Be sure to write down where you parked.

Upon entering the park, consult your *Magic Kingdom Guidemap* to get your bearings. It details every shop, restaurant, and attraction in every Land. Also consult your **entertainment schedule** to see what's on for the day. There are parades, musical extravaganzas featuring Disney characters, fireworks, band concerts, barbershop quartets, Disney-character appearances, and more.

If you have questions, all park employees are very knowledgeable, and City Hall, on your left as you enter, is both an information center and, along with Toontown Fair (details below), a likely place to meet up with costumed characters.

HOURS   Generally 9am to 7pm with extended hours—sometimes as late as midnight—during major holidays and the summer months.

TICKETS & PRICES $40.81 for adults, $32.86 for children, children under 4 are free. See "Tickets" earlier in this chapter for information on 4- and 5-day passes.

SERVICES & FACILITIES IN THE MAGIC KINGDOM

ATMs   These machines honor cards from banks using the Cirrus, Honor, and Plus systems and are located at the main entrance, the SunTrust Bank on Main Street, and in Tomorrowland.

Baby Care   Located next to the Crystal Palace at the end of Main Street, the Baby Care Center is furnished with rocking chairs and toddler-size toilets. Disposable diapers, formula, baby food, and pacifiers are for sale. There are changing tables here as well as in all women's rest rooms and some men's rest rooms. Disposable diapers are also sold at Guest Services.

Cameras & Film   Film and Kodak's disposable Fun Saver cameras are available throughout the park. Although once available, 35mm cameras and camcorders are no longer for rent at the Magic Kingdom.

First Aid   The First Aid Center, staffed by registered nurses, is located alongside the Crystal Palace.

Lockers   Lockers can be found in an arcade underneath the Main Street Railroad Station. The cost is $6, including a $2 refundable deposit.

Lost Children   Lost children in the Magic Kingdom are usually taken to City Hall or the Baby Care Center where lost children logbooks are kept. Children under 7 should wear name tags.

Package Pickup   Any large package you purchase can be sent by the shop clerk to Guest Relations in the Entrance Plaza. Allow 3 hours for delivery.

Pet Care   The Transportation and Ticket Center at Magic Kingdom boards animals overnight for $8 a day. There are also four kennels in the WDW complex.

Strollers   These can be rented at the Stroller Shop near the entrance to the Magic Kingdom. The cost is $6 a day, including a $1 deposit.

Wheelchair Rental   For wheelchairs, go to the gift shop to the left of the ticket booths at the Transportation and Ticket Center or to the Stroller and Wheelchair Shop inside the main entrance to your right. Cost is $6 regular and $32 electric, including a $2 deposit.

MAIN STREET, U.S.A.

Designed to replicate an archetypical turn-of-the-century American street (okay, so it culminates in a 13th-century castle), this is the gateway to the Kingdom. Don't dawdle on Main Street when you enter the park; leave it for the end of the day when you're heading back to your hotel.

Main Street Cinema
Recommended ages: all ages

A mannequin is in charge of the ticket booth here, so you can sneak right in without paying. Just kidding—there's no charge for admission. Main Street Cinema is an air-conditioned hexagonal theater where vintage black-and-white Disney cartoons (including the 1928 *Steamboat Willie,* in which Mickey and Minnie debuted) are aired continually on two screens. Viewers have to watch these standing; there are no seats.

Walt Disney World Railroad & Other Main Street Vehicles
Recommended ages: 2–8

You can board an authentic 1928 steam-powered train here for a 15-minute journey clockwise around the perimeter of the park. There are stations in Frontierland and Mickey's Toontown. There are also horse-drawn trolleys, horseless carriages, jitneys, omnibuses, and fire engines plying the short route along Main Street from Town Square to Cinderella Castle.

SHOPPING IN MAIN STREET

The vast **Disneyana Collectibles** carries limited-edition movie cels, antique Disney clocks and porcelain figures, and collectible dolls and items such as a 1947 Donald Duck cookie jar that today is worth $2,000! Why did I ever let Mom throw out my old toys?

The Emporium, in Town Square, houses the park's largest selection of Disneyana, everything from Mickey-logo golf balls to Dumbo cookie jars. Note the Animatronic window displays.

Basically an old-fashioned candy store, the **Market House** also has an interesting line of pipes and tobaccos, as well as Disney-theme kitchenware—Mickey cupcake papers, ice-cube molds, and cookie cutters.

Over at the **Harmony Barber Shop,** where nostalgic men's grooming items are sold (mustache wax, spice colognes, shaving mugs), a barbershop quartet called The Dapper Dans performs on the hour all day (except at 3pm).

Autographed sports memorabilia and team clothing—Joe Namath–signed footballs, Pittsburgh Steeler T-shirts, Bulls jerseys, a Babe Ruth–autographed 1936 World Series program, and the like—are available at the **Main Street Athletic Club.**

At **Crystal Arts,** you can watch craftspeople create the intricate animals, cut-glass vases and bowls, and other glittering items sold here. And at the adjoining **Shadow Box,** silhouette artists create cut-out portraits of customers on black paper.

At the end of Main Street, the **King's Gallery,** inside Cinderella Castle, is cluttered with family crests, tapestries, suits of armor, and other medieval wares, as well as miniature carousels. An artisan here demonstrates *damascening,* a form of metal engraving that originated in Damascus circa A.D. 600.

ADVENTURELAND

Cross a bridge to your left and stroll into an exotic jungle of lush tropical foliage, thatch-roofed huts, and carved totems. Amid dense vines and stands of palm and bamboo, drums are beating, and swashbuckling adventures are taking place.

❓ Did You Know?

- The movie portion of Universal Studios' *Back to the Future* attraction took 2 years to make and was the most expensive film per minute ever made.
- Mickey Mouse has more than 80 different outfits, ranging from a scuba suit to a tuxedo. Minnie has only 50.
- There are enough Mickey Mouse–ear hats sold each year to cover the head of every man, woman, and child in Pittsburgh.
- You could fit New York's Empire State Building into the Vehicle Assembly Building at the Kennedy Space Center 3³/₄ times.
- Shamu, the killer whale at Sea World, eats more than 65,000 pounds of fish a year.
- Every day an average of 100 pairs of sunglasses are turned in to the Lost and Found at the Magic Kingdom.
- Since Walt Disney World opened in 1971, the total miles logged by monorail trains is equal to more than 24 trips to the moon.
- During launch, it takes just 8 minutes for the space shuttle to reach its orbiting speed of 17,500 miles per hour.
- Both Disneyland and Walt Disney World were built on former citrus groves in counties named Orange.

Note: If you're heading toward Adventureland or Frontierland first thing in the morning, wait for the gates to open at the bridge in front of the Crystal Palace, to your left as you enter.

Jungle Cruise
Recommended ages: 4–14

What a cruise! In the course of about 10 minutes, your boat sails through an African veldt in the Congo, an Amazon rain forest, the Mekong River in Southeast Asia, and along the Nile. Lavish scenery, with ropes of hanging vines, cascading waterfalls, and lush tropical and subtropical foliage (most of it real), includes dozens of AudioAnimatronic birds and animals—elephants, zebras, lions, giraffes, crocodiles, tigers, even fluttering butterflies. On the shore, you'll pass a *Raiders*-like Cambodian temple cave fronted by a Buddha and guarded by snakes, a rhino and jackal chasing terrified African beaters up a tree, and a jungle camp taken over by apes. But the adventures aren't all on shore. Passengers are menaced by everything from water-spouting elephants to fierce warriors who attack with spears. The guide keeps up an amusing patter.

✪ Pirates of the Caribbean
Recommended ages: 6–adult

Although the Disneyland version of this ride has been adapted to be more politically correct, the pirates still chase the wenches in Florida. You'll proceed through a long grottolike passageway to board a boat into a pitch-black cave. Therein, elaborate scenery and hundreds of AudioAnimatronic figures (including lifelike dogs, cats, chickens, pigs, and donkeys) depict a rambunctious pirate raid on a Caribbean town. To a background of cheerful "yo-ho-yo-ho" music, the sound of rushing waterfalls, squawking seagulls, and screams of terror, passengers pass through the line of fire in a raging pirate battle and view tableaux of fierce-looking pirates swigging rum, looting, and plundering. This might be scary for kids under 5.

In the Words of Walt Disney

Sheer animated fantasy is still my first and deepest production impulse. The fable is the best storytelling device ever conceived. . . . And, of course, animal characters have always been the personnel of fable—animals through which the foibles as well as the virtues of humans can best and most hilariously be reflected.

Never get bored or cynical. Yesterday is a thing of the past.

Swiss Family Treehouse
Recommended ages: 4–12

This attraction is based on the 1960 Disney movie version of Johann Wyss's *Swiss Family Robinson,* about a shipwrecked family of five who created an ingenious dwelling for themselves in the branches of a sprawling banyan tree. Using materials and furnishings salvaged from their downed ship, the Robinsons created bedrooms, a kitchen, a library, and a living room. Visitors traverse a rope-suspended bridge and ascend the 50-foot tree for a close-up look into these rooms. Note the Rube Goldberg rope-and-bucket device with bamboo chutes that dips water from a stream and carries it to treetop chambers. The "tree" itself, designed by Disney "Imagineers," has 330,000 polyethylene leaves sprouting from a 90-foot span of branches; although it isn't real, it is draped with actual Spanish moss.

Tropical Serenade
Recommended ages: 2–10

In a large hexagonal Polynesian-style dwelling, with a thatched roof, bamboo beams, and tapa-bark murals, 250 tropical birds, chanting totem poles, and singing flowers whistle, tweet, and warble. The audience is encouraged to sing along. The show is hosted by four feathered friends named José, Michael, Pierre, and Fritz—all with appropriate national accents—who perch atop an "enchanted" fountain. Highlights include a thunderstorm in the dark (The gods are angry!), a light show over the fountain, and, of course, the famous "in the tiki, tiki, tiki, tiki, tiki room" song. Like it or not, you'll find yourself singing it all day. This is a must for young children.

SHOPPING IN ADVENTURELAND

The exotic **Traders of Timbuktu** carries carved wooden and soapstone animals, masks, and cowhide drums from Kenya, among other ethnic wares.

Plaza del Sol Caribe, a Mexican mercado, has piñatas, baskets, straw hats, stuffed and papier-mâché toucans and parrots, and much more.

For the Indiana Jones look, check out the clothing and accessories at **Elephant Tales.** The little **Tiki Tropic Shop** carries surfer-theme merchandise.

Shell mobiles and hangings, plus a wide selection of straw hats, are sold at the **Zanzibar Shell Shop. Island Supply,** a Disney version of The Nature Company, offers nature-theme books, posters, toys, bird feeders, and more.

And both the **House of Treasure** and the adjoining **Lafitte's Portrait Deck** retail pirate merchandise: hats, Captain Hook T-shirts, ships in bottles, and toy muskets and daggers; the latter has a pirate ship photo setup.

FRONTIERLAND

From Adventureland, step into the wild and woolly past of the American frontier, where Disney employees (they're called "cast members") are clad in denim and calico, sidewalks are wooden, rough-and-tumble architecture runs to log cabins and rustic saloons, and the landscape is Southwestern scrubby with mesquite, saguaro cactus, yucca, and prickly pear. Across the river is Tom Sawyer Island, reachable via log rafts.

✪ Big Thunder Mountain Railroad
Recommended ages: 10–adult

This mining-disaster–theme roller coaster—its thrills deriving from hairpin turns and descents in the dark, rather than sudden steep drops—is situated in a 200-foot–high red-stone mountain with 2,780 feet of track winding through windswept canyons and bat-filled caves. You enter the ride via the ramshackle headquarters of the Big Thunder Mining Company and board a runaway train that careens through the ribs of a dinosaur, under a thundering waterfall, past spewing geysers and bubbling mud pots, and over a bottomless volcanic pool. Riders are threatened by flash floods, earthquakes, rickety bridges, and avalanches. AudioAnimatronic characters (such as the long john–clad fellow navigating the floodwaters in a bathtub) and animals (goats, chickens, donkeys, possums) enhance the scenic backdrop, and several-hundred-thousand dollars' worth of authentic antique mining equipment adds verisimilitude. *Note:* You must be 40 inches tall to ride.

✪ Country Bear Jamboree
Recommended ages: 4–adult

I've always loved the Country Bear Jamboree, a 15-minute show featuring a troupe of fiddlin', banjo strummin', harmonica playin' AudioAnimatronic bears belting out rollicking country tunes and crooning plaintive love songs. The chubby Trixie, decked out in a satiny skirt, laments lost love as she sings "Tears Will Be the Chaser for Your Wine." Teddi Barra descends from the ceiling in a swing to perform "Heart We Did All That We Could." Other star performers include a country-western group called the Five Bear Rugs, Liver Lips McGrowl, and the 7-foot–tall master of ceremonies, Henry. In the rousing show finale, the entire cast joins in a foot-stompin' sing-along. Wisecracking commentary comes from a mounted buffalo, moose, and deer on the wall. A special holiday show plays throughout the Christmas season each year.

✪ Diamond Horseshoe Saloon Revue & Medicine Show
Recommended ages: 6–adult

Sit yourself down in air-conditioned comfort and enjoy a rousing western revue at Dr. Bill U. Later's turn-of-the-century saloon. Marshall John Charles sings and banters with the audience, Jingles the Piano Man plays honky-tonk tunes, there's a magic act, and Miss Lucille L'Amour and her troupe of dance-hall girls do a spirited can-can—all with lots of humor and audience participation. There are seven shows daily; plan on going around lunchtime, so you can eat during the show. The menu features deli or peanut-butter-and-jelly sandwiches served with chips.

Frontierland Shootin' Arcade
Recommended ages: 8–adult

Combining state-of-the-art electronics with a traditional shooting-gallery format, this vast arcade presents an array of 97 targets (slow-moving ore cars, buzzards, and gravediggers) in a three-dimensional 1850s gold-mining town scenario. Fog creeps across the graveyard, and the setting changes as a calm, starlit night turns stormy with flashes of lightning and claps of thunder. Coyotes howl, bridges creak, and skeletal arms reach out from the grave. If you hit a tombstone, it might spin around and mysteriously change its epitaph. To keep the western ambiance authentic, newfangled electronic firing mechanisms loaded with infrared bullets are concealed in genuine Hawkins 54-caliber buffalo rifles. When you hit a target, elaborate sound and motion gags are set off. Fifty cents buys you 25 shots.

✪ Splash Mountain
Recommended ages: 10–adult

Themed after Walt Disney's 1946 film, *Song of the South,* Splash Mountain takes you on an enchanting journey in a hollowed-out log craft along the canals of a flooded mountain, past 26 brilliantly colored tableaux of backwoods swamps, bayous, spooky caves, and waterfalls. Riders are caught up in the bumbling schemes of Brer Fox and Brer Bear as they pursue the ever-wily Brer Rabbit, who, against the advice of Mr. Bluebird, has left his briar-patch home in search of adventure and the "laughing place." The music from the film forms a delightful audio backdrop. Your log craft twists, turns, and splashes—sometimes plummeting in total darkness—all leading up to a thrilling five-story, 45°-angle splashdown from mountaintop to briar-filled pond at 40 miles per hour! And that's not the end. The ride continues, and finally it's a Zip-A-Dee-Doo-Dah kind of day. *Note:* You must be 44 inches tall to ride.

Tom Sawyer Island
Recommended ages: 4–14

Board Huck Finn's raft for a 1-minute float across the river to the densely forested Tom Sawyer Island, where kids can explore the narrow passages of Injun Joe's cave (complete with scary sound effects, like whistling wind), a walk-through windmill, a serpentine abandoned mine, or Fort Sam Clemens, where an AudioAnimatronic drunk is snoring-off a bender. Maintaining one's balance while crossing rickety swing and barrel bridges is also fun. Narrow, winding dirt paths lined with oaks, pines, and sycamores create an authentic backwoods island feel. It's easy to get briefly lost and stumble upon some unexpected adventure. You might combine this attraction with lunch at **Aunt Polly's** restaurant, which serves light fare (fried chicken, sandwiches, and the like) and has outdoor tables on a porch overlooking the river. Adults can rest weary feet over coffee, while the kids explore the island.

SHOPPING IN FRONTIERLAND

Mosey into the **Frontier Trading Post** for western-look leather items, cowboy boots and hats, western shirts, coonskin caps, turquoise jewelry, belts, and toy rifles. **Prairie Outpost & Supply** sells Native American items such as drums, headdresses, and bows and arrows, many of them related to Pocahontas.

Visit the **Briar Patch,** under Splash Mountain, for Uncle Remus and Winnie the Pooh merchandise.

LIBERTY SQUARE

Serving as a transitional area between Frontierland and Fantasyland, Liberty Square evokes 18th-century America with Federal and Georgian architecture, Colonial Williamsburg–type shops, and neat flower beds bordering manicured lawns. Thirteen lanterns, symbolizing the colonies, are suspended from the Liberty Tree, an immense live oak. You might encounter a fife and drum corps marching along Liberty Square's cobblestone streets. The **Liberty Tree Tavern** here (details in chapter 6) is my favorite Magic Kingdom restaurant.

Boat Rides
Recommended ages: 6–adult

A steam-powered sternwheeler called the *Liberty Belle* and two Mike Fink Keelboats (the *Bertha Mae* and the *Gullywhumper*) depart (the latter, summers and holidays only) from Liberty Square for scenic cruises along the Rivers of America. The passing landscape evokes the Wild West. Both ply the identical route and make a restful interlude for foot-weary park goers.

Hall of Presidents
Recommended ages: 10–adult

In this redbrick colonial hall, a giant bell suspended in its tower, all American presidents—from George Washington to Bill Clinton (whose actual voice was recorded for this attraction)—are represented by AudioAnimatronic figures who act out important events in the nation's history, from the signing of the Declaration of Independence through the space age. The show begins with a film, projected on a 180°, 70mm screen, about the importance of the Constitution. The curtain then rises on the 42 assembled American leaders, and, as each is spotlighted, he nods or waves with presidential dignity. Lincoln then rises and speaks, occasionally even referring to his notes. In a stunning example of Disney thoroughness, painstaking research was done in creating the figures and scenery, with each president's costume reflecting not only period fashion but period fabrics and tailoring techniques! Poet and author Maya Angelou narrates.

✪ Haunted Mansion
Recommended ages: 6–adult

What better way to exhibit Disney special-effects wizardry than a haunted mansion? Macabre attendants harry groups of visitors past a graveyard, turning them over to a ghost host who encloses them in a windowless, doorless portrait gallery (Are those eyes following you around?) where the floor seems to be descending. Its ambiance enhanced by inky darkness, spooky music, eerie howling, and mysterious screams and rappings, this mansion is replete with bizarre scenes and objects: a ghostly banquet and ball, a graveyard band, a suit of armor that comes alive, cobweb-covered chandeliers, luminous spiders, a talking head in a crystal ball, weird flying objects, and much more. At the end of the ride, a ghost joins you in your car. The experience is more amusing than terrifying, so you can take small children inside.

SHOPPING IN LIBERTY SQUARE

Olde World Antiques' high-quality inventory might range from an 18th-century pine hutch to 19th-century Staffordshire Chinoiserie willow-pattern platters. The adjoining **Silversmith** carries Revere-style silver and pewter butter dishes, candlesticks, bowls, trays, jewelry, and picture frames.

The Yankee Trader is a charming country store, its shelves stocked with Lion King and Winnie the Pooh cookie jars, Mickey cookie cutters, and fancy food items.

And over at **Heritage House,** you can purchase parchment copies of famous American documents as well as actual historic framed letters (one signed by President Andrew Johnson in 1864 was priced at $2,350). Old campaign buttons, Civil War hats, and presidential signatures are here, too. A craftsperson on the premises makes jewelry cut from coins.

FANTASYLAND

The attractions in this happy land—themed after Disney film classics such as *Snow White, Peter Pan,* and *Dumbo*—are especially popular with young visitors. If your kids are 8 or under, you might want to make it (and Mickey's Toontown; details below) your first stop in the Magic Kingdom. *Note:* Mr. Toad's Wild Ride is a bit scary. If your under-5 frightens easily, skip it.

Cinderella's Castle
Recommended ages: 2–10

At the end of Main Street, in the center of the park, you'll come to a fairyland castle, 185 feet high and housing a restaurant (King Stefan's Banquet Hall) and shops.

Mosaic murals inside depict the Cinderella story, and Disney family coats of arms are displayed over a fireplace. Cinderella herself, dressed for the ball, often makes appearances in the lobby area. You'll be able to see shows on the Castle Forecourt Stage.

Cinderella's Golden Carousel
Recommended ages: all ages

It's a beauty, built by Italian wood-carvers in the Victorian tradition in 1917 and refurbished by Disney artists who added 18 hand-painted scenes from the Cinderella story on the wooden canopy above the horses. The carousel organ plays Disney classics such as "When You Wish Upon a Star."

Dumbo, the Flying Elephant
Recommended ages: 2–10

This is a very tame kiddie ride in which the cars—large-eared baby elephants (Dumbos)—go around and around in a circle gently rising and dipping. But it's very exciting for wee ones.

It's a Small World
Recommended ages: 2–14

You know the song—and if you don't, you will. It plays continually as you sail "around the world" through vast rooms designed to represent different countries. They're inhabited by appropriately costumed AudioAnimatronic dolls and animals—all singing "It's a small world after all. . ." in tiny, doll-like voices. This cast of thousands includes Chinese acrobats, Russian kazatski dancers, Indian snake charmers in front of the Taj Mahal, French cancan dancers, Irish leprechauns, singing geese and windmills in Holland, Arabs on magic carpets, mountain goats in the Swiss Alps, African drummers and lunging hyenas in the jungle, a Venetian gondolier, and Australian koala bears. Cute. Very cute. But it just wouldn't be a visit to Disney without it.

✪ Legend of the Lion King
Recommended ages: 4–12

This stage spectacular based on Disney's blockbuster motion-picture musical combines animation, movie footage, sophisticated puppetry, and high-tech special effects. The show is enhanced by the Academy Award–winning music of Elton John and Tim Rice. Other voices are provided by Whoopi Goldberg and Cheech Marin as laughing hyenas.

Mad Tea Party
Recommended ages: 4–16

This is a traditional amusement park ride à la Disney, with an *Alice in Wonderland* theme. Riders sit in oversized pastel-hued teacups on saucers that careen around a circular platform, tilt, and spin. In the center of the platform is a big teapot, out from which pops a mouse. Believe it or not, this can be a pretty wild ride—or a tame one. It depends on how much you spin, a factor under your control via a wheel in the cup.

Mr. Toad's Wild Ride
Recommended ages: 6–16

This ride is based on the 1949 Disney film, *The Adventures of Ichabod and Mr. Toad,* which was itself based on an enduring children's classic, the divine *Wind in the Willows.* In colorful cars named for characters (Weasel, Toady, Moley), riders navigate a series of dark rooms, hurtling into solid objects—a fireplace, a bookcase, a haystack—and through barn doors into a coop of squawking chickens. They're menaced by falling suits of armor, snorting bulls, and an oncoming locomotive in a pitch-black tunnel, and are sent to jail (for car theft), to hell (complete with pitchfork-wielding demons), and through a fiery volcano. The ride's interior space is illuminated by invisible ultraviolet light, which makes whites and neons in the scenery glow.

Peter Pan's Flight
Recommended ages: 4–10

Riding in airborne versions of Captain Hook's ship, passengers careen through dark passages while experiencing the story of *Peter Pan*. The adventure begins in the Darlings's nursery and includes a flight over nighttime London to Never-Never Land, where riders encounter mermaids, Indians, a ticking crocodile, the lost boys, Princess Tiger Lilly, Tinker Bell, Hook, Smee, and the rest—all to the movie music "You Can Fly, You Can Fly, You Can Fly." It's fun.

Skyway
Recommended ages: all ages

Its entrance close to Peter Pan's Flight, the Skyway is an aerial tramway to Tomorrowland that makes continuous trips throughout the day. A good chance to let those tired feet rest and catch one of the rare Florida breezes.

Snow White's Adventures
Recommended ages: 6–14

This attraction used to focus only on the more sinister elements of Grimm's fairy tale—most notably the evil queen and the cackling, toothless witch—leaving small children screaming in terror. It's been toned down now, with Snow White appearing in a number of pleasant scenes—at the castle-courtyard wishing well, in the dwarfs' cottage, receiving the prince's kiss that breaks the witch's spell, and riding off with the prince to live "happily ever after." There are new AudioAnimatronic dwarfs, and the interior colors have also been brightened up and made less menacing. Even so, this could be scary for kids under 7.

SHOPPING IN FANTASYLAND

It's always the holiday season at **Mickey's Christmas Carol,** supply central for Disney-motif ornaments, caroler dolls, Mickey Christmas stockings, and charming Christmas-theme music boxes.

And little girls will adore **Tinker Bell's Treasures,** its wares comprising Peter Pan merchandise, costumes (Tinker Bell, Snow White, Cinderella, Pocahontas, and others), and collector dolls.

MICKEY'S TOONTOWN FAIR

Head off those cries of "Where's Mickey?" by taking the kids to this 2-acre replacement for Mickey's Starland, which was unveiled during the 25th Anniversary celebration in 1996. Toontown Fair offers kids a chance to meet their favorite Disney characters including Mickey, Minnie, Donald Duck, and Goofy. Set in a whimsical collection of candy-striped tents harking back to those turn-of-the-century county fairs, highlights include the **Toontown Hall of Fame,** animated shorts hosted by the stars, and both **Mickey's** and **Minnie's country houses.** Everything is brightly colored and kid-friendly in the best Disney tradition; there is even a **kid-sized roller coaster.** Toontown Fair has its own stop on the **WDW Railroad.**

TOMORROWLAND

This land focuses on the future—most notably, space travel and exploration. In 1994, the Disney people decided that Tomorrowland (originally designed in the 1970s) was

In the Words of Walt Disney

Fantasy, if it's really convincing, can't become dated, for the simple reason that it represents a flight into a dimension that lies beyond the reach of time. . . nothing corrodes or gets run down. . . . And nobody gets any older.

We have never lost our faith in family entertainment—stories that make people laugh, stories about warm and human things, stories about historic characters and events, and stories about animals.

beginning to look like "Yesterdayland." (Although something looking suspiciously like some of the old polyester ride uniforms can be found hanging in The Gap.)

It's now been revamped to reflect the future as a galactic, science fiction–inspired community inhabited by humans, aliens, and robots. A vast state-of-the-art video-game arcade has also been added.

✪ Alien Encounter
Recommended ages: 10–adult

Director George Lucas, of *Star Wars* fame, contributed his space-age vision to this major Tomorrowland attraction. The action begins at the Interplanetary Convention Center where a mysterious corporation called X-S Tech—a company from a distant planet—is marketing a "teletransporter" to Earthlings. The device is capable of beaming living beings between planets light-years apart. After a slick corporate presentation, S.I.R., a rather sinister robot, demonstrates the product on Skippy, a cute and fuzzy alien, though not with total success; Skippy ends up discombobulated and with singed fur! Despite this dubious beginning, X-S technicians try to teleport their sinister corporation head, Chairman Clench, to Earth. But the machine malfunctions, sending Clench instead to a distant planet and, inadvertently, teleporting a fearsome extraterrestrial to earth. Dark and truly scary, it is not your typical thrill ride. It's no fantasy that your heart is racing as you work your way through lots of high-tech effects—from the alien's breath on your neck to a mist of alien slime. *Note:* You must be 48 inches tall to ride.

Astro Orbiter
Recommended ages: 8 and under

This is a tame, typical amusement-park ride. The "rockets" are on arms attached to "the center of the galaxy," and they move up and down while orbiting spinning planets.

Skyway
Recommended ages: all ages

Located near the Tomorrowland entrance just west of Space Mountain, this aerial tramway to Fantasyland makes continuous round-trips throughout the day.

✪ Space Mountain
Recommended ages: 10–adult

Space Mountain entertains visitors on its long lines with space-age music, exhibits, and meteorites, shooting stars, and space debris whizzing about overhead. These "illusioneering" effects, enhanced by appropriate audio, continue during the ride itself, which is a cosmic roller coaster in the inky, starlit blackness of outer space. Your rocket climbs high into the universe before racing through a serpentine complex of aerial galaxies, making thrilling hairpin turns and rapid plunges. (Though it feels as though you're going at breakneck speed, your car actually never goes faster than 28 miles per hour.) Nab the front seat of the train for the best ride. Now that Alien Encounters has come on line, the queues to Space Mountain, which accommodates 3,000 people an hour, are usually relatively short. *Note:* You must be 44 inches tall to ride.

Take Flight
Recommended ages: 6–adult

A breezy look through the story of flight. High-tech special effects and 70mm live-action film footage add dramatic 3-D–style verisimilitude. Guests travel from a futuristic airport up a hillside to witness a flying circus, parachutists, stunt flyers, wing walkers, crop dusters, and aerial acrobats. The action moves on to the ocean-hopping age of commercial flight, as passengers are transported to a Japanese tea garden, Mount Fuji, and Paris at sunset. Finally, your vehicle is pulled into a giant jet engine and sent into hypersonic flight through psychedelic tunnels of light for a journey to outer space at a simulated speed of 300 miles per hour.

The Timekeeper
Recommended ages: 10–adult

This Jules Verne/H. G. Wells–inspired multimedia presentation combines Circle-Vision™ and IMAX footage with AudioAnimatronics. It's hosted by Timekeeper, a mad-scientist robot and his assistant, 9-EYE, a flying female camera-headed droid and time machine test pilot. In an unpredictable jet-speed escapade, the audience hears Mozart as a young prodigy playing his music to French royalty, visits medieval battlefields in Scotland, watches Leonardo at work, and floats in a hot-air balloon above Moscow's Red Square. Can you pick out the famous voices of Jeremy Irons, Robin Williams, Michael Piccoli, and Rhea Perlman?

Tomorrowland Speedway
Recommended ages: 6–16

This is a great thrill for kids (including teens still waiting to get their driver's licenses) who get to put the pedal to the metal, steer, and *vroom* down a speedway in an actual gas-powered sports car. Maximum speed on the 4-minute drive around the track is about 7 miles per hour, and kids have to be 4 feet 4 inches tall to drive alone.

Tomorrowland Transit Authority
Recommended ages: all ages

A futuristic means of transportation, these small five-car trains have no engines. They work by electromagnets, emit no pollution, and use little power. Narrated by a computer guide named Horack I, TTA offers an overhead look at Tomorrowland, including a pretty good preview of Space Mountain. If you're in the Magic Kingdom for only 1 day, you can skip this.

Walt Disney's Carousel of Progress
Recommended ages: all ages

This 22-minute show in a revolving theater features an AudioAnimatronic family in various tableaux demonstrating a century of development (beginning in 1900) in electric gadgetry and contraptions from Victrolas to virtual reality.

SHOPPING IN TOMORROWLAND

Kids love browsing over **Merchant of Venus**'s space-themed *Alien Encounter* and *Star Wars* merchandise. Also here: **Mickey's Star Traders,** a large Disneyana shop.

PARADES, FIREWORKS & MORE

You'll get an *Entertainment Show Schedule* when you enter the park, which lists all kinds of special goings-on for the day. These include concerts (everything from steel drums to barbershop quartets), encounters with Disney characters, holiday events, and the three major happenings listed below.

During the fireworks and the parades, there are designated viewing spots roped off for those with disabilities and their parties. Consult your park map or a park employee at least an hour before the parade. Like all space along the parade route, the spaces for those with disabilities also fill up quickly.

✪ Fireworks
Recommended ages: all ages

It's the Fourth of July every night with Fantasy in the Sky Fireworks, probably the most explosive display you have ever seen. Pyrotechnics is another thing that Disney has down to an art. Although the water-walking creatures in the Sea World closing show are certainly worth seeing, this is clearly the best way to end your day. It is preceded by Tinker Bell's magical flight from Cinderella Castle, and takes place nightly in summer, on selected nights during Christmas and Easter vacation times, and during other special celebrations. Consult your *Entertainment Show Schedule* for details. Suggested viewing areas are Liberty Square, Frontierland, and Mickey's Toontown Fair. Many of the Disney hotels close to the park also offer excellent views.

✪ SpectroMagic
Recommended ages: all ages

If you have time to see only one parade, see this one. Along a darkened parade route (the same one as below), 72,000 watts of dazzling high-tech lighting effects (including holography) create a glowing array of pixies and peacocks, sea horses and winged horses, flower gardens and fountains. Roger Rabbit is the eccentric conductor of an orchestra producing a rainbow of musical notes that waft magically into the night air. There are dancing ostriches from *Fantasia,* whirling electric butterflies, flowers that evoke Tiffany glass, bejeweled coaches, luminescent ElectroMen atop spinning whirlyballs, and, of course, Mickey, surrounded by a sparkling confetti of light. Remember the suit in the Electric Horseman? Multiply that by 1,000 and you've got SpectroMagic. It's unlike anything you've ever seen. The music and choreography are on a par with the technology.

Once again, very early arrival is essential to get a seat on the curb. SpectroMagic takes place nightly in summer, on selected nights during Christmas and Easter vacation times, and during other special celebrations. Consult your *Entertainment Show Schedule* for details.

✪ The 3 O'Clock Parade "Remember the Magic"
Recommended ages: all ages

You haven't really seen a parade until you've seen one at Walt Disney World. This spectacular daily event kicks off at 3pm year-round on Main Street and meanders through Liberty Square and Frontierland. The route is outlined on your *Entertainment Show Schedule.*

The only problem: Even in slow seasons, you have to snag a seat along the curb a good half hour before it begins; earlier during peak travel times. That's a long time to sit on a hard curb. You might want to consider bringing along an inflatable pillow. And remember, *stay off the grass,* or the Disney lawn police will shoo you away from what you thought was a prime viewing spot.

Top 10 Orlando-Area Attractions for Grown-Ups

1. **Innoventions**   Epcot, generally, is more geared to adults than the other Disney parks, but this display of future technologies is especially intriguing, providing a cogent preview of life in the 21st century.
2. **Sea World**   With its lush landscaping and laid-back pace, Sea World is a nice change from the go-go world of the other attractions. Mixing education with entertainment and lots of hands-on animal interaction, this is one of Orlando's most adult attractions, although kids love it too.
3. **World Showcase Pavilions**   Experience a 'round-the-world journey visiting 11 nations in microcosm—with authentically reproduced architectural highlights, restaurants, shops, and cultural performances.
4. **Universal Studios**   Okay, I'm an adult, but sometimes this really is a great place to play. The thrill rides can't be beat, the shows are fast-paced and funny, and now even the Terminator is back.
5. **Swimming with the Manatees**   Sign up for a 5-day program with a manatee biologist for an ecotour on the Crystal River that also includes bird watching, snorkeling, and informative lectures.
6. **Cypress Gardens**   Stroll 200 acres of gorgeous botanical gardens—roses, bougainvillea, crape myrtles, and magnolias—amid ponds, lagoons, waterfalls, Italian fountains, and manicured lawns.
7. **Kennedy Space Center**   Acquaint yourself with the history, present state, and future of America's space program. The kids will like this too.
8. **A Day in Winter Park**   This charming town has a recently expanded museum filled with masterpieces by Louis Comfort Tiffany and other noted 19th-century artists, great upscale shopping, and fine restaurants. Stay overnight at the Langford and arrange a day of beauty at its multifacility spa. Stroll through the shops on Park Avenue and lunch at one of the sidewalk bistros.
9. **A Resort Vacation**   Top-of-the-line accommodations, fine restaurants, magnificent grounds, golf, tennis, swimming, first-rate health clubs, and other elements of a plush resort vacation are available at the Hyatt Regency Grand Cypress, Marriott's Orlando World Center, the Peabody Orlando, and Disney's Grand Floridian.
10. **A Night on the Town**   Visit an Orlando restaurant and enjoy a night on the town, a carriage ride through downtown Orlando, a few hours at a club, or at Church Street Station. This is the other Orlando, the one for grown-ups.

In addition to Mickey and all his Disney pals—everyone from Minnie to Winnie (the Pooh)—there are elaborate floats, stunning costumes, special effects, and a captivating cavalcade of dancers, singers, and other talented performers. Great music, too.

WHERE TO FIND CHARACTERS

Mickey's Toontown Fair was designed as a place where kids can meet and mingle with their favorite characters all day. This is a sure thing and it doesn't hurt that it's air-conditioned. Mickey, Minnie, Goofy, and Donald Duck are stars in residence. In **Fantasyland** up to eight Disney characters, including Chip 'n' Dale, are available for autographs in a covered area across from Mr. Toad's Wild Ride. Ariel from *The Little Mermaid* can be found in Ariel's Grotto.

4 Epcot

In 1982, Walt Disney World opened its second major theme park, the world's fair–like Epcot (Experimental Prototype Community of Tomorrow). Its aims are described in a dedication plaque: "May Epcot entertain, inform and inspire. And, above all. . . instill a new sense of belief and pride in man's ability to shape a world that offers hope to people everywhere." Ever growing and changing, Epcot today occupies 260 acres so stunningly landscaped as to be worth visiting for botanical beauty alone—so stop and smell the roses. There are two major sections, Future World and World Showcase.

Epcot is huge, and walking around it can be exhausting (some people say its acronym stands for "Every Person Comes Out Tired"). Don't try to do it all in 1 day. And conserve your energy by taking launches across the lagoon from the edge of Future World to Germany or Morocco. There are also double-decker buses circling the World Showcase Promenade and making stops at Norway, Italy, France, and Canada.

Unlike the Magic Kingdom, Epcot's parking lot is right at the gate. Sections of the parking lot are named for Epcot themes (Harvest, Energy, etc.), and aisles are numbered.

Stop by the **Guest Relations lobby** to the left of Spaceship Earth to pick up an **Epcot Guidemap** and **entertainment schedule,** and, if you so desire (and haven't already done so by calling ☎ **407/WDW-DINE** [939-3463]), make reservations for lunch or dinner at WorldKey terminals just outside the lobby. (Many Epcot restaurants are described in chapter 6.) Then check out your show schedule and incorporate shows you want to see into your itinerary.

HOURS   Generally 9am to 9pm with extended hours—sometimes as late as midnight—during major holidays and the summer months.

TICKET PRICES $40.81 for adults, $32.86 for children, free for children under 4. See "Tickets," earlier in this chapter, for 4- and 5-day passes.

SERVICES & FACILITIES AT EPCOT

ATMs   These machines accept cards issued by banks using the Cirrus, Honor, and Plus systems and are located at the front of the park, in Germany, and on the bridge between World Showcase and Future World.

Baby Care   Epcot's Baby Care Center is located near the Odyssey Restaurant in Future World. It is furnished with rocking chairs and disposable diapers, formula, baby food, and pacifiers are for sale. There are also changing tables in all women's rest rooms, as well as in some of the men's rest rooms. Disposable diapers are available at Guest Services.

Cameras & Film   Kodak's disposable Fun Saver cameras are available throughout the park. Video camcorders are available for rent from the Kodak Camera Center at the Entrance Plaza. You can also rent from the Lagoon's Edge World Traveler, at the end of the promenade between Future World and the World Showcase, and at Cameras and Film at Journey into Imagination. Cost for camcorder rental is $25, plus a $300 deposit.

First Aid   The First Aid Center, staffed by registered nurses, is located near the Odyssey Restaurant in Future World.

Lockers   Lockers can be found to the west of Spaceship Earth, outside the entrance Plaza, and in the Bus Information Center by the bus parking lot. The cost is $3 a day, plus a $2 deposit.

Lost Children   Lost children in Epcot are usually taken to Earth Center or the Baby Care Center where lost children logbooks are kept. Children under 7 should wear name tags.

Package Pickup   Any large package you purchase can be sent by the shop clerk to Guest Relations in the Entrance Plaza. Allow 3 hours for delivery.

Pet Care   Day accommodations are offered at kennels just outside the Entrance Plaza at Epcot for $6. Proof of vaccination is required. There are also four kennels in the WDW complex.

Strollers   These can be rented from special stands on the east side of the Entrance Plaza and at World Showcase's International Gateway. The cost is $6, including a $1 refundable deposit.

Wheelchair Rental   Rent wheelchairs inside the Entrance Plaza to your left, to the right of ticket booths at the Gift Shop, and at World Showcase's International Gateway. The cost for regular chairs is $6, including a $1 refundable deposit. Electric chairs cost $32 a day, including a $2 refundable deposit.

FUTURE WORLD

The northern section of Epcot (where you enter the park) comprises Future World, centered on a giant geosphere known as Spaceship Earth. Future World's 10 themed areas, sponsored by major corporations, focus on discovery, scientific achievements, and tomorrow's technologies in areas running the gamut from energy to undersea exploration.

Horizons
Recommended ages: 8–adult

The theme of this pavilion is the future, which presents an unending series of new horizons. You board gondolas for a 15-minute journey into the next millennium. The first tableau honors visionaries of past centuries (like Jules Verne) and looks at outdated visions of the future and classic sci-fi movies. You ascend to an area where an IMAX film projected on two 80-foot–high screens presents a kaleidoscope of brilliant micro and macro images—growing crystals, colonies in space, a space shuttle launching, DNA molecules, and a computer chip. You then travel to 21st-century cityscapes, desert farms, floating cities under the ocean's surface, and outer-space colonies populated by AudioAnimatronic denizens. For the return to 20th-century earth, you can select one of three futuristic transportation systems: a personal spacecraft, a desert Hovercraft, or a minisubmarine.

Innoventions
Recommended ages: 8–adult

The pair of crescent-shaped buildings to your right and left just beyond Spaceship Earth house a constantly evolving 100,000-square–foot exhibit that showcases cutting-edge technologies and future products. Leading manufacturers sponsor ever-changing exhibit areas here. Visitors get a chance to preview virtual reality, electric cars, experience interactive television, and try out more than 200 new computer programs and games. Kids will be thrilled to preview new Sega video games. It is a chance to feel, hear, and see the future, hands-on.

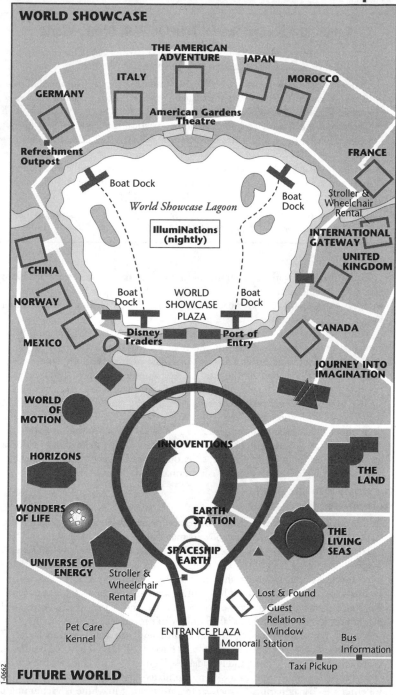

WORLD SHOWCASE

THE AMERICAN ADVENTURE

ITALY

JAPAN

GERMANY

MOROCCO

American Gardens Theatre

Refreshment Outpost

FRANCE

Boat Dock

World Showcase Lagoon

Boat Dock

Stroller & Wheelchair Rental

IllumiNations (nightly)

INTERNATIONAL GATEWAY

UNITED KINGDOM

CHINA

NORWAY

Boat Dock

WORLD SHOWCASE PLAZA

Boat Dock

Disney Traders

Port of Entry

CANADA

MEXICO

JOURNEY INTO IMAGINATION

WORLD OF MOTION

INNOVENTIONS

THE LAND

HORIZONS

WONDERS OF LIFE

EARTH STATION

THE LIVING SEAS

UNIVERSE OF ENERGY

SPACESHIP EARTH

Stroller & Wheelchair Rental

Lost & Found

Guest Relations Window

Pet Care Kennel

ENTRANCE PLAZA
Monorail Station

Bus Information

Taxi Pickup

1-0662

FUTURE WORLD

Behind the Scenes: Special Tours in Walt Disney World

In addition to the greenhouse tour in Epcot's Land pavilion, the Disney parks offer a number of walking tours and learning programs. These include:

* The 3-hour **Hidden Treasures of World Showcase,** focusing on the architecture and entertainment offerings of Epcot's international pavilions ($25 per person; ☎ **407/939-8687** for information).
* **Gardens of the World,** a 3-hour tour of the extraordinary landscaping at Epcot led by a Disney horticulturist ($25 per person; ☎ **407/939-8687** for information).
* The 4-hour **Keys to the Kingdom,** providing an orientation to the Magic Kingdom and a glimpse into the high-tech operational systems behind the magic ($45 per person; ☎ **407/WDW-TOUR** [939-8687]).

There are also **learning programs** on subjects ranging from animation to international cultures. For details, call ☎ **407/363-6000.**

The virtual-reality offerings—from swimming with the sharks at the Vivid Group pod or a walking tour of St. Peter's Basilica by ENEL—are the latest high-tech wonders and a chance to experience what you have been reading about in science magazines.

There are several show areas: You can be interviewed by Jay Leno on TV. Sky Cyberguy takes you on a tour of the future of wireless communication. At the Honeywell's Home Automation at the House of Innoventions Tour, visit the computer-controlled abode of the future. The computer literate will find this a fascinating place to play. The technologically challenged will find it less rewarding.

The two-story **Discovery Center,** located on the right side of Innoventions, includes an information resource area where guests can get answers to all their questions about Epcot attractions in particular and Walt Disney World in general. For instance, if after visiting The Land, you would like to learn more about hydroponics, they can print out an information sheet on it. The Discovery Center also houses a shop called **Field Trips,** featuring educational products and software.

✪ Journey Into Imagination
Recommended ages: 6–adult

In this terrific pavilion, even the fountains are magical, with arching streams of water that leap into the air like glass rods. Its major attraction is:

Honey I Shrunk the Audience: This 3-D attraction is based on the Disney hit *Honey I Shrunk the Kids* films. The audience, after being menaced by hundreds of mice and a 3-D cat, is shrunk and given a good shaking by a gigantic 5-year-old. Dramatic 3-D action is enhanced by vibrating seats and creepy tactile effects. Finally, everyone returns to proper size—everyone but the family dog, which creates the final, not altogether pleasant, special effect (I won't reveal it).

Visitors board slow-moving cars for a **Journey Into Imagination Ride.** The 14-minute excursion (recommended for ages 6 to adult), hosted by a red-bearded adventurer named Dreamfinder and his sidekick, Figment—a mischievous baby dragon with a childlike ability to dream. After a simulated flight across the nighttime sky, we enter the "Imaginarium," where a dream-catching machine is vacuuming up "sparks of imagination, ideas, and natural elements" into a giant storage bag. We then ride past whimsical tableaux in which AudioAnimatronic characters explore the creative worlds of the fine arts, literature, the performing arts (complete with laser-light dancers), science (Dreamfinder's lab is filled with magical gadgetry), and image technology (a.k.a. movies). The ride culminates at Image Works.

Image Works is where you can activate musical instruments by stepping on hexagons of colored light (remember Tom Hanks in *Big?*), participate in a TV drama, paint on a magic palette, draw patterns with laser beams, operate a giant kaleidoscope, wend your way through the Rainbow Corridor of a sensor maze, and conduct an electronic philharmonic orchestra.

The Land
Recommended ages: 8–adult

This largest of Future World's pavilions highlights man's relation to food and nature.

Living with the Land: A 13-minute boat ride takes you through three ecological environments (a rain forest, an African desert, and windswept American plains), each populated by appropriate AudioAnimatronic denizens. New farming methods and experiments—ranging from hydroponics to plants growing in simulated Martian soil!—are showcased in real gardens. If you'd like a more serious overview, take a 45-minute guided walking tour of the growing areas, offered daily. Sign up at the **Green Thumb Emporium** shop near the entrance to Food Rocks. The cost is $5 for adults, $3 for children 3 to 9, free for children 2 and under. It's not, by the way, really geared to children.

Circle of Life: Combining spectacular live-action footage with animation, this 15-minute, 70mm motion picture based on *The Lion King* is a cautionary environmental tale. Timon and Pumbaa are building a monument to the good life called Hakuna Matata Lakeside Village, but their project, as Simba points out, is damaging the savannah for other animals. The message: Everything is connected in the great circle of life. Recommended age group: 6 to 16.

In **Food Rocks,** AudioAnimatronic mock rock performers deliver an entertaining message about nutrition. Neil Moussaka sings "Don't Take My Squash Away from Me," the Refrigerator Police perform "Every Bite You Take," and the Peach Boys harmonize a rendition of "Good Vibrations" ("Good, good, good, good nutrition. . ."), while Excess, a trio of disheveled, obnoxious hard rockers, counters by extolling the virtues of junk food. Rapper Tone Loc (as Füd Wrapper, the show's host), Chubby Checker, Neil Sedaka, Little Richard, and the Pointer Sisters perform the actual voice-over parodies of their music. Recommended age group: 6 to 14.

✪ The Living Seas
Recommended ages: 12–adult

This United Technologies–sponsored pavilion contains the world's sixth "ocean," a 5.7-million–gallon saltwater aquarium (including a complete coral reef) inhabited by more than 4,000 sea creatures—sharks, barracudas, parrot fish, rays, and dolphins among them. While waiting on line, visitors pass exhibits tracing the history of undersea exploration, including a glass diving barrel used by Alexander the Great in 332 B.C., and Sir Edmund Halley's first diving bell (1697).

A 2½-minute multimedia preshow about today's ocean technology is followed by a 7-minute film demonstrating the formation of the earth and seas as a means to support life.

After the films, visitors enter hydrolators for a rapid descent to the sunlit ocean floor. Upon arrival, they board Seacabs that wind around a 400-foot–long tunnel to enjoy stunning close-up views (through acrylic windows) of ocean denizens in a natural coral-reef habitat. The ride concludes in the Seabase Concourse, which is the visitor center of Seabase Alpha, a prototype ocean-research facility of the future. Here exhibits include a 22¹/₂-foot scuba tube used by Seabase Alpha scientists to enter and leave the waters. And seven informational modules contain numerous exhibits focusing on ocean ecosystems, harvestable resources grown in controlled undersea environments, marine mammals (dolphins, sea lions, manatees), earth systems (the relationship between the planet's seas and its land masses), the study of oceanography from space, undersea exploration (featuring an AudioAnimatronic deep-sea submersible robot), and life in a coral-reef community. Many of these exhibits are hands-on. You can step into a diver's JIM Suit and use controls to complete diving tasks, and expand your knowledge of oceanography via interactive computers. *Note:* Via a program called Epcot DiveQuest, certified divers can participate in a program that includes a 30- to 40-minute scuba dive in the Living Seas aquarium; for details, call ☎ **407/WDW-TOUR** (937-8687).

✪ Spaceship Earth
Recommended ages: all ages

This massive, silvery geosphere symbolizes Epcot, so it is a must-do. But long lines can be avoided by saving it until later in the day when you can, more than likely, simply walk on in. The show/ride takes visitors on a 15-minute journey through the history of communications. You board time-machine vehicles to the distant past, where an AudioAnimatronic Cro-Magnon shaman recounts the story of a hunt while others record it on cave walls. You advance thousands of years to ancient Egypt, where hieroglyphics adorn temple walls and writing is recorded on papyrus scrolls. You'll progress through the Phoenician and Greek alphabets, and the Gutenberg printing press and the Renaissance (trying not to notice that several of these guys look an awful lot like Barbie's dream date Ken). Technologies develop at a rapid pace, through the telegraph, telephone, radio, movies, and TV. It's but a short step to the age of electronic communications. You are catapulted into outer space to see "spaceship earth" from a new perspective, returning for a finale that places the audience amid interactive global networks. High-tech special effects, animated sets, and laser beams create an exciting experience.

At the end of this journey through time, AT&T invites guests to sample an interactive computer-video wonderland that includes a motion-simulator ride through the company's electronic network. This exhibit complements Innoventions, detailed below.

Test Track
Recommended ages: 8–adult

Called a mix of General Motors engineering and Disney imagineering, the newest Epcot attraction has guests in the driver's seat to experience the rigors of automobile testing. During a preshow—essentially a GM commercial—guests will learn how the company works to promote automotive safety, reliability, and performance. Then they'll board full-scale, six-passenger test cars and travel upon what appears to be an actual roadway, accelerating on long straightaways, hugging hairpin turns, climbing steep hills, and braking abruptly—often on less-than-perfect road conditions. The ride will culminate with a terrifying high-speed outdoor run along the track's steeply banked "speed loop," which extends far beyond the pavilion facility. Cars will go at a top speed of 65 miles per hour. This was formerly World of Motion.

Universe of Energy
Recommended ages: 8–adult

Sponsored by Exxon, this pavilion—its roof glistening with solar panels—aims to better our understanding of America's energy problems and potential solutions via a 32-minute ride-through attraction. Recently refurbished, it's called **Ellen's Energy Adventure** and features comedian and television sitcom star Ellen DeGeneres as an energy expert tutored by Bill Nye the Science Guy to be a "Jeopardy" contestant. On a massive screen in Theater I, an animated motion picture depicts the earth's molten beginnings, its cooling process, and the formation of fossil fuels. You move from Theater I to travel back 275 million years into an eerie, storm-wracked landscape of the Mesozoic era, a time of violent geological activity. Here, you're menaced by giant AudioAnimatronic dragonflies, pterodactyls, dinosaurs, earthquakes, and streams of molten lava before entering a steam-filled tunnel deep through the bowels of the volcano to emerge back in the 20th century in Theatre II. In this new setting, which looks like a NASA Mission Control room, a 70mm film projected on a massive 210-foot wraparound screen depicts the challenges of the world's increasing energy demands and the emerging technologies that will help meet them. Your moving seats now return to Theatre I, where swirling special effects herald a film about how energy impacts our lives. It ends on a dramatically upbeat note—with a vision of an energy-abundant future and Ellen as a new "Jeopardy" champion.

✪ Wonders of Life
Recommended ages: 8–adult

Housed in a vast geodesic dome fronted by a 75-foot replica of a DNA molecule, this pavilion offers some of Future World's most engaging shows and attractions.

The Making of Me starring Martin Short is a captivating 15-minute motion picture combining live action with animation and spectacular in-utero photography to create the sweetest introduction imaginable to the facts of life. Don't miss it, although the presentation may prompt some questions from young children (recommended for ages 10 and up). Short travels back in time to witness his parents as children, their meeting at a college dance, their wedding, and their decision to have a baby. Along with him, we view his development inside his mother's womb and witness his birth.

You're miniaturized to the size of a single cell for a medical rescue mission inside the immune system of a human body during **Body Wars.** Your objective: to save a miniaturized immunologist who has been accidentally swept into the bloodstream. This motion-simulator ride takes you on a wild journey through gale-force winds (in the lungs) and pounding heart chambers (recommended for ages 6 and up). Although you know they are part of the Disney show, if you've ever seen the movie *Outbreak,* it is a little eerie passing through dermatopic purification stations in order to undergo miniaturization. Leonard Nimoy directed.

In the hilarious, multimedia **Cranium Command,** Buzzy, an AudioAnimatronic brain-pilot-in-training, is charged with the seemingly impossible task of controlling the brain of a typical 12-year-old boy. The boy's body parts are played by Charles Grodin, Jon Lovitz, Bob Goldthwait, Kevin Nealon and Dana Carvey (as Hans and Franz), and George Wendt. It's another must-see attraction (recommended for ages 8 and up). The audience is seated inside Bobby's head as Buzzy guides him through a day of typical preadolescent traumas—running for the school bus, meeting a girl, fighting bullies, and a run-in with the school principal.

There are large areas filled with fitness-related shows, exhibits, and participatory activities, including a film called **Goofy About Health,** and **Coach's Corner,** where your tennis, golf, or baseball swing is analyzed by experts, and the **Sensory Funhouse** where you can test your perceptions. Grown-ups and kids will enjoy playing here, in air-conditioned comfort. Try working out on a video-enhanced exercise bike, get a computer-generated evaluation of your health habits, and take a video voyage to investigate the effects of drugs on your heart. There's much, much more. You could easily spend hours here.

WORLD SHOWCASE

Surrounding a 40-acre lagoon at the park's southern end is World Showcase—a permanent community of 11 miniaturized nations, all with authentically indigenous landmark architecture, landscaping, background music, restaurants, and shops. The cultural facets of each nation are explored in art exhibits, dance performances, and innovative rides, films, and attractions. And all of the employees in each pavilion are natives of the country represented.

✪ The American Adventure
Recommended ages: 10–adult

Housed in a vast, Georgian-style structure, **The American Adventure** is a 29-minute dramatization of U.S. history, utilizing a 72-foot rear-projection screen, rousing music, and a large cast of lifelike AudioAnimatronic figures, including narrators Mark Twain and Ben Franklin. The "adventure" begins with the voyage of the *Mayflower* and encompasses major historic events. We view Jefferson writing the Declaration of Independence, the expansion of the frontier, Mathew Brady photographing a family about to be divided by the Civil War, the stock market crash of 1929, Pearl Harbor, and the *Eagle* heading toward the moon. John Muir and Teddy Roosevelt discuss the need for national parks, Susan B. Anthony speaks out on women's rights, Frederick Douglass on slavery, Chief Joseph on the situation of Native Americans. While waiting for the show to begin, you'll be entertained by the wonderful Voices of Liberty Singers performing American folk songs in the Main Hall. Note the quotes from famous Americans on the walls here.

Formal gardens shaded by live oaks, sycamores, elms, and holly complement the pavilion's 18th-century architecture. A shop called Heritage Manor Gifts sells signed presidential photographs, needlepoint samplers, afghans and quilts, pottery, candles, Davy Crockett hats, books on American history, historically costumed dolls, classic political campaign buttons, and vintage newspapers with banner headlines like "Nixon Resigns!" An artisan at the shop makes jewelry out of coins.

Note: International cultural performances take place here in the America Gardens Theater.

✪ Canada
Recommended ages: 8–adult

Our neighbors to the north are represented by diverse architecture ranging from a mansard-roofed replica of Ottawa's 19th-century French-style Château Laurier (here called the Hôtel du Canada) to a British-influenced rustic stone building modeled after a famous landmark near Niagara Falls.

An Indian village—complete with rough-hewn log trading post and 30-foot replicas of Ojibwa totem poles—signifies the culture of the Northwest, while the Canadian wilderness is reflected by a steep mountain (a Canadian Rocky), a waterfall cascading into a whitewater stream, and a "forest" of evergreens, stately cedars, maples, and birch trees. Don't miss the stunning floral displays of azaleas, roses, zinnias, chrysanthemums, petunias, and patches of wildflowers inspired by the Butchart Gardens in Victoria, British Columbia.

The pavilion's highlight attraction is **O Canada!**—a dazzling, 360° Circle-Vision film that reveals Canada's scenic splendor from sophisticated Montréal to the thundering flight of thousands of snow geese departing an autumn stopover near the St. Lawrence River. The film is 18 minutes in length.

Canada pavilion shops carry sandstone and soapstone carvings, fringed leather vests, duck decoys, moccasins, a vast array of Eskimo stuffed animals and Native

In the Words of Walt Disney

In my view, wholesome pleasure, sport, and recreation are as vital to this nation as productive work and should have a large share in the national budget.

American dolls, Native American spirit stones, rabbit-skin caps, heavy knitted sweaters, and, of course, maple syrup.

✪ China

Recommended ages: 10–adult

Bounded by a serpentine wall that snakes around its outer perimeter, the China pavilion is entered via a vast, triple-arched ceremonial gate inspired by the Temple of Heaven in Beijing, a summer retreat for Chinese emperors. Passing through the gate, you'll see a half-size replica of this ornately embellished red and gold circular temple, built in 1420 during the Ming dynasty. Gardens simulate those in Suzhou, with miniature waterfalls, fragrant lotus ponds, groves of bamboo, corkscrew willows, and weeping mulberry trees.

The highlight here is **Wonders of China,** a 20-minute, 360° Circle-Vision film that explores 6,000 years of dynastic and communist rule and the breathtaking diversity of the Chinese landscape. Narrated by 8th-century Tang dynasty poet Li Bai, it includes scenes of the Great Wall (begun 24 centuries ago!), a performance by the Beijing Opera, the Forbidden City in Beijing, rice terraces of Hunan Province, the Gobi Desert, and tropical rain forests of Hainan Island. Adjacent to the theater, an art gallery houses changing exhibits of Chinese art.

A bustling marketplace—the **Yong Feng Shangdian Shopping Gallery**—offers an array of merchandise including silk robes, lacquer and mother-of-pearl–inlay furniture, jade figures, cloisonné vases, tea sets, silk rugs and embroideries, dolls, fans, wind chimes, and Chinese clothing. Artisans here demonstrate calligraphy.

✪ France

Recommended ages: 8–adult

Focusing on La Belle Epoque (1870–1910)—a flourishing period for French art, literature, and architecture—this pavilion is entered via a replica of the beautiful cast-iron Pont des Arts footbridge over the "Seine." It leads to a park with pleached sycamores, Bradford pear trees, flowering crape myrtles, and sculptured parterre flower gardens inspired by Seurat's painting *A Sunday Afternoon on the Island of La Grande Jatte.* A one-tenth replica of the Eiffel Tower constructed from Gustave Eiffel's original blueprints looms above *les grands boulevards,* and period buildings feature copper mansard roofs and casement windows.

The highlight is **Impressions de France.** Shown in a palatial (mercifully sit-down) theater à la Fontainebleau, this 18-minute film is a breathtakingly scenic journey through diverse French landscapes projected on a vast, 200°-view wraparound screen and enhanced by music of French composers.

Emporia in the covered shopping arcade, with art-nouveau Métro facades at either end, have interiors ranging from a turn-of-the-century bibliothèque to a French château. Merchandise includes French art prints and original art, cookbooks, cookware, wines (there's a tasting counter), fancy French foodstuffs, Madeline and Babar books and dolls, perfumes, and original letters of famous Frenchmen ranging from Jean Cocteau.to Napoleon. Another marketplace/tourism center revives the defunct Les Halles, where Parisians used to sip onion soup in the wee hours. The heavenly aroma of a *boulangerie* (bakery) penetrates the atmosphere, and mimes, jugglers, and strolling *chanteurs* (singers) entertain.

✪ Germany
Recommended ages: 8–adult

Enclosed by towered castle walls, this festive pavilion is centered on a cobblestoned *Platz* (square) with pots of colorful flowers girding a fountain statue of St. George and the Dragon. An adjacent clock tower is embellished with whimsical glockenspiel figures that herald each hour with quaint melodies. The pavilion's outdoor **Biergarten**—where it's Oktoberfest all year long—was inspired by medieval Rothenberg. And 16th-century building facades replicate a merchant's hall in the Black Forest and the town hall in Frankfurt's Römerberg Square.

Shops here carry Hummel figurines, crystal, glassware, cookware, cuckoo clocks, cowbells, Alpine hats, German wines (there's a tasting counter) and specialty foods, toys (German Disneyana, teddy bears, dolls, and puppets), and books. An artisan demonstrates molding and painting Hummel figures; another paints detailed scenes on eggs. Background music runs from oom-pah bands to Mozart symphonies.

Italy
Recommended ages: 10–adult

One of the prettiest World Showcase pavilions, Italy lures visitors over an arched stone footbridge to a replica of Venice's intricately ornamented pink and white Doge's Palace. Other architectural highlights include the 83-foot Campanile (bell tower) of St. Mark's Square, Venetian bridges, and a central piazza enclosing a version of Bernini's Neptune Fountain. A garden wall suggests a backdrop of provincial country-side, and Mediterranean citrus, olive trees, cypress, and pine frame a formal garden. Gondolas are moored on the lagoon.

Shops here carry cameo and filigree jewelry, Armani figurines, kitchenware, Italian wines and foods, Murano and Venetian glass, alabaster figurines, and inlaid wooden music boxes. A troupe of street actors performs a contemporary version of 16th-century commedia dell'arte in the piazza.

Japan
Recommended ages: 8–adult

Heralded by a flaming red *torii* (gate of honor) on the banks of the lagoon and the graceful, blue-roofed Goju No To pagoda (inspired by a shrine built at Nara in A.D. 700), this pavilion focuses on Japan's ancient culture. In a traditional Japanese garden, cedars, yew trees, bamboo, "cloud-pruned" evergreens, willows, and flowering shrubs frame a contemplative setting of pebbled footpaths, rustic bridges, waterfalls, exquisite rock landscaping, and a pond of golden koi. The **Yakitori House** is based on the renowned 16th-century Katsura Imperial Villa in Kyoto, designed as a royal summer residence and considered by many to be the crowning achievement of Japanese architecture. Exhibits ranging from 18th-century Bunraki puppets to samurai armor take place in the moated White Heron Castle, a replica of the Shirasagi-Jo, a 17th-century fortress overlooking the city of Himeji.

And the **Mitsukoshi Department Store** (Japan's answer to Macy's) is housed in a replica of the Shishinden (Hall of Ceremonies) of the Gosho Imperial Palace, built in Kyoto in A.D. 794. It sells lacquerware, kimonos, kites, fans, dolls in traditional costumes, origami books, samurai swords, Japanese Disneyana, bonsai trees, Japanese foods, Netsuke carvings, and pottery—even modern electronics. In the courtyard, artisans demonstrate the ancient arts of *anesaiku* (shaping brown rice candy into dragons, unicorns, and dolphins), *sumi-e* (calligraphy), and *origami* (paper folding).

Be sure to include a show of traditional Japanese music and dance at this pavilion in your schedule. It's one of the best in the World Showcase.

Mexico

Recommended ages: 8–adult

You'll hear the music of marimbas and mariachi bands as you approach the festive showcase of Mexico, fronted by a towering Mayan pyramid modeled on the Aztec temple of Quetzalcoatl (God of Life) and surrounded by dense Yucatán jungle landscaping. Upon entering the pavilion, you'll find yourself in a museum of pre-Colombian art and artifacts.

Down a ramp is a small lagoon, the setting for **El Rio del Tiempo** (River of Time), where visitors board boats for 8-minute cruises through Mexico's past and present. Passengers get a close-up look at the above-mentioned pyramid and the erupting Popocatepetl volcano. Dance performances focusing on the cultures of Mayan, Toltec, Aztec, and colonial Mexico are presented in film segments and by an AudioAnimatronic cast in vignettes ranging from a *Day of the Dead* skeleton band to children breaking a piñata. Additional film footage focuses on Mexican tourist spots. The show culminates in a Mexico City fiesta with exploding fiber-optic fireworks.

Shops in and around the Plaza de Los Amigos (a "moonlit" Mexican *mercado* with a tiered fountain and street lamps) display an array of leather goods, baskets, sombreros, piñatas, pottery, embroidered dresses and blouses, maracas, jewelry, serapes, paper flowers, colorful papier-mâché birds, and blown-glass objects (an artisan gives demonstrations). La Casa de Vacaciones, sponsored by the Mexican Tourist Office, provides travel information.

Morocco

Recommended ages: 10–adult

This exotic pavilion—its architecture embellished with intricate geometrically patterned tile work, minarets, hand-painted wood ceilings, and brass lighting fixtures—is heralded by a replica of the Koutoubia Minaret, the prayer tower of a 12th-century mosque in Marrakesh.

The Medina (old city), entered via a replica of an arched gateway in Fez, leads to Fez House (a traditional Moroccan home) and the narrow, winding streets of the *souk,* a bustling marketplace where all manner of authentic handcrafted merchandise is on display. Here you can peruse or purchase pottery, brassware, hand-knotted Berber carpets, colorful Rabat carpets, ornate silver and camel-bone boxes, straw baskets, and prayer rugs. There are weaving demonstrations in the souk throughout the day. The Medina's rectangular courtyard centers on a replica of the ornately tiled Najjarine Fountain in Fez, the setting for musical entertainment.

The pavilion's Royal Gallery contains an ever-changing exhibit of Moroccan art, and the Center of Tourism offers a continuous three-screen slide show. Morocco's landscaping includes a formal garden, citrus and olive trees, date palms, and banana plants.

Norway

Recommended ages: 10–adult

Centered on a picturesque cobblestone courtyard, this pavilion evokes ancient Norway. A *stavekirke* (stave church), styled after the 13th-century Gol Church of Hallingdal, its eaves embellished with wooden dragon heads, houses changing exhibits. A replica of Oslo's 14th-century Akershus Castle, next to a cascading woodland waterfall, is the setting for the pavilion's featured restaurant. Other buildings simulate the red-roofed cottages of Bergen and the timber-sided farm buildings of the Nordic woodlands.

Find the Hidden Mickeys

Hiding Mickeys in designs began as an inside joke with early Walt Disney World "Imagineers" and became a park tradition. Today, dozens of subtle hidden Mickeys—the world-famous set of ears, profiles, and full figures—are concealed in attractions and resorts throughout Walt Disney World. No one even knows their exact number. See how many you can locate during your visit. A few to look for include the following:

In the Magic Kingdom

In the Haunted Mansion banquet scene, check out the arrangement of plate and adjoining saucers on the table.

In the Africa scene of It's a Small World, note the purple flowers on a vine on the elephant's left side.

While riding Splash Mountain, look for Mickey lying on his back in the pink clouds to the right of the steamboat.

Hint: There are four HMs in The Timekeeper and five in the Carousel of Progress.

At Epcot

In Journey into Imagination, check out the little girl's dress in the lobby film of *Honey I Shrunk the Audience,* one of five HMs in this pavilion.

In The Land pavilion, don't miss the small stones in front of the Native American man on a horse and the baseball cap of the man driving a harvester in the *Circle of Life* film.

As your boat cruises through the Mexico pavilion on the El Rio del Tiempo attraction, notice the arrangement of three clay pots in the marketplace scene.

In Maelstrom, in the Norway pavilion, a Viking wears Mickey ears in the wall mural facing the loading dock.

There are four HMs in Spaceship Earth, one of them in the Renaissance scene, on the page of a book behind the sleeping monk. Try to find the other three.

At Disney–MGM Studios

On the Great Movie Ride, there's an HM on the window above the bank in the gangster scene, and four familiar characters are included in the hieroglyphics wall opposite Indiana Jones.

At Jim Henson's Muppet*Vision 4D, take a good look at the TOP FIVE REASONS FOR TURNING IN YOUR 4-D GLASSES sign, and note the balloons in the film's final scene.

At the Monster Sound Show, check out Jimmy Macdonald's bolo tie and ring, in the preshow video.

In the Twilight Zone Tower of Terror, note the bell for the elevator behind Rod Serling in the film. There are five other HMs in this attraction.

There are also HMs at many Disney resorts. The best place to look for them is at Wilderness Lodge, which has over a dozen that I know about.

There's a two-part attraction here. **Maelstrom,** a boat ride in a dragon-headed Viking vessel, traverses Norway's fjords and mythical forests to the music of *Peer Gynt*— an exciting journey during which you'll be menaced by polar bears prowling the shore and trolls who cast a spell on the boat. The watercraft crashes through a narrow gorge and spins into the North Sea, where a violent storm is in progress. But the storm abates, and passengers disembark safely in a 10th-century Viking village to view the

70mm film **Norway,** which documents a thousand years of history. Featured images include *Oseberg bat* (a 1,000-year-old Viking ship), a small fishing village, festive national-holiday celebrations in Oslo, and soaring jumps at the Holmenkollen ski resort.

Shops feature hand-knit wool hats and sweaters, toys (there's a Lego table where kids can play while you shop), wood carvings, Scandinavian foods, pewterware, and jewelry.

United Kingdom
Recommended ages: 10–adult

Centered on Britannia Square—a formal London-style park, complete with copper-roofed gazebo bandstand and a statue of the Bard—the U.K. pavilion evokes Merry Olde England. Four centuries of architecture are represented along quaint cobble-stoned streets; troubadours and minstrels entertain in front of a traditional British pub; and a formal garden with low box hedges in geometric patterns, flagstone paths, and a stone fountain replicates the landscaping of 16th- and 17th-century palaces.

High Street and Tudor Lane shops display a broad sampling of British merchandise—toy soldiers, Paddington bears, personalized coats of arms, tobaccos and pipes, Scottish clothing (cashmere and Shetland sweaters, golf wear, tams, knits, and tartans), fine English china, Waterford crystal, and pub items (tankards, dart-boards, and the like).

A tea shop occupies a replica of Anne Hathaway's thatch-roofed 16th-century cottage in Stratford-upon-Avon, while other emporia represent the Georgian, Victorian, Queen Anne, and Tudor periods. Background music ranges from "Greensleeves" to the Beatles.

ILLUMINATIONS

IllumiNations, a 16½-minute spectacular using high-tech lighting effects, darting laser beams, fireworks, strobes, and rainbow-lit dancing fountains, takes place nightly. A backdrop of classical music by international composers (representing World Showcase nations) enhances the drama. Each nation is highlighted in turn. Colorful kites fly over Japan, the giant Rockies loom over Canada, a gingerbread house rises in Germany, and so on. Find a seat around the lagoon about a half hour before show time.

OTHER SHOWS

Live shows, especially those in World Showcase, make up an important part of the Epcot experience. Among others, these might include Chinese lion dancers and acrobats, German oom-pah bands, Caledonian bagpipers, Mexican mariachi bands, Moroccan storytellers and belly dancers, Italian "living statues" and stilt walkers, colonial fife and drum groups, and much more. Two especially good shows are the Voices of Liberty singers at the American Adventure pavilion and the traditional music and dance displays in Japan. Check your show schedule when you come in and plan your day to include some of them.

SHOPPING AT EPCOT

The most fascinating shops are found in World Showcase pavilions, which comprise an international bazaar selling everything from Berber rugs to Japanese kimonos. Noshing and shopping is the only reason to walk around the World Showcase. You'll find descriptions of merchandise available in these pavilions in the World Showcase listings, above.

5   Disney–MGM Studios

Disney–MGM Studios offers exciting movie and TV-themed shows and behind-the-scenes "reel-life" adventures. You see the eerie Tower of Terror and the Earrfel Tower, a water tower with mouse ears, off in the distance. Once inside, its main streets include Hollywood Boulevard and Sunset Boulevard, with art-deco movie sets evocative of Hollywood's glamorous golden age. There's also a New York Street lined with Gotham landmarks (the Empire State, Flatiron, and Chrysler buildings) and typical New York characters including peddlers hawking knock-off watches. This is some of the best street performing you find in any of the Disney parks. More important, this is a working movie-and-TV studio, where shows are in production even as you tour the premises.

Arrive at the park early, tickets in hand. Unlike the Magic Kingdom and Epcot, MGM's 110 acres of attractions can pretty much be seen in 1 day. The parking lot is right at the gate, although trams do run. Pay attention to your parking location, which is not as distinctly marked as in the Magic Kingdom.

If you don't get a *Disney–MGM Studios Guidemap* and entertainment schedule when you enter the park, you can pick them up at Guest Services (MGM's information center). First thing to do is check show times and work out an entertainment schedule based on highlight attractions and geographical proximity. My favorite MGM restaurants are described in chapter 6.

ESSENTIALS

HOURS   Generally 9am to 7pm with extended hours—sometimes as late as midnight—during major holidays and the summer months.

TICKET PRICES   A 1-day park ticket is $40.81 for adults, $32.86 for children, free for children under 4.

SERVICES & FACILITIES IN THE PARK

ATMs   ATM machines accepting cards from banks using the Cirrus, Honor, and Plus systems are located at the main entrance.

Baby Care   MGM has a small Baby Care Center where you'll find facilities for nursing and changing and disposable diapers, formula, baby food, and pacifiers are for sale. Changing tables are also in all women's rest rooms and some men's rest rooms. Disposable diapers are also available at the Guest Services Building.

Cameras & Film   Kodak's disposable Fun Saver cameras are available throughout the park. Video camcorders are available for rent at Hollywood Boulevard for $30 a day, plus a $450 deposit.

First Aid   The First Aid Center, staffed by registered nurses, is in the Entrance Plaza adjoining Guest Services.

Lockers   Lockers are alongside Oscar's Classic Car Souvenirs, to the right of the Entrance Plaza after you pass through the turnstiles. The cost is $3 to $5 a day, depending on the size.

Lost Children   Lost children at Disney–MGM are taken to Guest Services where lost-children logbooks are kept. Children under 7 should wear name tags.

Package Pickup   Any large package you purchase can be sent by the shop clerk to Guest Services in the Entrance Plaza. Allow 3 hours for delivery.

Disney-MGM Studios Theme Park

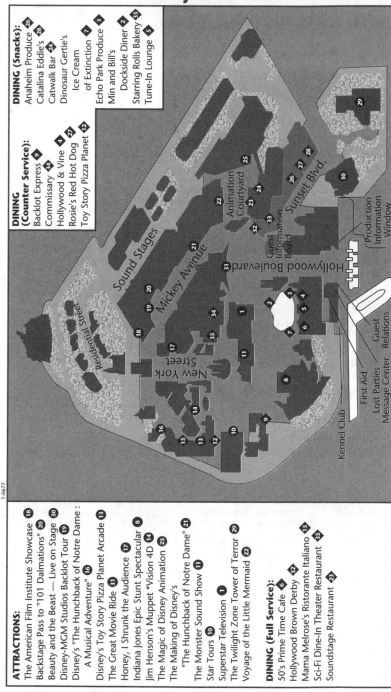

ATTRACTIONS:

The American Film Institute Showcase **18**
Backstage Pass to "101 Dalmations" **20**
Beauty and the Beast — Live on Stage **30**
Disney-MGM Studios Backlot Tour **19**
Disney's "The Hunchback of Notre Dame :
   A Musical Adventure" **16**
Disney's Toy Story Pizza Planet Arcade **13**
The Great Movie Ride **31**
Honey, I Shrunk the Audience **17**
Indiana Jones Epic Stunt Spectacular **8**
Jim Henson's Muppet *Vision 4D **14**
The Magic of Disney Animation **25**
The Making of Disney's
   "The Hunchback of Notre Dame" **21**
The Monster Sound Show **11**
Star Tours **10**
Superstar Television **1**
The Twilight Zone Tower of Terror **29**
Voyage of the Little Mermaid **22**

DINING (Full Service):

50's Prime Time Cafe **6**
Hollywood Brown Derby **32**
Mama Melrose's Ristorante Italiano **15**
Sci-Fi Dine-In Theater Restaurant **35**
Soundstage Restaurant **23**

**DINING
(Counter Service):**

Backlot Express **9**
Commissary **24**
Hollywood & Vine **4**
Rosie's Red Hot Dog **27**
Toy Story Pizza Planet **12**

DINING (Snacks):

Anaheim Produce **26**
Catalina Eddie's **28**
Catwalk Bar **24**
Dinosaur Gertie's
   Ice Cream
   of Extinction **7**
Echo Park Produce **3**
Min and Bill's
Dockside Diner **2**
Starring Rolls Bakery **33**
Tune-In Lounge **5**

1-0677

161

Pet Care   Day accommodations are offered at kennels just outside the entrance for $6 a day. There are also four kennels in the WDW complex.

Strollers   Strollers can be rented at Oscar's Super Service, inside the main entrance, for $6.

Wheelchair Rental   Wheelchairs are rented at Oscar's Super Service inside the main entrance. The cost for regular chairs is $6 a day. Electric chairs rent for $35.

MAJOR ATTRACTIONS & SHOWS

The American Film Institute Showcase
Recommended ages: 10–adult

This exhibit brings into focus the efforts all of those folks—editors, cinematographers, producers, and directors—whose names blur by as the credits roll. Created in 1996 in partnership with the Los Angeles–based American Film Institute, this walk-through tour also highlights some of the organization's winners of the Lifetime Achievement Award. They include Bette Davis, Jack Nicholson, and Elizabeth Taylor.

❂ Backstage Pass to 101 Dalmatians
Recommended ages: all ages

Have a De Vil of a good time spotting Cruella and the other stars of Disney's live-action remake of the animated classic. The stark, eerie sets from Cruella's movie are among the top attractions during this short tour. Wizzer, the most fluid of the canine actors, is featured in a film about the dog's life of a four-pawed star. Taking a cue from Universal, where you Ride the Movies, the special-effects show allows one lucky—usually tall and male—spectator to ride in the movies by re-creating Jeff Daniels' runaway-bike scene. Real Dalmatians are also on display. But don't call PETA yet. The pups pull only 2-hour shifts, treated better, one employee grumbled, than most two-legged "cast" members.

Note: This exhibit changes as Disney unveils its latest release. Hercules may have muscled into the spot by the time of your visit.

Backstage Studio Tour
Recommended ages: 10–adult

This 25-minute tram tour takes you behind the scenes for a close-up look at the vehicles, props, costumes, sets, and special effects used in your favorite movies and TV shows. You'll see costumers at work in the wardrobe department (Disney has the world's largest costume collection—more than 2 million garments), house facades of "The Golden Girls" and "Empty Nest" on Residential Street, and carpenters building sets. Most of the props are from short-lived series that you've never heard of, but it's still interesting. The real fun begins once the tram ventures into Catastrophe Canyon, where an earthquake in the heart of desert oil country causes canyon walls to rumble, and riders are threatened by a raging oil fire, massive explosions, torrents of rain, and flash floods! Then you're taken behind the scenes to see how filmmakers use special effects to create such disasters. Almost as interesting as the ride is the preshow. While waiting on line, you can watch entertaining videos—hosted by Tom Selleck and Carol Burnett—of well-known actors and directors, on overhead monitors: Penny Marshall talking about the piano scene in *Big,* Richard Dreyfuss sharing how he landed the role in *Jaws* that launched his movie career, Mel Brooks on why he was "forced" to become a director/producer, and many more. After the tram tour, visit Studio Showcase, a changing walk-through display of sets and props from popular and classic movies.

The Great Movie Ride
Recommended ages: 10–adult

Film footage and AudioAnimatronic replicas of movie stars are used to re-create some of the most famous scenes in filmdom on this thrilling ride through movie history. You'll relive magic moments from the 1930s through the present—Bergman and Bogart's classic airport farewell in *Casablanca,* Rhett carrying Scarlett up the stairs of Tara for a night of passion, Brando bellowing "Stellllaaaa," Sigourney Weaver fending off slimy *Alien* foes, Gene Kelly singin' in the rain, Johnny Weissmuller's trademark Tarzan yell and vine-swing across the jungle, and many more. Action is enhanced by dramatic special effects, and your tram is always highjacked en route by outlaws or gangsters. "Fasten your seat belts. It's going to be a bumpy night." The setting for this attraction is a full-scale reproduction of Hollywood's famous Mann's Chinese Theatre, complete with handprints of the stars out front.

✪ Indiana Jones Epic Stunt Spectacular
Recommended ages: 6–adult

Visitors get a glimpse into the world of movie stunts in this dramatic 30-minute show, which re-creates major scenes from the *Indiana Jones* series. The show opens on an elaborate Mayan temple backdrop. Indiana Jones crashes dramatically onto the set via a rope, and, as he searches with a torch for the golden idol, he encounters booby traps, fire and steam, and spears popping up from the ground, before being chased by a vast rolling boulder! The set is dismantled to reveal a colorful Cairo marketplace where a sword fight ensues and the action includes virtuoso bullwhip maneuvers, lots of gunfire, and a truck bursting into flame. An explosive finale takes place in a desert scenario. Throughout, guests get to see how elaborate stunts are pulled off and wonder how close the actors really do come to peril. (Here it is, another opportunity to be part of the fun. Arrive early and sit near the stage for your shot at short-lived stardom. Go ahead, you're running out of chances—*this time you get to wear a turban.*)

The action is enhanced by movie theme music and entertaining narrative, and throughout, guests get to see how elaborate stunts are pulled off.

Inside the Magic
Recommended ages: 10–adult

Movie and TV special effects and production facets are the focus of this behind-the-scenes walking tour of studio facilities. You'll see how a naval battle—complete with burning ships, torpedoes, and undersea explosions—is created and then view the results on videotape. Two young volunteers from the audience help demonstrate how miniaturization was achieved in *Honey, I Shrunk the Kids.* You'll visit three studio soundstages (on some tours, you'll get to see movies or TV shows being filmed from a soundproof catwalk); view a short comedy called *The Lottery* starring Bette Midler and learn how its special effects were achieved; and head to the Walt Disney Theater where, blessed relief, you'll get to sit down and enjoy a behind-the-scenes look at the company's latest animation feature. To find the entrance to this attraction, follow the big pink footsteps of Roger Rabbit.

✪ Jim Henson's Muppet*Vision 4D
Recommended ages: 4–adult

They added an additional D and some additional zany effects to this delightful film starring Kermit and Miss Piggy. The film combines Jim Henson's puppets with Disney AudioAnimatronics and special-effects wizardry, 70mm film, and cutting-edge 4D technology. Wow! The coming-right-at-you action includes flying Muppets, cream pies, cannonballs, high winds, fiber-optic fireworks, bubble showers, even an actual spray of water. Kermit is the host, Miss Piggy sings "Dream a Little Dream of Me," Statler and Waldorf critique the action (which includes numerous mishaps and disasters) from a mezzanine balcony, and Nicki Napoleon and his Emperor Penguins (a full Muppet orchestra) provide music from the pit. Kids in the first row get to interact with the characters. In the preshow area, guests view an entertaining Muppet video on overhead monitors and see movie props belonging to Muppet superstars. Note the cute Muppet fountain out front, and the Muppet take on a Rousseau painting inside.

✪ The Magic of Disney Animation
Recommended ages: 8–adult

You'll see Disney characters come alive at the stroke of a brush or pencil as you tour actual, glass-walled animation studios and watch artists at work. Walter Cronkite and Robin Williams (guess who plays straight man?) explain what's going on via video monitors, and they also star in a very funny 8-minute Peter Pan–theme film about the basics of animation. It's painstaking work: To produce an 80-minute film, the animation team must complete more than a million individual *cels* (drawings/paintings on clear celluloid sheets) of characters and scenery! Original cels from famous Disney movies, and some of the many Oscars won by Disney artists, are on display here. The tour also includes very entertaining video talks by animators and a grand finale of magical moments from Disney classics such as *Pinocchio, Snow White, Bambi, Beauty and the Beast,* and *The Hunchback of Notre Dame.*

✪ Monster Sound Show
Recommended ages: all ages

Scream. Wave your hands. Making a little noise is likely to help get you from the audience onto the stage where you will then take part in creating the sound effects for a short film starring Chevy Chase and Martin Short. The rumble includes thunder, rain, and creaking doors, but the real stars are the tourists trying to make it all happen like the professionals. Volunteer. You're on vacation. You'll *probably* never see these people again. If you can't muster the gumption to go on stage, the postshow, Soundworks, provides the opportunity of a little joyful noise on interactive computers and away from the maddening crowd.

Four "Foley artists" (Foley is the Hollywood sound-effects system named for its creator, Jack Foley) are chosen from the audience to create sound effects for a 2-minute comic Gothic thriller starring Chevy Chase and Martin Short. We see the film three times, first with professional sound, then without sound as volunteers frantically try to create an appropriate track, and finally with the sound effects they've provided. The show features some of the 20,000-plus ingenious gadgets created by sound master Jimmy Macdonald during his 45 years with Disney Studios. In a postshow area called Soundworks, guests can attempt to reproduce flying-saucer sounds from the film *Forbidden Planet,* dub the voice of Roger Rabbit, and create the gallop of the Headless Horseman in *Legend of Sleepy Hollow.*

Star Tours
Recommended ages: 8–adult

A wild galactic journey based on the *Star Wars* trilogy (George Lucas collaborated on its conception), this action-packed adventure uses dramatic film footage and flight-simulator technology to transform the theater into a vehicle careening through space. We enter a preshow area—where R2-D2 and C-3PO are running an intergalactic travel agency—and board a 40-passenger "spacecraft" for a voyage to the Moon of

Endor. En route, we encounter robots, aliens, and droids, among them our inexperienced pilot, RX-24. No sooner has he extricated our spaceship from an asteroidlike tunnel of frozen ice fragments than he's drawn into combat with a massive Imperial Star Destroyer. The ship lurches out of control, and passengers experience sudden drops, violent crashes, and oncoming laser blasts. The harrowing ride ends safely, and we exit into a *Star Wars* merchandise shop. One of the better thrill rides in the Disney parks, and because it has been around a while the lines are usually short.

Superstar Television
Recommended ages: 10–adult

This 30-minute show takes guests through a broadcast day that spans TV history. During the preshow, "casting directors" choose volunteers from the audience to re-enact 15 famous television scenes (arrive early if you want to snag a role, and *wave that hand!*). The broadcast day begins with a 1955 black-and-white "Today" show featuring Dave Garroway and continues through "Late Night with David Letterman," including scenes from a classic "I Love Lucy" episode (the candy factory), "General Hospital," "Bonanza," "Gilligan's Island," "Cheers," and "The Golden Girls," among others. Real footage is mixed with live action, and though occasionally a star is born, there's plenty of fun watching amateur actors freeze up, flub lines, and otherwise deviate from the script.

✪ Theater of the Stars
Recommended ages: 4–adult

This 1,500-seat, covered amphitheater is currently presenting a 25-minute live Broadway-style production of *"Beauty and the Beast"* adapted from the movie version. Musical highlights from the show range from the rousing "Be Our Guest" opening number to the poignant title song featured in a romantic waltz-scene finale complete with the release of white doves. A highlight is "The Mob Song" scene in a dark forest, in which villagers led by Gaston (the beast's rival for Belle) and armed with axes, hoes, and pitchforks set out on a rampage to "kill the beast," setting up the emotional climax. Sets and costumes are lavish, production numbers spectacular. Consider going to the last show; it makes for a feel-good (and sit-down) ending to your day. Arrive early to get a good seat.

When is someone going to do a version of this tale in which the beast is a woman and a man loves her for her inner qualities?

Note: Beauty and the Beast has been enjoying a long run here; a new show, based on a more recent Disney hit, may be in progress by the time you visit. *Hunchback of Notre Dame: A Musical Adventure* will probably be a major priority; for the latter, get in line 30 minutes prior at the Backlot Theater.

✪ The Twilight Zone Tower of Terror
Recommended ages: 10–adult

Legend has it that during a violent storm on Halloween night of 1939, lightning struck the Hollywood Tower Hotel, causing an entire wing—along with an elevator full of people—to disappear. And you're about to meet them as you become the star in a special episode of. . . *The Twilight Zone*. En route to this formerly grand hotel, guests walk past overgrown landscaping and faded signs that once directed them to stables and tennis courts; the vines over the entrance trellis are dead, and the hotel itself is a crumbling ruin. Eerie corridors lead to a dimly lit library, where you can hear a storm raging outside. After various spooky adventures, the ride ends in a dramatic climax: a terrifying 13-story fitful, free-fall plunge into *The Twilight Zone!* The best thrill ride at Disney with a "preshow" so authentic that maintenance crews

In the Words of Walt Disney

A family picture is one the kids can take their parents to see and not be embarrassed.

I don't like downbeat pictures, and I cannot believe that the average family does either. . . when I go to the theater, I don't want to come out depressed.

kept fixing leaking pipes designed to drip as part of the ambiance. *Note:* You must be 40 inches tall to ride.

✪ Voyage of the Little Mermaid
Recommended ages: 4–adult

Hazy lighting, creating an underwater effect in a reef-walled theater, helps set the mood for this charming musical spectacular based on the Disney feature film. The show combines live performers with more than 100 puppets, movie clips, and innovative special effects. Sebastian sings the movie's Academy Award–winning song, "Under the Sea"; the ethereal Ariel shares her dream of becoming human in a live performance of "Part of Your World"; and the evil, tentacled Ursula, 12 feet tall and 10 feet wide, belts out "Poor Unfortunate Soul." It all has a happy ending, as most of the young audience knows it will; they've seen the movie.

PARADES, SHOWS, FIREWORKS & MORE

Disney plugs its newest animated, soon-to-be classic Hercules in the daily **parade.** It features all of the movie's adorable cast and songs from the soundtrack that you and your children will, undoubtedly, soon have memorized. The parade takes place daily; check your entertainment schedule for route and times.

The **Sorcery in the Sky** fireworks show is presented nightly during summer and peak seasons. Check your entertainment schedule to see if it's on.

The **Visiting Celebrity** program features frequent appearances by stars such as Betty White, Burt Reynolds, Joan Collins, Leonard Nimoy, and Billy Dee Williams. They appear at attractions, record their handprints in front of the Chinese Theatre, and appear at question-and-answer sessions with park guests. Check your entertainment schedule to see if it's on. Kids ages 10 and up will enjoy it.

The **Honey, I Shrunk the Kids Movie Set,** an 11,000–square-foot playground based on the film, is located near New York Street. Everything in it is larger than life and will appeal to kids ages 2 to 10. A thicket of grass is 30 feet tall, mushroom caps are three stories high, and a friendly "ant" makes a suitable seat. Play areas—enhanced by sounds such as the buzzing of giant crickets and bees—include a massive cream cookie, a 52-foot garden hose (with leaks), cereal loops 9 feet in diameter (cushioned for jumping), a waterfall cascading from a leaf to a dell of fern sprouts (the sprouts form a musical stairway, activated when guests step from sprout to sprout), a root maze with a flower-petal slide, a "filmstrip" slide in a giant Kodak film can, and a huge spider web with 11 levels to climb.

Centering on a gleaming $14^1/_2$-foot bronze Emmy, the **Academy of Television Arts & Sciences Hall of Fame Plaza,** adjacent to SuperStar Television, honors TV legends. Bronze statues of television luminaries Carol Burnett, Sid Caesar, James Garner, Andy Griffith, Barbara Walters, Rod Serling, Bill Cosby, Mary Tyler Moore, Red Skelton, Danny Thomas, and Milton Berle are displayed, along with one of Walt Disney. This is really for adults; kids may not know all these names yet. Additional statues will be added each year. ATAS holds its annual Hall of Fame induction ceremonies at the Disney–MGM Studios.

Ace Ventura—When Nature Calls is a 20-minute show featuring a Jim Carrey look-alike who roars onto the set in an old jalopy, coming to a crashing halt. He performs his typically zany antics, does stunts, and gives wiseass answers to an interviewer. After the show, he poses for photos and signs autographs. For ages 6 to 14.

SHOPPING AT DISNEY–MGM STUDIOS

There's some really interesting shopping here. The **Animation Gallery** carries collectible cels, books about animation, arts-and-crafts kits for future animators, and collector figurines.

Sid Cahuenga's One-of-a-Kind sells autographed photos of the stars, original movie posters, and star-touched items such as a bracelet that once belonged to Joan Rivers.

Over at **Cover Story,** you can have your photograph put on the cover of your favorite magazine, anything from *Forbes* to *Psychology Today* to *Golf Digest.* Costumes are available.

Celebrity 5 & 10, modeled after a 1940s Woolworth's, has movie-related merchandise: *Gone With the Wind* memorabilia, MGM Studio T-shirts, movie posters, Elvis mugs, and more.

And major park attractions all have complementary merchandise outlets selling Indiana Jones adventure clothing, *Little Mermaid* stuffed characters and logo-wear, *Star Wars* souvenirs, and so on.

6 Animal Kingdom

Disney's fourth major park combines animals, elaborate landscapes, and rides to create yet another reason not to venture outside of the Disney world.

Slated to open in early 1998, Animal Kingdom is divided into three "regions," one dedicated to the wildlife in Africa today, one to mythical creatures such as unicorns and dragons, and the third focusing on extinction. The park covers more than 500 acres, nearly twice the size of Epcot.

At the heart of it all is a 14-story "Tree of Life," an intricately carved free-form representation of animals hand-crafted by Disney artists. This impressive landmark is nearly as tall and as imposing as the silver golf-ball dome, also known as Spaceship Earth, that has come to best symbolize Epcot.

Things are hush-hush about the exact nature of the wildlife and exhibits, but it is obvious from the heavy emphasis on conservation and education that Disney is directly entering into competition with the other animal parks, Sea World and Busch Gardens. The preopening publicity has centered on the heavily credentialed experts who have been brought in to run the park, and the emphasis has been on its zoological aspects over its entertainment value.

Although it's uncertain whether it can immediately challenge those parks, which over the years have honed their eco-entertainment theme, it will be interesting to see how Disney integrates the wonders of nature with the magic of make-believe. At press time, individual attractions and rides were still being kept under wraps. In the next edition of *Frommer's Walt Disney World & Orlando,* we'll give you the complete rundown of each attraction and show by name, with all the useful details you've come to expect from us.

7 Other WDW Attractions

TYPHOON LAGOON

Ahoy swimmers, floaters, run-aground boaters!
A furious storm once roared 'cross the sea
Catching ships in its path, helpless to flee. . .
Instead of a certain and watery doom
The winds swept them here to TYPHOON LAGOON.

Such is the Disney legend relating to Typhoon Lagoon, which you'll see posted on consecutive signs as you enter the park. Located off Lake Buena Vista Drive, half-way between Walt Disney World Village and Disney–MGM Studios, this is the ultimate in water theme parks. Its fantasy setting is a palm-fringed tropical island village of ramshackle, tin-roofed structures, strewn with cargo, surfboards, and other marine wreckage left by the "great typhoon." A storm-stranded fishing boat dangles precariously atop the 95-foot–high Mount Mayday, the steep setting for several major park attractions. Every half hour the boat's smokestack erupts, shooting a 50-foot geyser of water into the air.

ESSENTIALS

HOURS   The park is open from 10am to 5pm most of the year (with extended hours during some holiday periods), 9am to 8pm in the summer.

ENTRANCE FEES   A 1-day ticket to Typhoon Lagoon is $26.45 for adults, $20.67 for children.

HELPFUL HINTS   In summer, arrive no later than 9am to avoid long lines. The park is often filled to capacity by 10am and closed to later arrivals. Beach towels and lockers can be obtained for a minimal fee, and all beach accessories can be purchased at Singapore Sal's. Light fare is available at two eateries—**Leaning Palms** and **Typhoon Tillie's Galley and Grog**—a beach bar called **Let's Go Slurpin'** sells beer and soft drinks, and there are also picnic tables (consider bringing picnic fare; you can keep it in your locker until lunchtime). Guests are not permitted to bring their own flotation devices into the park.

ATTRACTIONS IN THE PARK

Castaway Creek

Hop onto a raft or inner tube and meander along this 2,100-foot lazy river. Circling the lagoon, Castaway Creek tumbles through a misty rain forest, past caves and se-cluded grottoes. It has a theme area called Water Works, where jets of water spew from shipwrecked boats and a Rube Goldberg assemblage of broken bamboo pipes and buckets sprays and dumps water on passersby. There are exits along the route where you can leave the creek; if you do the whole thing, it takes about a half hour. Tubes are complimentary.

Ketchakiddie Creek

Many of the other attractions require guests to be at least 4 feet tall. This section of the park is a kiddie area exclusively for those *under* 4 feet. An innovative water playground, it has bubbling fountains to frolic in, mini–water slides, a pint-size white-water tubing adventure, spouting whales and squirting seals, rubbery crocodiles to climb on, grottoes to explore, and waterfalls to loll under.

Shark Reef

Guests are given free snorkel equipment (and instruction) for a 15-minute swim through this 362,000-gallon simulated coral-reef tank populated by about 4,000 rainbow parrot fish, queen angelfish, yellowtail damselfish, rock beauties, blue tang, puddingwife fish, and other colorful denizens of the deep. Underwater scenery includes shipwrecked boats, and there's a rock waterfall at one end. If you don't want to get in the water, you can observe the fish via portholes in a walk-through area. Shark Reef is housed in a sunken upside-down tanker.

Typhoon Lagoon

This large and lovely lagoon, the size of two football fields and surrounded by white sandy beach (complete with volleyball setup), is the park's main swimming area. The chlorinated water's turquoise hue evokes the Caribbean. Large waves for surfing and bobbing crash against the shore every 90 seconds. A foghorn sounds to warn you when a wave is coming. Young children can wade in the lagoon's more peaceful tidal pools—Blustery Bay or Whitecap Cove.

Water Slides

Humunga Kowabunga consists of two 214-foot Mount Mayday water slides that drop you down the mountain before rushing into a cave and out again at 30 miles per hour. Three longer (about 300 ft. each) but less steep slides—Jib Jammer, Rudder Buster, and Stern Burner—take you on a serpentine route through waterfalls and bat caves, past nautical wreckage at about 20 miles per hour before depositing you in a bubbling catch pool; each offers slightly different views and thrills. There's seating for nonparticipatory parents whose kids have commissioned them to "watch me."

White-Water Rides

Mount Mayday is the setting for three white-water rafting adventures—Keelhaul Falls, Mayday Falls, and Gangplank Falls—all of them offering steep drops, coursing through caves, and passing lush scenery. Keelhaul Falls has the most winding spiral route, Mayday Falls the steepest drops and fastest water, while the slightly tamer Gangplank Falls uses large tubes so the whole family can ride together.

BLIZZARD BEACH

Blizzard Beach is Disney's newest water park—a 66-acre "ski resort" in the midst of a tropical lagoon. The park centers on a 90-foot snowcapped mountain (Mount Gushmore), which swimmers ascend via chairlifts, and the on-premises restaurant resembles a ski lodge. At the base of Mount Gushmore is a sandy beach with several other attractions, including a wave pool and a scaled-down version of Mount Gushmore for younger children. The park is located on World Drive, just north of the All-Star Sports and Music resorts.

ESSENTIALS

HOURS   The park is open from 10am to 5pm most of the year (with extended hours during some holiday periods), 9am to 8pm in the summer.

ENTRANCE FEES   A 1-day ticket to Blizzard Beach is $26.45 for adults, $20.67 for children.

HELPFUL HINTS   Arrive at or before park opening to avoid long lines and to be sure you get in. Beach towels and lockers are available for a small charge, and you can buy beach accessories at the Beach Haus.

MAJOR ATTRACTIONS IN THE PARK

Cross Country Creek
Inner tubers can float lazily along this meandering 2,900-foot creek, which circles the entire park, but beware: It will take you inside a mysterious cave.

Runoff Rapids
An inner-tube run, where guests can careen down four different twisting, turning flumes—sometimes in total darkness.

Ski-Patrol Training Camp
Designed for preteens, it features a rope swing, a T-bar drop over water, slides (including the wet and slippery Mogul Mania), and a challenging ice-floe walk along slippery floating icebergs.

Slush Gusher
Another Mount Gushmore speed slide (a bit tamer than the above) that travels along a snowbanked mountain gully.

Snow Stormers
Three flumes descending from the top of Mount Gushmore and following a switchback course through ski-type slalom gates.

Summit Plummet
Starting 120 feet up, this is a speed slide/thrill ride that makes a 55-mph plunge straight down to a splash landing at the base of the mountain.

Teamboat Springs
The world's longest white-water raft ride, with six-passenger rafts twisting down a 1,200-foot series of rushing waterfalls.

Toboggan Racers
An eight-lane water slide that sends guests racing head first over exhilarating dips as they descend a snowy slope.

RIVER COUNTRY

One of the many recreational facilities at the Fort Wilderness Resort campground, this mini–water park is themed after Tom Sawyer's swimming hole. Kids can scramble over boulders that double as diving platforms for a 330,000-gallon pool. Two 16-foot water slides also provide access to the pool. Attractions on the adjacent Bay Lake, which is equipped with ropes and ships' booms for climbing, include a pair of flumes—one 260 feet long, the other 100 feet—that corkscrew through Whoop-N-Holler Hollow; White Water Rapids, which carries inner tubers along a winding, 230-foot creek with a series of chutes and pools; and The Ol' Wading Pool, a smaller version of the swimming hole designed for young children.

There are pool and beachside areas for sunning and picnicking, plus a 350-yard boardwalk nature trail through a cypress swamp. Beach towels and lockers can be obtained for a minimal fee. Light fare is available at **Pop's Place.** To get here without a car, take a launch from the dock near the entrance to the Magic Kingdom or a bus from its Transportation and Ticket Center. River Country is generally open from 10am to 5pm most of the year (with extended hours during holidays), 10am to 7pm during the summer. A 1-day admission to River Country is $16.91 for adults, $13.25 for children.

DISCOVERY ISLAND

This lush, tropical 11½-acre zoological sanctuary—just a short boat ride away from the Magic Kingdom entrance, the Contemporary Resort, or Fort Wilderness Resort—provides a tranquil counterpoint to Disney World dazzle.

Plan to spend a leisurely afternoon strolling its scenic, mile-long nature trail, which, shaded by a canopy of trees, winds past gurgling streams, groves of palm and bamboo, ponds and lagoons filled with ducks and trumpeter swans, a bay that is a breeding ground for brown pelicans, and colonies of rose-hued flamingos. Peacocks roam free, and aviaries house close to 100 species of colorful exotic birds, including macaws, cockatoos, roseate spoonbills, scarlet ibis, kookaburras, bald eagles, toucans, parrots, partridges, king vultures, East African crowned cranes, and white-crested hornbills. Discovery Island denizens also include Patagonian cavies (they're a kind of guinea pig), alligators and caimans, Galápagos tortoises, small primates, and muntjac miniature deer from Southeast Asia.

Two different bird shows and a reptile show are scheduled several times throughout the day; they take place outdoors with seating on log benches. Guests can also look through a viewing area to see the nursery complex of the island's animal hospital, where baby birds and mammals are often hand-raised. Also new is a miniature golf course designed in the spirit of the Disney Classic *Fantasia*. Discovery Island is generally open from 10am to 5pm most of the year (with extended hours during holidays), 10am to 7pm during the summer. A 1-day admission to Discovery Island is $12.67 for adults, $6.89 for children.

8 What to See & Do Beyond Disney: Universal Studios, Sea World & Other Orlando Attractions

Locals call it the theme-park wars, the ongoing "anything-you-can-do-I-can-do-better" tussle between the Walt Disney properties and the many other Orlando-area attractions. Universal Studios Florida is the biggest challenger to Disney, opening its own nighttime entertainment complex and (soon) its first on-property resort and (in 1999) a second theme park. But, recognizing there is strength in numbers, Universal, Sea World, and several other major attractions each now offer their own multiday passes to compete with WDW.

And while the wars rage on in the traditional tourist areas, it seems—finally—it has dawned on the rest of Orlando that central Florida is one of the world's favorite vacation destinations.

Downtown Orlando has in the last decade undergone a major resurgence, with thousands regularly crowding its streets, nightclubs, and restaurants. Recent multimillion-dollar expansions at the Orlando Museum of Art and the Orlando Science Center show that the city is stepping up to compete.

This all means that visitors can enjoy the spoils: more variety, greater opportunities, and a world beyond Disney.

1 Universal Studios Florida

Universal Studios Florida bills itself as the "No. 1 Movie Studio and Theme Park in the World." While it is a working motion-picture and television production studio, most of the production goes on inside on the Nickelodeon soundstages, so for all intents and purposes, this is a theme park. Remember cable's "The Swamp Thing," "Clarissa Explains It All," or the short-lived "SeaQuest"? Those television series were shot on the property. Occasionally, visitors will come upon an actual working shoot. But every day you will amble amid reel history displayed in the form of some 40 actual sets displayed along "Hollywood Boulevard" and "Rodeo Drive." On hand to greet visitors are Hanna-Barbera characters (Yogi Bear, Scooby Doo, Fred Flintstone, and others) and a talented group of actors representing Universal stars from Harpo Marx to the Blues Brothers.

Orlando Area Attractions

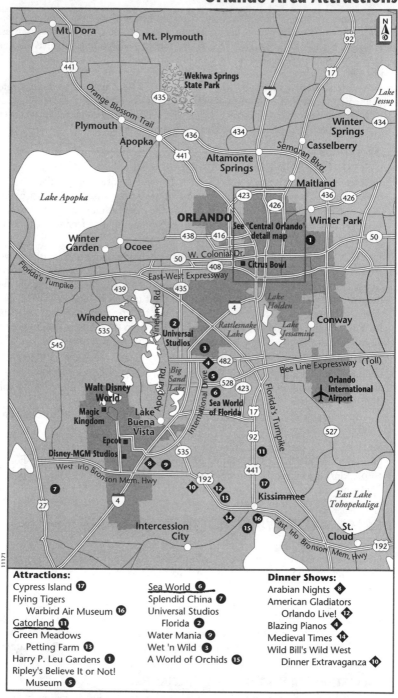

Attractions:

Cypress Island ⑰
Flying Tigers
  Warbird Air Museum ⑯
Gatorland ⑪
Green Meadows
  Petting Farm ⑬
Harry P. Leu Gardens ❶
Ripley's Believe It or Not!
  Museum ❺

Sea World ❻
Splendid China ❼
Universal Studios
  Florida ❷
Water Mania ❾
Wet 'n Wild ❸
A World of Orchids ⑮

Dinner Shows:

Arabian Nights ❽
American Gladiators
  Orlando Live! ⑫
Blazing Pianos ❹
Medieval Times ⑭
Wild Bill's Wild West
  Dinner Extravaganza ❿

The long-running Ghostbusters attraction has been closed. (Now who we gonna call?) Blowing into its place is an attraction based on one of 1996's blockbusters: "Twister, the Ride," is based on *Twister,* the movie, which brought Universal more than $245 million at the box office. The breezy encounter with a tornado will open in 1998.

A more impressive expansion will continue in 1999 as Universal opens its second theme park, Islands of Adventure. It will also go head-to-head with the competition with its first on-site resort property, à la Disney. We'll give you all the inside information on both of these as soon as information becomes available.

ESSENTIALS

GETTING TO UNIVERSAL BY CAR   Universal is about half a mile north of I-4 Exit 30B, Kirkman Road or Route 435. This is the exit leading to the main entrance, but it is very confusing because you follow the signs past the entrance, turn right, and continue to follow the signs around the block. After getting off the interstate, get into the far right lane and, although you are right in feeling that you are going in the wrong direction, follow the signs.

PARKING   Universal's surface lot is not overwhelmingly large and is also not well marked, so write down where you leave your car. If you park in the new, multilevel garage (which opened in December 1996), remember the theme and music on your floor to help you later identify your car. Or, do it the old-fashioned way: Write it down. Parking costs $5 for cars, $7 for RVs and trailers. Valet parking is available for $11. (By the way, this garage is one of the largest in the country, holding nearly 20,000 cars; a second will open along with the new theme park in 1999.)

TICKET PRICES   A **1-day ticket** costs $40.81 for ages 10 and over, $32.86 for children 3 to 9; a **2-day ticket** is $55 for ages 10 and over, $44 for children 3 to 9; an **annual pass** (admission for a full year) is $69 for ages 10 and over, $59 for children 3 to 9; children 2 and under enter free.

There is also a **VIP tour** available, which includes line-cutting privileges for about $100 per person.

HOURS   The park is open 365 days a year, generally from 9am to 7pm. Closing hours vary seasonally and depending on special activities within the park. For example, during Halloween Horror Nights the park closes around 5pm, reopens at 7pm, and remains open until at least midnight. The best bet is to call before you go so as not to be caught by surprise.

TIPS FOR MAKING YOUR VISIT MORE ENJOYABLE
PLAN YOUR VISIT

Get information before you leave by calling **Guest Relations** at (☎ **407/363-8000**). Request information about the new travel packages, as well as theme-park information.

ON-LINE   Information about Universal Studios can be found at **http://www.usf.com**. Orlando's daily newspaper, the *Orlando Sentinel,* also produces *Orlando Sentinel Online* at **http://www.oso@aol.com**. Once there, click into "Theme Park Central" for a variety of information and updates on what is going on at local attractions.

INFORMATION FOR VISITORS WITH SPECIAL NEEDS

Guests with disabilities should go to Guest Services located just inside the main entrance for a *Disabled Guest Guidebook,* a Telecommunications Device for the Deaf (TDD), or other special assistance. Wheelchairs are for rent at the park.

BEST TIME OF YEAR TO VISIT

As with Walt Disney World, there is really no "off" season for Universal, but during the winter months, usually from January through April, the park crowds are smallest, the weather coolest, and the air least humid. The summer months, when the masses throng to the park, are not only crowded but uncomfortably hot, sticky, and humid. During the cooler months, you also don't have to worry about the daily summer storms. Avoid spring-break months.

THE BEST DAYS TO VISIT

Go near the end of the week, Thursday or Friday. The pace is somewhat faster between Monday and Wednesday, with heavy crowds on weekends.

CREATE AN ITINERARY

Pick three or four things that you must see or do and plan your day, along a rough geographical guide. Universal is relatively small, so walking from one end of the park to the other is not that daunting.

CHOOSE AGE-APPROPRIATE RIDES/SHOWS

Here, as in Disney, height and age restrictions are not bent to accommodate your screaming child. Some of the Universal shows contain loud music and pyrotechnics that can frighten children. The same is true of the end-of-the day "Stuntacular." Check the attraction descriptions below to make sure your child won't be unduly disappointed or frightened.

SUGGESTED INTINERARY

A single day is usually sufficient to see the park if you arrive early. Skip the city sidewalks of the main gate and **Terminator 2: 3-D Battle Across Time** and veer to the left (clockwise) toward **Murder She Wrote Mystery Theatre, Alfred Hitchcock: The Art of Making Movies,** or the **Funtastic World of Hanna-Barbera.** Continue around the park in this direction, beating the crowd to the blockbuster rides **Kongfrontation, Jaws,** and **Earthquake.** Take a break for lunch, watch the **Wild West Stunt Show,** and move on to **Back to the Future** and **ET Adventure.** Let the kids burn off some energy in **Fievel's Playland** and go to **Terminator 2.** You may have some time before the stunt show to visit a few other attractions. If speed boats and explosions don't excite you, skip the show and revisit your favorite attractions, or beat the crowd to the parking lot.

A second day will allow you to revisit some of the blockbuster rides. Most of them, especially **Back to the Future,** are worth a second trip. With the pressure to hit all the major rides lessened, tour **Nickelodeon Studios.** This is a must if you have kids, who no doubt will be able to tell you a thing or two about this kids' network. Visitors often have a chance to participate in the taping of some of Nick's often sloppy game shows. Also visit the **Gory, Gruesome & Grotesque Horror-Makeup Show,** and take a break at **Mel's Diner** and shows such as the **Beetlejuice Graveyard Revue.**

SERVICES & FACILITIES IN THE PARK

ATMs   Machines accepting cards from banks using the Cirrus, Honor, and Plus systems are located outside of the main entrance and just inside the main entrance.

Baby Care   Changing tables are in both men's and women's rest rooms; there are nursing facilities at Guest Relations just inside the main entrance and to the right.

Universal Studios Theme Park

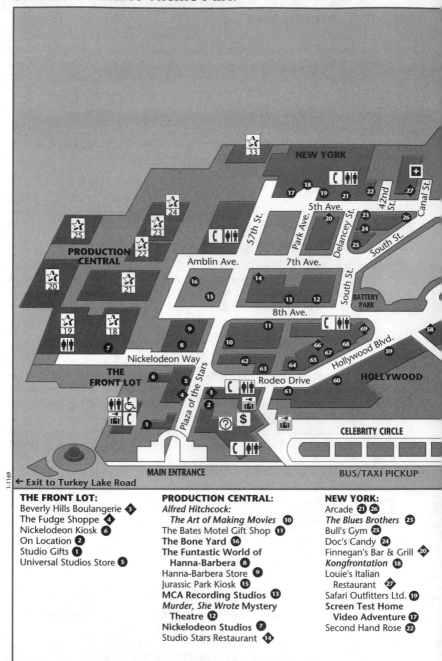

THE FRONT LOT:
Beverly Hills Boulangerie **3**
The Fudge Shoppe **4**
Nickelodeon Kiosk **6**
On Location **2**
Studio Gifts **1**
Universal Studios Store **5**

PRODUCTION CENTRAL:
Alfred Hitchcock:
   The Art of Making Movies **10**
The Bates Motel Gift Shop **11**
The Bone Yard **16**
The Funtastic World of
   Hanna-Barbera **8**
Hanna-Barbera Store **9**
Jurassic Park Kiosk **15**
MCA Recording Studios **13**
Murder, She Wrote **Mystery**
   Theatre **12**
Nickelodeon Studios **7**
Studio Stars Restaurant **14**

NEW YORK:
Arcade **21 26**
The Blues Brothers **23**
Bull's Gym **25**
Doc's Candy **24**
Finnegan's Bar & Grill **20**
Kongfrontation **18**
Louie's Italian
   Restaurant **27**
Safari Outfitters Ltd. **19**
Screen Test Home
   Video Adventure **17**
Second Hand Rose **22**

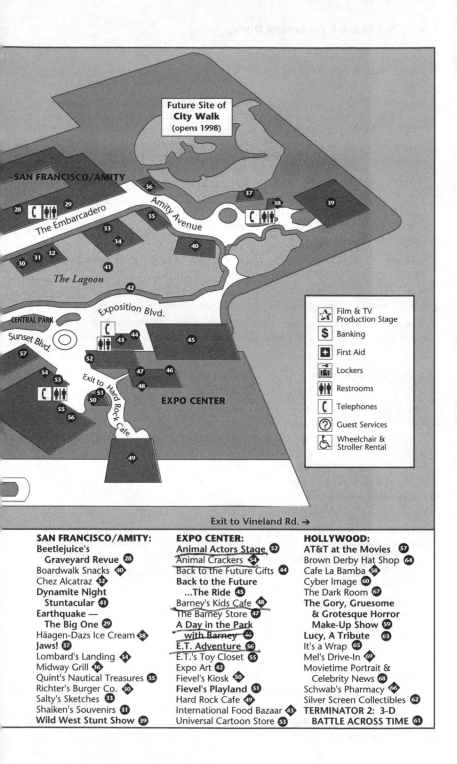

Future Site of City Walk (opens 1998)

SAN FRANCISCO/AMITY

28 **C** 🚻 29
The Embarcadero
36
Amity Avenue
37
38 **C** 🚻
39
35
33
34
40
30 31 32
41
The Lagoon
42
Exposition Blvd.
CENTRAL PARK
Sunset Blvd.
C
43 44
45
57
52
47 46
54 53
48
Exit to Hard Rock Cafe
C 🚻
50 51
EXPO CENTER
55 56
49

Exit to Vineland Rd. →

⭐	Film & TV Production Stage
$	Banking
➕	First Aid
🖼️	Lockers
🚻	Restrooms
C	Telephones
?	Guest Services
♿	Wheelchair & Stroller Rental

SAN FRANCISCO/AMITY:
Beetlejuice's
 Graveyard Revue 28
Boardwalk Snacks 40
Chez Alcatraz 32
Dynamite Night
 Stuntacular 41
Earthquake —
 The Big One 29
Häagen-Dazs Ice Cream 48
Jaws! 37
Lombard's Landing 34
Midway Grill 36
Quint's Nautical Treasures 35
Richter's Burger Co. 30
Salty's Sketches 33
Shaiken's Souvenirs 31
Wild West Stunt Show 39

EXPO CENTER:
Animal Actors Stage 52
Animal Crackers 54
Back to the Future Gifts 44
Back to the Future
 ...The Ride 45
Barney's Kids Cafe 48
The Barney Store 47
A Day in the Park
 with Barney 46
E.T. Adventure 56
E.T.'s Toy Closet 55
Expo Art 42
Fievel's Kiosk 50
Fievel's Playland 51
Hard Rock Cafe 49
International Food Bazaar 43
Universal Cartoon Store 53

HOLLYWOOD:
AT&T at the Movies 57
Brown Derby Hat Shop 64
Cafe La Bamba 58
Cyber Image 60
The Dark Room 67
The Gory, Gruesome
 & Grotesque Horror
 Make-Up Show 59
Lucy, A Tribute 63
It's a Wrap 65
Mel's Drive-In 69
Movietime Portrait &
 Celebrity News 68
Schwab's Pharmacy 66
Silver Screen Collectibles 62
TERMINATOR 2: 3-D
 BATTLE ACROSS TIME 61

177

No diapers are sold on the premises, but complimentary diapers are available to guests in need at the Animal House, Doc's Candy Store, and the Universal Studios Store.

Cameras & Film   Camcorders are for rent, and film and disposable cameras are available at the Lights, Camera, Action shop in the Front Lot, just inside the main entrance. One-hour photo developing is available in the Darkroom.

First Aid   The First Aid Center is located between New York and San Francisco, next to Louie's Italian Restaurant.

Lockers   Lockers are across from Guest Relations near the main entrance and cost $1 a day.

Lost Children   If you lose a child, go to Guest Relations near the main entrance or to Security (behind Louie's, between New York and San Francisco). Children under 7 should wear name tags.

Pet Care   An indoor/outdoor kennel is available for $5 a day near the newest parking lot. Ask the attendant for directions upon entering the toll plaza.

Stroller Rental   Strollers can be rented in Amity and at Guest Relations just inside the entrance to the right. The cost is $6 for a single, $12 for a double.

Wheelchair Rental   Regular wheelchairs can be rented for $6 in Amity and at Guest Relations just inside the main gate. Electric wheelchairs are $30, with a $25 deposit.

MAJOR ATTRACTIONS

Rides and attractions utilize cutting-edge technology—such as OMNIMAX 70mm film projected on seven-story screens—to create terrific special effects. While waiting in line, you'll be entertained by excellent preshows, better even than those at that *other* theme park. Universal, as a whole, takes itself less seriously than the Mouse that Roared, and the atmosphere is peppered by subtle reminders that in the competitive 1990s it is not a small world after all.

Back to the Future: The Ride
Recommended ages: 8–adult

Visitors blast through the space-time continuum, plummeting into volcanic tunnels ablaze with molten lava, colliding with Ice Age glaciers, thundering through caves and canyons, and briefly being swallowed by a dinosaur in a spectacular multisensory adventure. You twist, you turn, you dip and dive, and feel like you are really flying. Stick to seats in the back of the car to avoid ruining the illusion by glimpsing your neighbors careening hydraulically in the next bay. This is a very bumpy ride and might not be appropriate for those with certain health problems. Note the posted warnings displayed at the ride. Children must be 40 inches tall.

The Beetlejuice Graveyard Revue
Recommended ages: 6–adult

Dracula, Wolfman, the Phantom of the Opera, Frankenstein and his bride, and Beetlejuice put on a funky—and very funny—rock musical with pyrotechnic special effects and MTV-style choreography. Loud and lively enough to scare some small children.

A Day in the Park with Barney
Recommended ages: all ages

City Walk

While many details were not available at press time, this 12-acre entertainment complex could easily be renamed theme-restaurant heaven. Not only is it home to the world's largest **Hard Rock Cafe**—the grande dame of all theme restaurants—but also the **NASCAR Cafe,** the **Motown Cafe,** and **Marvel Mania,** a theme send-up to villains and superheroes. City Walk, which opens in early 1998, also contains a hearty dose of Cajun spice with **Pat O'Brien's,** a re-creation of the joint in New Orleans, and **Emeril's of New Orleans,** featuring the Creole-based cuisine of chef Emeril Lagasse. If that's not enough to keep you busy, there is the **Down Beat Jazz Hall of Fame,** a tribute to reggae *mon* Bob Marley, and a 5,000-seat **Cineplex Odeon Megaplex.**

Finally, celebrity hounds may catch a live taping involving one of their favorite stars at the **E! Entertainment Television Production Center.**

Detailed reviews of all these establishments will appear in the next edition of *Frommer's Walt Disney World & Orlando.*

Set in a parklike theater-in-the-round, this musical show—starring the popular purple one, Baby Bop, and BJ—uses song, dance, and interactive play to deliver an environmental message. For young children, this could be the highlight of the day.

✪ Earthquake—The Big One
Recommended ages: 6–adult

You board a BART train in San Francisco for a peaceful subway ride, but just as you pull into the Embarcadero station there's an earthquake—the big one, 8.3 on the Richter scale! As you sit helplessly trapped, vast slabs of concrete collapse around you, a propane truck bursts into flames, a runaway train comes hurtling at you, and the station floods (60,000 gallons of water cascade down the steps). Children must be 40 inches tall and must ride with an adult.

E.T. Adventure
Recommended ages: all ages

Visitors are given a passport to E.T.'s planet, which needs his healing powers to rejuvenate it. You'll soar with E.T. on a mission to save his ailing planet, through the forest and into space, aboard a star-bound bicycle—all to the accompaniment of that familiar movie theme music. A cool, wooded forest serves to create one of the most pleasant waits for any ride in central Florida. This is a wait worth the ride; a pleasure for kids of all ages.

The Funtastic World of Hanna-Barbera
Recommended ages: 5–adult

This motion-simulator ride takes guests careening through the universe in a spaceship piloted by Yogi Bear to rescue Elroy Jetson. Prior to this wild ride, you'll learn about how cartoons are created. After it, in an interactive area, you can experiment with animation sound effects—*boing! plop! splash!*—and color in your own cartoons. This is a great place for kids of all ages to take some time and play. Although it doesn't make a lot of sense (since this is the park's most blatant kiddie ride), children must be 40 inches tall.

Jaws
Recommended ages: 8–adult

Did you really think it was safe to go back into the water? As your boat heads out to the open seas, an ominous dorsal fin appears on the horizon. What follows is a series of terrifying attacks from a 3-ton, 32-foot–long great white shark that tries to sink its teeth into passengers. And there's more trouble ahead. The boat is surrounded by a 30-foot wall of flame from burning fuel that lets you truly feel the heat. I won't tell you how it ends, but let's just say, blackened shark, anyone? (The effects are more startling after dark.)

✪ Kongfrontation
Recommended ages: 6–adult

It's the last thing the Big Apple needed: King Kong is back! As you stand in line in a replica of a grungy, graffiti-scarred New York subway station, CBS newsman Roland Smith reports on Kong's terrifying rampage. Everyone must evacuate to Roosevelt Island, so it's all aboard the tram. Cars collide and hydrants explode below, police helicopters hover overhead putting you directly in the line of fire, the tram malfunctions, and, of course, you encounter Kong—32 feet tall and 13,000 pounds. He emits banana breath in your face and menaces passengers, dangling the tram over the East River. A great thrill—or just another day in New York. Children must be 40 inches tall to ride alone. Younger children may be frightened by the dark waiting area.

Nickelodeon Studios Tour
Recommended ages: all ages

You'll tour the soundstages where Nick shows are produced, view concept pilots, visit the kitchen where gak and green slime are made, play typical show games, and try out new Sega video games. There's lots of audience participation, and a volunteer will get slimed.

Terminator 2: 3-D Battle Across Time
Recommended ages: 8–adult

He's back. . . at least in Orlando. This is billed as "the quintessential sight and sound experience for the 21st century!" The same director who made the movie, Jim Cameron, has overseen this production. It features the Big Man himself, along with other original cast members, and combines 70mm 3-D film (utilizing three 23- by 50-foot screens) with live stage action and thrilling technical effects. This ride is probably rated PG for violence and loud noise. Small children may find it to be too much.

Wild, Wild, Wild West Show
Recommended ages: all ages

Stunt people demonstrate falls from three-story balconies, gun and whip fights, dynamite explosions, and other oater staples. This is a well-performed, lively show that is especially popular with foreign visitors who have celluloid visions of the American West. Kids, do not try this at home. *Warning:* Heed the splash zone or you will get very wet.

ADDITIONAL ATTRACTIONS

Other park attractions include the **Gory, Gruesome & Grotesque Horror-Makeup Show** for a behind-the-scenes look at the transformation scenes from movies like *The Fly* and *The Exorcist;* **"I Love Lucy," A Tribute,** a remembrance of America's queen of comedy; **Fievel's Playland,** an innovative western-themed playground based on the Spielberg movie *An American Tail;* the **"Murder She Wrote" Mystery Theatre,** which puts you on the set with Angela Lansbury and lets you make postproduction executive decisions via computer; and **Alfred Hitchcock: The Art of Making Movies,** a tribute to the "master of suspense" in which Tony Perkins narrates a reenactment of the famous shower scene from *Psycho,* and *The Birds*—as if it weren't scary enough—becomes an in-your-face 3-D movie. You might also catch the **Blues Brothers show** or take a look at old movie props in the **Bone Yard.**

Descendants of Lassie, Benji, Mr. Ed, and other animal superstars perform their famous pet tricks in the **Animal Actors Show.** During **Screen Test Home Video Adventure,** a director, crew, and team of "cinemagicians" put visitors on the screen in an exciting video production. And **Dynamite Nights Stuntacular,** a nightly show, combines death-defying stunts with a breathtaking display of fireworks.

SHOPPING AT UNIVERSAL

Every major attraction here (thoughtfully) has a themed store attached. Although the prices are relatively high when you consider you are buying a T-shirt, the **Hard Rock Cafe** shop is extremely popular and has a small but diverse selection of Hard Rock everything. When City Walk opens, the store will relocate along with the Hard Rock Cafe. If you've often longed for a pair of Fred Flintstone boxer shorts or, perhaps, some plastic Scooby snacks, visit the **Hanna-Barbera Shop.**

More than 25 other shops in the park sell everything from Lucia collectibles to Bates Motel towels, and restaurants run the gamut from **Mel's Drive-In** (of *American Graffiti* fame) to the **Hard Rock Cafe,** to **Schwab's.** Be warned, unlike WDW where Mickey is everywhere, these shops are specific to the individual attraction. If you see something you like, buy it. You probably won't find it in another store.

2 Sea World

This popular 200-plus–acre marine-life park explores the mysteries of the deep in a format that combines entertainment with wildlife-conservation awareness. Its beautifully landscaped grounds, centering on a 17-acre lagoon, include flamingo and pelican ponds and a lush tropical rain forest. Shamu, a killer whale, is the star of the park along with his expanding family, which includes several baby whales. The pace is much more laid-back than either Universal or Disney, and it's a good way to end a long week of trudging through other parks. Be sure to budget some extra money to buy smelt to feed the animals. The close encounters offered at many wading and feeding pools are the real attraction here and more than half the fun. Sea World can't compete with the high-tech wonders abounding elsewhere, but where else can you discover that a stingray feels like crushed velvet or learn the song of a seal?

The last several years have seen the park not only expand but renovate. If you haven't been there in a while, it is worth a visit. During 1997 Sea World will open its first major thrill ride, a major roller coaster with record-breaking twists and turns. Although details of the new attraction weren't available at press time, word is that Sea World, owned by Anheuser-Busch, the same folks who operate Busch Gardens, got some pointers from the engineers who have created wonderful, gut-wrenching thrill rides such as Kumba.

ESSENTIALS

GETTING TO SEA WORLD BY CAR   Take I-4 to the Bee Line Expressway (Fla. 528) and follow the signs. It may look like you are going the wrong way, but don't despair, as long as you see the signs.

PARKING   Parking costs $5 per car, $7 for RVs and trailers. The lots are not huge, and you can walk into the park. Trams also run. Note the location of your car. Sections are marked by Sea World characters like Wally Walrus.

TICKET PRICES   A **1-day ticket** costs $39.95 for ages 10 and over, $32.80 for children 3 to 9; a **2-day ticket** is $44.95 for ages 10 and over, $37.40 for children 3 to 9; children 2 and under enter free.

HOURS   The park is open from 9am to 7pm 365 days a year, and later during summer and holidays when there are additional shows at night. Call before you go.

TIPS FOR MAKING YOUR VISIT MORE ENJOYABLE

Get information before you leave by writing to **Guest Services** at 7007 Sea World Dr., Orlando, FL 32801, or call ☎ **407/351-3600.**

ON-LINE   Sea World information is available at **http://www.4adventure.com**. The Orlando daily newspaper, the *Orlando Sentinel,* also produces *Orlando Sentinel Online* at **http://www.oso@aol.com**. Once there, click on "Theme Park Central" for a variety of information and updates on what is going on at local attractions.

FOR GUESTS WITH SPECIAL NEEDS

The park publishes a guide for guests with disabilities, although most of its attractions are easily accessible to those in wheelchairs. Sea World also provides a Braille guide for the visually impaired. It also provides a very brief synopsis of shows for the hearing impaired. For information call ☎ **407/351-2600.**

BEST TIME OF YEAR TO VISIT

Since this is a mostly outdoor, water-related park, even in Florida it can get a tad nippy during February and March. As at the other parks, crowds at Sea World are smaller during the winter months; usually from January through April the park crowds are smallest, the weather coolest, and the air least humid.

BEST DAYS TO VISIT

Monday and Wednesday are busy days at this park. Thursday and Sunday are the best times to visit.

CHOOSE AGE-APPROPRIATE ACTIVITIES

Since it has few thrill rides, Sea World has few restrictions, but you may want to check out special tour programs offered through the education department.

Sea World lives up to its reputation for making education fun with a variety of tours. One of the newest, and most interesting, is the **Polar Expedition Guided Tour.** For information call ☎**407/351-2600.**

BUDGET YOUR TIME

Sea World has a naturally leisurely pace since the major attraction here is taking time to enjoy up-close encounters with the animals. Don't be in a rush. Sea World's many attractions can easily be enjoyed in a single day. The layout of the park amplifies a feeling of space, and the many outdoor exhibits give it an open feel. Because of the large capacity and walk-through nature of many attractions, crowds are generally not a concern. Although you do need to be in Shamu stadium in plenty of time for the show and Wild Arctic draws a crowd, lines seldom reach Disney proportions. So, relax. Isn't that what a vacation is supposed to be about?

Now that you know your way around, let's move on to something simple.

1 8 0 0
C A L L
A T T®

For card and collect calls.

AT&T

SERVICES & FACILITIES IN THE PARK

ATMs   An ATM machine is located at the front of the park. It accepts Cirrus, Honor, and Plus.

Baby Care   Changing tables are in or near most women's rest rooms and at the men's rest room at the front entrance near Shamu's Emporium. You can buy diapers in machines located near all changing areas and at Shamu's Emporium. There is a special area for nursing mothers near the women's rest room at Friends of the Wild gift shop, near the center of the park.

Cameras & Film   Disposable cameras are available at stores throughout the park.

First Aid   First Aid Centers staffed with registered nurses are behind Stingray Lagoon and near Shamu's Happy Harbour.

Lockers   Lockers are located next to Shamu's Emporium, just inside the park entrance. The cost is $1 a day.

Lost Children   Lost children are taken to the Information Center. A parkwide paging system helps reunite guests. Children under 7 should wear name tags.

Pet Care   A kennel is available between the parking lot and the main gate. The cost is $4 a day.

Strollers   Strollers, in the shape of dolphins, can be rented at the Information Center near the entrance. The cost is $5 for a single, $10 for a double.

Wheelchair Rental   Regular wheelchairs are available at the Information Center. Regular chairs cost $5, electric $25 with a $25 deposit and a driver's license.

MAJOR ATTRACTIONS

Baywatch Nights
Recommended ages: all ages

Actors and stunt drivers recreate some of the high-powered drama of the most popular syndicated television show in the world. Sorry, no Pamela Sue Anderson (is she still Lee?) look-alikes, but plenty of zooming motor boats. It's appropriate for everyone, but the thrill may be lost on very young children who may also find the noise unsettling. You may have read about safety problems with this show at one of the other Sea World parks—namely a boat crashing into the crowd. Following that 1996 incident, Baywatch shows in all the Sea World parks were closed while an investigation was undertaken. Some minor safety adjustments were made, and the shows have continued without problem.

Hotel Clyde & Seamore
Recommended ages: all ages

Two sea lions, along with a cast of otters and walruses, appear in this fishy "Fawlty Towers" comedy with a conservation theme. Arrive early to catch the mime doing the preshow.

✪ Key West at Sea World
Recommended ages: all ages

It's not quite the way Ernest Hemingway saw it, but this 5-acre paved paradise dotted with palms, hibiscus, and bougainvillea is set in a Caribbean village offering island cuisine, street vendors, and entertainers. The attraction comprises three naturalistic animal habitats: Stingray Lagoon, where visitors enjoy hands-on encounters with harmless southern diamond and cownose rays; Dolphin Cove, a massive habitat for bottlenose dolphins set up for visitor interaction; and Sea Turtle Point, home to threatened and endangered species such as green, loggerhead, and hawksbill sea turtles. Shortly after opening, dolphins showed their intelligence by realizing how easy humans are to tease. They'd routinely swim just out of arm's reach but discovered that there are advantages to coming in a little closer, namely smelt.

Key West Dolphin Fest
Recommended ages: all ages

At the Whale and Dolphin Stadium—a big, partially covered open-air stadium—whales and Atlantic bottlenose dolphins perform flips and high jumps, swim at high speeds, twirl, swim on their backs, and give rides to trainers—all to the accompaniment of calypso music. The tricks are impressive, but go before the show-stopping behemoth, Shamu, puts these little mammals to shame.

✪ Manatees: The Last Generation
Recommended ages: all ages

Today the Florida manatee is in danger of extinction, with as few as 2,000 remaining. Underwater viewing stations, innovative cinema techniques, and interactive displays combine to create an exciting format for teaching visitors about the manatee and its fragile ecosystem. Also on display here are hundreds of other native fish as well as alligators, turtles, and shore birds. It's amazing to watch the huge beast move effortlessly through the water. There is something about this mammoth, slow-moving vegetarian that really appeals to children.

✪ Mermaids, Myths & Monsters
Recommended ages: 3–adult

This nighttime multimedia spectacular is a must-see, featuring fireworks and hologramlike imagery against a towering 60-foot screen of illuminated water. King Neptune rises majestically from the deep, as do terrifying sea serpents, storm-tossed ships, and frolicking mermaids. It is one of the most innovative closing shows in recent years. While it doesn't have the explosive power of the Disney fireworks, its quieter grace is in keeping with the overall laid-back Sea World theme. Small children may be frightened by the large, moving figures (which appear quite real) walking over the water.

✪ Penguin Encounter
Recommended ages: all ages

This display of hundreds of penguins and alcids, another species of aquatic birds (including adorable babies) native to the Antarctic and Arctic regions, also serves as a living laboratory for protecting and preserving polar life. On a moving walkway, you'll view six different penguin species congregating on rocks, nesting, and swimming underwater. There's an additional area for puffins and murres (flying Arctic cousins of penguins).

Shamu's Happy Harbor
Recommended ages: children of all ages

This 3-acre play area has a four-story net tower with a 35-foot crow's-nest lookout, water cannons, remote-controlled vehicles, and a water maze. It's one of the most extensive play areas at any park and a great place to burn off some energy between sitting in shows. Bring extra clothes for the tots (or for yourself) because this place isn't designed to keep you dry.

Shamu: World Focus
Recommended ages: all ages

Sea World trainers develop close relationships with killer whales, and in this partly covered open-air stadium, they direct performances that are extensions of natural cetacean behaviors—twirling, waving tails and fins, rotating while swimming, and splashing the audience. Splash zones are clearly marked. Sit in the upper tiers if you don't want to get soaked. The evening show here, called "Shamu: Night Magic," utilizes rock music and special lighting effects. There is no reason to attend both shows unless you really like whales. The tricks are much the same. I'd opt for the evening show, taking advantage of shorter lines as others flock to the stadium in the afternoon. If you do decide on the afternoon show, arrive at least 30 minutes early. The stadium does fill up.

Shamu: Close Up!, an adjoining exhibit, lets you get close up to killer whales and talk to trainers; don't miss the underwater viewing area here and a chance to see a mother whale with her offspring. Talk about a big baby.

Swim with the Dolphins
Recommended ages: adults

Since late 1996 a few lucky visitors have been able to don wet suits and join some of Flipper's cousins for an up-close encounter. This effort is modeled after a similar program started in Sea World San Diego in 1995. Animal-rights activists have voiced some concerns, but Sea World argues that the health and well-being of the dolphins is of the utmost importance and is maintained. Most guests pay about $125 for a chance to interact with the dolphins under the watchful eyes of their trainers. (Annual-pass holders pay less.) Call ahead for information.

Terrors of the Deep
Recommended ages: 3–adult

This exhibit houses 220 specimens of venomous and otherwise scary sea creatures in a tropical-reef habitat. Immense acrylic tunnels provide close encounters with slithery eels, three dozen sharks, barracudas, lionfish, and poisonous puffer fish. A theatrical presentation focusing on sharks puts across the message that pollution and uncontrolled commercial fishing make humankind the ultimate "terror of the deep." This is not the ride for the claustrophobic, since you walk under a Plexiglas tube under hundreds of millions of gallons of water. Also, small children may find the glowing eels and skimming sharks a little too much to handle.

✪ Wild Arctic
Recommended ages: exhibit, all ages; ride, 6–adult

Enveloping guests in the beauty, exhilaration, and danger of a polar expedition, Wild Arctic combines a high-definition adventure film with flight-simulator technology to evoke breathtaking Arctic panoramas. After a hazardous flight over the frozen north, visitors emerge at a remote research base—home to four polar bears (including star residents and polar twins Klondike and Snow), seals, walruses, and white beluga whales. Kids may find the bumpy ride a little much. There is a separate line for those who want to skip the thrill-ride section.

Window to the Sea
Recommended ages: all ages

A multimedia presentation takes visitors behind the scenes at Sea World and explores a variety of marine subjects. These include an ocean dive in search of the rare six-gilled shark, a killer whale giving birth, babies born at Sea World (dolphins, penguins, walruses), dolphin anatomy, and underwater geology.

ADDITIONAL ATTRACTIONS

Although details have yet to be officially announced at press time, Sea World during late 1997 is expected to, for the first time, enter into direct competition for the ride most likely to make you loose your lunch. Rumors have it that a **roller coaster** with record-breaking turns, loops, and twists is the latest attraction.

The park's other attractions include: **Pacific Point Preserve,** a $2^1/2$-acre naturalistic setting that duplicates the rocky northern Pacific Coast home of California sea lions and harbor and fur seals; and a **Tropical Reef,** a tide pool of touchables, such as sea anemones, starfish, sea cucumbers, and sea urchins, plus a 160,000-gallon man-made coral-reef aquarium, home to 1,000 brightly hued tropical fish displayed in 17 vignettes of undersea life.

A **Hawaiian dance troupe** entertains in an outdoor facility at Hawaiian Village; if you care to join in, grass skirts and leis are available. You can ascend 400 feet to the top of the **Sea World Sky Tower** for a revolving 360° panorama of the park and beyond (there's an extra charge of $3 per person for this activity). And at the 5.5-acre **Anheuser-Busch Hospitality Center** you can try free samples of Anheuser-Busch beers and snacks, and stroll through the stables to watch the famous Budweiser Clydesdale horses being groomed. (Remember, the Bud-men of Anheuser-Busch own Sea World.)

The **Aloha! Polynesian Luau Dinner and Show,** a full-scale dinner show featuring South Seas food, song, and fire dancing, takes place nightly at 6:30pm. Park admission is not required. The cost is $29.65 for adults, $20.10 for children 8 to 12, $10.55 for children 3 to 7, and free for children 2 and under. Reservations are required (☎ **800/227-8048** or 407/363-2559).

Visitors can take 90-minute **behind-the-scenes tours** of the park's breeding, research, and training facilities and/or attend a 45-minute presentation about Sea World's animal behavior and training techniques. The cost for either tour is $5 for ages 10 and over, $4 for children 3 to 9, and free for children 2 and under. While there are several tours throughout the day, you should make a reservation when you enter the park.

SHOPPING AT SEA WORLD

This is one area where Sea World really knows better than to compete with Universal and the WDW parks. There aren't nearly as many shops, but there are lots of surprisingly cuddly aquatic-based sea creatures. Where else can you get a stuffed manatee but **Manatee Cove?** The **Friends of the Wild** gift shop near Penguin Encounters is also nice, as is the shop attached to **Wild Arctic.** And, because of the Anheuser-Busch connection, the gift shop outside the entrance to the park offers a staggering array of Budweiser-related items.

3 Other Area Attractions

IN KISSIMMEE

Kissimmee sights are close to the Walt Disney World area—about a 10- to 15-minute drive.

✪ Cypress Island

1541 Scotty's Rd., Kissimmee. ☎ **407/935-9202.** Admission $24 adults for an all-day pass, including boat ride; $17 children 3–12, under 3 free. Call for rates for additional activities. Daily 9am–5pm. Take U.S. 192 east, make a right at Shady Lane, and follow the signs.

About 12 miles from Walt Disney World, you can get a feel for old-time Florida at Cypress Island, located on Lake Tohopekaliga, the second-largest lake in central

Florida. Throughout the 1800s, the 200-acre island was a Seminole fort site, and it was the childhood home of Cacoochee, one of the last great chiefs of that tribe.

Visitors reach the island via an excursion boat that offers an ecotour narrative en route (there are frequent departures throughout the day). On arrival, you can explore (on foot or in a safari cart) 2 miles of pristine signposted nature trail lined with ancient live oaks and cypress. Another island attraction is abundant wildlife. Emus, peacocks, Sicilian donkeys, Barbados mountain sheep, African pygmy goats, and llamas freely roam grassy savannahs, and avian residents include American bald eagles, osprey, blue herons, white egrets, hummingbirds, cranes, cardinals, ibis, hawks, and owls. Bring your camera and binoculars.

By prior reservation, you can also arrange airboat and swamp buggy rides, waterskiing, jet skiing, tubing, and horseback riding here. And there are nighttime gator safaris (led by experienced guides) through marshy areas of the lake. On-premises facilities include volleyball, horseshoes, picnic tables, a country store, and a concession that sells barbecued burgers and other fare.

Flying Tigers Warbird Air Museum

231 N. Hoagland Blvd. (off U.S. 192, 1 traffic light west of Armstrong Blvd. and Yates Rd.). ☎ 407/933-1942. Admission $6 adults, $5 seniors over 60 and children 6–12, under 6 free. Daily 9am–5 or 6pm (hours vary seasonally).

Flying Tigers is actually a World War II aircraft restoration facility where vintage planes are rebuilt and test-flown. Seventy-five percent of the displays—which run the gamut from 1920s antiques to 1970s fighter jets—are permanent; the rest are in the shop on a temporary basis.

On guided tours, which depart at intervals throughout the day, you'll visit the rebuilding facility where planes in various stages of assemblage are being restored. Exhibits include a U.S. Navy pilot trainer, many World War II bombers (including B-17s), Navy helicopters, torpedo bombers, cargo planes, and a rare World War II Paisacki Hup 1, as well as actual bombs, military jeeps and command cars from World War II and the Korean War, a large display of World War II memorabilia, and much, much more.

Visitors can sit in the cockpit of a jet-fighter simulator, or—for a more realistic Red Baron fantasy experience—arrange to go up in a 1935 three-seat open biplane (call ahead for information on the latter, as well as other flight and piloting opportunities, some for families).

Gatorland

14501 S. Orange Blossom Trail (U.S. 441; between Osceola Pkwy. and Hunter's Creek Blvd.). ☎ 800/393-JAWS or 407/855-5496. Admission $11.95 adults, $9.56 seniors over 65, $8.95 children 3–9, under 3 free. Daily 8am–dusk. Free parking.

Founded in 1949 with a handful of alligators living in huts and pens, Gatorland today features thousands of alligators and crocodiles on a 70-acre spread. Breeding pens, nurseries, and rearing ponds are situated throughout the park, which also displays monkeys, snakes, deer, goats, birds, sheep, Florida lake turtles, a Galápagos tortoise, and a bear. A 2,000-foot boardwalk winds through a cypress swamp and a 10-acre breeding marsh with an observation tower. Or you can take the free Gatorland Express Train around the park.

There are three shows scheduled throughout the day—Gator Wrestlin', the Gator Jumparoo, and Snakes of Florida. Facilities include an open-air restaurant (where you can try smoked gator ribs and nuggets), a shop (Gatorland also functions as an alligator-breeding farm for meat and hides; you'll find a wide array of alligator leather products here, not to mention canned gator chowder), and a picnic area.

Green Meadows Petting Farm

1368 S. Poinciana Blvd. (off U.S. 192 between Polynesian Blvd. and S.R. 535). ☎ **407/846-0770.** Admission $13, children under 3 free. Daily 9:30am–5:30pm, with tours departing throughout the day until 4pm. Free parking.

Though kids of any age will enjoy it, if your children are 8 or younger, a visit to this delightful 40-acre farm—home to over 200 animals—will give you better value for your money than any major theme park. On guided 2-hour farm tours, visitors view, learn about, and in some cases feed or pet, sheep, goats, exotic chickens, turkeys, ducks, llamas, pigs, donkeys, ostriches, peacocks, and bison. Kids especially love to see the baby animals, and for parents it's really fun to watch the kids in this setting. Everyone also gets a turn to milk a cow, and a hayride, miniature train ride, and pony ride are included in the entrance fee.

Call before you go to find out about special events such as shows, pumpkin harvesting, and barn dances. There's a large, shaded picnic area, so pack your lunch and make a day of it.

Splendid China

Formosa Gardens Blvd. (off W. Irlo Bronson Memorial Hwy./U.S. 192, between Entry Point Blvd./Sherbeth Rd. and Black Lake Rd.). ☎ **407/396-7111.** Admission $23.55 adults, seniors $21.20, $13.90 children 5–12, under 5 free. Daily from 9:30am. Closing hours vary seasonally; call ahead. Free parking.

This 76-acre outdoor attraction features more than 60 miniaturized replicas of China's most noted man-made and natural wonders, spanning 5,000 years of history and culture. Visitors enter via a bustling commercial street in the "water city" of Suzhou (the Venice of the East) circa A.D. 1300 to view a short orientation film about China. Park highlights include a half-mile–long copy of the 4,200-mile Great Wall; the Forbidden City's 9,999-room Imperial Palace, built in 1420; Tibet's sacred Potala Palace, former mountain home of the Dalai Lama; carved Buddhist grottoes with statuary dating from A.D. 477 to A.D. 898; the massive Leshan Buddha, carved out of a mountainside between A.D. 713 and A.D. 803; the Stone Forest of Yunan, a natural formation of towering limestone peaks; and the Mongolian mausoleum of Genghis Khan.

Live shows (acrobats, martial-arts demonstrations, storytelling, dance, puppetry, and more) take place throughout the day on stages around the park, in the indoor 800-seat Golden Peacock Theater, and in a 900-seat open-air amphitheater; check your entertainment schedule when you come in.

Over a dozen shops sell Chinese merchandise. Food concessions, a gourmet restaurant, and a Chinese cafeteria are on the premises.

Two-hour guided walking tours, departing several times a day, cost $5 per person (children under 12 free), and 1-hour golf-cart tours ($45 per six-person cart) depart every half hour. Or you can board a free tram that circles the park, stopping at major points for pickup and drop-off. There is also recorded commentary at each attraction.

Water Mania

6073 W. Irlo Bronson Memorial Hwy. (U.S. 192), just east of I-4. ☎ **407/396-2626.** Admission $23.95 adults, $17.95 children 3–12, under 3 free. Nov–Feb daily 11am–5pm; other times daily 9:30am–7pm with extended hours on some weekends and during spring break. From Nov–Feb admission is half-price after 3pm. Parking $3.

This conveniently located 36-acre water park offers a variety of aquatic thrill rides and attractions. You can boogie-board or bodysurf in continuous-wave pools, float lazily along an 850-foot river, enjoy a white-water tubing adventure, and plummet down spiraling water slides and steep flumes. Or dare to ride the Abyss an enclosed tube slide that corkscrews through 300 feet of darkness, exiting into a splash pool. There's a rain forest–theme water playground for children. A miniature golf course and wooded picnic area—with arcade games, a beach, and volleyball—adjoin. Water Mania, smaller than many similar parks, lives up to its billing as being family-friendly. There are lots of opportunities for smaller children, and there tend to be fewer rowdy teenagers and young adults than at parks such as Wet 'n' Wild.

A World of Orchids

2501 Old Lake Wilson Rd. (C.R. 545), off U.S. 192. ☎ **407/396-1887.** Admission $8.95 adults, $7.95 seniors, 15 and under free. Daily 9:30am–5:30pm. Closed New Year's Day, July 4, Thanksgiving, and Christmas.

Lovers of horticulture will enjoy touring this conservatory filled with tropical trees (including 64 varieties of palms and 21 of bamboo), ferns, lush tropical foliage, and, most notably, thousands of orchids—many of them rare—magnificently abloom at all times. Streams, waterfalls, koi ponds, and birds enhance this little enchanted garden. Also on the premises: a nature walk through a wooded area, aquariums of exotic fish, and a small aviary. Free guided tours are given by resident horticulturists at 11am and 3pm weekdays, 11am and 1 and 3pm on weekends.

Note: If this is the kind of attraction you enjoy, be sure to also visit Harry P. Leu Gardens in Orlando (details below).

ON INTERNATIONAL DRIVE

Like Kissimmee attractions, these are about a 10- to 15-minute drive from the Disney area.

Ripley's Believe It or Not! Museum

8201 International Dr. (1½ blocks south of Sand Lake Rd.). ☎ **407/345-0501.** Admission $9.95 adults, $6.95 children 4–12, under 4 free. Daily 10am–noon.

It's always fun to peruse a Ripley collection of oddities, curiosities, and fascinating artifacts from faraway places. Among the hundreds of items and mannequins on display here are a 1,069-pound man, a two-headed kitten, a five-legged cow, a three-quarter–scale model of a 1907 Rolls-Royce made from a million matchsticks, a mosaic of the *Mona Lisa* created from 1,426 pieces of toast, torture devices from the Spanish Inquisition, a Tibetan flute made from human bones, an Ecuadorean shrunken head, a painting on a grain of rice, a "disappearing" nude bather (they do it with mirrors), Ubangi women with wooden plates in their lips, and Burmese Padaung women who stretch their necks up to 15 inches long by wearing heavy brass rings around them. There are exhibits on Houdini and Florida sinkholes, and a film documents people swallowing unusual items. . . coat hangers, a lightbulb, and, most notably, a padlock, ring, and keys (when the latter three items are—ahem!—evacuated, the ring is locked into the padlock!). Museum visitors are greeted by a hologram of Robert Ripley. *Warning:* A few years back there was a mini–baby boom among employees that was attributed to the statue of a fertility god on display.

Wet 'n' Wild

6200 International Dr. (at Republic Dr.). ☎ **800/992-WILD** or 407/351-WILD (9453). Admission $24.95 adults, $19.95 children 3–9, under 3 free. Age 55 and older always half price; half-price admission for all after 3pm. Daily 10am–5pm. Parking: cars $4, RVs $6. Take I-4 east to Exit 30A and follow the signs.

Who knew people came in such a variety of shapes and sizes? Stacked or stubby, tan or terribly white, all kinds of people come to Wet 'n' Wild. According to industry polls, Wet 'n' Wild is one of the hottest tourist attractions in the country. When temperatures soar, head for this 25-acre water park and cool off by jumping waves, careening down steep flumes, and running rapids. When temps aren't soaring, you'll be pleased to know that all the pools are heated. Among the highlights: Fuji Flyer, a six-story, four-passenger toboggan ride through 450 feet of banked curves; The Surge, one of the longest, fastest multipassenger tube rides anywhere in the Southeast, with 580 feet of exciting banked curves; Bomb Bay (enter a bomblike casing 76 feet in the air for a speedy vertical flight straight down to a target pool); Black Hole (step into a spaceship and board a two-person raft for a 30-second, 500-foot, twisting, turning, space-themed reentry through total darkness propelled by a 1,000-gallon-a-minute blast of water!); Raging Rapids, a simulated white-water tubing adventure with a waterfall plunge; and Lazy River, a leisurely float trip. This is the park that really started it all. Disney built its own water parks to compete with Wet 'n' Wild, and the originator still has plenty to offer. Bomb Bay ranks among one of the best thrill rides in central Florida.

There are additional flumes, a vast wave pool, a large and innovative children's water playground where the above rides are re-created in miniature, a sunbathing area, and a picnic area. Food concessions are located throughout the park, lockers and towels can be rented, and you can purchase beach accessories at the gift shop. *Bring or buy sunscreen.*

IN ORLANDO

The rest of the sights and attractions are spread out around Orlando. Loch Haven Park, the location of the Orange County Historical Museum, Orlando Museum of Art, and Orlando Science Center, is about 35 minutes by car from the Disney area. You might also wish to incorporate a trip to Winter Park in the same day (see chapter 11 for details).

✪ Harry P. Leu Gardens

1920 N. Forest Ave. (between Nebraska St. and Corrine Dr.). ☎ **407/246-2620.** Fax 407/246-2849. Admission $3 adults, $1 children 6–16, under 6 free. Daily 9am–5pm. Leu House tours Tues–Sat 10am–3:30pm, Sun–Mon 1–3:30pm. Closed Christmas. Take I-4 east to Exit 43 (Princeton St.), follow Princeton St. east, make a right on Mills Ave. and a left on Virginia Dr.; look for the gardens on your left, just after you go around the curve in the road.

This delightful, 50-acre botanical garden on the shores of Lake Rowena offers a serene respite from theme-park razzle-dazzle. Meandering paths lead through forests of giant camphors, moss-draped oaks, palms, cycads, and camellias (one of the world's largest collections, comprising some 2,000 plants in 50 species; they bloom October through March). Exquisite formal rose gardens (the largest in Florida, displaying 75 varieties) are enhanced by Italian fountains, a gazebo, and statuary. Other highlights include orchids, azaleas, desert plants, beds of colorful annuals and perennials, and a 50-foot floral clock. The gardens were created by Orlando businessman Harry P. Leu, who donated his 49-acre estate to the city in the 1960s.

Free 20-minute tours of the Leu House, built in 1888 and restored to reflect the period between 1910 and 1930, take place on the hour and half hour. The house is a decorative arts museum filled with Victorian, Chippendale, and Empire pieces and other furnishings and objets d'art. It takes about 2 hours to see the house and gardens. Inquire about lectures and workshops, including some for children. A new visitor center was added a few years ago, expanding the gift shop and adding a little luster to this laid back attraction.

Orange County Historical Museum

812 E. Rollins St. (between Orange and Mills aves.), in Loch Haven Park. ☎ **407/897-6350.** Fax 407/897-6409. Admission $2 adults, $1.50 seniors 65 and over, $1 children 6–12,

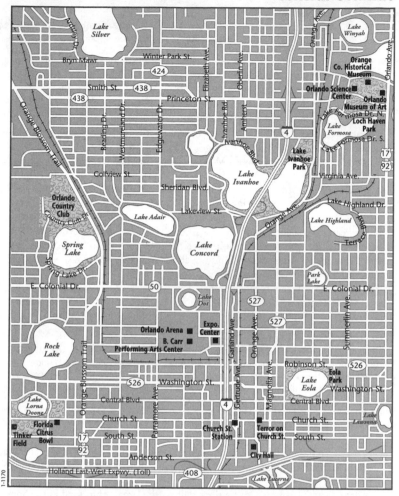

under 6 free. Mon admission is by donation. Mon–Sat 9am–5pm, Sun noon–5pm. Closed Martin Luther King, Jr. Day, Memorial Day, July 4, Labor Day, Thanksgiving, Christmas, and New Year's Day. Take I-4 east to Exit 43 (Princeton St.) and follow the signs to Loch Haven Park.

Like everything else in Orlando, this museum is soon to get a lift and a make over. It focuses mainly on central Florida history, beginning with prehistoric projectile points, a Timucuan canoe, and tooled animal bones from hunting cultures that existed here 12,000 years ago.

Other exhibits include displays of Seminole pottery and clothing; items from a pioneer kitchen; artifacts from an 1892 courthouse; a chronicle of the citrus industry and the role it played in the development of central Florida; and re-creations of a turn-of-the-century country store, a Victorian parlor, and the old *Orlando Sentinel* composing room. Also on the premises is Fire Station No. 3, a restored 1926 firehouse containing historic fire trucks, equipment, and memorabilia. The permanent collection is supplemented by changing exhibits of local, national, and international significance. Best enjoyed by true history buffs.

✪ Orlando Museum of Art

2416 N. Mills Ave. (in Loch Haven Park off Hwy. 17/92). ☎ **407/896-4231.** Admission $4 adults, $2 children 4–11, under 4 free. Tues–Sat 9am–5pm, Sun noon–5pm. Art Encounter hours are Tues–Fri and Sun noon–5pm, Sat 10am–5pm. Free parking. Closed Mon, New Year's Day, Memorial Day, July 4, Labor Day, Thanksgiving, and Christmas. Take I-4 east to Exit 43 (Princeton St.) and follow the signs to Loch Haven Park.

After closing for a 4-month, multimillion-dollar makeover, the Orlando Museum of Art opened in 1997 ready to handle some of the most prestigious exhibits traveling the nation. The improved and expanded museum is worth a look, especially if it is hosting a traveling exhibit, such as the "Imperial Tombs of China," which had an extended stay in the 31,000-square-foot expansion during 1997.

Founded in 1924, the Orlando Museum of Art displays its permanent collection of 19th- and 20th-century American art, pre-Colombian art dating from 1200 B.C. to A.D. 1500, and African art on a rotating basis. These holdings are augmented by long-term loans focusing on Mayan archaeology and art of the African sub-Saharan region. **Art Encounter** is an interactive hands-on area for young children, where they might weave on a giant loom, piece together a pre-Colombian pot, or play African instruments. And temporary exhibits here range from Hudson River School landscapes to works of Andy Warhol. Inquire about guided tours, workshops for adults and children, gallery talks, and other activities.

From Diego Rivera refrigerator magnets to Georgia O'Keefe cards, and original jewelry and pottery by local artists, the gift shop alone is worth visiting the museum. Where else could you find Mark Harding birth announcements?

✪ Orlando Science Center

777 E. Princeton St. (between Orange and Mills aves.), in Loch Haven Park. ☎ **407/896-7151.** Admission for all exhibits: $8 for adults, $7 for seniors, $6.50 for children 3–11, under 3 free. For exhibits and either a CineDome film or planetarium show: $12 for adults, $11 seniors, $9.50 for children 3–11. For all exhibits and both a CineDome film and planetarium show: $14 for adults, $13 for seniors, $11.50 for children 3–11. Open Mon–Thurs and Sat 9am–5pm, Fri 9am–9pm, Sun noon–5pm. Closed Thanksgiving and Christmas. Parking is available in a garage across the street from the new building and costs $3.50. Take I-4 east to Exit 43 (Princeton St.), and cross Orange Ave.

Dan Rather and the CBS evening news gave America a peek at the newly renovated Orlando Science Center when it was unveiled in February 1997 after a $44-million renovation.

It drew Dan's attention because the facility is the largest of its kind in the Southeast. (It probably didn't hurt that the show meant a trip to Florida in February.) Those familiar with the Orlando Science Center's previous incarnation as stepsister sharing a building with the Orange County Historical Society will be amazed at the Cinderella that has evolved. The new center provides 10 exhibit halls that allow visitors to spend the whole day exploring everything from the swamplands of Florida to the arid plains of Mars.

One of the major additions is actually just beneath that Trojan helmet–shaped silver dome that has loomed over Orlando for months. The **Dr. Phillips CineDome,** a 310-seat theater, uses the latest technology to present large-format films, planetarium shows, and laser light shows

In **KidsTown,** little folks wander around in exhibits representing a miniature version of the big world around them. In one section is a pint-sized community including a construction site, park, and wellness center. Nearby is **Science City,** which includes a power plant, suspension bridge, and the Inventor's Workshop, a garagelike station for creative play. Children stopping by at **123 Math Avenue** work on puzzles and play with math-based toys that teach while entertaining.

Both the **Virtual Reality Theater** and the **New Media Living Room** show the real advances that will soon become as commonplace as the once-exotic VCR.

4 Staying Active

Recreational facilities of every description abound in Walt Disney World and the surrounding area. These are especially accessible to guests at Disney-owned resorts, official hotels, and the Fort Wilderness Resort and Campground, though many other large resort hotels also offer comprehensive facilities (see details in chapter 5). The Disney facilities listed below are all open to the public, no matter where you're staying. For further information about WDW recreational facilities, call ☎ 407/824-4321. Guests at Disney properties can inquire when making hotel reservations or at guest services/concierge desks.

BICYCLING

Bike rentals (single and multispeed bikes for adults, tandems, and children's bikes) are available from the **Bike Barn** (☎ **407/824-2742**) at Fort Wilderness Resort and Campground. Rates are $5 per hour, $12 per day; overnight rentals are $15. Both Fort Wilderness and Disney's Village Resort offer good bike trails.

Most of the best biking is done in Lake County, north of the Disney Area. *Florida Backroads* by Robert Howard (under $20 in the bookstore) offers detailed descriptions of favorite biking paths throughout Florida.

BOATING

Walt Disney World, with its many man-made lakes and lagoons, owns the nation's largest fleet of pleasure boats. At the **Walt Disney World Village Marina,** you can rent Water Sprites, canopy boats, and 20-foot pontoon boats. For information call ☎ **407/828-2204.**

The **Bike Barn** at Fort Wilderness (☎ **407/824-2742**) rents canoes ($6 per hour, $10 per day) and paddleboats ($6 per half hour, $10 per hour).

See hotel facilities listings in chapter 5 for additional boating options.

FISHING

Fishing excursions on Lake Buena Vista—mainly for largemouth bass—may be arranged from 2 to 14 days in advance by calling the **Walt Disney World Village Marina** (☎ **407/828-2621**). No license is required. The fee is $137 for up to five people for 2 hours; those rates include gear, guide, bait, and tax.

A less expensive alternative: Rent fishing poles at the **Bike Barn** (☎ **407/824-2742**) to fish in Fort Wilderness canals. No license is required.

FLYING

The **Flying Tigers Warbird Air Museum** offers rides in a 1934 open-cockpit barnstormer, and hands-on dual-instruction adventures in a historic World War II fighter trainer. Call ☎ **407/933-1942** for details.

A slightly more offbeat experience is offered by **Fighter Pilots USA.** Ever dreamed of suiting up, jumping into a fighter plane, and engaging in high-speed one-on-one dogfighting? This is your chance to experience the excitement of aerial combat. Actual F-16 pilots are your instructors. To schedule a "mission," call ☎ **800/56-TOPGUN** or 407/931-4333. No license is required. Cost is $795 per person.

See Orlando from a different perspective. Hover over tourist hot spots on a ride with **Falcon Helicopter Service.** Located at 8990 International Dr., the service offers nine different aerial tour packages ranging from $15 to $395. (You get 4 minutes for $15.) For information call ☎ **407/396-7222.**

Hot Links: Orlando's Top Golf Courses

Like most of Florida, Orlando is a golfer's paradise, with 123 courses within a 45-minute drive of downtown. . . . courses designed by Arnold Palmer, Jack Nicklaus, Tom Fazio, Pete Dye, Robert Trent Jones, and other major players. Its most famous courses include the following:

- The legendary **Arnold Palmer's Bay Hill Club,** 9000 Bay Hill Blvd. (☎ **800/ 523-5999** or 407/876-2429), site of the Bay Hill Invitational. Its 18th hole, nicknamed the Devil's Bathtub, is supposed to be the toughest par-4 on the tour.
- **Falcon's Fire Golf Club,** 3200 Seralago Blvd., in Kissimmee (☎ **407/ 239-5445**), a challenging Ree Jones course with 136 bunkers and water on 10 holes.
- **Walt Disney Resorts** facilities (see details above), comprising 99 holes. Their most famous hazard is a sand trap on Magnolia Course's 6th hole in the shape of Mickey Mouse.

Also notable are two beautifully landscaped facilities: the award-winning 45-hole/ par-72 Jack Nicklaus–designed course at the **Villas of Grand Cypress** (☎ **800/ 835-7377** or 407/239-4700) and the 18-hole/par-71 Joe Lee–designed championship course at **Marriott's Orlando World Center** (☎ **800/621-0638** or 407/ 239-4200). See details on both properties in chapter 5.

GOLF

Walt Disney World operates five championship 18-hole, par-72 golf courses and one 9-hole, par-36 walking course. All are open to the general public and offer pro shops, equipment rentals, and instruction. For tee times and information, call ☎ **407/ 824-2270** up to 7 days in advance (up to 30 days for Disney-resort and official-property guests). Call ☎ **407/W-DISNEY** (934-7639) for information about golf packages.

Also consider calling **Golfpac** (☎ **800/327-0878** or 407/260-2288), an organization that packages golf vacations (with accommodations and other features) and prearranges tee times at over 40 Orlando-area courses. The further in advance you call (I'm talking months here), the better your options.

Nick Faldo, three-time winner of the British Open, shares his skills with the average duffer at the new **Faldo Golf Institute** by Marriott. The "institute," as those involved like to call it, will feature a 9-hole course, a 27-hole putting course, and one of the largest learning centers in the country. Prices begin at $40 for 30-minute private instruction to $195 for a half day and $950 for a 5-day swing-a-thon. You will mostly be dealing with pros trained in the Faldo method, although you may occasionally glimpse the man himself. The school will be located at Marriott's Grande Vista Resort, 11301 International Dr., Orlando, FL 32821 (☎ **407/ 238-6800**).

HAYRIDES

The hay wagon departs from Pioneer Hall at **Fort Wilderness** nightly at 7 and 9:15pm for hour-long, old-fashioned hayrides with singing, jokes, and games. Cost is $6 for adults, $4 for children ages 3 to 10, free for children under 3. Children under 12 must be accompanied by an adult. No reservations; it's first-come, first-served.

HORSEBACK RIDING

Disney's Fort Wilderness Resort and Campground offers 45-minute scenic guided-tour trail rides daily, with four to six rides per day. Cost is $17 per person. Children must be at least 9 years old. For information and reservations up to 5 days in advance, call ☎ **407/824-2832.**

ICE-SKATING

Rock on Ice! Skating Arena, in the Dowdy Pavilion, 7500 Canada Ave., between Sand Lake Road and Carrier Drive (☎ **407/352-9878**), is a gorgeous, Olympic-size indoor rink with high-tech lighting and sound systems. A DJ spins Top 40 tunes. There are ice-skating games with prizes throughout the day. Facilities include video games, a snack bar, and a complete skate shop offering a large selection of figure-skating and hockey equipment. Rental skates are $2. Admission is $4.50 to $6, depending on the season. Hours vary seasonally; call ahead.

To get here from the Disney World area, take International Drive north, turn right at Sand Lake Road and left on Canada Avenue. It's about a 10-minute drive.

JOGGING

Many of the Disney resorts have scenic jogging trails. For instance, the **Yacht and Beach Club** resorts share a 2-mile trail, the **Disney Institute** has a 3.4-mile course with 32 exercise stations, the **Caribbean Beach Resort's** 1.4-mile promenade circles a lake, **Dixie Landings** has a 1.7-mile riverfront trail, and **Fort Wilderness's** tree-shaded 2.3-mile jogging path has exercise stations about every quarter mile. Pick up a jogging trail map at any Disney property's guest-services desk.

SWIMMING WITH THE MANATEES

An organization called **Oceanic Society Expeditions** (☎ **800/326-7491** or 415/441-1106) offers a "Swim with the Manatees" program in the Crystal River area, 2 hours east of Orlando. A manatee biologist leads 5-day Monday-to-Friday trips aboard a 12-person skiff, which include swimming with manatees, bird watching, snorkeling, slide presentations, and an excursion to a facility for the care of injured and orphaned wildlife. Cost is $985, including accommodations, excursions, and most meals. Reserve as far in advance as possible.

TENNIS

Seventeen lighted tennis courts are located throughout the Disney properties. Most are free and available on a first-come, first-served basis. If you're willing to pay, courts can be reserved up to several months in advance at two Disney resorts: the **Contemporary** (☎ **407/824-3578**) and the **Grand Floridian** (☎ **407/824-2435**). Both charge $12 per hour; you can also reserve lesson times with resident pros. The Contemporary offers a large pro shop, a ball machine, rebound walls, and equipment rentals.

WATER PARKS/SWIMMING

See section 7 of chapter 7, "Other WDW Attractions," for information on River Country, Typhoon Lagoon, and Blizzard Beach, as well as water parks listed in section 3, "Other Area Attractions," above.

WATERSKIING

Waterskiing trips (including boats, drivers, equipment, and instruction) can be arranged at Walt Disney World by calling ☎ **407/824-2621.** Make reservations up to 14 days in advance. Cost is $82 per hour for up to five people.

5   Spectator Sports

Disney doesn't want to give the competition a sporting chance, branching out with a multimillion-dollar **Walt Disney World International Sports Center,** a 200-acre facility. The Mouse hopes to hit a home run with a 7,500-seat baseball stadium that will be a spring-training home to the 1996 almost–World Champs, the Atlanta Braves, beginning in 1998. In addition there is a 5,000-seat field house featuring six basketball courts, a fitness center, and training rooms; major-league practice fields and pitcher mounds; four softball fields; 12 tennis courts, including a 2,000-seat stadium center court; a track-and-field complex; a golf driving range; and much more. A variety of sporting events have been held there since the center opened in May 1997. For information about events during your stay, call ☎ **407/363-6262** or 407/363-6100.

The **Orlando Centroplex** administers six public sports and entertainment facilities in the downtown area. These include three major sporting arenas: the Florida Citrus Bowl, the Orlando Arena, and Tinker Field.

ARENA FOOTBALL

Orlando is home to the **Orlando Predators,** who play from April until August. For the uninitiated, arena football is an indoor cross between rugby and football played by eight-man teams on a much-abbreviated field. You don't necessarily need to know the rules to enjoy the up-close crunching and beer-fest atmosphere. The Predators are the Buffalo Bills of arena football, coming close but never quite winning a championship. They have a loyal and rowdy following. Sold-out games are common, but single tickets are often available the day of the game at the Orlando Arena box office. For information call ☎ **407/648-4444.**

BASEBALL

From April to September, the **Orlando Rays**—the Tampa Devil Rays' Class AA Southern league affiliate—play at Tinker Field, 287 S. Tampa Ave., between Colonial Drive (Highway 50) and Gore Street (☎ **407/649-7297** for information and to charge tickets). Tickets are $3 to $7. To get there, take I-4 east to the East–West Expressway and head west to Highway 441; make a left on Church Street and follow the signs. Tinker Field adjoins the Citrus Bowl. Parking is $2.

BASKETBALL

The 17,500-seat Orlando Arena, (the "O-rena"), 600 W. Amelia St., between I-4 and Parramore Avenue (☎ **407/896-2442** for information, 407/839-3900 to charge tickets), is home to the **Orlando Magic** during their October-to-April season. Some of the Magic dimmed when the team was left by star center (and marketing phenomenon) Shaquille O'Neal, but it's still the NBA. Tickets to games (about $13 to $50) have to be acquired far in advance; they usually sell out by September before the season starts. Several hundred individual seats, sometimes in the nosebleed sections, can usually be obtained before games against some of the league's less-well–known teams, like the Timberwolves. To get there, take I-4 east to Amelia Avenue, turn left at the traffic light at the bottom of the off-ramp, and follow signs. For up-to-the-minute parking information, turn your car radio to 1620 AM.

FOOTBALL

The Florida Citrus Bowl, 1 Citrus Bowl Place, at West Church and Tampa streets (☎ **407/473-2476** for information, 407/839-3900 to charge tickets), hosts the annual **CompUSA Florida Citrus Bowl** game, college football games, and NFL pre-season games. Tickets to all football events are hard to come by, but you may have some luck if you try far enough in advance. To get there, take I-4 east to the East-West Expressway and head west to Highway 441, make a left on Church Street, and follow the signs. Parking is $5.

GREYHOUND RACING

The **Sanford-Orlando Kennel Club,** 301 Dog Track Rd., between Fla. 427 and U.S. 17/92, in Longwood (☎ 407/831-1600), offers a pleasant way to spend a day or evening, especially if you opt to watch the races over lunch or dinner in the glassed-in clubhouse restaurant. The restaurant is moderately priced and has a full bar; reservations are suggested. There are a variety of ways to bet on the greyhounds; if you've never done it before, pick up a free brochure that explains trifectas, quinelas, boxing, and wheeling and also shows you how to read your ticket. You can also buy tip sheets here recommending computer and expert picks. Each meet includes 14 races. You must be at least 18 years old to enter the track. This facility also offers simulcast wagering of greyhound, thoroughbred, and harness racing at other Florida tracks and at Aqueduct.

Admission is $1, plus $1 admission to the clubhouse restaurant. Parking is free, preferred parking (closer to the entrance) is $1, and valet parking is $2.

It's open from November to early May. Nighttime races are held Monday through Saturday at 7:30pm; matinees are Monday, Wednesday, and Saturday at 12:30pm. From the Walt Disney World area, take I-4 east, make a right at Maitland Boulevard, go north on 17/92, and make a left onto Dog Track Road. It's about a 40-minute drive.

Seminole Greyhound Park, 2000 Seminola Blvd., just east of U.S. 17/92, in Casselberry (☎ 407/699-4510), offers a very similar setup to the above. Its attractive third-floor restaurant, Osceola Terrace, has tiered seating with big picture windows overlooking the track and TV monitors enhancing the view at higher tables. Prices are moderate, and there's a full bar; reservations are suggested. Each meet here includes 14 or 15 races. Children are welcome but must be at least 18 years old to enter the betting area.

Admission is $1, free for seniors 55 and over at matinees, $2 for clubhouse seating, and $3 for restaurant seating. Children under 18 pay half-price throughout. Parking is free, preferred parking (closer to the entrance) is $1, and valet parking is $2.

Open May to October. Nighttime races are held Monday through Saturday at 7:30pm; matinees are Monday, Wednesday, and Saturday at 1pm. From the Walt Disney World area, take I-4 east, make a right at Exit 48 (Fla. 436), a left at U.S. 17/92, and a right on Seminola Boulevard, which dead-ends at the track. It's about a 40-minute drive.

Unfortunately, when past their racing prime, these graceful greyhounds are often callously put to death by track owners. There have always been animal-rescue agencies promoting greyhound adoption, but their effectiveness greatly increased in the early 1990s when the ASPCA and the American Greyhound Council joined together to support existing programs and to get the word out that greyhounds make intelligent (they're easy to train), gentle (they're good around kids), and loving—not to mention very handsome—pets. And since they've lived with other greyhounds their entire lives, they adapt well to your other dogs. If you're interested in adopting (and possibly saving the life of) a greyhound, call ☎ 800/366-1472 or 212/876-7700, ext. GREY.

HOCKEY

Ice Hockey? Orlando? Well, sure, why not? There is an ice rink under the floor at the downtown Orlando Arena; the regular floor is replaced for Orlando Magic games. An International Hockey League team, the **Orlando Solar Bears,** plays from October through April, longer if they do well in the playoffs. Ticket prices are a professional sports bargain beginning at $6 and topping out at $26 for prime lower-bowl seats. For information call ☎ **407/872-7825.**

JAI ALAI

Orlando Jai Alai, 6405 S. U.S. 17/92, at S.R. 436 in Fern Park (☎ **407/339-6221**), offers the action-packed Basque sport of jai alai (it's the world's fastest game). It's played on a 180-foot court with three walls. The ball is hurled at speeds of up to 150 miles an hour from baskets strapped to the players' wrists, and the object of the game is to throw the ball with such force, spin, and/or placement that the opponent is unable to return it before it bounces twice. A score of seven points wins. There are two opposing singles or doubles teams on the court at all times.

Your program offers extensive information about how the game is played and how to wager, and the public-address announcer explains what is happening on the court.

Best bet is to watch the action from the moderately priced, and very attractive, open-air Terrace Restaurant, with some tables as close as 20 feet from the court. There's a color TV monitor at every table. Fare is American/continental; there's a full bar; reservations are suggested. Children 39 inches and taller are admitted into the fronton with parents, but are not allowed in the betting area.

Note: The fronton also features intertrack wagering; you can place bets here on thoroughbred and harness races as well as Miami jai alai.

Admission is $1, reserved seats are $2, restaurant seating is $3, and box seats are $3 to $5. Seniors 55 and older get free admission to matinees. Parking is free; valet parking is $1.50. Open year-round Wednesday to Sunday. Evening games are held at 7:30pm Wednesday to Saturday, matinees at noon Thursday and Saturday, and at 1pm Sunday. From the Walt Disney World area, take I-4 east, make a right at Exit 47A (Maitland Exchange), a right at U.S. 17/92, and look for the fronton 2 miles along on your right. It's about a 40-minute drive.

Shopping 9

What is a vacation without a little shopping. . . okay, without a lot of shopping. Not only do you really *need* a few extra (bags of) souvenirs, who knows what native Florida treasures you may find?

Of course, the theme parks carry just about everything you can imagine embossed with their name. (Even quite a few things you'd never imagine.) And, we all know, you are really paying more than you should. When searching for deals at home, do you hightail it to the tourist areas? I didn't think so. Although I'm not knocking the staggering number of ways Mickey Mouse can be merchandised, there are plenty of other places to shop and plenty of things to purchase in Orlando that don't carry the initials M.M. The shopping opportunities at the theme parks are outlined in chapters 7 and 8.

Get out and explore some of them, especially if you're making a repeat visit to the theme parks or your first trip to the United States.

One word of advice: If you are traveling during the Christmas holiday season, from the end of November to December 25, it is best to avoid local shopping malls on the weekends.

1 Orlando-Area Malls

FACTORY OUTLETS

Belz Factory Outlet World, 5401 W. Oak Ridge Rd., at the north end of International Drive (☎ **407/354-0126** or 407/352-9600), is the largest of these, with 180 stores in two huge, enclosed malls and four shopping annexes. It offers an immense range of merchandise at savings up to 75% off retail prices. There's even an old-fashioned carousel for the kids (and adults).

At its emporia: 18 shoe stores (including Bass, Bally, and Capezio); 14 housewares shops (including Fieldcrest/Cannon, Corning, Oneida, and Mikasa); and more than 60 clothing shops for men, women, and children (including London Fog, Van Heusen, Jonathan Logan, Guess Jeans, Aileen, Danskin, Jordache, Leslie Fay, Carole Little, Harvé Benard, Calvin Klein, and Anne Klein). You can also shop for books and records, electronics, sporting goods, health and beauty aids, jewelry, toys, gifts, accessories, lingerie, and hosiery here. It's open Monday through Saturday from 10am to 9pm, Sunday from 10am to 6pm.

Close to the above is the **Quality Outlet Center,** on International Drive a block east of Kirkman Road (☎ **407/423-5885**). It has about 20 outlets, including Arrow, American Tourister, Corning–Revere (glassware and cookware), Florsheim shoes, Magnavox, Laura Ashley, Adidas, Great Western Boots, Totes, Le Creuset (cookware), Linens 'n' Things, Mikasa, Royal Doulton, and Villeroy & Boch. Once again, big savings. It's open Monday through Saturday from 10am to 10pm, Sunday from 11am to 6pm.

Continuing a quarter of a mile north on International Drive, you'll come to the **International Drive Value Center,** under the same auspices as the Quality Outlet Center (same phone, same hours). Its 15 stores include T.J. Maxx; other women's clothing stores; Old Navy Clothing Company (a Gap concept); Lane Bryant; Linea Garbo (Italian shoes); Converse; Perfumania; Books A Million; and Bed, Bath, & Beyond.

Manufacturer's Outlet Mall, U.S. 192, a mile east of Fla. 535 in Kissimmee (☎ 407/396-8900), houses about 35 stores, including Van Heusen, Nike, London Fog, Fieldcrest/Cannon, Bass Apparel, Geoffrey Beene, American Tourister, Westport (women's fashions), Acme Boot, and Levi's. Open Monday through Saturday from 10am to 9pm, Sunday from 11am to 5pm.

INTERNATIONAL DRIVE–AREA MALLS

The Mercado, 8445 International Dr., just south of Sand Lake Road (☎ 407/ 345-9337)—a Mediterranean-style shopping center with brick and cobblestone streets, terra-cotta–roofed buildings, brightly colored awnings, and splashing fountains—is home to the Orlando/Orange County Visitor Information Center. A video-game arcade here keeps the kids amused while you shop, and there's live entertainment evenings (jazz, country rock, and reggae bands) in the central courtyard.

More than 60 specialty shops include Swings 'N' Things (everything from hammocks to wind chimes), Kandlestix (handcrafted candles), American Cola Company (Coca-Cola and Anheuser-Busch memorabilia), House of Ireland (china, crystal, claddagh jewelry), Historic Families (find your family's coat of arms), Earth Matters (conservation/ecology-theme merchandise), Lady Bug (needlecrafts), The Magic Shop (novelties, tricks, and pranks), and The Looking Glass (blown glass). It makes good browsing, and there are over a dozen restaurants and bars on the premises.

Stop by Guest Services to get a free "Privilege Card" for discounts at mall stores. Guest Services also offers airline ticketing, discounted attraction tickets (including Disney parks), car rental, help with accommodations, and more. The mall is open daily from 10am to 10pm, until 11pm late spring through the end of August.

SUBURBAN MALLS

The Florida Mall, 8001 S. Orange Blossom Trail, at Sand Lake Road (☎ 407/ 851-6255), is, aside from the Saks Fifth Avenue, your basic massive American shopping mall with more than 200 shops, restaurants, and services. It's a little unusual because of the 500-room Sheraton Hotel plopped in its center. Plus, it's anchored by six department stores—Saks Fifth Avenue, *two* Dillard's stores, JC Penney, Gayfers, and Sears. In addition, there are more than 10 jewelry shops, about 50 clothing and accessory shops (including mall regulars such as Benetton, the Warner Bros. Studio Store, Gap/Gap Kids, The Limited, and Victoria's Secret), over a dozen shoe stores, bookstores, electronics stores, eateries (among them, a food court), and much, much more. Open Monday through Saturday from 10am to 9:30pm, Sunday from 11am to 6pm.

Under the Walt Disney World auspices, the **Crossroads of Lake Buena Vista** at Exit 27 off I-4 (☎ 407/827-7300) is anchored by a 24-hour Goodings supermarket with a full-service pharmacy. Other shops sell sportswear, electronics, books, cards,

---

Going Upscale

Orlando, dubbed by city founders as "The City Beautiful," is beginning to attract more upscale retailers catering to the beautiful people.

Saks Fifth Avenue, Versace, and FAO Schwarz aren't exactly names usually associated with Orlando, but all three have recently come to Orlando. Saks Fifth Avenue, one of the nation's premier retailers, carries a variety of exclusive designer labels. It opened in the Florida Mall in late 1996.

FAO Schwarz, which some call the Saks Fifth Avenue of the toy business, is scheduled to open a 35,600-square-foot flagship store in a new development called Pointe Orlando. Although details weren't available at press time, the development will be located at the corner of International and Republic drives along the I-Drive tourist corridor.

Pointe Orlando will also be home to Versace, the name that always seems to be attached to today's most glamorous stars. The to-die-for designer label is scheduled to open its first boutique outside of New York in late 1997.

Both the Versace store and FAO Schwarz are expected to be appointed in the lavish style of the extravagant New York stores. Versace will feature Italian marble, mosaic, and painted frescos. Although details weren't available, FAO Schwarz should echo the wacky decor of the New York store, which has a giant, singing clock tower.

---

gifts, shoes, and Disney merchandise. There's also a post office, and restaurants/fast-food outlets include, among others, T.G.I. Friday's, Johnny Rockets, Pebbles (see chapter 6), Pizzeria Uno, and Red Lobster. Shops are open daily 10am to 10pm. It's just like a shopping center in the real world.

The **Orlando Fashion Square Mall** underwent a major renovation in the mid-1990s, and with marblelike walkways, indoor palm trees, and high ceilings, its a comfortable place to shop. Major stores include Burdines, Gayfers, JC Penney and Sears. There are 165 stores, plus an expansive food court. You'll also find several arcades for the kiddies, and there are two multiplex theaters nearby. Easily accessible, the mall is about 5 miles from downtown Orlando. Take I-4 east to Exit 41, the Colonial Drive/Highway 50 Exit. Take Colonial about 3 miles east, the main entrance is just past Maquire Boulevard. It's open Monday through Saturday 10am to 9pm, Sunday 11am to 6pm.

Just as Disney brought new life to Orlando, the **Altamonte Mall** brought new life to the little one-stoplight town of Altamonte Springs. The mall, built in the early 1970s, underwent a major renovation in 1989 and added a food court in 1990. It is the area's second largest mall, just behind the newly expanded Florida Mall. It includes major department stores such as Gayfers, Burdines, and JC Penney as well as 175 specialty shops. This is a multilevel mall with a light, airy feel and benches and indoor palm trees that make for a relaxing atmosphere (except during the Christmas holiday shopping rush). The mall is located at 451 Altamonte Blvd., just east of I-4. Take I-4 east to the Altamonte Springs, Route 436 Exit, Exit 48. Turn right. The mall is on the left. Hours are Monday through Saturday, 10am to 9pm; Sunday from noon to 5:30pm.

Just down the street, the **Renaissance Center** includes an AMC theater complex with eight screens and a large Book Stop and Blockbuster Music. Also located in this center is a small branch of **FanAttic,** a store specializing in all sorts of paraphernalia featuring the NBA's Orlando Magic, including the typical jerseys and hats to more obscure things like ties, table lamps, and even Magic alarm clocks. Be warned: This can be a very congested area during rush hour, so avoid traveling in the morning between 8 and 9am and in the evening between 5 and 6pm.

Seminole Towne Centre opened in September 1995. Although this is not the largest mall in the area, it is one of the newest and worth a visit if you are a true mall aficionado. It's anchored by Dillard's, Sears, JC Penney, Burdines, and Parisian, an upscale clothing store. It contains 100 retailers and a food court. Strollers and wheelchairs are available for rent. This mall is located about 40 minutes north of the attractions, so it is best to visit as part of a day trip. To get there take I-4 east to Exit 51. Follow the signs. For information call ☎ **407/323-2262.** It is open Monday through Saturday from 10am to 9pm, and Sunday from noon to 6pm.

2 Other Shopping in Orlando

IN DOWNTOWN ORLANDO

If you can think of nothing better than a relaxing afternoon of bargain hunting or scouring thrift and antiques shops, check out **Antique Row** in downtown Orlando. This collection of about two dozen shops and a couple of restaurants is about as far away as you can get from the manufactured fun of Disney. The shops are an interesting collection of the old, the new, and the unusual.

Stores such as **Fee Fi Faux** offer colorful, hand-painted furniture or other funky, original works of art. **Flo's Attic, Inc.** and **Pieces of Eight Emporium** sell more traditional antiques.

Down the road a handful of shops sell upscale clothing, cigars, or traditional works of art such as wildlife sculptures. **Art's Cigars** is a two-story leather-and-tweed kind of place where patrons are encouraged to light up and enjoy the view of Lake Ivanhoe across the street. **Wildlife Gallery** sells pricey, original works of wildlife art, including sculpture.

The Fly Fisherman sells—guess what?—fly-fishing equipment. You can sometimes see people taking lessons in the park across the street.

Stores are spread out for about 3 miles along Orange Avenue. The heaviest concentration is along Orange Avenue between Princeton Street and New Hampshire Avenue, although Fee Fi Faux and a few others are scattered between New Hampshire and Virginia avenues. The more upscale shops extend a few blocks beyond Virginia. To get there from the theme parks, take I-4 east to Princeton Street (Exit 43). Turn right on Orange Avenue. Parking is limited, so stop wherever you find a space along the street. The shops are usually open from about 8am to 6pm, Monday to Saturday. (The owners usually run these shops, so hours can vary. A small number of stores are open on Sunday.)

Built in an ornate Victorian style with hardwood oak floors and hand-painted tin ceilings, **The Exchange Shopping Emporium** is part of Church Street Station. The Exchange offers 50 specialty shops spread over several floors. Although there are some American mall standards such as **Victoria's Secret,** most stores offer more unusual wares. Places to visit include **Black Market Minerals,** which sells an infinite variety of things made of stone—polished semiprecious gems and beads and even big slabs of quartz in a variety of colors. **The Gothic Shop** sells everything plaster, concentrating on angel figures, gargoyles, and Greek and Roman images. **Udderly Country**—you guess the theme.

Just across the tracks is **Church Street Market,** a collection of another 30 shops and restaurants. The Market includes **Behr's Chocolates,** which sells a variety of homemade confections, along with retailers like **Hit or Miss,** a woman's clothing store, and **Brookstone,** an upscale shop specializing in electronic equipment like massage chairs and computerized toys of all sorts. All of the merchandise is on display for you to play with, um, try out. Restaurants include **The Olive Garden, Pizzeria Uno,** and **Hooter's,** a restaurant known for scantily clad, shapely waitresses serving up hot wings, curly fries, and suds. (The name, company officials claim with a straight face, in no way refers to a slang term for a certain part of the female anatomy.)

Church Street Market is open from Monday through Saturday, 10am to 10pm; Sunday, noon to 6pm. Restaurants are open later.

To get to the shopping complexes from the attractions, take I-4 east to downtown Orlando. Get off at Anderson Street (Exit 38). Turn left on Boone Avenue, then left on South Street. Turn right on Garland Avenue. Parking is available in a city-owned lot between South Street and Garland Avenue. Note your parking space and pay at the machines located at the end of the lot.

A FLEA MARKET

The largest flea market in the world, that's what you'll find in Sanford, about 40 minutes north of the attractions.

Flea World is pretty much exactly what the name implies, a huge flea market with everything from dentist's and lawyer's offices to lingerie and lamps. Although some folks have affectionately called the place the "white-trash mall," the politically correct term would be "economically challenged shopping emporium." Car tires, plants, ginsu knives, gourmet coffee, fresh produce, leather chaps. . . the array of merchandise is impressive even if the surroundings aren't. Unlike flea markets in some regions, this one sells mostly new merchandise in its nearly 2,000 booths. (A couple folks set up booths to sell old auto parts or garage-style finds.) Among this babble of bargains are many shops selling Florida T-shirts and souvenir-worthy knickknacks. Entertainment as diverse as live demonstrations by lions and tigers to Elvis impersonators and bingo games is regularly featured on the Flea World stage.

Nearby **Fun World** offers miniature golf courses, a miniature race track with gas-powered cars for the kiddies, a video arcade, and a small collection of carnival rides.

Although it is about 40 minutes from the theme parks, Flea World is more American than apple pie and a good place for bargains. Be warned: Some of the barnlike buildings are not air-conditioned, so this is not the best place to shop in the hot summer months. Business is good enough that it is open only from Friday through Sunday from 8am to 5pm. To get there take I-4 to Exit 50, Lake Mary Boulevard. Go about 3 miles to U.S. 17/92 and turn left. Continue for about 1 mile. Flea World will be on your right. You will be directed to parking in an unpaved lot. For information call ☎ 407/321-1792.

A MORE HOMESPUN ALTERNATIVE

Mount Dora is a haven for artists and retirees and a wonderful day trip, not to mention a wonderful alternative to Disney. (Parents: Put the kids in one of the day-long camp programs—see chapter 2—and take a day to yourselves.) Mount Dora, established in 1874, has the genuine feel of an old Florida town with an authentic Main Street like the one Disney tries to re-create. The 19th-century buildings still lining the streets are a perfect postcard picture leading up to the calm dark-green waters of Lake Dora. Unlike most of Florida, this town actually includes rolling hills, adding to the charm.

Stroll through the dozens of shops featuring crafts, art and antiques, and collectibles and then take a break with lunch at the **Beauclair Dining Room** at the historic **Lakeside Inn.** Enjoy lemonade and cookies while rocking on the front porch overlooking the lake.

For information call the Mount Dora Area Chamber of Commerce (☎ 352/ 383-2165).

To get there take I-4 to U.S. 441 and go west. Take Old U.S. 441 or Route 44B into town. Look for signs directing you to the "business district."

SPORTS STORES

Sports fans aching to add to their collection can tackle that shopping obsession at several stores specializing in merchandise for the Orlando Magic, the University of Florida Gators, and the Florida State University Seminoles.

There are four locations of the **Magic FanAttic,** which sells every conceivable item embossed with the logo of the NBA's Orlando Magic. From lamps to alarm clocks to jerseys from the Magic's most popular player, "Penny" Hardaway, the **FanAttic** delivers. (Check the discount clearance bin for merchandise bearing Shaquille O'Neal, who defected to the L.A. Lakers in 1996.) The store also carries merchandise featuring the cool images of the shades-wearing polar-bear mascot of Orlando's ice-hockey team, the Solar Bears. (Yes, I said ice hockey.)

The main branch of the store is located in downtown Orlando at 715 N. Garland Ave. (☎ 407/649-2222). Take I-4 east to Exit 41 (Amelia Street). Stay to the right as the road goes around the bend. At the next light, go straight. The parking lot is on the left. The store is open daily from 10am to 6pm. Other locations are in the **Renaissance Center** near the Altamonte Mall (see above), at the **Orlando International Airport,** and in the **West Oaks Mall** in Ocoee.

The name **Gatorstuff** gives you a hint as to what is sold here. The growling gator and the orange and blue of the 1996 National Champion University of Florida is the *sole* color scheme. The store is located east of downtown Orlando at 1021 E. Colonial Dr. (☎ 407/898-2129). Take I-4 east to Exit 41 (Amelia Street). Stay to the right as the road goes around the bend. At the next light, turn right. Look for the multistoried purple and yellow "Cruises Only" building. Gatorstuff is on the left side of the road and is open from 10am to 6pm.

It's a wonder how they keep peace among the rabid fans of UF and FSU (Florida State University) but the **University Store** sells merchandise of both the Florida Gators and their arch rival the FSU Seminoles. The store is located near downtown Orlando, at 1406 N. Mills Ave. (☎ 407/896-9391). To get there from the theme parks take I-4 east to Princeton Street (Exit 43). Turn right on Orange Avenue. Turn left at Virginia Avenue. The store is at the corner of Mills and Virginia avenues. Look for the painting of a Seminole Indian rasslin' with a gator on the side of the building. Open from Monday through Friday 10am to 6pm; Saturday, 10am to 4pm.

Walt Disney World & Orlando After Dark

10

The opening of Universal's nighttime entertainment complex, **City Walk,** shows that people in charge seem to feel visitors need more places to go after a long day of schlepping around the theme parks.

My hat's off to those of you who after a long day traipsing around amusement parks still have the energy to venture out at night in search of entertainment. You'll find plenty to do. And this being a kid's world, many of the theme-park evening shows are geared to families. There is, however, plenty of adults-only entertainment both at the parks and beyond in downtown Orlando.

Check the "Calendar" section of Friday's **Orlando Sentinel** for up-to-the-minute details on local clubs, visiting performers, concerts, and events. Also check out the *Orlando Sentinel Online* at **http://www.oso@aol.com**. It has hundreds of listings. The *Orlando Weekly* is a free magazine circulated in boxes throughout Central Florida that highlights more offbeat and often more up-to-date performers and performances. Also, *Downtown Orlando Monthly* highlights cultural events, sports, and entertainment in downtown Orlando; it is available in boxes throughout the downtown area.

Tickets to many performances are handled by **TicketMaster** (☎ **407/839-3900** to charge tickets).

1 What's New in 1998 (& What's in the Works)

This figures to be a big year for nightlife in Orlando as Disney and Universal begin to compete head-to-head, with Disney expanding Pleasure Island and Universal opening City Walk. Plus, bars and clubs in downtown Orlando continue to flourish, offering locals and tourists something to do in addition to Church Street Station.

Disney is expanding Pleasure Island (details below), to include Dan Aykroyd's **House of Blues,** which is scheduled to open in early 1998. Based on the likes of Jake and Elwood, the Blues Brothers, the hot spot will offer live music (blues, R&B, jazz, and country) nightly and a New Orleans–style menu. Also included will be **Lario's,** created by Gloria Estefan and her husband Emilio, which, like its popular Miami Beach sister club, will feature sizzling Latin American rhythms; **Disney's Entertainment Theater,** a new performing-arts venue to showcase Disney productions and visiting headliners; and 14 new screens at the already-extant multiplex **AMC Theatres,** bringing its total to 24 and making it the largest such complex in the state. Also coming is **The Cirque Du Soleil,** a 1,650-seat theater in the Pleasure Island entertainment district. The unique venue will feature circus-style performances that have been very popular in Montreal, New York City, Las Vegas, and Berlin.

There are also exciting developments under way at Universal Studios Florida, where a multibillion-dollar expansion (due for completion in January 1998) will include a dynamic, high-energy 12-acre entertainment complex called **City Walk.** Occupying a two-tiered promenade with authentic streetscapes, a 4-acre lagoon, waterfalls, and lush landscaping, City Walk could easily be renamed theme-restaurant heaven. Not only is it home to the world's largest **Hard Rock Cafe**—the grande dame of all theme restaurants—but also the **NASCAR Cafe,** the **Motown Cafe,** and **Marvel Mania,** a theme send-up to villains and superheroes. City Walk will also contain a hearty dose of Cajun spice with **Pat O'Brien's,** a re-creation of the joint in New Orleans, and **Emeril's of New Orleans,** featuring the Creole-based cuisine of chef Emeril Lagasse. If that's not enough to keep you busy, there is the **Down Beat Jazz Hall of Fame,** a tribute to reggae *mon* Bob Marley, and a 16-screen, 5,000-seat **Cineplex Odeon Megaplex** with a cutting-edge projection and sound system; finally, there will be a floating outdoor theater to be used for special shows and concerts.

2 Walt Disney World Dinner Shows

Two distinctly different dinner shows are hosted by Walt Disney World. Other night-time park options include SpectroMagic, fireworks, and IllumiNations (details in chapter 7).

Hoop-Dee-Doo Musical Revue

At Disney's Fort Wilderness Resort and Campground, 3520 N. Fort Wilderness Trail. ☎ **407/ WDW-DINE** (939-3463). Reservations required. $37 adults, $19.50 children 3–11. Taxes and gratuities extra. Show times at 5, 7:15, and 9:30pm nightly. Free self-parking.

Fort Wilderness's rustic log-beamed Pioneer Hall is the setting for this 2-hour foot-stompin', hand-clappin', down-home musical revue. It's a high-energy show, with 1890s costumes, corny vaudeville jokes, rousing songs, and lots of good-natured audience participation.

During the show, the audience chows down on an all-you-can-eat barbecue dinner, including chips and salsa, salad, smoked ribs, country-fried chicken, corn on the cob, baked beans, loaves of fresh-baked bread with honey butter, and a big slab of strawberry shortcake for dessert. Beverages (coffee, tea, beer, sangria, and soda) are included.

Reservations are required. If you catch an early show, stick around for the Electrical Water Pageant at 9:45pm, which can be viewed from the Fort Wilderness Beach.

Polynesian Luau Dinner Show

At Disney's Polynesian Resort, 1600 Seven Seas Dr. ☎ **407/WDW-DINE** (939-3463). Reservations required. $37 adults, $19.50 children 3–11. Taxes and gratuities are extra. Show times 6:45 and 9:30pm nightly. Free self- and valet parking.

This delightful 2-hour dinner show is a big favorite with kids, who are all invited up on the stage. It features a colorfully costumed cast of entertainers from New Zealand, Tahiti, Hawaii, and Samoa performing authentic hula, warrior, ceremonial, love, and fire dances on a flower-bedecked stage. The show also includes a Hawaiian/Polynesian fashion show.

It all takes place in an open-air theater (dress for nighttime weather) with candlelit tables, red-flame lanterns suggesting torches, and tapa-bark paintings adorning the walls. Arrive early; there's a preshow highlighting Polynesian crafts and culture (lei making, hula lessons, and more).

The all-you-can-eat meal includes a big platter of fresh island fruits, barbecued chicken, corn on the cob, other vegetables, roasted red potatoes and sweet potatoes, pull-apart cinnamon bread, beverages, and a tropical ice-cream sundae.

Reservations are required. There's also a 4:30pm version daily called Mickey's Tropical Luau (see character-meal listings in chapter 6).

3 More Dinner Shows

American Gladiators Orlando Live!

Gladiator Arena, 5515 W. Irlo Bronson Memorial Hwy. (U.S. 192, between I-4 and Fla. 535), Kissimmee. ☎ **800/BATTLE-4** or 407/240-0069. Reservations recommended. Snack show: adults $27.95, children 3–12 $15.95, under 3 free; dinner show: adults $39.95, children 3–12 $21.50. Sun–Thurs 7:30pm, Fri–Sat 6:30 and 9:30pm; the 2-show weekend time schedule is also in effect mid-Feb to mid-Apr, the 3rd week of June–the 3rd week of Aug, and Christmas week. Free parking.

This 90-minute, action-packed show features qualified contenders battling in areas such as assault, breakthrough and conquer, joust, powerball, the wall, and whiplash. If you don't know what all that means, watch it on TV before you decide whether or not it's your thing. Shows at 6:30 and 7:30pm include a full chicken dinner, while snack fare is served at the later show.

Arabian Nights

6225 W. Irlo Bronson Memorial Hwy. (or U.S. Hwy. 192, just east of I-4 at Exit 25A), Kissimmee. ☎ **800/553-6116** or 407/239-9223. Reservations recommended. Admission $36.95 adults, $23.95 children 3–11. Shows nightly at 7:30pm. Free parking.

Entering its 10th year, Arabian Nights offers a little bit of everything from prancing Royal Lipizzaner Stallions to chariot races. The 2-hour show claims to have more characters, costumes, and lights than any show on Broadway. You certainly won't find the "land of the mythical unicorn" on the Great White Way.

The menu includes salad, prime rib, vegetables, new potatoes, dinner rolls, dessert, and beer, wine, and soft drinks. The price of admission covers the cost of the dinner and the show.

Medieval Times

4510 W. Irlo Bronson Memorial Hwy., (or U.S. Hwy. 192, 11 miles east of the main Disney entrance, next to Super Wal-Mart) in Kissimmee. ☎ **800/229-8300** or 407/239-0214. Reservations recommended. Admission $36.95 adults, $22.95 children 3–12. Daily at 8pm. Free parking.

Jim Carrey fans know that the Cable Guy went to a California branch of Medieval Times to duel with his hapless friend. A longtime favorite for Orlando visitors, the Kissimmee-based show is billed as "dinner and tournament." Living up to its name, it includes jousting contests, armored clashes, and 80 Andalusian stallions performing with military precision. It's all put on for you and 1,000 of the "special" guests of the castle, who eat off heavy metal plates while watching the tournament contestants tumble about before them. Dark and cavernous, Medieval Times has an ambiance all its own. The menu includes a wine cocktail, fresh-vegetable soup, a whole roasted chicken, spare ribs, herb-basted potatoes, and dessert. The price includes

Blazing Pianos: A Perfect Hell for the Shy

A rambunctious crowd of all ages hangs out at this popular sing-along club, where a talented cast of singers and musicians—on fire-engine–red grand pianos—perform classic rock tunes, do a bit of comedy, and try to embarrass audience members. Most of the songs they select are on the lively side—"Great Balls of Fire," "The Twist," "Jailhouse Rock," and the like, as well as TV theme songs.

Audience members occasionally get up on the stage—or are dragooned there—to dance. And probably once a night everyone stands up to perform "Hand Jive." Blazing Pianos promotes audience participation to the max; it's an exhibitionist's paradise, and perhaps unbearable for the sensitive (you might be spotlighted if they see you're not singing!). The ambiance is slick and upscale; special effects include smoke, mirror balls, and strobe lights. A fairly extensive bar menu lists items such as fried calamari and buffalo wings, plus gourmet desserts.

Blazing Pianos is located in the Mercado at 8445 International Blvd., just south of Sand Lake Road (☎ **407/363-5104**).

Admission is $5. Though it opens earlier, the action begins about 9:30pm and continues until 2am nightly. No one under 21 is admitted weekend nights. Sunday through Thursday, children are welcome, and it makes for a fun family outing.

---

dinner, beverages, and the show. The castle is air-conditioned and accessible to the handicapped. Medieval Times is very popular, so reservations are suggested.

Wild Bill's Wild West Dinner Extravaganza

5260 U.S. 192 (just east of I-4). ☎ **800/883-8181** or 407/351-5151. Reservations recommended. Admission $35.92 adults, $22.50 children 3–11, under 3 free. Nightly at 7pm, with 9:30pm shows on selected nights. Free parking.

Located at Fort Liberty, a 22-acre western-themed shopping/dining/entertainment complex, this rambunctious dinner show takes place in a big, barnlike wooden building. You'll be given a cardboard cowboy hat when you sit down, which identifies you as a shepherd or cowherd for audience-participation activities (there are a lot of these). The show includes rousing song-and-dance numbers ("Annie Get Your Gun," "Oklahoma," "Back in the Saddle Again"); rodeo roping, knife-throwing, and archery demonstrations; sing-alongs; a cancan; and Comanche ceremonial and war dances. All the children in the audience get to go up on the stage.

Dinner—served on pewterware—is a hearty four-course meal consisting of salad, soup, beef stew, fried chicken, barbecued pork ribs, biscuits with honey butter, corn, beans, a baked potato, and hot apple pie. Beer, wine, and Coca-Cola are included.

4 Entertainment Complexes: Pleasure Island & Church Street Station

Pleasure Island

In Walt Disney World, adjacent to Walt Disney World Village. ☎ **407/934-7781**. Free admission before 7pm, $19.03 after 7pm. Admission included in the 5-Day World-Hopper Pass. Clubs daily 7pm–2am; shops 11am–2am. Free self-parking; valet parking $5.

This Walt Disney World theme park is a rollicking 6-acre complex of nightclubs, restaurants, shops, and movie theaters where, for a single admission price, you can enjoy a night of club-hopping until the wee hours.

Due to double in size in the near future (see section 1 for more details), the park is designed to evoke an abandoned waterfront industrial district with clubs in "converted" ramshackle lofts, factories, and warehouses, but the streets are festive with brightly colored lights and balloons. Dozens of searchlights play overhead, and rock music emanates from the bushes. You'll be given a map and show schedule when you enter the park; take a look at it, and plan your evening around shows that interest you.

The mood here is always festive. For one thing, every night at Pleasure Island is New Year's Eve, celebrated on the stroke of midnight with a high-energy street party, live entertainment, a barrage of fireworks, and showers of confetti.

Although this is Disney, it is essentially a bar district where liquor is served, so when sending out your teens, use the same rules that you use at home. This is the place at which the singer Bobby Brown got arrested for fighting. They must be 18 to get in unless accompanied by a parent or legal guardian.

The clubs are:

Pleasure Island Jazz Company: This big, barnlike club—purported to be an abandoned waterfront carousel factory—features contemporary and traditional live jazz. Performers are mostly locals, but about once a month there are big names such as Kenny Rankin, Lionel Hampton, Maynard Ferguson, the Rippingtons, and Billy Taylor. Light fare, international coffees, and a variety of foreign and domestic wines are available.

Mannequins Dance Palace: Housed in a vast dance hall with a small-town movie-house facade, Mannequins is supposed to be a converted theatrical mannequin warehouse (remember, you're still in Disney World). It's a high-energy club with a large rotating dance floor and is a favorite of locals. Three levels of bars and hangout space are festooned with elaborately costumed mannequins and moving scenery suspended from overhead rigging. A DJ plays contemporary tunes at ear-splitting decibel levels, and there are high-tech lighting effects. You must be 21 to get in, and they're very serious about it. Have your ID ready, even if you learned to dance to the Platters.

Neon Armadillo Music Saloon: You guessed it: This trilevel club is country—with neon beer signs, rustic tables mounted on beer barrels, walls hung with spurs and saddles, and a spur-shaped neon chandelier. Live country bands play nightly, and dancers whirl around the floor doing the Texas Two-Step or Cotton-Eyed Joe (lessons are given Sunday from 7 to 8pm). Sometimes name stars come in and take the stage. The staff is in cowboy/cowgirl garb. A specialty at the bar is Jell-O shooters—Jell-O cubes laced with rum, vodka, and other alcoholic beverages. You can also order Southwestern fare here such as chili and fajitas.

Adventurers Club: The most unique—and my personal favorite—of Pleasure Island's clubs occupies a multistory building that, according to Disney legend, was designed to house the vast library and archaeological trophy collection of island founder and compulsive explorer Merriweather Adam Pleasure. It's also headquarters for the Adventures Club, which Pleasure headed up until he vanished at sea in 1941. The plushly furnished club is chock-full of artifacts—early aviation photos, hunting trophies, shrunken heads, Buddhas, Indian goddesses, spears, and a mounted "yakoose" (half yak, half moose) who occasionally speaks. He's not the only one. In the eerie Mask Room, strange sounds are often heard, and more than 100 masks move their eyes, jeer, and make odd pronouncements. Also on hand are Pleasure's zany band of globe-trotting friends and club servants, played by skilled actors who interact with guests and always stay in character. Improvisational comedy shows take place throughout the evening in the main salon, diverse 20-minute cabaret shows/ events in the library (during which "volunteers" are dragooned from the audience).

You could easily hang out here all night imbibing potent tropical drinks in the library and at the bar—where elephant-foot barstools rise and sink mysteriously.

Comedy Warehouse: Housed in the island's former power plant, the Comedy Warehouse—another favorite of mine—has a rustic interior with tiered seating. A very talented troupe performs 45-minute improvisational comedy shows based on audience suggestions. There are five shows a night, and bar drinks are available. Arrive early.

Rock & Roll Beach Club: Once the laboratory in which Pleasure developed a unique flying machine, this three-story structure today houses a dance club where live bands play "classic rock from the 60s through the 90s." There are bars on all three floors, including one serving international beers. The first level contains the dance floor. The second and third levels offer air hockey, pool tables, basketball machines, pinball, video games, darts, and a pizza and beer stand.

8 Trax: This 1970s-style club, with about 50 TV monitors airing diverse shows and videos over the dance floor, occupies three levels, all with bars. Period movie posters (*Bananas, Star Wars*) adorn the walls, and the top-floor lounge is vaguely psychedelic in decor. A DJ plays disco music, and guests engage in games of Twister.

In addition, live bands—including occasional big-name groups—play the **West End Plaza** outdoor stage and the **Hub Stage;** check your schedule for show times. You can star in your own music video at **SuperStar Studios.** And there are carnival games, a video-game arcade, virtual-reality games, a Velcro wall (don a jumpsuit over your clothes, bounce on a trampoline, and stick yourself on), and an Orbitron (a "21st-century workout machine," originally developed for NASA, that lets you experience weightlessness). Shops and eateries (with outdoor umbrellaed tables) are found throughout the park. **Planet Hollywood** (see chapter 6 for details) is adjacent.

Church Street Station

129 W. Church St. (off I-4, between Garland and Orange aves. in downtown Orlando). ☎ 407/ 422-2434. Free admission prior to 5pm, after which you have to pay $16.95. Clubs open nightly until 2am; shops until 11pm. There are several parking lots nearby (call for specifics). Take I-4 east to Exit 38 (Anderson St.), stay in the left lane, and follow the signs. Most hotels offer transportation to and from Church St., and, since you'll probably be drinking, I advise it.

Though not part of Walt Disney World, Church Street Station in downtown Orlando operates on a similar principle to Pleasure Island (in fact, it started the concept).

Occupying a cobblestoned city block lined with turn-of-the-century buildings (real ones), it, too, is a shopping/dining/nightclub complex offering a diverse evening of entertainment for a single admission price. There are 20 live shows nightly (consult your show schedule upon entering), plus an array of street performers. Major blowout celebrations are held for special events such as St. Patrick's Day and the Super Bowl.

Stunning interiors are the rule here. It's worth coming by just to check out the magnificent woodwork, stained glass, and thousands of authentic antiques. And capitalizing on the traffic Church Street generates, many other clubs have opened in the immediate area, further enlarging your bar-hopping potential.

Entry to restaurants, the Exchange Shopping Emporium, and the Midway game area is free. Highlights include:

Rosie O'Grady's Good Time Emporium: This 1890s-style gambling hall–cum-saloon, with beveled- and leaded-glass panels, etched mirrors, and vast globe chandeliers suspended from a high pressed-tin ceiling, is filled with interesting antiques. The train benches came from an old Florida rail station, back-bar mirrors from a

Glasgow pub, and bank tellers' cages from a 19th-century Pittsburgh bank. Dixieland bands, banjo players, singing waiters, and cancan dancers entertain nightly. Light fare (deli sandwiches, chili dogs) is available. The house specialty drink is a rum and fruit concoction called the Flaming Hurricane (served in a souvenir glass). The "Good Time Piano Man" plays at 1:30, 2:30, 3:30 and 4:30pm; visitors are encouraged to sing along.

Apple Annie's Courtyard: Adjoining Rosie's, this brick-floored establishment, domed by arched trusses from an early 19th-century New Orleans church, evokes a Victorian tropical garden. The room is further embellished by 12-foot hand-carved filigree mirrors created in Vienna circa 1740 and magnificent 1,000-pound chandeliers suspended from an ornate vaulted cherry-wood ceiling. An 18th-century French communion rail serves as the front bar. Seating is in wicker peacock chairs at English pub tables. Patrons sip potent tropical fresh fruit and ice-cream drinks while listening to folk and bluegrass music.

Lili Marlene's Aviator's Pub & Restaurant: Its plush, oak-paneled interior is embellished with World War I memorabilia, stained-glass transoms, and accoutrements from an 1850 Rothschild town house in Paris, the latter including a walnut fireplace and wine cabinets. Eclectic seating ranges from hand-carved oak pews that came from a French church to a place at a large drop-leaf mahogany table where Al Capone once dined. Model airplanes and marvelous Victorian chandeliers are suspended from a beamed pine ceiling with a stained-glass skylight. The menu features premium aged steaks, prime rib, and fresh seafood.

Phineas Phogg's Balloon Works: This whimsical bar, with hot-air balloons and airplanes over the dance floor, is a high-energy club playing loud, pulsating music. It doubles as a virtual ballooning museum housing photographs and artifacts from historic flights, including Orlando native Joe Kittinger—the first man to cross the Atlantic in a gas balloon. Every Wednesday from 6:30 to 7:30pm, beers cost just 5¢ here. No one under 21 is admitted.

Cheyenne Saloon and Opera House: This stunning trilevel balconied saloon, crowned by a lofty stained-glass skylight, is constructed of golden oak lumber from a century-old Ohio barn. Quality western art is displayed throughout, including many oil paintings and 11 Remington sculptures. Balcony seating, in restored church pews, overlooks the stage—the setting for entertainment ranging from country bands (some big names) to clogging exhibitions—and the dance floor. There are free country-dance lessons in the saloon on Friday, Saturday, and Sunday from 2pm to 5:30pm. The menu features steaks, barbecued chicken and ribs, and hickory-smoked brisket.

Orchid Garden Ballroom: This stunning space, with ornate white wrought-iron arches and Victorian lighting fixtures suspended from an elaborate oak-paneled ceiling, is the setting for an oldies dance club. A DJ plays rock 'n' roll classics like "Great Balls of Fire" and "Let's Go to the Hop," interspersed with live bands. As the evening progresses, so do the musical decades.

Crackers Oyster Bar: Brick columns, oak paneling, and a gorgeous antique oak and mahogany bar characterize this cozy, late 1800s–style dining room. Fresh Florida seafood is featured, along with more than 50 imported beers. You can nibble on appetizers such as oysters Rockefeller, smoked fish dip, and steamed mussels. Or opt for more serious entrees ranging from crab cakes rémoulade to paella.

In addition, the 87,000-square–foot Exchange houses the carnival-like **Commander Ragtime's Midway of Fun, Food, and Games** (including an enormous video-game arcade), a food court, and more than 50 specialty shops. You can rent a horse-drawn carriage out front for a drive around the downtown area and Lake Eola. And hot-air balloon flights can be arranged (☎ 407/841-8787).

5 Other Downtown Hot Spots

There are dozens of clubs and restaurants along the main street in downtown, Orange Avenue. A free public transportation system called **Lymmo** runs in a designated lane that connects many of these clubs, but since Lymmo stops running at about 11pm, it may stop moving before you do. Keep enough money for a taxi.

Eight Seconds

100 W. Livingston Ave., Orlando. ☎ **407/839-4800.** Cover charge varies.

What used to be the hottest concert spot in downtown has been transformed into a honky-tonk, complete with "Buckin' Bull Nights" and a mechanical bull, à la *Urban Cowboy.* Yeeehaaaawww. (Eight seconds is the time a cowboy or cowgirl needs to stay atop his or her steer to score.)

Jani Lane's Sunset Strip

25 S. Orange Ave. (corner of Orange and Pine), Orlando. ☎ **407/649-4803.** Cover charge varies but is usually between $5 and $10.

Big hair, leather, and heavy-metal music are the standards at this large, loud downtown favorite. Local acts predominate, and you'll find occasional special concerts by hard-rocking bands. A balcony overlooks busy Orange Avenue.

Kit Kat Club/Go Lounge/Yab Yum

23 Wall St. Plaza (off of Orange Ave.), Orlando. ☎ **407/422-6990.** No cover for the Kit Kat; cover varies, usually under $10 for Go Lounge; Yab Yum cover varies, but is usually under $5.

Plush red-velvet couches, pool tables, and the feel of a swinging joint of a different era—complete with a cigarette girl—this is a magnet for Generation-X types who dig the Tony Bennett on the jukebox. The Kit Kat Club is attached to the coffeehouse Yab Yum, which features delicious javas and a variety of sandwiches, and the Go Lounge, a small alternative dance club.

Renaissance

22. S. Magnolia Ave. (1 block off Orange Ave.), Orlando. ☎ **407/422-3595.** Cover charge $5.

One of the newer arrivals to downtown, this is a large, popular dance club with bars on three levels. You'll find lots of retro-70s clothes and kids trying to look older than their age. Reggae is played on an open-air rooftop on the weekends.

Sapphire Supper Club

54 N. Orange Ave., Orlando. ☎ **407/246-1419.** Cover charge varies.

Local and national acts both perform at this laid-back club with vintage brick walls. Jazz legend and transplanted Orlando resident Sam Rivers is a regular. This place is as cool and jazzy as the music it often features and offers specials like "Martini and Cigar" nights. It's popular with young professionals and music-lovers of all ages.

Scruffy Murphy's

9 W. Washington St. (off of Orange Ave.). ☎ **407/648-5460.** No cover.

Here you'll find Irish beers, special events like the "Celtic Throw Down," and bartenders with authentic Irish brogues saying there is "no, never" a cover charge. A good place to hang out and enjoy some unusual—for Florida at least—entertainment. But it's more watering hole than wild dance palace.

Sloppy Joe's

41 W. Church St. (between Church Street Station and Orange Ave.). ☎ **407/843-5825.** No cover Sun–Thurs; $3 Fri–Sat.

Based loosely, very loosely, on the Key West bar where Papa Hemingway liked to hang, this place caters mainly to a college and tourist crowd. The live music is always loud, the lines are always long, and the drink specials help give a different meaning to the "sloppy" in the name. Everybody rushes to get in so they can sit on the patio and watch the Church Street traffic stream before them. Go figure.

Zuma Beach

46 N. Orange Ave. ☎ **407/648-8363.** Open to those 18 and over. Under 21, generally a $5 cover. Over 21, no cover charge.

The bouncers are well muscled, and servers wear G-strings. One local newspaper dubbed Zuma Beach the "Best Pickup Place," that is if you are hot, hot, hot like the pumping dance music. Located in the former Becham Theater, this is still the site of occasional special live performances.

Terror on Church Street

135 S. Orange Ave. (at Church St. in downtown Orlando, a block from Church Street Station). ☎ **407/649-FEAR** or 407/649-1912. Admission $12 adults, $10 children under 17. Sun–Thurs 7pm–midnight, Fri–Sat 7pm–1am. Most hotels offer transportation to the area. There are several lots nearby (call for specifics). Take I-4 east to Exit 38 (Anderson St.), stay in the left lane, and follow the signs to Church Street Station parking.

Terror on Church Street is a multimedia, high-tech house of horrors incorporating innovative special effects and 23 highly theatrical sets on two floors. On a labyrinthine 25-minute tour of the darkened premises, guests are menaced by cleaver- and chain-saw–wielding maniacs, ghoulish monks, assorted cadavers, vicious dogs, Freddie Kreuger, and Dracula, among others—all convincingly portrayed by actors. Children under 10 are not admitted without an adult. A gift shop on the premises sells stick-on warts and burn scars, coffin banks, and the like.

6 Gay & Lesbian Nightspots

Same-sex dancing is not expressly forbidden anywhere in Orlando—even in WDW—but although there is a lot of pixie dust floating around, we are still in Dixieland. Travelers interested in sampling some of the gay and lesbian hot spots might check out some of the places listed below.

The Club

578 N. Orange Ave. (at Concord St., in a converted garage still bearing the Firestone sign). ☎ **407/426-0005** for information and a weekly schedule. Cover varies.

Go-go boys dance on lifts converted into raised platforms and a diverse group boogies on the hard concrete dance floor. Rooms to the side with couches offer a place for conversations, along with some upstairs warrens, one with a pool table.

Partners

916 N. Mills Ave. (about 5 miles from downtown, next to a dry cleaners). ☎ **407/896-4348.**

Low-key and laid-back, this place has the feel of a neighborhood bar rather than a pickup spot. Located in a nondescript concrete block building, you have to be looking for the Partners sign. This is the place for a relaxing evening.

Southern Nights

375 S. Bumby Ave. (between Anderson St. and Colonial Dr.). ☎ **407/898-0424.**

Voted "Best Gay Bar" by the readers of a local alternative weekly paper, theme nights pack in women on Saturdays and men on Sundays. On Friday night there are three female-impersonator shows.

7   More Entertainment

A SPORTS BAR

Champions

In Marriott's Orlando World Center, 8701 World Center Dr. ☎ **407/239-4200.** Open nightly until 2am. Free self-parking; valet parking $7. No cover.

Champions is a sports-bar chain—one so appealing, it's easy to see why the concept has succeeded. Its interior is chockablock with $25,000 worth of signed sports photos, posters, and artifacts such as Lou Gehrig's baseball bat, a golf bag autographed by Dallas Cowboys coach Jimmy Johnson, and (of local interest) a wet suit belonging to Cypress Gardens' famed barefoot waterskiing star, Banana George. Some nights a DJ plays music (mostly Motown and oldies) for dancing. Otherwise, entertainment includes three pool tables, video games, Foosball, darts, coin-op football and basketball, and blackjack tables. In addition, sporting events are aired on large-screen TVs and on smaller monitors around the room (a calendar at the entrance lists all game times). Champions offers a fairly extensive bar-food menu.

Note to single women: Men outnumber women about five to one, so this is a good place to meet guys—if you can distract them from the sports action on the screen.

AN ALCOHOL-FREE ALTERNATIVE

Club Soda

6341 N. Orange Blossom Trail (about 35 miles from the heart of tourist central, near the intersection of Clarcona–Ocoee Rd. and Orange Blossom Trail), Orlando. ☎ **407/523-1556.**

Those looking to party away from the (at times) alcohol-drenched tourist areas can have an alcohol-free night at Club Soda. Sunday and Tuesday are karaoke nights. Live music with a house band on Wednesday. There is a DJ and dancing on the weekends. Weekend dances are sometimes sponsored by various local 12-step groups. This place is very laid-back, very low-key. Crowds are small.

MOVIES

Pleasure Island AMC Theater

In Walt Disney World adjacent to the Pleasure Island nightclub complex. ☎ **407/827-1300.** Matinees $4.50 adults, $3.75 seniors and children 2–13, under 2 free; twilight shows (4:30–6pm) $3.25 for all seats; evening shows $6.50 adults, $4.50 students, $3.75 seniors (over 55) and children 2–13, under 2 free.

This 10-screen AMC theater complex—equipped with state-of-the-art Dolby-digital sound systems and 70mm projection capability—extends the variety of nighttime entertainment available to Disney World guests and will soon extend it further; it's adding 14 new screens to become Florida's largest multiplex! A bridge connects the theater complex with Pleasure Island clubs. New Disney films premiere here, and first-run films are shown; check the *Orlando Sentinel* for show times.

8   Major Concert Halls & Auditoriums

Three large entertainment facilities, administered by the Orlando Centroplex, host the majority of big-name performers playing the Orlando area.

The **Florida Citrus Bowl,** 1610 W. Church St., at Tampa Street (☎ 407/ 849-2020 for information, 407/839-3900 to charge tickets), with 70,000 seats, is the largest. This is the setting for major rock concerts and headliners like Billy Joel, Elton John, The Eagles, Guns 'n' Roses, Paul McCartney, Metallica, and the Rolling Stones. To reach the Citrus Bowl, take I-4 east to the East–West Expressway and head west to Highway 441; make a left on Church Street and follow the signs. Parking is $5.

The 17,500-seat **Orlando Arena** at 600 W. Amelia St., between I-4 and Parramore Avenue (☎ 407/849-2020 for information, 407/839-3900 to charge tickets), also hosts major performers (Elton John, Bruce Springsteen, Billy Joel, Bette Midler) in addition to an array of family-oriented entertainment: Ringling Bros. Barnum & Bailey Circus every January, Discover Card Stars on Ice in February, Tour of World Figure-Skating Champions in April or May, and Walt Disney's World on Ice in September. To reach the arena, take I-4 east to Amelia Avenue, turn left at the traffic light at the bottom of the off-ramp, and follow the signs. Parking is $5.

The area's major cultural venue is the **Bob Carr Performing Arts Centre,** 401 W. Livingston St., between I-4 and Parramore Avenue (☎ 407/849-2020 for information, 407/839-3900 to charge tickets). Concert prices vary with performers: ballet tickets are $15 to $35, opera tickets $12 to $45, Broadway Series $24.50 to $46.50. This 2,500-seat facility is home to the Orlando Opera Company and the Southern Ballet Theater, both of which have October-to-May seasons. The Orlando Broadway Series (September to May) features original-cast Broadway shows such as *Carousel, The Who's Tommy, Damn Yankees,* and *Cats.* Also featured at the Bob Carr are concerts and comedy shows; a recent year's performers included Patti LaBelle, Lyle Lovett, Julio Iglesias, and Crosby, Stills, and Nash. To get here, take I-4 east to Amelia Avenue, turn left at the traffic light at the bottom of the off-ramp, and follow the signs. Parking is $5.

11 Short Trips in the Orlando Area

Get away from the glitter and glitz that characterize most Orlando attractions. Stroll through Cypress Gardens—a serene botanical paradise that was central Florida's first major tourist draw, or head to Winter Park, a charming upscale town with some exquisite attractions.

1 Cypress Gardens

40 miles SW of Walt Disney World, 45 miles SW of Orlando

Founded in 1936 when Dick and Julie Pope hired a crew of laborers to dig canals and drain swamps, **Cypress Gardens,** located on Fla. 540 at Cypress Gardens Boulevard in Winter Haven (☎ **800/ 282-2123** or 941/324-2111), came into being as a 16-acre public garden along the banks of Lake Eloise with cypress-wood–block pathways and thousands of tropical and subtropical plants. Today it has grown to over 200 acres, with ponds and lagoons, waterfalls, classic Italian fountains, topiary, bronze sculptures, and manicured lawns. Ancient cypress trees shrouded in Spanish moss form a backdrop to ever-changing floral displays of 8,000 varieties of plants from more than 90 countries. Southern belles in Scarlett O'Hara costumes stroll the grounds or sit on benches under parasols in idyllic, tree-shaded nooks. They symbolize Florida's old-fashioned Southern hospitality.

In 1995, the park, once owned by Anheuser-Busch, was sold to a collection of one-time park managers. Little has changed, but the new team seems to be working hard to lure tourists to their little piece of paradise. New additions include a small tropical zoo, a nighttime show projecting animated characters onto a 35-by-70-foot water screen, and "Biblical Gardens," which features more than 25 plants, fruits, and spices mentioned in the Bible. (Now that's something you don't find at WDW.)

In the late winter and early spring, more than 20 varieties of bougainvillea, 40 of azalea, and hundreds of roses burst into bloom. Crape myrtles, magnolias, and gardenias perfume the late-spring air, while brilliant birds of paradise, hibiscus, and jasmine brighten the summer landscape. And in winter, the goldenrain trees, floss silk trees, and camellias of autumn give way to millions of colorful chrysanthemums and red, white, and pink poinsettias. Tip for allergy sufferers: Be sure to bring along your medicine; this place, though beautiful, can wreck your sinuses, especially on a windy day.

ESSENTIALS

GETTING THERE   Take I-4 west to U.S. 27 south and proceed west on to Fla. 540. If you don't have a car, inquire about public transportation at your hotel. Parking is free.

ADMISSION & HOURS   Admission to Cypress Gardens is $27.95 for adults, $17.45 for children 3 to 9, free for kids under 3. There are discounts for seniors, and in recent years there have been specials allowing children to come free with a paying adult. Cypress Gardens is open 365 days a year, from 9:30am to 5:30pm, with extended hours during peak seasons.

EXPLORING THE GARDENS

Strolling the grounds is, of course, the main attraction (there are over 2 miles of winding botanical paths, and half of the park's acreage is devoted to floral displays), but this being central Florida, it's not the only one.

Shows are scheduled several times each day. The world-famous **Greatest American Ski Team** performs daring freestyle jumps, swivel skiing, barefooting, ski ballet, and slalom exhibitions on Lake Eloise in a show augmented by an awesome hang-gliding display. **Moscow on Ice Live!** is the Russian answer to America's Ice Capades. And **Variété Internationale** features specialty acts from all over the world.

And there's still more. An enchanting exhibit called **Wings of Wonder** surrounds visitors with more than 1,000 brightly colored free-flying butterflies (representing more than 50 species) in a 5,500-square-foot Victorian-style glass conservatory filled with tropical plantings, orchids, and waterfalls.

Electric boats navigate a maze of lushly landscaped canals in the original botanical gardens area. You can ascend 153 feet to the **Island in the Sky** for a panoramic vista of the gardens and a beautiful chain of central Florida lakes.

Carousel Cove, with eight kiddie rides and arcade games, centers on an ornate turn-of-the-century–style carousel. It adjoins another kid pleaser, **Cypress Junction,** an elaborately landscaped model railroad (scenery includes everything from a burning house to Mount Rushmore) that travels 1,100 feet of track with up to 20 trains moving at one time.

Cypress Roots, a museum of park memorabilia, displays photographs of famous visitors (Elvis on water skis, Tiny Tim tiptoeing through the roses) and airs ongoing showings of *Easy to Love* starring Esther Williams (it was filmed here). Another museum commemorates the **age of radio,** with a display of hundreds of vintage radios, radio memorabilia, and recordings of radio shows and music from the 1920s to the 1950s.

Wind up your visit with a relaxing 30-minute narrated **pontoon cruise** on scenic Lake Eloise, past virgin forest, bulrush, and beautiful shoreline homes. En route, you're likely to spot cormorants, osprey, ducks—maybe even an alligator or two. There's an additional $4-per-person charge for this attraction.

WHERE TO DINE

Your options range from a food court to the **Crossroads Restaurant,** a cheerful full-service facility serving American fare and offering alfresco seating at umbrellaed tables on a terrace. I also like the more casual **Lakeview Terrace,** with covered outdoor seating overlooking Lake Eloise; it offers great views of the ski show.

Fresh strawberries are sold throughout the park in season. And if you care to pack a basket, there are picnic tables. Over a dozen shops sell everything from quaint country-store merchandise to gardening books and paraphernalia.

2 Winter Park

20 miles N of Walt Disney World, 5 miles N of Orlando

The beautiful lakefront community of Winter Park was created in the early 1880s as "a first-class place" for "men and women of intelligence, culture, character, taste and means." Developers Loring A. Chase and Oliver E. Chapman priced their lots accordingly. The town was incorporated in 1887. To this day it remains an affluent haven—Florida's answer to Greenwich, Connecticut. You can visit on a day trip, or you can spend a relaxing night or two here away from theme-park hubbub.

Its attractions include a lovely Beverly Hills–like shopping strip (Park Avenue) lined with posh boutiques and art galleries; golf courses; fine old homes along winding, tree-shaded streets; shimmering lakes and canals (Winter Park has been called the "Venice of America"); Central Park, a large village green with lush lawns, stately moss-draped live oaks, and rose gardens; and a museum housing a treasure trove of Tiffany windows, lamps, and objets d'art. And though (actually, *because*) refined Winter Park takes no official notice of the fact, the town attracts numerous celebrities looking for a quaint and quiet retreat.

ESSENTIALS

GETTING THERE   Take I-4 east to Fairbanks Avenue (Exit 45), exit right and proceed east for about a mile, turn left on Park Avenue, and follow the signs to public parking.

Amtrak service (☎ 800/USA-RAIL) is available from Orlando and Kissimmee (see chapter 2 for locations). The Winter Park station is located right in the center of town at 150 W. Morse Blvd. (☎ 407/645-5055).

Take **LYNX bus no. 4** from the Osceola Square Mall at Columbia Street and Hoagland Avenue in Kissimmee. It will take you to the Orlando downtown terminal where you can transfer to bus no. 1 or 9, either of which makes several stops along Park Avenue in Winter Park. Call ☎ 407/841-8240 for a schedule.

VISITOR INFORMATION   For further information about·Winter Park, contact the **Chamber of Commerce,** 150 N. New York Ave., just north of Morse Boulevard (P.O. Box 280), Winter Park, FL 32790 (☎ 407/644-8281). Hours are 9am to 4pm Monday through Friday.

PARKING   Street parking is sometimes difficult. There are convenient and free municipal lots on South New York Avenue on either side of Morse Boulevard.

SEEING THE SIGHTS

Stroll Winter Park's main street, browse its boutiques, visit its museums, play a few rounds of golf, and take a leisurely lake cruise. Do note that most of the town's museums are closed on Monday.

✪ Charles Hosmer Morse Museum of American Art

445 Park Ave. (between Canton and Cole aves.). ☎ 407/645-5311. Admission $3 adults, $1 students of any age. Tues–Sat 9:30am–4pm, Sun 1–4pm. Closed Mon, Memorial Day, July 4, Labor Day, Thanksgiving, Christmas, and New Year's Day.

Anyone who loves the sinuous, nature-inspired art-nouveau genre (and who doesn't?) will be amazed and thrilled by this gem of a gallery. Even those who aren't usually big fans of art will be intrigued by the mammoth scale of these works marked by the intricate detail and brilliant colors of the individual panes. This gallery alone justifies a trip to Winter Park.

It was founded by Hugh and Jeannette McKean in 1942 to display their peerless collection (more than 4,000 pieces), including 40 magnificent windows and 21 paintings created by Louis Comfort Tiffany. Some of the treasures had in fact languished, unseen, in storage for years after a fire destroyed the Tiffany home.

But Tiffany is not the only artist displayed here. There are non-Tiffany windows by William Morris, Frank Lloyd Wright, Frederick Stymetz Lamb, and 15th- and 16th-century German masters; leaded lamps by Tiffany and Emile Gallé; paintings by John Singer Sargent, Samuel F.B. Morse, Maxfield Parrish, Thomas Hart Benton, and Arthur B. Davies; jewelry designed by Tiffany, Lalique, and Fabergé; sculptures by Hiram Powers and Daniel Chester French (of Lincoln Memorial fame); prints by Cézanne, Childe Hassam, Rembrandt, Whistler, Winslow Homer, Mary Cassatt, and Grant Wood; photographic works by Tiffany and other 19th-century artists; and art-nouveau furnishings by Tiffany, Gallé, and others. The collection, which is shown on a rotating basis, also includes Tiffany memorabilia— letters, furnishings, personal effects, and photographs used by his studio as source materials.

And furniture and accessories by Gustav Stickley and his contemporaries—plus a major collection of American art pottery—make the Morse arts and crafts collection one of the most important in the Southeast.

Be sure to peek into the gift shop, where unique items include art-nouveau gift wrap, Maxfield Parrish stationery, and much more.

Cornell Fine Arts Museum

At the eastern end of Holt Ave., on the campus of Rollins College at Lake Virginia. ☎ **407/ 646-2526.** Free admission. Tues–Fri 10am–5pm, Sat–Sun 1–5pm. Free parking in adjacent lot "H." Closed Mon, July 4, Thanksgiving, Christmas Eve, Christmas Day, New Year's Eve, and New Year's Day.

Rollins College was the first home of Hugh and Jeannette McKean's (see listing above) Tiffany glass. Today, with close to 4,000 square feet of exhibition space, it houses an impressive century-spanning collection that includes works by Hiram Powers, Childe Hassam, Tiffany, Thomas Sully, William Glackens, Reginald Marsh, Leonard Baskin, and the studio of Peter Paul Rubens. Also displayed here: 19th-century silver, 17th-century Dutch Delftware, French rococo decorative panels, and Chippendale furniture. Traveling exhibits supplement the collection.

A SCENIC BOAT TOUR

Since 1938, tourists have been boarding pontoons at the eastern end of Morse Boulevard for leisurely hour-long cruises on Winter Park's beautiful chain of natural lakes. The ride traverses Lake Osceola (which flows north into the St. John's River), Lake Virginia, and Lake Maitland, winding through canals built by loggers at the turn of the century and tree-shaded fern gullies lined with bamboo and lush tropical foliage.

You'll view magnificent lakeside mansions and villas (Margaret Mitchell used to winter on Lake Maitland), pristine beaches, cypress swamps, ancient trees draped with Spanish moss, and dozens of marsh birds—white herons, grackle, cormorants, osprey, and gallinule, possibly even an American bald eagle. The captain regales passengers with local lore. It's a delightful trip. You can also rent canoes and small fishing boats here.

For information, call ☎ **407/644-4056.** The price is $6 for adults, $3 for children ages 2 to 11 (children under 2 ride free). Weather permitting, tours depart daily between 10am and 4pm, every hour on the hour, except on Christmas.

WHERE TO STAY

Though you could visit Winter Park on a day excursion from Orlando, you might also consider an overnight stay at one of the following properties.

Langford Resort Hotel

300 E. New England Ave. (at Interlachen Ave.), Winter Park, FL 32789. ☎ **407/644-3400.** Fax 407/628-1952. 209 rms, 9 suites. A/C TV TEL. $75–$115 double; $200 suite. Extra person $10. Children 17 and under stay free in parents' room. Rooms with kitchenettes $10 extra. AE, DC, MC, V. Free self-parking.

In pre-Disney days, Winter Park was one of central Florida's most-visited resorts, and the Langford was the place to stay. Vaughn Monroe entertained in the lounge, and the guest roster listed people like Eleanor Roosevelt, Mamie Eisenhower, Lillian Gish, Vincent Price, and Dina Merrill. Ronald and Nancy Reagan celebrated their 25th wedding anniversary here.

Today, though it's no longer glamorous, this friendly, family-run resort does offer extensive resort facilities at very reasonable rates. Most notably, its on-premises spa offers sauna, steam, massage (shiatsu, Swedish, and deep athletic), body wraps, seaweed wraps, salt glows, facials, manicures, pedicures, and day-of-beauty packages. And its central location, on a lovely street shaded by tall oaks draped with Spanish moss, is another plus. Room decor varies and is notably eclectic. Many rooms have balconies and/or fully equipped kitchenettes with two-burner stoves and small refrigerators.

Dining/Entertainment: The nautical/tropical Bamboo Room serves reasonably priced American fare; steak and seafood are featured at dinner. The adjoining Del Prado bar/lounge provides piano-bar entertainment and complimentary hors d'oeuvres from 5 to 8pm nightly and dancing to live band music Tuesday through Saturday from 8pm to midnight. The elegant Empire Room offers a lavish buffet champagne Sunday brunch and Saturday-night mystery dinner theater.

Services: Concierge (sells tickets, many of them discounted, to Walt Disney World and other Orlando attractions), room service, *Orlando Sentinel* delivered to your room Monday through Friday, baby-sitters.

Facilities: Olympic-size heated swimming pool, kiddie pool, car-rental service, small video-game arcade, unisex hair salon. Golf and tennis are close by.

Park Plaza Hotel

307 Park Ave. S. (at New England Ave.), Winter Park, FL 32789. ☎ **800/228-7220** or 407/647-1072. Fax 407/647-4081. 16 rms, 11 suites. A/C TV TEL. $80–$135 double; $150–$185 suite. During special events, rates may be higher. Rates include continental breakfast. AE, DC, MC, V. Free self- and valet parking.

Centrally located in the heart of the Park Avenue shopping and restaurant district, this small, elegant hotel dates to 1921. Owners John and Sandra Spang bought the property in 1975 and did an exquisite renovation, fitting out rooms bed-and-breakfast–style with antique furnishings, Persian rugs, patchwork quilts, and beautiful floral-print bedspreads. Wide wooden Bermuda shutters on the windows and wood-bladed ceiling fans add tropical ambiance, and homey touches include live plants in white wicker baskets and magazines in the rooms.

Most rooms open onto a wicker-furnished, plant-filled balcony, and many have cozy parlor areas. Especially lovely is the Balcony Suite, which has Victorian-reproduction wallpaper and a brass bed made up with a Ralph Lauren spread, throw pillows, and white dust ruffle. There are also four luxurious honeymoon suites with oversized oak beds and private balconies. In-room amenities include complimentary fruit baskets at check-in.

The hotel's Park Plaza Gardens restaurant (see "Where to Dine," below) adjoins. The front desk offers conciergelike service. Other amenities here include room service, complimentary daily newspaper, and nightly bed turndown; transport to/from Disney parks and the Orlando airport can be arranged. A beauty shop is just behind the property, and, for a fee, guests can use the nearby Winter Park Wellness Center, an extensively equipped health club. A complimentary continental breakfast with fresh-squeezed orange juice and fresh-baked muffins is served daily in the European-style lobby (or in your room). Golf and tennis are close by.

WHERE TO DINE

There are so many fine restaurants in Winter Park that Orlandoans often drive over just to dine and stroll the tree-lined streets or enjoy an ice cream in the park while window shopping.

VERY EXPENSIVE

Park Plaza Gardens

319 Park Ave. S. (between Lyman and New England aves.). ☎ **407/645-2475.** Reservations recommended. Main courses $7.95–$12.95 at lunch (sandwiches and salads $5.95–$8.95), $19.95–$26.95 at dinner. AE, CB, DC, DISC, MC, V. Mon–Sat 11:30am–3pm; Mon–Thurs 6–10pm, Fri–Sat 6–11pm; Sun 11am–3pm and 6–9pm. Free parking at city lot at New England and S. New York aves. CONTEMPORARY AMERICAN/FLORIDIAN SEAFOOD.

This charming patio garden restaurant—with tables shaded by a striped canvas awning and seating amid a small forest of ficus trees—offers the feeling of outdoor dining in air-conditioned comfort. During the day, sunlight streams in through a skylit ceiling; at night, tables are romantically candlelit. Exposed-brick walls hung with changing exhibits serve as gallery space for local artists. There are also cafe tables on Park Avenue.

Chef Luis Colon's culinary creations—served on large, white platters—are as exquisitely presented as they are delicious. Good beginnings here include smoked duck pâté drizzled with goat-cheese cream and velvety lobster bisque beautifully marbleized with crème fraîche. Entrees include broiled sea bass wrapped in banana leaves, served with bulgur-wheat pilaf and wild-berry preserves. Also excellent are the rack of lamb dijonnaise with rosemary-thyme sauce and crisp, cherry-wood–smoked Muscovy duck served with sweet-potato haystack. For dessert, ebony and ivory is a sweet dream—espresso chocolate mousse and thin, semisweet chocolate leaves on a mirror of marbleized white chocolate sauce with blackberry garnish. The well-chosen wine list offers many by-the-glass selections, and there's page after page of after-dinner cordials, cognacs, ports, sherries, and brandies.

The lunch menu adds pasta, sandwich, and salad options. Brunch—including complimentary champagne, mimosa, or Kir royale—includes an appetizer, soup or salad, and entrees ranging from a seafood frittata topped with creamy velouté and caviar to sesame-seared Maui snapper glazed with Hawaiian fruit chutney and served on a bed of rice.

MODERATE

✪ La Venezia Cafe

142 Park Ave. S. (between Morse Blvd. and Welbourne Ave.). ☎ **407/647-7557.** Reservations not accepted. Breakfast pastries $1.75; main courses $5.95–$9 lunch/brunch, $5.95–$18.50 at dinner; prix-fixe afternoon teas $7, $10, and $15. AE, DISC, MC, V. Mon–Thurs 8am–9:30pm, Fri–Sat 8am–10pm, Sun 8am–9:30pm. Parking on street only. ITALIAN/COSMOPOLITAN COFFEEHOUSE.

La Venezia Cafe is the highlight of a Winter Park visit, for continental breakfast, British-style afternoon tea, or a full meal. It's a charming place, with flower-bedecked tables (white-linen cloth and candlelit at night) and cream stucco walls hung with photographs of Italy. There's an open-air patio overlooking Central Park here, but the pièce de résistance is inside: a collection of six authentic Tiffany windows.

La Venezia fresh-brews 52 different kinds of coffee and offers an extensive choice of gourmet teas. Come by in the morning for a steaming pot of fragrant Ethiopian Yrgacheffe with a fresh-baked croissant, jalapeño corn bread, or brown-sugar–topped streusel coffee cake. At lunch and dinner, menu options include delicious salads (I love the chicken curry tossed with greens, mango chutney, raisins, coconut, and peanuts), sandwiches, pizzas, pastas, quesadillas, and quiches. The evening meal also features more serious entrees, such as pistachio-crusted baked salmon served with wild mushrooms in pink-champagne butter sauce.

Other enticements here are coffee/ice-cream drinks and frappes and a wide selection of liqueurs, aperitifs, and international beers. And save some room for oven-fresh desserts like buttered rum apple pie and amaretto-praline butter-cream torte. A $15 afternoon tea includes finger sandwiches, freshly baked scones and pastries, berries, tea, and champagne.

INEXPENSIVE

The Briarpatch

252 Park Ave. N. (at Garfield Ave.). ☎ **407/628-8651.** Reservations not accepted. Breakfast $2.95–$6.95; lunch and dinner main courses and sandwiches $4.95–$8.95. AE, MC, V. Mon–Thurs 7am–9pm, Fri–Sat 7am–10pm, Sun 8am–5pm. Street parking only. AMERICAN.

A delightful way to start your day in Winter Park is with breakfast on the Briarpatch's open-air patio overlooking Central Park. If it's raining or chilly, the rustic gardenlike interior is also alluring. Breakfast fare includes great coffee and fresh-baked biscuits, muffins, and cinnamon buns. Other options are buttermilk pancakes, a Brie and parsley omelet, a bagel with Nova and cream cheese, or hot oatmeal with berries and bananas.

Later in the day, come by for sandwiches, salads, stuffed baked potatoes, burgers, or pasta dishes—or for cappuccino with fresh-baked desserts such as Kahlua praline cream squares and mile-high chocolate-layer or carrot cake.

Beach Vacations in Central Florida

by Victoria Pesce Elliott & Bill Goodwin

Victoria Pesce Elliott is a freelance journalist who contributes to many local and national newspapers and magazines. A native of Miami, she returned there after nearly a decade in New York City, where she graduated from Barnard College and the Columbia Graduate School of Journalism. She is also the author of *Frommer's Miami & the Keys*.

Bill Goodwin began his career as an award-winning newspaper reporter before becoming legal counsel and speechwriter for two U.S. senators. Now based in Virginia, he is also the author of *Frommer's South Pacific* and *Frommer's Virginia*.

1 Daytona Beach

50 miles NE of Orlando   *by Victoria Pesce Elliott*

Daytona is known as many things and has yet to really figure out exactly what it is. It is at once the "World's Most Famous Beach," the "World Center of Racing," and a mecca for spring break. One thing is for sure: Daytonans love their cars. Recent debate over the environmental impact of unrestricted driving on the sand has caused an uproar from citizens who can't imagine it any other way—sea turtles or not. It has been a destination for racing enthusiasts since the days when cars were called horseless carriages and raced on the hard-packed–sand beach.

Today, hundreds of thousands of race enthusiasts come to the home of The National Association for Stock Car Auto Racing (NASCAR) for the Daytona 500, The Pepsi 400, and other races throughout the year. New at the speedway is the $18-million state-of-the-art motor-sports entertainment attraction—**Daytona USA**—worth a visit even by non–racing fans.

Daytona Beach Shores even provides a drive-in church where a dedicated following flocks to hear Sunday morning sermons from speakers hooked to their car windows.

But you don't have to be a car aficionado to enjoy Daytona. It has 23 miles of sandy beach, an active nightlife, surprisingly good museums, and good shopping options. Be sure to find out when the town belongs to college students during spring break, hundreds of thousands of leather-clad motorcycle buffs during bike week, or racing enthusiasts for big competitions. Don't bother trying to find a hotel room, drive the highways, or enjoy a peaceful vacation at those times. You won't be able to.

ESSENTIALS

GETTING THERE　From Orlando, take I-4 East and follow the Daytona Beach signs to I-95 North to U.S. 92. From northwestern Florida, take I-10 East to I-95 South to U.S. 92.

Daytona-Orlando Transit Service (DOTS) (☎ **800/231-1965** or 904/ 257-5411) provides van transportation to or from Orlando. The fare is $26 for adults one way, $46 round-trip; children 11 and under are charged half price. The service brings passengers to the company's terminal at 1598 N. Nova Rd., at 11th Street (LPGA Blvd.) or, for an additional fee, to beach hotels. In Orlando, the vans depart from the airport.

VISITOR INFORMATION　The **Daytona Beach Area Convention & Visitors Bureau,** 126 E. Orange Ave. (just west of the Silver Beach Bridge; P.O. Box 910), Daytona Beach, FL 32115 (☎ **800/854-1234** or 904/255-0415; fax 904/255-5478; e-mail daytonabea@aol.com), can help you with information on attractions, accommodations, dining, and events. Call in advance for maps and brochures, or visit the office when in town. It also maintains a branch at the new Daytona USA attraction at 1801 W. International Speedway Blvd.

CITY LAYOUT　Daytona Beach is surrounded by water. The Atlantic Ocean borders its east coast and the Halifax River flows north to south through the middle of the city. There are actually four little towns along its beach: **Ormond Beach** to the north, the centrally located **Daytona Beach** and **Daytona Beach Shores,** and **Ponce Inlet** at the southern tip, just above New Smyrna Beach.

Fla. A1A (Atlantic Avenue) runs along the beach north to south. **U.S. 1** runs inland paralleling the west side of the Halifax River, and I-95 vaguely parallels the river still farther west. **International Speedway Boulevard (U.S. 92)** is the main east–west artery.

GETTING AROUND　Although it's primarily a driver's town, VOTRAN, Volusia County's public transit system, runs **buses** throughout downtown and the beaches Monday to Saturday until 7:30pm and on Sunday until 7pm. Also, between January and September turn-of-the-century–style **trolleys** run along S.R. A1A Monday to Saturday from noon to midnight. Adults pay 75¢, seniors and children 5 to 16 pay 35¢, and children 5 and under with an adult ride free.

Call for **bus or trolley** routing information (☎ **904/761-7700**).

A VISIT TO THE WORLD CENTER OF RACING

Opened in 1959 with the first Daytona 500, the 480-acre ✪ **Daytona International Speedway complex,** at 1801 W. International Speedway Blvd. (U.S. 92 at Bill France Boulevard; P.O. Box 2801), Daytona Beach, FL 32120-2801 (☎ **904/253-RACE** for tickets, or 904/254-2700 for information), is certainly the keynote of the city's fame. It presents about 9 weekends of major racing events annually, featuring stock cars, sports cars, motorcycles, and go-carts, and is also used for automobile testing. Its grandstands seat over 120,000.

Big events sell out months in advance (the Daytona 500, held in February, as early as a year in advance), so plan far ahead and also reserve accommodations well before your trip.

To learn more about racing, head for the **World Center of Racing Visitors' Center** at the east end of the speedway and NASCAR office complex. Open daily from

Daytona Beach

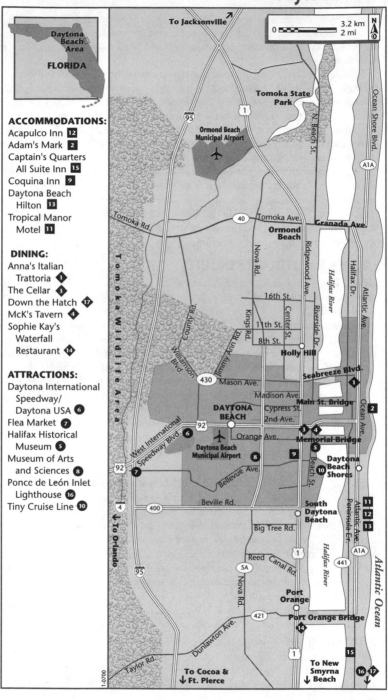

ACCOMMODATIONS:
Acapulco Inn **12**
Adam's Mark **2**
Captain's Quarters
  All Suite Inn **15**
Coquina Inn **9**
Daytona Beach
  Hilton **13**
Tropical Manor
  Motel **11**

DINING:
Anna's Italian
  Trattoria **1**
The Cellar **3**
Down the Hatch **17**
McK's Tavern **4**
Sophie Kay's
  Waterfall
  Restaurant **14**

ATTRACTIONS:
Daytona International
  Speedway/
  Daytona USA **6**
Flea Market **7**
Halifax Historical
  Museum **5**
Museum of Arts
  and Sciences **8**
Ponce de León Inlet
  Lighthouse **16**
Tiny Cruise Line **10**

9am to 5pm, the center is also the departure site for entertaining 25-minute guided tram tours of the facility. Admission is $5, free for children 6 and under. Tours depart daily every 30 minutes between 9:30am and 4pm, except during races and special events.

Opened in late 1996 on speedway grounds is the phenomenally popular 50,000-square-foot ✪ **Daytona USA**—a state-of-the-art interactive motor-sports entertainment attraction presenting the history, color, and excitement of stock-car, go-cart, and motorcycle racing in Daytona. Bring your video camera. There are lots of colorful photo-ops here. Visitors can participate in a pit stop on a NASCAR Winston Cup stock car, see the actual winning Daytona 500 car still covered in track dust, talk via video with favorite competitors, and play radio or television announcer by calling the finish of a race. The highlight of the attraction is the action-packed IMAX film that puts you in the winner's seat of a Daytona 500 race. Allow at least $3^1/_2$ hours to enjoy this new theme attraction, which is open daily, except Christmas Day, from 9am to 6pm. Admission for adults is $12, seniors $10, children 6 to 12 $6, and children 5 and under free. Discounted combination tickets are available for those who also want to take the tour of the facilities.

BEACHES & OUTDOOR PURSUITS

BEACHES   The beach near the **Adam's Mark** and **Main Street Pier,** popular with families, is the hub of activity, putting you close to concessions, a boardwalk, and a small amusement park. Couples seeking greater privacy usually prefer the northern or southern extremities of the beach. Especially peaceful is **Ponce Inlet** at the very southern tip of the island where there is precious little commerce or traffic to disturb the silence. Surfers and bikers congregate near the **Main Street and Sun Glow piers.**

Although regulations are in the works, for now, you can drive and park directly on the sand along most of Daytona Beach's 500-foot-wide beaches. There's a $5 access fee, although in some areas like Ponce Inlet, the fee is waived in winter.

If Daytona's beaches aren't enough, you can venture south. **New Smyrna Beach** has 7 miles of hard-packed white sand, a quiet historic downtown, an active arts community, and excellent accommodations. **Flagler Beach** to the north is another pristine beach for those looking for solitude and natural beauty away from the condos and hotels.

CRUISES   Take a leisurely cruise on the Halifax River aboard the 14-passenger, 25-foot *Fancy,* a replica of the old fantail launches used at the turn of the century. It's operated by **A Tiny Cruise Line River Excursions,** 425 S. Beach St., at Halifax Harbor (☎ 904/226-2343). Captain Jim regales passengers with river lore and points out dolphins, manatees, herons, diving cormorants, pelicans, egrets, osprey, oyster beds, and other natural phenomena during the morning cruise. Cruises are $10 to $15 for adults, $7.50 to $9.50 for children 4 to 12, and free for children 3 and under. Weather permitting, cruises depart year-round (with a brief hiatus during the holidays), Monday to Saturday at 11:30am. A 1-hour tour of riverfront homes is at 2pm and of historic downtown at 3:30pm; there are no Monday cruises in winter months. Call for reservations. Romantic sunset cruises are also available.

FISHING   If you're interested in deep-sea fishing (for marlin, sailfish, king mackerel, grouper, red snapper, and more) and/or whale watching, contact **Critter Fleet,** 4950 S. Peninsula Dr., Ponce Inlet (☎ 800/338-0850 or 904/767-7676). **Sea Love Marina,** 4884 Front St., Ponce Inlet (☎ 904/767-3406), also offers deep-sea fishing.

Save the cost of a boat and fish with the locals from the **Main Street Pier,** near the Adam's Mark (☎ 904/253-1212). Bait and fishing gear are available, and no license is required.

GOLF   There are a dozen excellent courses within 25 minutes of the beach, and most hotels can arrange starting times for you. Or call **Golf Daytona Beach** (☎ 800-881-7065 or 904/239-7065) for advice and bookings.

Opened in July of 1994, the **LPGA course,** 300 Championship Dr. (☎ 904/274-3880), is one of the top-rated courses in the country, especially for women golfers. The 7,088-yard course, designed by Rees Jones, boasts five sets of tees and a number of challenging holes. Just down the street from the LPGA headquarters, this center for professional and amateur women golfers has workshops, teaching programs, and a great selection of ladies' equipment and clothing. Greens fees are usually under $75, and less than $50 in summer.

Also recommendable are the **Daytona Beach Club,** 600 Wilder Blvd. (☎ 904/258-3119), the city's largest, with 36 holes; and the centrally located 18-hole, par-72 **Indigo Lakes Golf Course,** 2620 W. International Speedway Blvd. (☎ 904/254-3607), designed by Lloyd Clifton with flat fairways and large bunkered Bermuda greens.

HORSEBACK RIDING   Shenandoah Stables, 1759 Tomoka Farms Rd., off U.S. 92 (☎ 904/257-1444), offers daily trail rides and lessons between 10am and 4pm.

WATER SPORTS   For jet-ski rentals, contact **Daytona High Performance—MBI,** 925 Sickler Dr., at the Seabreeze Bridge (☎ 904/257-5276).

Additional water-sports equipment, as well as bicycles, beach buggies, and mopeds, can be rented along the beach in front of major hotels. A good place to look is in front of the Adam's Mark at 100 N. Atlantic Ave.

MUSEUMS

✪ Halifax Historical Museum

252 S. Beach St. (just north of Orange Ave.). ☎ **904/255-6976.** Admission $2 adults, 50¢ children 11 and under; free for everyone Sat. Tues–Sat 10am–4pm.

This local history museum is housed in a former bank and is worth seeing just for the 1912 neoclassical architectural details. A mural of old Florida wildlife graces one wall, the stained-glass ceiling reflects the sunlight, and across the room, an old gold metal teller's window still stands. Its eclectic collection includes Native American artifacts, more than 10,000 historic photographs, possessions of past residents (such as a ball gown worn at Lincoln's inauguration), and, of course, model cars.

Museum of Arts and Sciences

1040 Museum Blvd. (off Nova Rd.). ☎ **904/255-0285.** Museum, $4 adults, $1 children and students with ID, free for children 5 and under; planetarium shows, $2. Tues–Fri 9am–4pm, Sat–Sun noon–5pm. Take International Speedway Blvd. west, make a left on Nova Rd., and look for a sign on your right.

Most impressive in this eclectic collection are the Cuban works—mostly paintings acquired in 1956, when Cuban dictator Fulgencio Batista donated his private collection to the city. One highlight of the collection is a portrait of Eva Perón (better known as Evita, since the Madonna film of 1996), said to be the only existing painting completed while she was alive. Other exhibits include "Masterworks of American Art," a gallery dedicated to the prehistory of Florida, and "Africa: Life and Ritual."

Ponce de León Inlet Lighthouse & Museum

4931 S. Peninsula Dr., Ponce Inlet. ☎ **904/761-1821.** Admission $4 adults, $1 children 11 and under. May–Aug, daily 10am–9pm; Sept–Apr, daily 10am–5pm (last admission an hour before closing). Follow Atlantic Ave. south, make a right on Beach St., and follow the signs.

If you are in the area, this 175-foot lighthouse—the second-tallest in the United States—is worth a quick stop. Built in the 1880s and restored in the 1970s, this brick-and-granite sentinel's beacon is visible for 16 nautical miles. The head lighthouse-keeper's cottage now houses a museum of exhibits of maritime artifacts. The first-assistant keeper's house is furnished to reflect turn-of-the-century occupancy. A concise 12-minute video details the structure's history.

SHOPPING

Daytona Beach's main riverside drag, Beach Street, is one of the only areas in town where people actually stroll. The street is wide and inviting, with decorative wrought-iron archways and fancy brickwork overlooking the Halifax River.

Today, between Bay Street and Orange Avenue, Beach Street offers more than a dozen antiques shops, a magic shop, an excellent historical museum (see "Museums," above), several good cafes, and the world-famous **Dunn Toys & Hobbies.**

Also look for antiques at the 13,500-square-foot **House of Gamble,** 1102 State Ave. at LPGA Boulevard (☎ **904/258-2889**), housing 50 diverse dealers under its roof.

The **Daytona Flea Market** is huge, with 1,000 covered outdoor booths plus 100 antiques vendors in an air-conditioned building. It's located on Tomoka Farms Road, a mile west of the speedway at the junction of I-95 and U.S. 92 (☎ **904/252-1999**), and is open year-round Friday to Sunday from 8am to 5pm (parking is free).

WHERE TO STAY

Daytona Beach hotels fill to the bursting point during major events at the speedway, during bikers' gatherings, and whenever college students are on break. Room rates will skyrocket, if you can find a room at all, and there's often a minimum-stay requirement. If you're planning to be in town at one of these busy times, reserve far in advance.

In addition to the listings below, there are dozens of chain hotels along Atlantic Avenue. Among the choices are three oceanfront **Howard Johnsons** (☎ **800/446-4656**), but the best option is the **Days Inn** (☎ **800/224-5056** or 904/255-4492) at 1909 S. Atlantic Ave. (at Flamingo Ave.) in Daytona Beach. At this nine-story beachfront hotel the pretty rooms all have ocean views and balconies. Facilities include a swimming pool/kiddie pool and a sundeck overlooking the beach. There's also the **Ramada Inn Surfside,** 3125 S. Atlantic Ave. (☎ **800/255-3838** or 904/788-1000), which boasts a prime beachfront location; all its rooms have ocean views and balconies. Families will appreciate the efficiency units with fully equipped eat-in kitchens and, in summer, free children's activities. Facilities include a large swimming pool, oceanfront picnic tables, and more.

All the accommodations listed below are on or near the beach and close to the speedway. *Note:* In addition to the 6% state sales tax, Daytona levies a 4% tax on hotel bills.

EXPENSIVE

Adam's Mark Daytona Beach Resort

100 N. Atlantic Ave. (between Earl St. and Auditorium Blvd.), Daytona Beach, FL 32118. ☎ **800/872-9269** or 904/254-8200. Fax 904/253-0275. 388 rms, 25 suites. A/C MINIBAR

TV TEL. $99–$295 double (the high end reflects special-event periods); $250–$1,000 suite. Additional person $20. Children 17 and under stay free in parents' room. AE, CB, DC, DISC, MC, V. Valet parking $8; free self-parking in lot across the street.

This is Daytona's most central beachfront hotel—and one of its most luxurious—designed so that every room has an ocean view. Although the lobby and common areas are more elegantly detailed, guest rooms are not as spacious or well laid out as the less expensive and quieter Hilton further south (see below). It's right at the band shell, and, in season, its beach and boardwalk concessions offer parasailing, bicycle rentals, motorized four-wheelers, surfboards, boogie boards, cabanas, and umbrellas.

Dining/Entertainment: The hotel's premier dining room features steak and seafood dinners. Another facility, with picture windows overlooking the beach and umbrellaed tables outside, serves all meals. There's also a complex of small beachfront restaurants and bars with outdoor cafe seating. The sophisticated lounge offers piano-bar or other live music nightly.

Services: Concierge, room service, dry cleaning and laundry service, free newspapers in executive-level rooms, baby-sitting, secretarial services, express checkout, valet parking $8.

Facilities: Spectravision movie channels, Indoor/outdoor heated swimming pool and kid's pool, beach, complete health club, two whirlpools, steam and sauna, bicycle rental, children's center and programs, business center or programs, conference rooms, self-service Laundromat, sundeck, water-sports equipment, sand volleyball court, playground, gift shops.

MODERATE

Captain's Quarters All-Suite Inn

3711 S. Atlantic Ave. (about a quarter mile south of The Port Orange Bridge), Daytona Beach, FL 32127. ☎ **800/332-3119** or 904/767-3119. Fax 904/767-0883. 26 suites, 1 penthouse suite. A/C TV TEL. $80–$100 suite double; $145–$185 oceanfront penthouse suite. During special events, rates are nearly double. Additional person $5. Children 16 and under stay free in parents' suite. Lower rates available for extended stays. AE, DISC, MC, V. Free parking.

A great choice down on the quiet southern part of Daytona Beach, this five-story beachfront inn has spacious suites, all with ocean or river views and large living/dining-room areas, balconies, and fully equipped kitchens. The country-look bedrooms have French doors that open onto balconies or patios with wooden rockers. Each is equipped with two cable TVs and VCRs (movies can be rented). The penthouse suite has a fireplace, a spa tub, and a big picture window overlooking the ocean.

On-premises facilities include a heated swimming pool, a sundeck with love seat swings and barbecue grills, and coin-op washers/dryers. The restaurant, which has an outdoor deck overlooking the ocean, is open for breakfast and lunch daily. Daily newspapers are complimentary.

✪ Coquina Inn

544 S. Palmetto Ave. (at Cedar St.), Daytona Beach, FL 32114. ☎ **800/805-7533** or 904/254-4969. Fax 904/254-4969. 4 rms. A/C TV. $80–$110 double Mon–Thurs, $110–$200 double Fri–Sun, $150–$175 double during special events. Rates include full breakfast. Additional person $15. AE, MC, V. Free parking. Children 11 and under are not accepted.

Daytona's best bed-and-breakfast, this charming coquina and cream-stucco house sits on a tranquil, shady street half a block west of the Halifax River and is convenient to Beach Street and about a 5-minute drive to the beaches.

The crystal-chandeliered dining room is the setting for breakfast, served on fine china, and a sitting room outfitted in a mish-mash of antiques is a tranquil spot to enjoy the fireplace and a selection of books and magazines.

Each of the rooms is decorated differently. In the Hibiscus Room, French doors lead to a private plant-filled balcony overlooking an ancient live oak draped with Spanish moss. The Hibiscus Room and next door Jasmine Room can be combined to create a two-bedroom/two-bath suite. All rooms have cable TVs. Phones are available on request. Complimentary tea and sherry are served in the parlor throughout the day. Beach cruiser bikes are available at no charge. New in 1997 were two octagonal wooden decks, one with a large whirlpool under a Victorian gazebo, and a gift shop.

✪ Daytona Beach Hilton Oceanfront Resort

2637 S. Atlantic Ave. (between Florida Shores Blvd. and Richard's Lane), Daytona Beach, FL 32118. ☎ **800/525-7350** or 904/767-7350. Fax 904/760-3651. 212 rms, 2 suites. A/C TV TEL. $95–$159 river-view double; $115–$189 oceanfront double; suites from $250. Rates increase for special events. Additional person $15. Children of any age stay free in parents' room. AE, CB, DC, DISC, JCB, MC, V. Free parking.

Perhaps the best accommodation choice in Daytona Beach, the Hilton welcomes guests in an elegant terra-cotta–tiled lobby with comfortable seating areas, a fountain, and potted palms. The large, balconied guest rooms are furnished in airy tropical furnishings and pretty print fabrics. All have ocean and/or river views and have major convenient extras like safes, coffeemakers, irons, full-size ironing boards, hair dryers, small refrigerators, and satellite TVs offering pay-movie options. The hotel also has a small fitness room, unisex hair salon, and gift shop. Daily newspapers are complimentary.

Kids appreciate the video-game room with pool table and the kiddie pool on the beautiful oceanfront sundeck where you can often see seagulls drinking from the large heated pool.

A surprisingly good lobby restaurant—one of Daytona's most beautiful—serves all meals; patio dining is an option. A comfy bar/lounge with game tables adjoins; it's the setting for nightly entertainment—a pianist or jazz combo. In summer, reggae bands play near the poolside bar.

INEXPENSIVE

✪ Acapulco Inn

2505 S. Atlantic Ave. (between Dundee Rd. and Seaspray St.), Daytona Beach, FL 32118. ☎ **800/874-7420** or 904/761-2210. Fax 904/253-9935. 42 rms, 91 efficiencies. A/C TV TEL. $50–$100 double; $54–$124 efficiency. The higher rates reflect high season and oceanfront accommodations. Additional person $6–$10. Children 17 and under stay free in parents' room. Rates may be higher during special events. Monthly rates available. Inquire about packages. AE, DC, DISC, MC, V. Free parking.

This Mayan-themed hotel is one of six beachfront hostelries managed by Oceans Eleven Resorts and is a great choice for families. It's especially popular with Canadian snowbirds, who return year after year for the warm hospitality, clean ocean-view rooms with balconies, and organized activities like Bingo, bridge, and mah-jongg. All rooms have balconies, small refrigerators, in-room safes, and cable TV with Spectravision pay movies. Efficiencies have fully equipped eat-in kitchens.

A large dining room overlooks the ocean, serving American fare at breakfast and lunch; a comfortable lounge adjoins. Facilities include a heated oceanfront swimming pool, two whirlpools, a kiddie pool, a picnic area, a coin-op laundry, and a video-game room. An on-staff PGA pro helps guests plan golf vacations and will arrange lessons and tee times.

Tropical Manor Motel

2237 S. Atlantic Ave., Daytona Beach, FL 32118. ☎ **800/253-4920** or 904/252-4920. 40 rms, 30 efficiencies/suites, 1 three-bedroom suite. A/C TV TEL. Winter $33–$43 double, $34–$100 efficiencies/suites, $95–$135 three-bedroom suite. High-season $52–$63 double, $54–$127 suite, $165–$237 three-bedroom suite. Additional person $5. Rates higher during holidays. AE, CB, DISC, M, V. Free parking.

This Caribbean-tinted motel wins points for its unique and colorful murals, pleasant staff/owners, and meticulous upkeep. Located square in the middle of Daytona's nicest beach, these funky accommodations also offer sundecks, umbrella-covered tables, lounge areas, a large heated pool, a water slide, a shuffleboard court, a cookout area, a heated kiddie pool, and two gazebos, all surrounded by lush tropical foliage. The rooms are not large or particularly fancy, but many come with cable TV, kitchens, and ocean views. Especially good for families are the two- and three-bedroom suites.

WHERE TO DINE

Perhaps as a concession to the spring-break crowd, Daytona Beach has a profusion of fast-food places that line the major thoroughfares, especially along International Speedway Boulevard, near the race track. You'll find many new restaurants on and around Beach Street, where more than two dozen other start-up businesses opened in 1996. An old favorite is the little diner inside Dunn's Toy Store. Also check out the Main Street Pier, where a casual oceanfront restaurant serves burgers and chicken wings and lots of beer.

MODERATE

✪ Anna's Italian Trattoria

304 Seabreeze Blvd. (at Peninsula Dr.). ☎ **904/239-9624.** Reservations recommended. Full dinners $8.50–$16. AE, DISC, MC, V. Mon–Sat 5–10pm. ITALIAN.

The Triani family lends a warm, friendly air to this simple yet comfortable trattoria. The pastas, many of which are homemade, include a scrumptious *fettuccine alla campagniola*—pasta tossed with strips of sautéed eggplant and chunks of sausage in tomato-cream sauce. I also recommend salmon scampi and risotto alla Anna (similar to a Spanish paella). Portions are hearty; main courses come with soup or salad and a side dish of angel-hair pasta or a vegetable. There's a good selection of Italian wines to complement your meal. Free parking is available in a lot on Seabreeze Boulevard across Peninsula Drive.

✪ The Cellar

220 Magnolia Ave. (between Palmetto and Ridgewood aves.). ☎ **904/258-0011.** Reservations accepted only for large lunch parties. Main courses $10–$16. AE, CB, DC, DISC, MC, V. Mon–Fri 11am–3pm and 5–10pm. Dinner by reservation during high season. AMERICAN.

Housed in a National Historic Register Victorian home built in 1907 for Warren G. Harding, the Cellar couldn't be more charming. Its low-ceilinged interior, with fresh flowers on every table and back-lit stained-glass windows, draws a genteel luncheon crowd and a few businessmen willing to brave a tearoom ambiance in pursuit of good food. In the warm months there's outdoor seating at umbrellaed tables on a covered garden patio.

A small but varied menu includes fresh seafood, chicken, and pastas. Crab cakes—available at lunch and dinner—are fluffy and delicious, drizzled with remoulade sauce and served with seasoned rice and fresh vegetables. At lunch a salad sampler is a good bet; order some banana bread on the side.

McK's Tavern

218 S. Beach St. ☎ **904/238-3321.** Reservations not accepted. Main courses $9–$13, salads and sandwiches $4–$6. AE, MC, V. Daily 11am–3am. IRISH/AMERICAN.

Especially worth knowing about because it serves food until 3am, this upscale Irish tavern has a highly eclectic menu. Choices include Mexican and Spanish dishes like vegetarian burritos and black-bean soup as well as hearty Irish favorites like shepherd's pie. Club sandwiches and burgers round out the large and reasonably priced selection. The food is not exceptional, but it's perfectly acceptable, especially once you've had a few Bass ales. The service is sometimes rushed, but usually pleasant. McK's is known as the downtown meeting place for businesspeople, especially at lunch and happy hour.

Sophie Kay's Waterfall Restaurant

3516 S. Atlantic Ave. (at Raymond Ave.). ☎ **904/756-4444.** Reservations recommended. Main courses $6–$24; early-bird menu served 4–6:30pm, $7–$10. AE, DC, DISC, MC, V. Mon–Thurs 4–10pm, Fri–Sat 4–11pm, Sun noon–10pm. (Bar serves light fare, Sun–Thurs to midnight, Fri–Sat to 1am.) CONTINENTAL.

Longtime Daytona restaurateur, cookbook author, and local television personality Sophie Kay has created a faux-tropical atmosphere with romantic details like a rock waterfall that cascades into a goldfish pond, full-size palm trees, candles, and soft piano music.

Oysters Rockefeller (bubbling with cheese) or shrimp scampi makes an excellent starter. Sophie has a great hand with pasta, and her primavera linguine in delicate white-wine sauce is perfection. Also very good is the baked seafood served *en papillote* in a creamy lobster béchamel sauce. Many people come here for filet mignon, roast prime rib au jus with creamy horseradish sauce, or surf-and-turf combinations. For dessert, don't pass up Sophie's delicious twice-baked cheesecake on a buttery graham-cracker crust. After dinner, adjourn to the piano bar for cocktails.

INEXPENSIVE

Down the Hatch

4894 Front St., Ponce Inlet. ☎ **904/761-4831.** Reservations not accepted; call ahead for priority seating. Main courses mostly $8–$15; early-bird menu served 11am–5pm, $5–$7. Kids' menu. AE, MC, V. Daily 7am–10pm. Take Atlantic Ave. south, make a right on Beach St., and follow the signs. SEAFOOD.

Occupying a half-century–old fish camp on the Halifax River, Down the Hatch serves up fresh fish and seafood (note its shrimp boat docked outside). During the day, picture windows provide scenic views of boats and shore birds; you might even see dolphins frolicking. At night, arrive early to catch the sunset over the river, and also to beat the crowd at this very popular place. In summer, light fare is served outside on an awninged wooden deck.

Start your meal with an order of piquant buffalo shrimp served with chunky homemade bleu-cheese dressing. Lightly breaded, deep-fried grouper fingers, served with tartar sauce, are also tasty. Portions are large.

DAYTONA BEACH AFTER DARK

In addition to the following, the piano bar at **Sophie Kay's Waterfall Restaurant** (see "Where to Dine," above) is worth a visit. Especially during biker festivities, Main Street is a happening area where dozens of bars and restaurants catering to the leather set are in full swing.

A popular beachfront bar for more than 40 years, **Ocean Deck,** 127 S. Ocean Ave., next to the Mayan Inn (☎ **904/253-5224**), is packed with a mix of locals and tourists, young and old, who come for live music and cheap drinks. Often reggae or ska bands will play after 9:30pm. Park across Ocean Avenue at the beach and surf shop, Reggae Republic (under the same ownership).

At press time, two popular nightspots in downtown Daytona, **The Coliseum** and **The Spot,** both at 176 N. Beach St. (at Bay Street) (☎ **904/257-9982**), were due to close because of landlord troubles. No doubt, though, that the spaces (one a converted movie theater) will reemerge as some other dance clubs. Call or stop by to see.

A typical spring-break party spot, **Razzles,** 611 Seabreeze Blvd., between Grandview and South Atlantic avenues. (☎ **904/257-6236**), plays Top 40 tunes and high-energy music till 3am nightly. There's plenty to keep you occupied if you're not dancing—10 pool tables, a blackjack table, air hockey, electronic darts, pinball, and video games. The crowd is young—18 and up—and the scene is wild.

2 Cocoa Beach & the Kennedy Space Center

35 miles SE of Orlando   *by Victoria Pesce Elliott*

This once-sleepy area, known as "The Space Coast" after its most famous occupant, the NASA space program, is a place where city-dwellers used to flock to escape the crowds from the exploding urban centers of Miami and Jacksonville. Now, the area has grown to accommodate its own crowds, especially the tourists who come in droves for the 72 miles of beaches, as well as the fishing, surfing, golfing, and tennis—and most especially for The Kennedy Space Center.

ESSENTIALS

GETTING THERE   From Orlando, take the Beeline Expressway (S.R. 528) east, and where the road divides, go left on S.R. 407, make a right on S.R. 405, and follow the signs to the Space Center. Cocoa Beach, your best bet for a place to stay, is about a half-hour drive south of the Space Center.

VISITOR INFORMATION   Contact the **Cocoa Beach Chamber of Commerce,** 400 Fortenberry Rd., Merritt Island, FL 32952 (☎ **407/633-2100**; fax 407/ 459-2232), for information about Cocoa Beach, Cape Canaveral, Merritt Island, and nearby communities. Also, the **Office of Tourism Development** (☎ **800/936-2326** or 407/633-2110; fax 407/633-2112) at 2725 Judge Fran Jamison Way (right off of I-95 on the west side of Exit 73) sends out information packages on hotels and area attractions.

TOURING KENNEDY SPACE CENTER/SPACEPORT USA

More than 56 million people have visited NASA's ✪ **John F. Kennedy Space Center** (☎ **407/452-2121**; Internet: http://www.kscvisitor.com) since it opened to the public in 1963. Whether or not you're a space buff, you're sure to appreciate the sheer grandeur of the facilities and the achievement of technology displayed here. Astronauts departed Earth at this site en route to the most famous "small step" in history—man's first voyage to the moon.

And, yes, this is where television's most famous astronaut, Major Anthony Nelson, worked. He and his bottle-dwelling Jeannie lived in nearby Cocoa Beach.

Arrive early and make your first stop at Information Central at the **Visitor Center,** which opens at 9am. Pick up a schedule of events and a map to help plan your day. The offerings can be confusing, so I've summarized the highlights below. A knowledgeable and helpful staff is on duty to answer questions and give advice. You'll need at least a full day to see and do everything.

The best way to get an overview of the area, and the only way to see actual working facilities on the grounds, is by taking a bus tour. Two main tours are offered; each departs the visitor center every 15 minutes starting at 9:45am, with the last tour leaving late in the afternoon (call for details). The tours will take at least 2 hours, depending on how interested you are in hanging out at the stops along the way. Buses run continuously, so you can reboard as you wish.

The most recommendable of the two is the **Kennedy Space Center Tour,** which visits facilities now in use on the grounds, including the Complex 39 Space Shuttle launch pads and the massive Vehicle Assembly Building where shuttles are made. New on the tour is a just-completed, impressive **Apollo/Saturn V Center.** This $37-million, 100,000-square-foot exhibit includes the most powerful rocket ever launched by the United States, the 363-foot-tall Saturn V. Videos, artifacts, photos, and interactive exhibits bring the history of the Apollo program to life.

The **Cape Canaveral Tour** is more historical and stops at the Cape Canaveral Air Station, where America's first satellites and astronauts were launched into space. Other stops include the launch pads currently used for unmanned launches, the original site of Mission Control, and The Air Force Space Museum.

For the same price as the longer tours mentioned above, you can take the **Saturn Express Tour.** A scenic 15-minute drive to the new **Apollo/Saturn V Center** (described above) is a worthwhile abbreviated trip for those with no patience for lengthy bus tours.

A $79-million renovation due to be completed in early 1998 has already added the impressive Apollo/Saturn V Center and a not-to-be-missed 3-D IMAX movie, *L-5: First City in Space,* which depicts future life among the stars. Still to come is an observation tower as well as other interactive exhibits.

Two other IMAX films are also shown on the 5 1/2-story-high screens every day. The 37-minute *Dream is Alive* gives an insider's view of the space shuttle program with in-flight footage shot by astronauts on various missions. Leonard Nimoy narrates *Destiny In Space,* an odyssey of the universe with exterior shots of shuttle flights.

As part of the extensive renovations, several dining options were added. A cafeteria-style breakfast and lunch area serves bacon and eggs, yogurt, sandwiches, pizzas, burgers, and BBQ. A new sit-down diner, **Mila's,** serves an extensive selection of home-style foods. Cart vendors sell snacks like pretzels, hot dogs, and Space Dots (a cool new ice cream that consists of tiny pinhead-size spheres).

Admission to the center is free, but tickets for the bus tours cost $8 for adults, $5 for children 3 to 11, and are free for children 2 and under. IMAX films cost $5 for adults, $3 for children 3 to 11, and are free for children under 3. The 3-D IMAX movie costs $6 for adults and $4 for children. The center is open from 9am to dusk every day except Christmas Day and some launch days.

There are more than two dozen launches each year. If you'd like to **see a launch,** call ☎ 407/449-4343. Tickets cost $10 to $15. You can reserve tickets up to 7 days before a launch, but they must be picked up at least 2 days beforehand since the facilities close prior to launches.

BEACHES & OUTDOOR ACTIVITIES

BEACHES & NATURE WALKS   Adjoining the grounds of the Kennedy Space Center is **Canaveral National Seashore,** a protected stretch of coastline 24 miles long and backed by cabbage palms, sea grapes, and palmettos.

Port Canaveral Beach boasts bike paths, campsites, wide beaches, parks, and dozens of shops and restaurants for those seeking a more active beach experience. The beach at **Cocoa Beach Pier** is also a popular spot, especially for surfers. The pier has 842 feet of fishing, shopping, and food and drinks overlooking a wide, sandy beach.

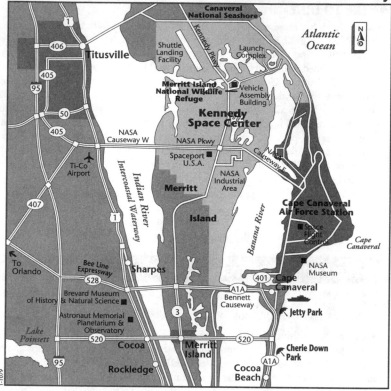

Cocoa Beach & Vicinity

CRUISES   **Port Canaveral** is where a handful of the major cruise lines depart, including the soon-to-be-launched *Disney Magic* and *Disney Wonder* due in late 1998.

Scenic day or evening charters are available with **Tradewinds Sail Charters,** at the Port Canaveral Seaport (☎ **407/635-1898**). From a 2-hour port excursion to weekend-long cruises to Daytona Beach, Larry Shoeman offers many different cruises. Prices start at $35 and can be as high as $140 per person for long private sails.

ECOTOURS   Call **Funday Discovery Tours** (☎ **407-725-0796**) to arrange backcountry kayaking, airboat rides, horseback tours, and bird-watching expeditions.

WHERE TO STAY

If you want to combine your space-center visit with some beaching, your best bet is to locate in Cocoa Beach, about a half-hour drive from the attraction. All the major chains have outposts here, including the **Holiday Inn Cocoa Beach Resort,** 1300 N. Atlantic Ave. (☎ **800/2-BOOK-US** or 407/783-2271), which lies on 30 oceanfront acres; and **The Inn at Cocoa Beach,** 4300 Ocean Beach Blvd. (☎ **800/343-5307** or 407/799-3460), offering large rooms with ocean views.

If you are more interested in watching a launch than laying on the beach, you might consider staying on the mainland in Titusville, where half a dozen chain hotels operate just 3 miles from the entrance to the Kennedy Space Center. Among these are a **Best Western** (☎ **800/523-7654** or 407/269-9100) at 3455 Cheney Hwy. (half a block east of I-95 off Exit 79) and a **Howard Johnson** (☎ **800/654-2000** or 407/267-7900) at 1829 Riverside Dr.

WHERE TO DINE

Cocoa Beach has more fast-food chains than you could ask for along Fla. A1A and S.R. 520, a profusion of bars serving bar snacks, Chinese restaurants, and of course, lots of BBQ joints. The few choices for really good food include one of the most highly acclaimed restaurants, **The Mango Tree,** 118 N. Atlantic Ave., Cocoa Beach (☎ 407/799-0513). Gourmet seafood, pastas, and chicken are served in a tropical garden atmosphere with elegant furnishings. Prices by local standards are high, with entrees from $13 to $27 (and a lobster special for $60). Check out the Cocoa Beach Pier for more casual beach restaurants. Many have menus outside so you can compare choices and prices. Or you can get fine seafood at ✪ **Mona's: More Than a Cafe,** 6615 N. Atlantic Ave. (Between S.R. 520 and S.R. 528 on A1A), in Cape Canaveral (☎ 407/784-8648). Main courses are priced from $7 to $13; salads are slightly less. Popular with Europeans and health-conscious locals tired of the institutional offerings elsewhere, this homey spot offers fresh vegetable-topped pastas, just-caught seafood, and big fresh salads. A thrift-store–style interior has only a dozen tables (all with price tags in case you are interested) and a small stage where you can catch live acoustic music Friday and Saturday from 7 to 10pm.

3 The Tampa Bay Area

Tampa: 74 miles SW of Orlando   *by Bill Goodwin*
St. Petersburg: 84 miles SW of Orlando
Clearwater: 94 miles SW of Orlando

Many families visiting Orlando's theme parks eventually drive an hour west on I-4 to another major kiddie attraction, Busch Gardens Tampa Bay. But Tampa and St. Petersburg are no mere side trips from Disney World; fact is, Tampa's stellar aquarium, dining scene, and museums, coupled with St. Pete's and Clearwater's mile upon mile of sugar-white beaches, make this region an exciting destination unto itself.

At the head of the bay, Tampa is the commercial center of Florida's west coast. It's the country's 11th busiest seaport and a center of banking, hi-tech manufacturing, and cigar making (half a billion drugstore stogies a year). Yet it has its charms, especially in the historic Cuban enclave of Ybor City, now an exciting entertainment and dining venue. Downtown Tampa may roll up its sidewalks after dark, but you can come here during the day to see the sea life at the Florida Aquarium and stroll through the Henry B. Plant Museum, housed in an ornate, Moorish-style hotel built a century ago to lure tourists to Tampa. And out in the suburbs, Busch Gardens may be best known for its scintillating rides, but it's also one of the world's largest zoos.

Two bridges and a causeway cross the bay to the Pinellas Peninsula, one of Florida's most densely packed urban areas. Over here on the bayfront, lovely downtown St. Petersburg is famous for wintering seniors, an unusual pier, and the world's largest collection of Salvador Dalí's surrealist paintings. Keep going west and you'll drive out onto a line of barrier islands where St. Pete Beach, Treasure Island, Clearwater Beach, and other gulfside communities boast 28 miles of sunshine, surf, and white sand. Yes, they're lined with resorts and condos of every description and price, but this strip also is anchored on each end by parks that preserve two of the nation's finest beaches. Drive north, and you'll go back in time at the old Greek sponge town of Tarpon Springs and at Weeki Wachee Springs, a tourist attraction where "mermaids" have been entertaining underwater for half a century.

TAMPA

Even if you stay at the beaches 20 miles to the west, you should consider driving into Tampa to see its sights. If you have children in tow, they will *demand* that you come into the city so they can ride the rides and see the animals at Busch Gardens. While here, you can educate them at the Florida Aquarium and the city's fine museums. And even if you don't have kids, historic Ybor City has the bay area's liveliest nightlife.

Tampa was a sleepy little port when Cuban immigrants founded Ybor City's cigar industry in the 1880s. A few years later Henry B. Plant put Tampa on the tourist map by building a railroad to town and the bulbous minarets over his garish Tampa Bay Hotel. During the Spanish-American War, Teddy Roosevelt trained his Rough Riders here and walked the Ybor City streets with Cuban Revolutionary José Marti. A land boom in the 1920s gave the city its charming, Victorian-style Hyde Park suburb, just across the Hillsborough River from downtown (once gone to seed, it has been gentrified by the baby boomers).

The downtown skyline we see today, however, is the product of a 1980s and early-1990s boom, when banks built skyscrapers and the city put up an expansive convention center, a performing-arts center, and the **Ice Palace,** a 20,000-seat bayfront arena, which is home to professional hockey's Tampa Bay Lightning. Alongside the new Florida Aquarium, the Garrison Seaport Center eventually should house a cruise-ship terminal and a shopping-and-dining complex. Baseball's New York Yankees helped things along by building their spring-training complex here, including a scaled-down replica of Yankee Stadium. And although the project has been plagued by controversy, the city fathers also hope to build a new stadium to satisfy the owners of football's Tampa Bay Buccaneers.

All this adds up to a fast-paced, modern city on the go. Tampa isn't a beach vacation destination, but there's plenty here to keep both adults and kids busy for a few days.

ESSENTIALS

GETTING THERE   Tampa is accessible via I-275, I-75, I-4, U.S. 19, U.S. 41, U.S. 92, and U.S. 301. The Busch Gardens area lies between I-75 and I-275 north of downtown; exit at Busch Boulevard and follow the signs. Downtown is south of I-275; take Exit 26 and go south on Ashley Street.

VISITOR INFORMATION   Contact the **Tampa/Hillsborough Convention and Visitors Association, Inc. (THCVA),** 400 N. Tampa St., Tampa, FL 33602-4706 (☎ **800/44-TAMPA** or 813/223-2752; fax 813/229-6616) for advance information. Its Internet site is at **http://www.thcva.com**. Once you're downtown, head to the THCVA's visitors information center at the corner of Ashley and Madison streets. It's open Monday to Saturday from 9am to 5pm.

Near Busch Gardens, the **Tampa Bay Visitor Information Center,** 3601 E. Busch Blvd., at N. Ednam Place (☎ **813/985-3601**), is actually a privately owned travel agency, but it offers free brochures about attractions in Tampa and sells discounted tickets to many attractions. You may be able to avoid waiting in long Busch Gardens ticket lines by buying here.

CITY LAYOUT   Most visitors to Tampa head north of downtown to the suburban area around **Busch Gardens Tampa Bay,** the city's major attraction. The main drag here is Busch Boulevard, which passes the park entrance as it runs east–west between I-75 and I-275. It's a busy commercial strip where you'll find dozens of restaurants and hotels.

Tampa & St. Petersburg

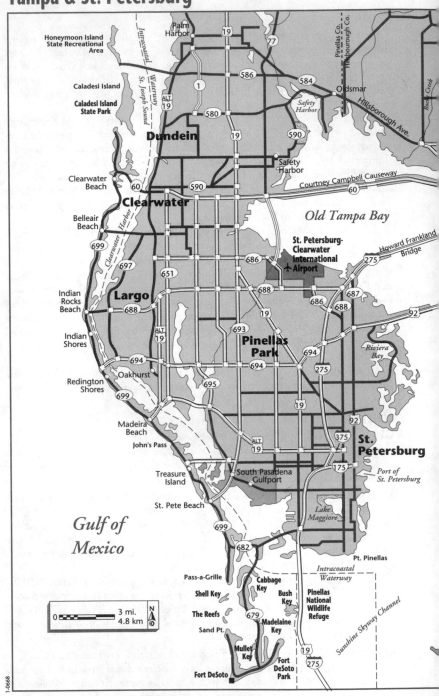

Honeymoon Island State Recreational Area

Palm Harbor

Intracoastal Waterway

St. Joseph Sound

Caladesi Island

Caladesi Island State Park

Dundein

Clearwater Beach

Clearwater

Belleair Beach

Clearwater Harbor

Indian Rocks Beach

Largo

Indian Shores

Redington Shores

Oakhurst

Madeira Beach

John's Pass

Treasure Island

St. Pete Beach

Gulf of Mexico

Pass-a-Grille

Shell Key

The Reefs

Sand Pt.

Mullet Key

Fort DeSoto

Cabbage Key

Bush Key

Madelaine Key

Fort DeSoto Park

Pinellas National Wildlife Refuge

Pinellas Park

South Pasadena

Gulfport

Lake Maggiore

St. Petersburg

Port of St. Petersburg

Pt. Pinellas

Intracoastal Waterway

Sunshine Skyway Channel

Riviera Bay

St. Petersburg-Clearwater International Airport

Old Tampa Bay

Howard Frankland Bridge

Courtney Campbell Causeway

Safety Harbor

Oldsmar

Pinellas Co.
Hillsborough Co.

Hillsborough Ave.

Rock Creek

0 3 mi.
   4.8 km

N

1-0668

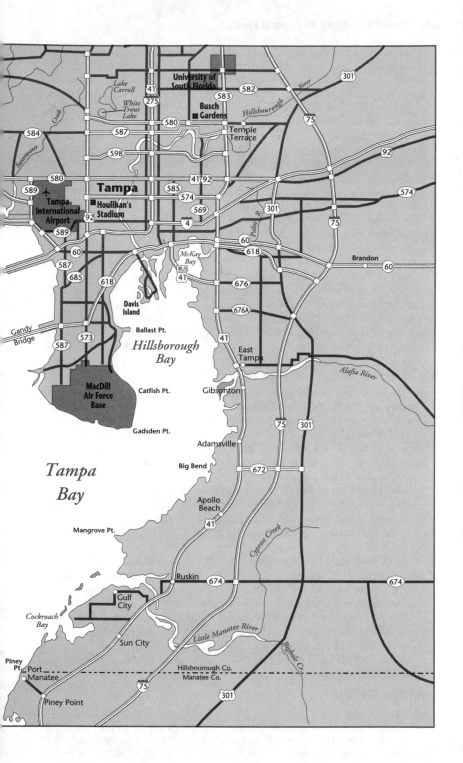

Tampa's compact **downtown** area is primarily a daytime business and financial hub. Here you'll find the Florida Aquarium and the Garrison Seaport Center, from which cruise ships depart. The grid streets are all one-way except for pedestrians-only Franklin Street. From the southern tip of Franklin, you can ride the People Mover, an elevated tram that automatically shuttles over to **Harbour Island** (see "Getting Around," below). Across the narrow Garrison Channel from downtown, Harbour Island is a struggling urban development project whose restaurants and shops were closed during my recent visit.

When the downtown sidewalks roll up at 5pm, **Ybor City** comes alive. On the northeastern edge of downtown, "Ybor" is Tampa's lively Latin Quarter, settled for more than 100 years by Cuban immigrants. Today it's home to hot new restaurants, clubs, arts-and-crafts shops, and hand-rolled cigars.

Just across the Hillsborough River from downtown, **Hyde Park** is the city's oldest and once again its poshest residential neighborhood, complete with the upscale shops and trendy restaurants of **Old Hyde Park Village.** This Victorian neighborhood is on the National Register of Historic Districts. **Bayshore Boulevard** runs from Hyde Park south along the shores of Hillsborough Bay; with a view across the water to the downtown skyline, it's the most beautiful part of Tampa, a gorgeous route for driving, biking, or in-line skating.

Kennedy Boulevard leads from downtown to the **Westshore** area, lying near the bay west of Hyde Park and south of Tampa International Airport. Westshore is a suburban commercial and financial hub, with office buildings, business-oriented hotels, and a shopping mall.

GETTING AROUND   Like most other Florida destinations, it's virtually impossible to see Tampa's major sights and enjoy the best restaurants without a car. Nevertheless, the **Tampa-Ybor Trolley** connects downtown, Harbour Island, the Florida Aquarium, the Garrison Seaport Center, and Ybor City daily from 9am to 4pm, with additional service between downtown and the aquarium daily from 7:30 to 9am and from 4 to 5:30pm. The fare is 25¢ per person. Get a route map at the visitor information center (see above), or call HARTline at ☎ 813/224-4278 for information. The 18 stops are marked with green and orange signs.

The **Harbour Island People Mover,** an automated tram on elevated tracks, runs between the third level of the Fort Brooke Parking Garage, on Whiting Street at Franklin Street, and Harbour Island continuously Monday to Saturday from 7am to midnight and Sunday from 8am to midnight (there's a shuttle bus off-hours). The fare is 25¢ each way.

The **Hillsborough Area Regional Transit/HARTline** (☎ 813/254-HART) provides regularly scheduled bus service between downtown Tampa and the suburbs. Fares are $1 for local rides, $1.50 for express routes; exact change is required. Pick up a route map at the visitor information center (see above).

Taxis in Tampa don't normally cruise the streets for fares, but they do line up at public loading places, such as hotels, the performing-arts center, and bus and train depots. If you need a taxi, call **Tampa Bay Cab** (☎ 813/251-5555), **Yellow Cab** (☎ 813/253-0121), or **United Cab** (☎ 813/253-2424). Fares are 95¢ at flagfall plus $1.50 for each mile.

WHAT TO SEE & DO

Adventure Island

10001 McKinley Dr. (between Busch Blvd. and Bougainvillea Ave.). ☎ 813/987-5600. Admission $20.95 adults, $18.95 children 3–9, plus tax. Free for children 2 and under. Lockers $1. Combination ticket including Busch Gardens Tampa Bay: $42.82 adults, $36.59 children 3 to

9, plus tax. Late-Mar to Labor Day, daily 10am–5pm; Sept–Oct, Fri–Sun 10am–5pm (extended hours in summer and on holidays). Closed Nov to late Mar. Take Exit 33 off I-275, go east on Busch Blvd. 2 miles to left on McKinley Dr. (N. 40th St.) to entry on right.

You can take a water-logged break at **Adventure Island,** a 36-acre outdoor water theme park adjacent to Busch Gardens Tampa Bay (see below). The Key West Rapids, Tampa Typhoon, Gulf Scream, and other exciting water rides will drench the teens, while other calmer rides are geared for kids. There are places to picnic and sunbathe, a game arcade, a volleyball complex, and an outdoor cafe. If you forget to bring your own, a surf shop sells bathing suits, towels, and suntan lotion.

✪ Busch Gardens Tampa Bay

3000 E. Busch Blvd. (at McKinley Drive/N. 40th St.). ☎ 813/987-5283. Admission $36.15 for adults, $28.75 for children 3 to 9, including tax. Free for children 2 and under. Parking $3. Combination ticket including Adventure Island: $42.82 adults, $36.59 children 3 to 9, plus tax. Daily 9:30am–6pm (extended hours in summer and holidays). Take I-275 north of downtown to Busch Blvd. (Exit 33) and go east 2 miles.

Predating Disney World, this 335-acre family theme park remains this area's most popular attraction. Although the thrill rides, live entertainment, shops, restaurants, and games get most of the ink, Busch Gardens ranks among the top zoos in the country, with several thousand animals living in naturalistic environments. This is a great place to show the kids what all those wild beasts they've seen on The Discovery Channel look like in person.

The animals help carry out an overall "Dark Continent of Africa" theme. The open **Serengeti Plain** has more than 500 African animals roaming freely in herds. This 80-acre natural grassy veldt may be viewed from the monorail, Trans-Veldt Railway, or sky ride. **Nairobi** is home to "Myombe Reserve: The Great Ape Domain," a natural habitat for various types of gorillas and chimpanzees, and a baby-animal nursery, as well as a petting zoo, reptile displays, and Nocturnal Mountain, a simulated environment that allows visitors to observe animals that are active in the dark. **The Congo** features a display of rare white Bengal tigers in a natural setting, plus Kumba (the largest steel roller coaster in the southeastern United States), Claw Island, and white-water raft rides. **Bird Gardens,** the park's original core, offers rich foliage, lagoons, and a free-flight aviary for hundreds of exotic birds, including golden and American bald eagles.

Timbuktu is an ancient desert trading center with African craftspeople at work, plus a sandstorm-style ride, a boat-swing ride, a roller coaster, and an electronic-games arcade. **Morocco,** a walled city with exotic architecture, has Moroccan craft demonstrations, a sultan's tent with snake charmers, and the Marrakesh Theaters. **Stanleyville,** a prototype African village, has a shopping bazaar and live entertainment, as well as two water rides: the Tanganyika Tidal Wave and Stanley Falls. **Crown Colony** is the home of a team of Clydesdale horses as well as the Anheuser-Busch hospitality center. Questor, a flight-simulator adventure ride, is also located in this area.

Egypt, the park's newest area, mirrors that country's culture and history, including a replica of King Tutankhamen's tomb. Older kids can ride Montu, the tallest and longest inverted roller coaster in the world, while youngsters can dig for their own ancient treasures in a sand area.

Land of the Dragons also entertains the younger set with a variety of play elements in a fairy-tale setting with just-for-kids rides. The area is dominated by Dumphrey, a whimsical dragon who interacts with visitors and guides children around a three-story tree house with winding stairways, tall towers, stepping stones, illuminated water geysers, and an echo chamber. To get the most from your visit,

Tampa

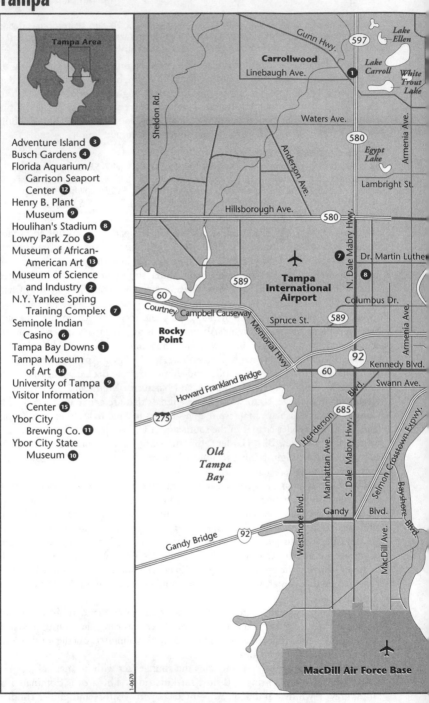

Tampa Area

Gunn Hwy.
597
Lake Ellen
Lake Carroll
White Trout Lake
Carrollwood
Linebaugh Ave.
❶
Waters Ave.
580
Egypt Lake
Armenia Ave.
Lambright St.
Sheldon Rd.
Anderson Ave.
Hillsborough Ave.
580
N. Dale Mabry Hwy.
Dr. Martin Luther
❼
Tampa International Airport
❽
Columbus Dr.
589
60
Courtney Campbell Causeway
Spruce St.
589
Rocky Point
Memorial Hwy.
92
Kennedy Blvd.
Armenia Ave.
60
Swann Ave.
Howard Frankland Bridge
685
Blvd.
Henderson Ave.
Manhattan Ave.
S. Dale Mabry Hwy.
Selmon Crosstown Expwy.
Bayshore Blvd.
275
Old Tampa Bay
Westshore Blvd.
Gandy
Blvd.
MacDill Ave.
Gandy Bridge
92
MacDill Air Force Base

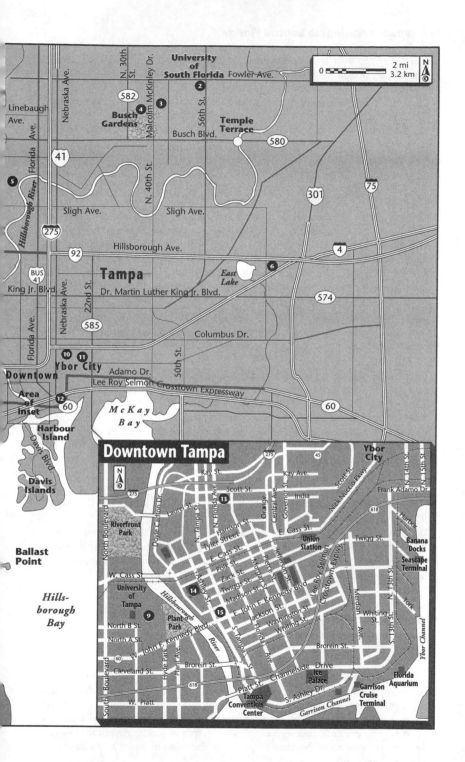

University
of
South Florida
Fowler Ave.

N. 30th St.
Malcolm McKinley Dr.
56th St.

582

Busch
Gardens

Temple
Terrace

Busch Blvd.

580

Linebaugh
Ave.

Nebraska Ave.

Florida Ave.

41

N. 40th St.

5

Hillsborough River

301

75

Sligh Ave.

Sligh Ave.

275

Hillsborough Ave.

92

4

BUS
41

Tampa

East
Lake

6

King Jr. Blvd.

Dr. Martin Luther King Jr. Blvd.

574

Nebraska Ave.

22nd St.

Florida Ave.

585

Columbus Dr.

50th St.

10 11

Ybor City

Adamo Dr.

Downtown

Lee Roy Selmon Crosstown Expressway

Area
of
inset

12

60

McKay
Bay

60

Harbour
Island

Davis Blvd.

Davis
Islands

Ballast
Point

Hillsborough
Bay

Downtown Tampa

N

Ybor
City

275

45

Kay St.

Kay Ave.

Scott St.

india

Scott St.

Nick Nuccio Pkwy.

14th St.

15th St.

Frank Adamo Dr.

275

North Boulevard

Doyle Carlton Dr.

Laurel St.

N. Tampa Ave.

N. Florida Ave.

13

Harrison St.

Orange

Central Ave.

Governor St.

618

Harbor

Riverfront
Park

Tyler Street

E. Cass St.

Union
Station

Twigg St.

Banana
Docks

Seascape
Terminal

W. Cass St.

Polk St.

Zack St.

Jefferson St.

Crosstown Expwy.

Lee Roy Selmon

University
of
Tampa

14

Twiggs St.

Morgan St.

Pierce St.

Meridian Ave.

Whiting
St.

N. 13th St.

Kok

Ybor Channel

N. Ashley St.

Madison St.

15

E. John F. Kennedy Blvd.

Jackson St.

Washington St.

Whiting St.

S. 13th St.

9

Plant
Park

North B St.

North A St.

Hillsborough River

S. Tampa Ave.

S. Florida Ave.

Brorein St.

W. John F. Kennedy Blvd.

60

Hyde Park Ave.

Plant Ave.

Cleveland St.

Brorein St.

S. Ashley Dr.

Channelside Drive

Ice
Palace

Florida
Aquarium

618

Platt St.

W. Platt

Tampa
Convention
Center

Garrison
Cruise
Terminal

Garrison Channel

arrive early and wear comfortable shoes. Many visitors pack a bathing suit because some of the rides get you totally soaked. Don't forget to bring extra money for snacks.

Helpful hints: Try to arrive early, pick up a map, and plan your visit carefully. You may be able to avoid some of the crowds by heading to the far reaches of the park first, then touring back toward the entrance. Bring comfortable shoes, and remember, you can get wet on some of the rides, so wear appropriate clothing. You can exchange foreign currency in the park, and interpreters are available.

✪ The Florida Aquarium

701 Channelside Dr. ☎ 813/273-4000. Admission $13.95 adults, $12.55 seniors and teens 13–18, $6.95 children 3–12, free for children under 3. Parking $3. Daily 10am–5pm. Closed Thanksgiving and Christmas Day.

Visitors here are introduced to more than 5,300 aquatic animals and plants that call Florida home. Various exhibits allow you to follow the pristine springs of the Florida Wetlands Gallery, go through a mangrove forest in the Bays and Beaches Gallery, and stand amazed at the Coral Reefs. The most impressive display is a 43-foot-wide, 14-foot-tall panoramic window with schools of fish and lots of sharks and stingrays. You can watch a diver twice a day. There's a half-million-dollar "Explore a Shore" playground to educate the kids.

Henry B. Plant Museum

401 W. Kennedy Blvd. (between Hyde Park and Magnolia aves.). ☎ 813/254-1891. Free admission; suggested donation, $3 adults, $1 children 12 and under. Tues–Sat 10am–4pm, Sun noon–4pm. Take Fla. 60 west of downtown.

You can't miss the 13 silver minarets and distinctive Moorish architecture—it's modeled after the Alhambra in Spain—which make this National Historic Landmark a focal point of the Tampa skyline. Originally built in 1891 as the 511-room Tampa Bay Hotel by railroad tycoon Henry B. Plant, it's filled with art and furnishings from Europe and the Orient. Other exhibits focus on the history of the original railroad resort, Florida's early tourist industry, and the hotel's role as a staging point for Teddy Roosevelt's Rough Riders during the Spanish-American War.

Lowry Park Zoo

7530 North Blvd. ☎ 813/932-0245. Admission $7.50 adults, $6.50 seniors, $4.95 children 3–11, free for children 2 and under. Daily 9:30am–5pm. Take I-275 to Sligh Ave. (Exit 31) and follow the signs to Lowry Park Zoo.

Watching the 2,000-pound manatees is the highlight here, although seeing a Komodo dragon from Indonesia might rival that experience. With lots of greenery, bubbling brooks, and cascading waterfalls, this 24-acre zoo displays animals in settings similar to their natural habitats. Other major exhibits include the Florida wildlife display, the Asian Domain, Primate World, an Aquatic Center, a free-flight aviary, and a children's petting zoo.

✪ Museum of African-American Art

1308 N. Marion St. (entry and parking lot face N. Florida Ave. between Scott and Laurel sts.), downtown. ☎ 813/272-2466. Admission $3 adults, $2 seniors and children grades K–12. Tues–Fri 10am–4:30pm, Sat 10am–5pm. Take Exit 26 off I-275.

Recently renovated to the tune of $2 million, the museum is touted as the first of its kind in Florida and one of four in the United States. It's the home of the Barnett-Aden collection, considered the state's foremost collection of African-American art. More than 80 artists are represented in the display, which includes sculptures and paintings that depict the history, culture, and lifestyle of African Americans from the 1800s to the present, with special emphasis on the works of artists active during the Harlem Renaissance.

Museum of Science and Industry (MOSI)

4801 E. Fowler Ave. (at N. 50th St.). ☎ 813/987-6300. Admission $8 adults, $7 seniors, $5 children 2–12, free for children under 2. Daily 9am–5pm or later. Head north of downtown, 1 mile east of Busch Gardens.

MOSI is the largest science center in the Southeast and has more than 450 interactive exhibits. Guests can step into the Gulf Hurricane and experience gale-force winds, defy the laws of gravity in the unique *Challenger* space experience, or cruise the mysterious world of microbes in LifeLab. "The Amazing You" allows visitors to explore the body, "Our Florida" focuses on environmental factors, and "Our Place in the Universe" introduces them to space, flight, and beyond. You can also watch stunning movies in MOSIMAX, Florida's first IMAX dome theater.

Tampa Museum of Art

600 N. Ashley St. (at Twiggs St.), downtown. ☎ 813/274-8130. Admission $5 adults, $4 seniors and college students, $3 children 6–18, free for children 5 and under; free for everyone Wed 5–9pm and Sun 1–5pm. Mon–Tues and Thurs–Sat 10am–5pm, Wed 10am–9pm, Sun 1–5pm. Take I-275 to Exit 25 (Ashley St.).

Located on the east bank of the Hillsborough River next to the round NationsBank building (locals facetiously call it the "Beer Can") and just south of the Tampa Bay Performing-Arts Center, this fine-arts complex offers eight galleries with changing exhibits ranging from classical antiquities to contemporary Florida art. There's also a new 7-acre riverfront park and sculpture garden. Museum tours are offered on Wednesday and Saturday at 1pm and on Sunday at 2pm.

YBOR CITY

A few short years ago the part of Tampa northeast of downtown was known simply as the Latin Quarter, the historic district famous for cigars and The Columbia, the largest Spanish restaurant in the world (see "Where to Dine," below). It takes its present name from Don Vicente Martinez Ybor, a Spanish cigar maker who arrived here in 1886 via Cuba and Key West. Soon his and other Tampa factories were producing more than 300,000 hand-rolled stogies a day.

It may not be the cigar capital of the world anymore, but "Ybor" is the happening part of Tampa, a cross between New Orleans's Bourbon Street, Washington's Georgetown, and New York's SoHo. By day, you can stroll past the art galleries, boutiques, and trendy new restaurants and cafes that line 7th Avenue. At night, when good food and great music dominate the scene, streets will be bustling until 4am. Unique shops offer a wide assortment of goodies, from silk boxer shorts to unique tattoos. Dozens of outstanding nightclubs and dance clubs have lines waiting out the door. Live-music offerings run the gamut from jazz and blues to indie rock. There are lots of police around in the wee hours, but be as cautious here as you would exploring any big city at night.

○ **Ybor City Walking Tours** are an ideal way to check out the highlights of this historic district. Free 1¹/₂-hour tours are sponsored by the Ybor City State Museum (see below) and are led by enthusiastic local volunteers. Tours start at the information desk in Ybor Square shopping center, on 13th Street between 8th and 9th avenues, and cover over three dozen points of interest before ending at the Ybor City State Museum. January to April the tours depart on Tuesday, Thursday, and Saturday at 10:30am; May to December, only on Thursday and Saturday.

Cigar smokers will enjoy a stroll through the **Ybor City State Museum,** 1818 9th Ave., between 18th and 19th streets. (☎ 813/247-6323), housed in the former Ferlita Bakery (1896–1973). You can take a self-guided tour around the museum to see a collection of cigar labels, cigar memorabilia, and works by local artisans.

Admission includes a guided tour of **La Casita,** a renovated cigar worker's cottage adjacent to the museum; it's furnished as it was at the turn of the century.

Another interesting stop here is the **Ybor City Brewing Company,** 2205 N. 20th St., facing Palm Avenue (☎ 813/242-9222). Housed in a 100-year-old, three-story former cigar factory, this microbrewery produces Ybor Gold and other brews, none with preservatives. Admission of $2 per person includes a tour of the brewery and a taste of the end result. Open Tuesday to Saturday from 11am to 3pm. The top floor is now occupied by **Nick's Cigar Company** (☎ 813/724-1075), which carries on the cigar-making tradition. Many of America's machine-made, "drugstore" cigars are still produced in Tampa, and though you can buy many fine imported cigars at Ybor City's shops, Nick's is the only factory where you can watch workers rolling them just like in the old days. Nick's is open Monday to Saturday from 8am to 4pm.

OUTDOOR PURSUITS & SPECTATOR SPORTS

BIKING, IN-LINE SKATING & JOGGING   Bayshore Boulevard, a 7-mile promenade is famous for its sidewalk right on the shores of Hillsborough Bay. Reputed to be the world's longest continuous sidewalk, it's a favorite for runners, joggers, walkers, and in-line skaters.

Rent bicycles and in-line skates at **Blades & Bikes,** in a pink-and-blue shop at 201-A W. Platt St., at S. Parker Street (☎ 813/251-0780), a block west of the northern end of Bayshore Boulevard. It's open Monday to Friday from 10:30am to 8pm, Saturday from 9am to 7pm, and Sunday from 11am to 6pm.

GOLF   Tampa has this area's largest selection of municipal golf courses, where you can play for a pittance when compared to the private courses in Florida.

The **Babe Zaharias Municipal Golf Course,** 11412 Forest Hills Dr., north of Lowry Park (☎ 813/932-8932), is an 18-hole, par-70 course with a pro shop, putting greens, and a driving range. Just south of the airport, the **Hall of Fame Golf Club,** 2222 N. Westshore Blvd. (☎ 813/876-4913), is an 18-hole, par-72 affair with a driving range. The **Rocky Point Municipal Golf Course,** 4151 Dana Shores Dr. (☎ 813/884-5141), located between the airport and the bay, is an 18-hole, par-71 course with a pro shop, practice range, and putting greens. On the Hillsborough River in north Tampa, the **Rogers Park Municipal Golf Course,** 7910 N. 30th St. (☎ 813/234-1911), is an 18-hole, par-72 championship course with a lighted driving and practice range.

Greens fees at the municipal courses range from $23 to $30. They all are open daily from 7am to dusk, and lessons and club rentals are available.

In addition, the **University of South Florida Golf Course,** Fletcher Avenue and 46th Street (☎ 813/632-6893), is just north of the USF campus. This 18-hole, par-71 course is nicknamed "The Claw" because of its challenging layout. It offers lessons and club rentals. Greens fees are $20, $32 with a cart. It's open daily from 7am to dusk.

Other courses open to the public include **Persimmon Hill Golf Club,** 5109 Hamey Rd. (☎ 813/623-6962); **Silver Dollar Trap & Golf Club,** 17000 Patterson Rd., Odessa (☎ 813/920-3884); and **Westchase Golf Club,** 1307 Radcliff Dr. (☎ 813/854-2331).

You can book starting times and get information about these and the area's other courses by calling **Tee Times USA** (☎ 800/374-8633).

SPECTATOR SPORTS   Okay, you **New York Yankees** fans, your Boys in Blue hold their spring training during February and March at Legends Field, opposite Houlihan's Stadium, at the southwest corner of Dale Mabry Highway and Dr. Martin Luther King, Jr. Boulevard (☎ 813/875-7753). A scaled-down replica of

Yankee Stadium, it's the largest spring-training facility in Florida, with a 10,000-seat capacity.

About a half-hour drive from downtown Tampa, the **Plant City Stadium,** Park Road, Plant City (☎ 813/757-9221), is the spring-training turf of the **Cincinnati Reds.** The season runs from mid-February to April and admission is $4 to $7.

National Football League fans can catch the improving **Tampa Bay Buccaneers,** for now at Houlihan's Stadium, 4201 N. Dale Mabry Hwy. (☎ 813/872-7977 or 813/879-BUCS). Local governments are planning to build the team a new $318-million stadium, but at press time, the project continued to be mired in controversy. Wherever the "Bucs" play, their season runs from September through December.

The National Hockey League's **Tampa Bay Lightning** play at the 20,000-seat **Ice Palace,** downtown between the Tampa Convention Center and the Florida Aquarium (☎ 813/229-8800).

The only oval thoroughbred race course on Florida's west coast, ✪ **Tampa Bay Downs,** 11225 Racetrack Rd., Oldsmar (☎ 813/855-4401), is the home of the Tampa Bay Derby. Races are held from December to May, and the track presents simulcasts year-round. Post time is 12:30pm on Tuesday, Thursday, and Friday, and at 1pm on Saturday and Sunday. Admission to the 10-race daily program is $1.50 to the grandstand, $3 to the clubhouse. Parking costs $1.

Professional players volley the lethal pelota at the **Tampa Jai-Alai Fronton,** 5125 S. Dale Mabry Hwy. (☎ 813/831-1411). Admission is $1 to $3 and parking is $1 or free. It's open year-round, with games Monday to Saturday beginning at 6:45pm, and matinees on Monday, Wednesday, Friday, and Saturday beginning at noon.

TENNIS The **City of Tampa Tennis Complex,** at Hillsborough Community College, 4001 Tampa Bay Blvd. (☎ 813/348-1173), across from Houlihan's Stadium, is the largest public complex in Tampa. On the water and overlooking Harbour Island, the **Sandra W. Freedman Tennis Complex,** in Marjorie Park, 59 Columbia Dr., Davis Islands (☎ 813/259-1664), has eight clay courts. Reservations are required.

SHOPPING

Hyde Park and Ybor City are two areas of Tampa worth some window-shopping, perhaps sandwiched around lunch at one of their fine restaurants (see "Where to Dine," below). ✪ **Old Hyde Park Village,** 1507 W. Swann Ave., at South Dakoda Avenue (☎ 813/251-3500), is a terrific alternative to cookie-cutter suburban malls. **Ybor City,** along East 7th Avenue between 14th and 22nd streets, has several shops worth browsing. Listed on the National Register of Historic Places, **Ybor Square,** 1901 13th St., at 8th Avenue (☎ 813/247-4497), consists of three brick buildings (dating from 1886) that once comprised the largest cigar factory in the world; today it's a specialty mall. If you want to stock up on fresh Florida fruits and vegetables, head to **Whaley's Markets,** 533 S. Howard Ave., at DeLeon, northwest of Hyde Park (☎ 813/254-2904).

WHERE TO STAY

If you're going to Busch Gardens, Adventure Island, Lowry Park Zoo, and the Museum of Science and Industry (MOSI), the motels near Busch Gardens are much more convenient than those about 7 miles to the south, in downtown. The downtown hotels are geared to business travelers, but staying there will put you near the Florida Aquarium, the Museum of African-American Art, the Tampa Museum of Art, the Henry B. Plant Museum, the Tampa Bay Performing-Arts Center, the Hyde Park historic district, scenic Bayshore Boulevard, and Ybor City's restaurants and nightlife.

The Westshore area, near the bay west of downtown and south of Tampa International Airport, is another commercial center, with a wide range of national chain hotels catering to business travelers and conventioneers. It's convenient to Houlihan's Stadium and the New York Yankees' spring-training complex. Here you'll find the Spanish-style **Doubletree Guest Suites,** 4400 W. Cypress St., at Manhattan Avenue (☎ **800/222-TREE** or 813/873-8675); **Courtyard by Marriott,** 3805 W. Cypress St., at Dale Mabry Highway (☎ **800/321-2211** or 813/874-0555); the **Hyatt Regency Westshore,** 6200 Courtney Campbell Causeway (☎ **800/233-1234** or 813/874-1234), nestled on a 35-acre bayside nature preserve; the **Sheraton Grand Hotel,** 4860 W. Kennedy Blvd., at Shore Boulevard (☎ **800/325-3535** or 813/286-4400), across the street from Westshore Plaza mall and home to one of former Miami Dolphins Coach Don Shula's steak houses; and the **Tampa Marriott Westshore,** 1001 N. Westshore Blvd. (☎ **800/228-9290** or 813/287-2555).

The high season in Tampa generally is January to April, but you won't find as large an increase here as at the beach resorts. Most hotels offer discounted package rates in the summer and weekend specials all year, dropping their rates by as much as 50%. Hotels often combine tickets to major attractions like Busch Gardens in their packages, so always ask about special deals.

Near Busch Gardens

In addition to the listings below, there's the **Days Inn Busch Gardens/Maingate,** 2901 E. Busch Blvd., at 30th Street (☎ **800/DAYS-INN** or 813/933-6471); it's great for families on a budget and you can walk to Busch Gardens from here. There's also a **Red Roof Inn,** 2307 E. Busch Blvd. (☎ **800/THE-ROOF** or 813/932-0073), less than a mile from Busch Gardens. Both motels have outdoor pools.

Best Western Resort Tampa at Busch Gardens

820 E. Busch Blvd., Tampa, FL 33612. ☎ **800/288-4011** or 813/933-4011. Fax 813/932-1784. 255 rms. A/C TV TEL. Winter, $99 double. Off-season $59 double. AE, DC, DISC, MC, V.

Right at the Busch Boulevard exit off I-275, this motel is fine for families on a budget. The lobby leads to an enclosed skylit atrium-style courtyard with fountains, streetlights, benches, a pool, and tropical foliage. Guest rooms in this wing open to walkways facing the indoor atrium or the parking lots. Newer units are in a four-story annex. They all have standard furnishings and coffeemakers.

The Palm Grill Restaurant off the lobby features a variety of dishes. Charades Nite Club offers themed happy hours. Services include a concierge desk, secretarial services, valet laundry, limited room service, and courtesy transport to Busch Gardens. There are indoor and outdoor heated swimming pools, two whirlpools, a sauna, four lighted tennis courts, exercise and game rooms, a coin-operated laundry, and a gift shop.

Budgetel Inn

9202 N. 30th St. (at Busch Blvd.), Tampa, FL 33612. ☎ **800/428-3438** or 813/930-6900. Fax 813/930-0563. 150 rms. AC TV TEL. Winter, $70 double. Off-season $50 double. Rates include continental breakfast. AE, DC, DISC, MC, V.

Fake banana trees and a parrot cage welcome guests to the terra-cotta–floored lobby of this comfortable and convenient member of a young but growing chain of budget-conscious motels. Formerly a Travelodge, this one opened in 1996 after its two- and three-story buildings were gutted and rebuilt. All rooms are spacious and have ceiling fans, bright wood furniture with tropical trim, desks, phones with long cords, and coffeemakers (Danish pastries or a blueberry muffin and juice are hung on your door knob before dawn). Rooms with king beds also have recliners. Outside, a courtyard with an unheated swimming pool has plenty of space for sunning. There's a game room and coin-operated laundry, and local telephone calls are free. There's no restaurant on the premises, but plenty are nearby.

✪ Quality Suites Hotel—USF/Busch Gardens

3001 University Center Dr., Tampa, FL 33612. ☎ **800/786-7446** or 813/971-8930. Fax 813/971-8935. 150 suites. A/C TV TEL. Winter, $99–$159 suite for 2. Off-season, $89–$139 suite for 2. Rates include full breakfast buffet and evening cocktail reception. AE, DC, DISC, MC, V.

Actually on North 30th Street, between Busch Boulevard and Fletcher Avenue, this hacienda-style all-suite hotel sits about a mile from the Busch Gardens entrance and is the pick of the hotels in this area. The complex encloses a lushly tropical courtyard surrounding a heated pool. Opening to this pleasant vista, each suite has a separate bedroom with built-in armoire and well-lit mirrored vanity area. Living/dining rooms have a sofa bed, Lazy Boy recliner, wet bar, coffeemaker, microwave, and stereo/VCR unit. The decor relies heavily on art-deco–style furnishings. Facilities also include a 24-hour gift shop/food store, VCR rentals, whirlpool, meeting rooms, and coin-operated laundry.

Downtown

Holiday Inn Select Downtown

111 W. Fortune St., Tampa, FL 33602. ☎ **800/ASK-VALUE** or 813/223-1351. Fax 813/221-2000. 311 rms. A/C TV TEL. Winter, $115–$140 double. Off-season, $79–$105 double. AE, DC, DISC, MC, V. Take Exit 25/Ashley St. exit off I-275, turn right on Tyler St., then right on W.C. McCandless Place to hotel.

This modern 14-story hotel is adjacent to the Tampa Bay Performing-Arts Center and within walking distance of the Tampa Museum of Art. The guest rooms are spacious, with dark-wood furnishings, full-length wall mirrors, coffeemakers, and irons and boards. Most rooms on the upper floors have views of the Hillsborough River. The lobby level offers three dining choices: the Backstage Restaurant, for moderately priced meals; the Deli, for light fare; and the Encore Lounge, for drinks and occasional live music. There's room service, airport courtesy shuttle, an outdoor heated swimming pool, whirlpool, fitness room, gift shop, and both laundry service and a coin-operated laundry.

✪ Hyatt Regency Tampa

2 Tampa City Center (corner of E. Jackson St.), Tampa, FL 33602. ☎ **800/233-1234** or 813/225-1234. Fax 813/273-0234. 518 rms. A/C TV TEL. Winter $194–$210. Off-season, $145–$160 double. Weekend packages available off-season. AE, DC, DISC, MC, V.

In the center of the downtown business district, it's not surprising that this Hyatt caters primarily to the corporate crowd. It's just off the Franklin Street pedestrian mall and a short walk from the Harbor Island People Mover. The Hyatt-signature eight-story atrium lobby has a cascading waterfall and lots of foliage. Many units on the upper floors have bay or river views.

Dining/Entertainment: Creative American cuisine is featured at City Center Cafe. Light lunches are offered at Deli Express. For libations with piano music, try Saltwaters Lounge (there's not much else going on downtown after dark).

Services: Concierge, room service (24 hours), valet laundry, airport courtesy shuttle.

Facilities: Outdoor heated swimming pool, whirlpool, health club.

✪ Wyndham Harbour Island Hotel

725 S. Harbour Island Blvd., Harbour Island, Tampa, FL 33602. ☎ **800/WYNDHAM** or 813/229-5000. Fax 813/229-5322. 300 rms. A/C MINIBAR TV TEL. Winter, $139–$219 double. Off-season, $99–$169 double. AE, DC, DISC, MC, V.

With the shops closed, there's not much action on this little island, but you'll enjoy quiet elegance at this 12-story luxury property. It has great views of the surrounding channels, which link the Hillsborough River and the bay. The bedrooms, all with views of the water, are furnished in dark woods and floral fabrics, and each has a well-lit marble-trimmed bathroom, executive desk, and work area, plus in-room conveniences such as a coffeemaker, iron, and ironing board.

Dining/Entertainment: Watch the yachts drift by as you dine at the Harbourview Room, or enjoy your favorite drink in the Bar, a clubby room with equally good views. Snacks and drinks are available during the day at the Pool Bar.

Services: Concierge, room service, secretarial services, notary public, evening turndown, valet laundry, courtesy airport shuttle.

Facilities: Outdoor heated swimming pool and deck, 50 boat slips, newsstand/gift shop, guest privileges at the Harbour Island Athletic Club.

WHERE TO DINE

Near Busch Gardens

You'll find the national fast-food and family restaurants east of I-275 on Busch Boulevard and along Flower Avenue near University Mall.

✪ Mel's Hot Dogs

4136 E. Busch Blvd., at 42nd St. ☎ **813/985-8000.** Main courses $3–$6.50. No credit cards. Mon–Sat 10am–10pm, Sun 11am–9pm. AMERICAN.

Catering primarily to area college students and hungry families craving inexpensive all-beef hot dogs, this red-and-white cottage offers everything from "bagel-dogs" and corn dogs to a bacon/cheddar Reuben. All choices are served on a poppy-seed bun and most come with french fries and a choice of coleslaw or baked beans. Even the decor is dedicated to wieners: The walls and windows are lined with hot-dog memorabilia. And just in case hot-dog mania hasn't won you over, there are a few alternative choices (sausages, chicken breast, and beef and veggie burgers).

Shells

11010 N. 30th St. (between Busch Blvd. and Fowler Ave.). ☎ 813/977-8456. Reservations not accepted. Main courses $5–$16 (most $8–$10). AE, DISC, MC, V. Mon–Thurs 11:30am–10pm, Fri–Sat 11:30am–11pm, Sun noon–10pm. SEAFOOD.

You'll see other Shells in the Tampa Bay area, and with good reason, for this casual, award-winning chain consistently provides good value, especially if you have a family to feed. Shells is particularly known for its spicy Jack Daniels Buffalo shrimp and scallop appetizers. Main courses range from the usual fried seafood platters to chargrilled shrimp, fish, steaks, and chicken. I counted 21 tender, bite-size shrimp in a light, garlic-tinged cream sauce and served over linguini—a bargain for $8.95.

Hyde Park

Bern's Steak House

1208 S. Howard Ave. (at Marjory Ave.). ☎ 813/251-2421. Reservations required. Main courses $18.50–$32.50. AE, DC, DISC, MC, V. Daily 5–11pm. AMERICAN.

The exterior of this famous steak house looks like a factory built almost under the Lee Roy Selmon Crosstown Expressway. Inside, however, you'll find eight ornate dining rooms with themes like Rhone, Burgundy, and Irish Rebellion. They set an appropriately dark atmosphere for meat lovers, for here you order and pay for chargrilled steaks (beef or buffalo) according to the thickness and weight. They come with onion soup, salad, baked potato, garlic toast, onion rings, and vegetables grown in Bern's own organic garden. The phone-book–size wine list offers more than 7,000 selections.

The big surprise here are the dessert quarters upstairs, where 50 romantic booths paneled in aged California redwood can privately seat from 2 to 12 guests. Each of these little chambers is equipped with a phone for placing your order and a closed circuit TV for watching and listening to a resident pianist. The dessert menu offers 94 delicious selections, plus 1,400 after-dinner drinks. It's possible to reserve a booth for dessert only, but preference is given to those who dine. (Bern's is planning to open a dessert-only restaurant nearby, so call to see if it's open yet.)

Cactus Club

In Old Hyde Park shopping complex, 1601 Snow Ave. (south of Swan St.). ☎ 813/251-4089. Reservations not accepted. Main courses $6.25–$15. AE, DC, MC, V. Sun–Thurs 11am–11:30pm, Fri–Sat 11am–12:30am. AMERICAN SOUTHWEST.

Watch all the shoppers go by at Old Hyde Park from this fun and casual cafe with a Southwestern accent. Dine inside or outside on tacos, enchiladas, chili, sizzling fajitas, hickory-smoked baby back ribs, Texas-style pizzas, Jamaican jerk chicken, guacamole/green-chili burgers, sandwiches, smoked chicken salad, and more. It's always packed at lunchtime—get there early.

The Colonnade

3401 Bayshore Blvd. (at W. Julia St.). ☎ 813/839-7558. Reservations accepted only for large parties. Main courses $7–$16. AE, DC, DISC, MC, V. Sun–Thurs 11am–10pm, Fri–Sat 11am 11pm. AMERICAN/SEAFOOD.

Locals have been flocking to this rough-hewn, shiplap place since the 1930s, primarily for the great view of Hillsborough Bay across Bayshore Boulevard. The food is a bit on the Red Lobsterish side, but get here early or wait for a windowside table; the vista is worth it. Fresh seafood is the specialty: grouper in lemon butter, crab-stuffed flounder, Maryland-style crab cakes, even wild Florida alligator as an appetizer. Prime rib, steaks, and chicken are also available.

Four Green Fields

205 W. Platt St. (between Parker St. and Plant Ave.). ☎ 813/254-4444. Main courses $3.95–$8.95. AE, MC, V. Mon–Sat 11am–2am, Sun noon–2am. IRISH/AMERICAN.

This thatched-roof pub may be surrounded by palm trees instead of potato fields, but it still offers the ambiance and tastes of Ireland, just across the bridge from the downtown convention center. Staffed by genuine Irish immigrants, the large room with a square bar in the center smells of Irish ale. The Gaelic stew is predictably bland, but the salads and sandwiches are passable. The crowd usually is young, especially for live Irish music on Thursday, Friday, and Saturday nights.

Le Bordeaux

1502 S. Howard Ave. (2 blocks north of Bayshore Blvd.). ☎ 813/254-4387. Reservations accepted only for parties of 6 or more. Main courses $10–$22. AE, DC, MC, V. Mon–Thurs 6–10pm, Fri 6–11pm, Sat 5:30–11pm, Sun 5:30–9:30pm. FRENCH.

This bistro's authentic French fare is some of the region's best, but keep a reign on your credit card—everything's sold à la carte, so you can ring up a hefty bill quickly. French-born chef/owner Gordon Davis offers seating in a living-room–style main dining room of this converted house expanded to include a plant-filled conservatory. His menu changes daily, but you can count on homemade pâtés and pastries, and the specials often include salmon en croûte, pot au feu, veal with wild mushrooms, and filet of beef au Roquefort. Part of the establishment is The Left Bank Jazz Bistro, with live entertainment.

✪ Mise en Place

In Grand Central Place, 442 W. Kennedy Blvd. (at S. Magnolia Ave., opposite the University of Tampa). ☎ 813/254-5373. Reservations accepted only for parties of 6 or more. Main courses

$11–$20. AE, DC, DISC, MC, V. Mon 11am–3pm, Tues–Thurs 11am–3pm and 5:30–10pm, Fri 11am–3pm and 5:30–11pm, Sat 5:30–11pm. NEW AMERICAN.

Look around at all those happy, stylish people soaking up the trendy ambiance and you'll know why chef Marty Blitz and his wife, Marianne, are the culinary darlings of Tampa. They continue to present the freshest of ingredients, with a creative "Floribbean" menu that changes daily. Main courses often include such choices as roast duck with Jamaican wild-strawberry sauce or grilled swordfish with trimelon mint salsa. There's valet parking at the rear of the building on Grand Central Place.

After dinner you can wander next door into "442," an upscale bar with live jazz and blues.

MoJo
238 E. Davis Blvd. (at Biscayne Ave.), Davis Island. ☎ 813/259-9949. Main courses $9.95–$12.95. AE, DC, DISC, MC, V. Tues–Thurs 11am–11pm, Fri–Sat 11am–midnight. SOUTH AMERICAN.

An offshoot of the popular Mise en Place (see above), this casual establishment livened up the dining scene in Davis Island's business district, across the bridge from Hyde Park. Bright-yellow colors shout "have fun" and paper tablecloths say "relax." The dishes are hot and spicy, so be prepared for Latin spices. You can dine inside or outdoors under large arches facing a courtyard with a fountain.

Selena's
In Old Hyde Park shopping complex, 1623 Snow Ave. (south of Swan St.). ☎ 813/251-2116. Reservations recommended. Main courses $7.95–$17.95. AE, MC, V. Sun–Wed 11am–10pm, Thurs 11am–11pm, Fri–Sat 11am–midnight. CREOLE/SICILIAN.

This charming restaurant seems straight out of New Orleans. Sit in the plant-filled Patio Room, the eclectic Queen Anne Room, or watch the world go by at the outdoor cafe. Local seafood, especially grouper and shrimp, top the menu at dinner, with many of the dishes served Creole style or blackened, as well as broiled or fried. Choices also include pastas, chicken, steaks, and veal. At night, jazz sounds enliven the proceedings, as musical groups perform in the upstairs lounge.

Ybor City

✪ Cafe Creole and Oyster Bar
1330 9th Ave. (at avenida de Republica de Cuba/14th St.). ☎ 813/247-6283. Reservations recommended. Main courses $9–$16. AE, DC, MC, V. Mon–Thurs 11:30am–10pm, Fri–Sat 11:30am–11pm. CREOLE/CAJUN.

Enjoy Tampa's great weather at this indoor/outdoor restaurant and breathe in the history. The building, dating back to 1896, was originally known as El Pasaje, the home of the Cherokee Club, a gentlemen's hotel and private club with a casino and a decor rich in stained-glass windows, wrought-iron balconies, Spanish murals, and marble bathrooms. Specialties include Louisiana crab cakes, oysters, blackened grouper, and jambalaya.

✪ The Columbia
2117 E. 7th Ave. (between 21st and 22nd sts). ☎ 813/248-4961. Reservations recommended. Main courses $11–$19. AE, DC, DISC, MC, V. Daily 11am–11pm. SPANISH.

Dating back to 1905, this hand-painted tile building occupies an entire city block in the heart of Ybor City. Tourists flock here to soak up the ambiance, and so do the locals, because it's so much fun to clap along during fire-belching floor shows in the main dining room. You can't help coming back time after time for the famous Spanish bean soup and original "1905" salad. The paella à la valenciana is outstanding, with more than a dozen ingredients from gulf grouper and gulf pink shrimp to calamari, mussels, clams, chicken, and pork. The decor throughout is graced with hand-painted tiles, wrought-iron chandeliers, dark woods, rich red fabrics, and stained-glass windows. You can breathe your own fumes in the Cigar Bar.

Frankie's Patio Bar & Grill

1905 E. 7th Ave. (between 19th and 20th sts.). ☎ 813/249-3337. Reservations accepted only for large parties. Main courses $8–$14; sandwiches $4.25–$6.50. AE, MC, V. Mon 11am–3pm, Tues 11am–10pm, Wed–Thurs 11am–1am, Fri–Sat 11am–3am, Sun 1–11pm. INTERNATIONAL.

Known mostly as a venue for outstanding musical acts, this Ybor City attraction is also fun at lunch and dinner. With exposed industrial pipes, the large three-story restaurant stands out from the usual Spanish-themed, 19th-century architecture of Ybor City. There's seating indoors, on a large outdoor patio, or on an open-air balcony overlooking the action on the street. It's a fun atmosphere, and the food blends Cuban, American, Creole, and Italian influences. Live jazz, blues, reggae, and rock add to the atmosphere Wednesday to Saturday.

Ovo Cafe

1901 E. 7th Ave. (at 19th St.). ☎ 813/248-6979. Reservations not accepted. Main courses $8–$15. AE, MC, V. Mon–Tues 11am–4pm, Wed–Sat 11am–2am, Sun 11am–10pm. INTERNATIONAL.

This cafe, popular with the business set by day and the club crowd at night, is Tampa's answer to SoHo. You'll find a blend of good food, eclectic art, and pleasing surroundings. Locals love the "menage à trois" omelets at breakfast. The fresh Ovo's chicken feta salad is a great lunch choice. An eclectic menu includes pierogies, smoked tuna sandwiches, and shrimp bisque soup. The big surprise is finding Dom Perignon on the menu, as well as root-beer floats made with Absolut vodka.

Silver Ring

1831 E. 7th Ave. (at 19th St.). ☎ 813/248-2549. Reservations not accepted. Sandwiches $3.25–$5. No credit cards. Mon–Sat 7am–7pm. SPANISH/AMERICAN.

This place has been an Ybor City tradition since 1947, and it looks it. The greasy walls are lined with dusty old pictures, vintage radios, fishing rods, a stuffed tarpon, and deer heads. Still, it's *the* place to get a genuine Cuban sandwich—smoked ham, roast pork, Genoa salami, Swiss cheese, pickles, salad dressing, mustard, lettuce, and tomato on crispy Cuban bread. Other menu items include Spanish bean soup, deviled crab, and other types of sandwiches.

Westshore

✪ Armani's

In the Hyatt Regency Westshore, 6200 Courtney Campbell Causeway. ☎ 813/281-9165. Reservations required. Jackets required for men. Main courses $14–$26.75. AE, DC, DISC, MC, V. Mon–Sat 6–11pm (bar opens 5pm). NORTHERN ITALIAN.

This is the most elegant dining room in town and the only one with a view—you can see the entire bay from its 14th-floor perch (come early for sunset). The candlelit ambiance is romantic and subdued. Outstanding dishes include the lamb and marinated salmon filet stuffed with spinach and fennel. When used together, the words "salad" and "bar" usually leave me cold, but Armani's create-your-own-antipasto table is something to behold.

Crawdaddy's

2500 Rocky Point Dr. (on Rocky Point Island, off Courtney Campbell Causeway). ☎ 813/281-0407. Reservations recommended. Main courses $15–$20. AE, DC, DISC, MC, V. Sun–Thurs 5–10pm, Fri–Sat 5–11pm. REGIONAL/SEAFOOD.

Overlooking Old Tampa Bay, this ramshackle, rusty tin establishment looks and feels like an old Florida fish camp. In fact, it's named for Beauregard "Crawdaddy" Belvedere, a Roaring Twenties tycoon who actually did own a fish camp on this site. The seven dining rooms are all bedecked with Victorian furnishings, books, pictures, and collectibles. The down-home menu ranges from beer-battered shrimp and fish camp fry (shrimp, scallops, and fresh fish, deep-fried in corn crisp and almond coating, with jalapeño hush puppies) to shrimp and chicken jambalaya, prime ribs, and steaks.

Also on the premises, Whiskey Joe's Pub offers lunches Monday to Friday from 11am to 2pm, and The Attic has dancing nightly.

✪ Lauro Ristorante Italiano

3915 Henderson Blvd. (between Watrous and Neptune aves.). ☎ **813/281-2100.** Reservations recommended. Main courses $10–$20. AE, DC, DISC, MC, V. Mon–Fri 11:30am–2pm and 6–10pm, Sat 6–11pm. ITALIAN.

Known for extraordinary sauces and pastas, chef/owner Lauro Medeglia is a native Italian who cooks with love. Though his restaurant is off the beaten track, Lauro's classic decor, soft music, and smartly attired waiters make it worth the detour (it's 2 blocks west of the Dale Mabry Highway). Try the caprese, putanesca, gnocchi, or agnoloeti.

TAMPA AFTER DARK

The Tampa/Hillsborough Arts Council maintains an **Artsline** (☎ **813/229-ARTS**), a 24-hour information service providing the latest on current and upcoming cultural events. Racks in many restaurants and bars have copies of *Tropical Breeze Arts & Life Styles* and *Tampa Tonight,* two free publications detailing what's going on in the entire bay area. And you can check the "Baylife" and "Friday Extra" sections of the *Tampa Tribune* and the Friday "Weekend" section of the *St. Petersburg Times.* The visitor center usually has copies of the week's newspaper sections (see "Essentials," above).

THE CLUB & MUSIC SCENE Ybor City is Tampa's favorite nighttime venue by far. All you have to do is stroll along 7th Avenue East between 15th and 20th streets to find a club or bar to your liking. The avenue is packed with people of every possible age and description on Fridays and Saturdays from 9pm to 3am, but you'll also find something going on from Tuesday to Thursday and even on Sundays. You don't need addresses or phone numbers; your ears will guide you along 7th Avenue.

Starting at 15th Street and heading east, you'll come first to **The Masquerade,** with retro and old-wave bands Friday to Sunday. The body-pierced twenty-something crowd gets primed at **Cherry's** before dancing at **The Rubb** across the avenue. You can hear the band playing outdoors at the **Ybor Market,** at the corner of 17th Street, from blocks away.

Between 17th and 18th streets, you'll smell the cigar smoke coming from the sidewalk tables of the **Green Iguana Bar & Grill,** a refined establishment frequented by young professionals. **The Irish Pub** is just that, while **Fat Tuesday** has a large dance floor and long bar. Between 18th and 19th streets you'll see **Harpo's,** which doesn't charge a cover. Keep going across 19th Street to **Bubba's Beach Club,** the kind of noisy joint that advertises "no panties" on Thursday. Upstairs over Bubba's is one of Ybor's best clubs, **Blues Ship Café on Top,** which features live blues, jazz, and reggae. And last but not least is the warehouselike **Frankie's Patio Bar & Grill,** known for its reasonably priced food as well as its outstanding musical acts (see "Dining," above).

Although not in the heart of Ybor's bar scene, the **Jazz Cellar,** on 9th Avenue East between 13th Street and Avenida de Republica de Cuba (14th Street), features contemporary jazz, rhythm and blues, and just plain blues. This basement establishment is on the north side of Ybor Square. Call ☎ **813/248-1862** for reservations.

Across town in the Westshore district, **Brothers Lounge,** in the Lincoln Center Building, 5401 W. Kennedy Blvd., at North Hoover Boulevard (☎ **813/286-8882**), has been around for more than 20 years, concentrating solely on jazz Tuesday to Saturday.

In the Busch Gardens/University of South Florida area, the **Brass Mug Pub,** 1441 E. Fletcher Ave., near USF (☎ **813/972-8152**), features nightly music, from heavy metal to rock 'n' roll. In North Tampa, **Skipper's Smokehouse Restaurant & Oyster Bar,** 910 Skipper Rd., off Bruce E. Downs Boulevard (☎ **813/971-0666** or 813/977-6474), is a prime spot for live reggae, blues, and zydeco Tuesday to Sunday. Locals call it the "Club That Washed Ashore."

Sidesplitters Comedy Club, 12938 N. Dale Mabry Hwy. (☎ **813/960-1197**), presents professional stand-up comedians on most nights. Shows begin at 8:30pm Tuesday to Thursday, at 8 and 10:30pm on Friday and Saturday, and at 8:30pm on Sunday.

You can loose your life savings playing bingo, poker, and the video slot machines at the **Seminole Indian Casino,** 5223 N. Orient Rd., at Hillsborough Road east of the city (☎ **813/621-1302** or 800/282-7016). It's open 24 hours every day of the year.

THE PERFORMING ARTS With a prime downtown location on 9 acres along the east bank of the Hillsborough River, the huge **Tampa Bay Performing-Arts Center,** 1010 N. MacInnes Place (☎ **800/955-1045** or 813/229-STAR), is the largest performing-arts venue south of the Kennedy Center in Washington, D.C. Accordingly, this four-theater complex is the focal point of Tampa's performing-arts scene, presenting a wide range of Broadway plays, classical and pop concerts, operas, cabarets, improv, and special events.

A sightseeing attraction in its own right, the restored ✪ **Tampa Theatre,** 711 Franklin St. (☎ 813/223-8981), dates from 1926 and is on the National Register of Historic Places. It presents a varied program of classic, foreign, and alternative films, as well as concerts and special events.

ST. PETERSBURG

On the western shore of the bay, St. Petersburg stands in contrast to Tampa, much like San Francisco compares to Oakland out in California. While Tampa is the area's business, industrial, and shipping center, St. Petersburg was conceived and built almost a century ago primarily for tourists and wintering snowbirds. Here you'll find one of the most picturesque and pleasant downtowns of any city in Florida, with a waterfront promenade and the famous, pyramid-shaped Pier offering great views out across the bay, plus quality museums, interesting shops, and fine restaurants.

Away from downtown, the city pretty much consists of strip malls dividing residential neighborhoods, but plan at least to have a look around the charming bayfront area. If you don't do anything else, go out on The Pier and take a pleasant stroll along Bayshore Drive.

All is not completely happy in this urban paradise, however, for St. Petersburg was rocked by riots after a white police officer shot and killed a black motorist in late 1996. Although all was calm at press time, you should avoid the area south of I-175 and east of I-275.

ESSENTIALS

GETTING THERE   To reach downtown from Tampa, take I-275 or the Gandy Causeway (U.S. 92) across the bay, then I-275 south to I-375 east to the waterfront. From points north, take congested U.S. 19 straight to downtown.

VISITOR INFORMATION   For information about both St. Petersburg and the beaches, contact the **St. Petersburg/Clearwater Area Convention & Visitors Bureau,** 14450 46th St. N., Clearwater, FL 34622 (☎ **800/345-6710,** or 813/464-7200 for advance hotel reservations). The office is south of Roosevelt Boulevard (Fla. 686) opposite St. Petersburg–Clearwater International Airport. The bureau's web site is at **http://www.stpete-clearwater.com**.

Information is also available from the **St. Petersburg Area Chamber of Commerce,** 100 2nd Ave. N., St. Petersburg, FL 33701 (☎ **813/821-4069**). This downtown main office and visitor center is open Monday to Saturday from 10am to 8pm, Sunday from 11am to 6pm. Ask for a copy of the chamber's visitor's guide, which lists hotels, motels, condominiums, and other accommodations. The chamber's Internet site is at **http://www.stpete.com**.

The chamber also operates the **Suncoast Welcome Center,** on Ulmerton Road at Exit 18 off I-275.

Also downtown, there are **walk-in information centers** on the first level of The Pier and in the lobby of the Florida International Museum (see "What to See & Do," below).

CITY LAYOUT   St. Petersburg's **downtown** is laid out according to a grid system, with streets running north–south and avenues running east–west. **Central Avenue** is the dividing line for north and south addresses. "Northeast" avenues—those designated NE—lie east of 1st Street North. With the exception of Central Avenue, most streets and avenues downtown are one way.

GETTING AROUND   You can see everything on the free **Looper: The Downtown Trolley** (☎ 813/571-3440), which runs out to the end of The Pier and past all of the downtown attractions daily from 11am to 5pm except Thanksgiving and Christmas Day.

The **Pinellas Suncoast Transit Authority/PSTA** (☎ 813/530-9911) operates regular bus service throughout Pinellas County. The fare is $1.

If you need a cab, call **Yellow Cab** (☎ 813/821-7777) or **Independent Cab** (☎ 813/327-3444).

SEEING THE SIGHTS

Florida International Museum

100 2nd St. N. (between 1st and 2nd aves. N.). ☎ **800/777-9882** or 813/822-3693. Admission $14.50 adults, $13.25 seniors, $5 children 5–16, children under 5 free. Daily 9am–6pm.

This facility attracted 600,000 visitors from around the world in 1995 when it opened its first exhibition, called "Treasures of the Czars." Its 1997 exhibit on Alexander the Great was also a smash. Call to see what's scheduled during your visit. The museum is housed in the former Maas Brothers Department Store, long an area landmark. Tickets should be reserved and purchased in advance to be sure of a specific time. Each visitor is provided with an audio guide as part of the admission price; allow at least 2 hours to tour a major exhibition.

Great Explorations

1120 4th St. S. (at 11th Ave. S.). ☎ **813/821-8885.** Admission $6 adults, $5.50 seniors, $5 children 4–17, free for children 3 and under. Mon–Sat 10am–5pm, Sun noon–5pm.

With a variety of hands-on exhibits, this museum is great for a rainy day or for kids who've overdosed on the sun and need to cool off inside. They can explore a long, dark tunnel; measure their strength, flexibility, and fitness; paint a work of art with sunlight; and play a melody with a sweep of the hand.

Museum of Fine Arts

255 Beach Dr. NE (at 3rd Ave. N.). ☎ **813/896-2667.** Admission Mon–Sat $5 adults, $3 seniors, $2 students. Free admission on Sun. Tues–Sat 10am–5pm, Sun 1–5pm; winter, 3rd Thurs of each month 10am–9pm.

Resembling a Mediterranean villa on the waterfront, this museum houses a permanent collection of European, American, pre-Columbian, and Far Eastern art, with works by such artists as Fragonard, Monet, Renoir, Cézanne, and Gauguin. Other highlights include period rooms with antiques and historical furnishings, plus a gallery of Steuben crystal, a new decorative-arts gallery, and world-class rotating exhibits.

The Pier

800 2nd Ave. NE. ☎ **813/821-6164.** Free admission to all the public areas and decks; donations welcome at the aquarium. Shops, Mon–Sat 10am–9pm, Sun 11am–7pm; restaurants, daily 11am–11pm; bars, daily 10am–midnight or 1am; aquarium, Mon and Wed–Sat 10am–9pm, Sun 11am–7pm. Parking Mon–Fri $2, Sat–Sun $1.

Walk out on The Pier and enjoy this festive waterfront complex overlooking Tampa Bay. Originally built as a railroad pier in 1889, today it's a modern inverted pyramid offering five levels of shops and restaurants, plus an aquarium, tourist information desk, observation deck, catwalks for fishing, boat docks, a small bayside beach, miniature golf, boat and water-sports rentals, sightseeing boats, and a food court. A free trolley service operates between The Pier and the parking lots on shore.

○ St. Petersburg Museum of History

335 2nd Ave. NE. ☎ **813/894-1052.** Admission $4 adults, $3.50 seniors, $1.50 children 7–17, free for children 6 and under. Mon–Sat 10am–5pm, Sun 1–5pm.

Located at the foot of The Pier, this museum features a permanent interactive exhibition chronicling St. Petersburg's history, ranging from prehistoric artifacts to documents, clothing, and photographs. There are also computer stations where you can "flip through the past." Walk-through exhibits include a replica of the Benoist airboat that made the world's first scheduled commercial flight from St. Petersburg in 1914.

○ Salvador Dalí Museum

1000 3rd St. S. (near 11th Ave. S.). ☎ **813/823-3767.** Admission $8 adults, $7 seniors, $4 students, free for children 9 and under. Mon–Sat 9:30am–5:30pm, Sun noon–5pm. Closed Thanksgiving and Christmas Day.

Located on Tampa Bay south of The Pier, this starkly modern museum houses the world's largest collection of works by the renowned Spanish surrealist. Valued at over $150 million, it includes 94 oil paintings, more than 100 watercolors and drawings, and 1,300 graphics, plus posters, photos, sculptures, objets d'art, and a 5,000-volume library on Dalí and surrealism.

Sunken Gardens

1825 4th St. N. (between 18th and 19th aves. NE). ☎ **813/896-3186.** Admission $14 adults, $8 children 3–11, free for children 2 and under. Daily 9:30am–5pm.

One of the city's oldest attractions, this 7-acre tropical garden park dating back to 1935 is a holdover from Florida's early tourist days. It contains a vast array of 5,000 plants, flowers, and trees, and there are bird and alligator shows.

St. Petersburg Area

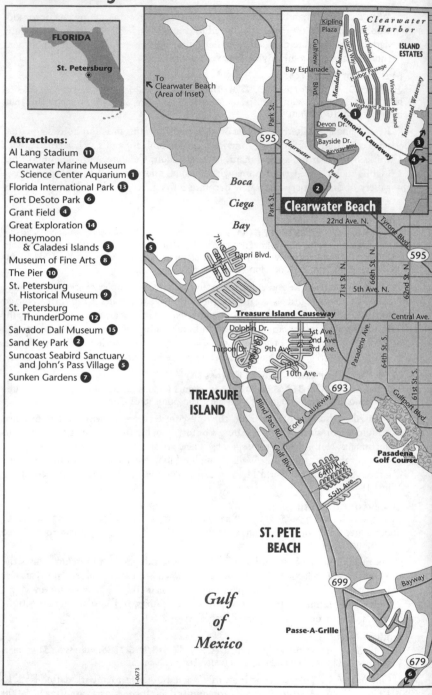

FLORIDA

St. Petersburg

Attractions:

Al Lang Stadium ⑪

Clearwater Marine Museum
Science Center Aquarium ①

Florida International Park ⑬

Fort DeSoto Park ⑥

Grant Field ④

Great Exploration ⑭

Honeymoon
& Caladesi Islands ③

Museum of Fine Arts ⑧

The Pier ⑩

St. Petersburg
Historical Museum ⑨

St. Petersburg
ThunderDome ⑫

Salvador Dalí Museum ⑮

Sand Key Park ②

Suncoast Seabird Sanctuary
and John's Pass Village ⑤

Sunken Gardens ⑦

To Clearwater Beach (Area of Inset)

Clearwater Harbor

Kipling Plaza

ISLAND ESTATES

Gulfview Blvd.

Bay Esplanade

Mandalay Channel

Island Way

Harbor Island

Harbor Passage

Windward Island

Windward Passage

Intercoastal Waterway

Memorial Causeway

Devon Dr.

Bayside Dr.

Bayway Blvd.

③

④

Clearwater Beach

②

Boca

Ciega

Bay

Park St.

595

Clearwater Pass

22nd Ave. N.

Tyrone Blvd.

595

N. 71st St.

N. 66th St.

62nd St. N.

5th Ave. N.

⑤

7th

Capri Blvd.

Treasure Island Causeway

Central Ave.

Dolphin Dr.

1st Ave.

2nd Ave.

3rd Ave.

9th Ave.

Tarpon Dr.

10th Ave.

Pasadena Ave.

64th St. S.

61st St. S.

TREASURE ISLAND

693

Gulfport Blvd.

Corey Causeway

Pasadena Golf Course

Blind Pass Rd.

Gulf Blvd.

64th Ave.

55th Ave.

ST. PETE BEACH

699

Bayway

Gulf

of

Mexico

Passe-A-Grille

679

⑥

258

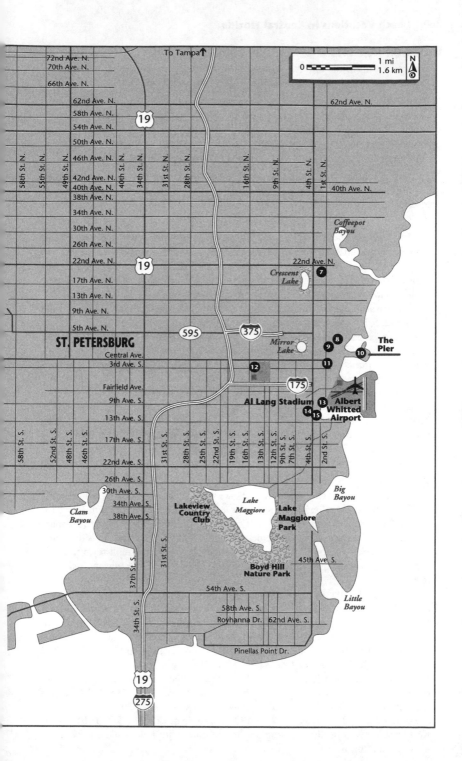

To Tampa↑

0 ⎯ 1 mi
1.6 km

N

72nd Ave. N.
70th Ave. N.
66th Ave. N.
62nd Ave. N.
62nd Ave. N.
58th Ave. N.
54th Ave. N.
50th Ave. N.
46th Ave. N.
42nd Ave. N.
40th Ave. N.
40th Ave. N.
38th Ave. N.
34th Ave. N.
30th Ave. N.
26th Ave. N.
22nd Ave. N.
22nd Ave. N.
17th Ave. N.
13th Ave. N.
9th Ave. N.
5th Ave. N.

19

19

58th St. N.
55th St. N.
49th St. N.
40th St. N.
34th St. N.
31st St. N.
28th St. N.
16th St. N.
9th St. N.
4th St. N.
1st St. N.

Coffeepot
Bayou

Crescent
Lake

7

ST. PETERSBURG

Central Ave.
3rd Ave. S.

595   375

Mirror
Lake

8
9   The
10   Pier
11

12

Fairfield Ave.
9th Ave. S.
13th Ave. S.

175

Al Lang Stadium 13   Albert
14   Whitted
15   Airport

17th Ave. S.
22nd Ave. S.
26th Ave. S.
30th Ave. S.
34th Ave. S.
38th Ave. S.

58th St. S.
52nd St. S.
48th St. S.
46th St. S.
31st St. S.
28th St. S.
25th St. S.
22nd St. S.
19th St. S.
16th St. S.
13th St. S.
12th St. S.
9th St. S.
7th St. S.
4th St. S.
2nd St. S.

Clam
Bayou

Lakeview
Country
Club

Lake
Maggiore

Lake
Maggiore
Park

Big
Bayou

45th Ave. S.

Boyd Hill
Nature Park

37th St. S.
31st St. S.
34th St. S.

54th Ave. S.

58th Ave. S.
Royhanna Dr.   62nd Ave. S.

Little
Bayou

Pinellas Point Dr.

19
275

259

OUTDOOR PURSUITS & SPECTATOR SPORTS

You can get up-to-the-minute recorded information about the city's sports and recreational activities by calling the **Leisure Line** (☎ 813/893-7500).

BOAT RENTALS   On The Pier, **Waterworks Rentals** (☎ 813/363-0000) rents Wave Runners and jet boats. A second location is at 200D 150th Ave., Madeira Beach (☎ 813/399-8989). Prices for Wave Runners begin at $25 for a half hour; for jet boats, from $45 per hour. Open daily from 9am to 6pm or later.

CRUISES   The *Caribbean Queen* (☎ 813/895-BOAT) departs from The Pier and offers 1-hour sightseeing and dolphin-watching cruises around Tampa Bay. Sailings are daily at 11:30am and 1, 3, and 5pm; they cost $10 for adults, $8 for seniors and juniors 12 to 17, $5 for children 3 to 11, and free for children 2 and under.

GOLF   One of the nation's top 50 municipal courses, the **Mangrove Bay Golf Course,** 875 62nd Ave. NE (☎ 813/893-7797), hugs the inlets of Old Tampa Bay and offers 18-hole, par-72 play. Facilities include a driving range; lessons and golf-club rental are also available. Fees are about $22, $32 including a cart in winter, slightly lower off-season. Open daily from 6:30am to 6pm.

The city also operates the challenging, par-3 **Twin Brooks Golf Course,** 3800 22nd Ave. S. (☎ 813/893-7445).

In Largo, the **Bardmoor Golf Club,** 7919 Bardmoor Blvd. (☎ 813/397-0483), is often the venue for major tournaments. Lakes punctuate 17 of the 18 holes on this par-72 championship course. Lessons and rental clubs are available, as is a Tom Fazio–designed practice range. Call the clubhouse for seasonal greens fees. Open daily from 7am to dusk.

Adjacent to the St. Petersburg–Clearwater airport, the **Airco Flite Golf Course,** 3650 Roosevelt Blvd., Clearwater (☎ 813/573-4653), is a championship 18-hole, par-72 course with a driving range. Golf-club rentals are also available. Greens fees including cart are $30 in winter, about $20 off-season. Open daily from 7am to 6pm.

Call **Tee Times USA** (☎ 800/374-8633) to reserve times at these and other area courses.

SPECTATOR SPORTS   Away from the waterfront, the city's skyline is dominated by **Tropicana Field,** alongside I-175 between 9th and 16th streets south (☎ 813/825-3100). Formerly known as the St. Petersburg ThunderDome before the orange-juice company paid to change its name, this 45,000-seat domed stadium is the home of the big league **Tampa Bay Devil Rays,** a new baseball expansion team that will start playing here in April 1998. Call ☎ 813/825-3187 for schedule and ticket information.

The area is also the **spring-training** home of several other major-league teams from mid-February through March. The **St. Louis Cardinals** had been training at Al Lang Stadium, on 2nd Avenue South at 1st Street South (☎ 813/822-3384), but the advent of the Devil Rays probably will send them elsewhere in 1998. The **Philadelphia Phillies** traditionally play their spring-training season at Jack Russell Stadium, 800 Phillies Dr. in Clearwater (☎ 813/442-8496). Admission is $8 to $9. The **Clearwater Phillies,** a Class A minor-league team, play in the stadium from April to September. Grant Field, 373 Douglas Ave. in Dunedin (☎ 813/733-0429), is the winter home of the **Toronto Blue Jays.** Admission is $8 to $9.

Founded in 1925, **Derby Lane,** 10490 Gandy Blvd. (☎ 813/576-1361), is the world's oldest continually operating greyhound track, with indoor and outdoor seating and standing areas.

SHOPPING

✪ **The Pier,** at the end of 2nd Ave. NE (☎ 813/821-6164), houses more than a dozen boutiques and craft shops. But there are many more on land in downtown, all of them listed in *The Quarter,* a brochure available from the St. Petersburg Area Chamber of Commerce (see "Essentials," above). Running along the waterfront, **Beach Drive** is one of the most fashionable downtown strolling and shopping streets. **Central Avenue** is another shopping venue, featuring the **Gas Plant Antique Arcade,** between 12th and 13th streets (☎ 813/895-0368), the largest antiques mall on Florida's west coast. Out in the suburbs, outlet shoppers can browse at the air-conditioned **Bay Area Outlet Mall,** at the intersection of U.S. 19 and East Bay Drive (☎ 813/535-2337), west of St. Petersburg–Clearwater International Airport.

WHERE TO STAY

Ask the **St. Petersburg Area Chamber of Commerce** (see "Essentials," above) for a copy of its visitor's guide, which lists a wide range of hotels, motels, condominiums, and other accommodations. In addition, the St. Petersburg/Clearwater Convention & Visitors Bureau has a free **reservations service** (☎ 800/345-6710).

You'll find plenty of chain motels along U.S. 19.

Price-wise, the high season is from January to April. The hotel tax rate in Pinellas County is 11%.

Bay Gables Bed & Breakfast

136 4th Ave. NE (between Beach Dr. and 1st St. N.), St. Petersburg, FL 33701. ☎ **800/ 822-8803** or 813/822-8855. Fax 813/824-7223. 9 rms. A/C. $85–$135 double. Rates include continental breakfast. MC, V.

You can walk to The Pier from this charming B&B, which was built in the 1930s. It overlooks a flower-filled garden with a gazebo and faces a fanciful Victorian-style house whose first floor is a tearoom/restaurant (see "Where to Dine," below). The guest rooms have been furnished with ceiling fans and Victorian pieces, including some canopy beds. All units have bathrooms with claw-foot tubs and modern showers; half of the rooms have a porch, while the rest have a separate sitting room and kitchenette. Continental breakfast is served in the common room, on the garden deck, or in the gazebo. This is a professionally managed operation; the owners don't live on premises.

✪ The Heritage/Holiday Inn

234 3rd Ave. N. (between 2nd and 3rd sts.), St. Petersburg, FL 33701. ☎ **800/283-7829** or 813/822-4814. Fax 813/823-1644. 71 rms. A/C TV TEL. Winter, $86–$107 double. Off-season, $57–$69 double. Rates include continental breakfast. AE, DC, DISC, MC, V.

No ordinary Holiday Inn, The Heritage dates to the early 1920s and is the closest thing to a Southern mansion you'll find in the heart of downtown. With a sweeping veranda, French doors, and tropical courtyard, it attracts an eclectic clientele, from young families to seniors. The furnishings include period antiques. There's a heated swimming pool and a whirlpool in a small tropical courtyard between the main building and the Heritage Grill next door, one of the area's most popular restaurants (see "Where to Dine," below).

Mansion House Bed & Breakfast

105 5th Ave. NE (at 1st St. N.), St. Petersburg, FL 33701. ☎ **800/274-7520** or 813/821-9391. Fax same as phone. 6 rms (all with bath). A/C. Winter $100–$125 double. Off-season, $85–$115 double. Rates include full breakfast. AE, MC, V.

This two-story, shingle-and-stucco house was built in 1904 by a local doctor and extensively renovated in 1991. Sporting a faux fireplace adorned with hand-painted tiles, the comfortable living room opens to a sunroom, off which a small screened porch provides mosquito-free lounging and the only place where guests can smoke here. There's another front parlor upstairs with a TV. Tall, old-fashioned windows let lots of light into the attractive guest rooms. The "Pembrooke" room actually is upstairs over the carriage house; it has its own refrigerator, phone, TV, and four-poster bed with mosquito net. In an unusual architectural twist, the "Harlech" room has a toilet and hand basin in one converted closet, a shower in another. Proprietors Rob and Rosie Ray serve a full breakfast in two formal dining rooms and keep fruit bowls and snacks available at all hours. There's a whirlpool bath in its own screened hut in the backyard.

✪ Renaissance Vinoy Resort

501 5th Ave. NE (at Beach Dr.), St. Petersburg, FL 33701. ☎ **800/HOTELS-1** or 813/894-1000. Fax 813/822-2785. 360 rms. A/C MINIBAR TV TEL. Winter, $249–$289 double. Off-season, $129–$169 double. Parking $7. AE, DC, DISC, MC, V.

Built as the Vinoy Park in 1925 during Florida's heyday of grand hotels, this elegant Spanish-style establishment reopened in 1992 after a total and meticulous $93-million restoration and refurbishment that has made it even more luxurious than ever. Dominating the northern part of downtown, it overlooks Tampa Bay and is within walking distance of The Pier, Central Avenue, museums, and other attractions. All the guest rooms, many of which enjoy lovely views of the bayfront, are designed to offer the utmost in comfort and include three phones, an additional TV in the bathroom, hair dryer, bath scales, and more; some units in the new wing also have whirlpools and private patios/balconies.

Dining/Entertainment: Marchand's Grille, an elegant room overlooking the bay, specializes in steaks, seafood, and chops. The Terrace Room is the main dining room for breakfast, lunch, and dinner. Casual lunches and dinners are available at the indoor-outdoor Alfresco, near the pool deck, and at the Clubhouse, at the golf course on Snell Isle. There are also two bar/lounges.

Services: Concierge, room service (24 hours), laundry service, tour desk, child care, complimentary coffee and newspaper with wake-up call.

Facilities: Two swimming pools (connected by a roaring waterfall), 14-court tennis complex (nine lighted), 18-hole private championship golf course on nearby Snell Isle, private 74-slip marina, two croquet courts, fitness center (with sauna, steam room, spa, massage, and exercise equipment), access to two bayside beaches, shuttle service to gulf beaches, hair salon, gift shop.

St. Petersburg Bayfront Hilton

333 1st St. S., St. Petersburg, FL 33701. ☎ **800/HILTONS** or 813/894-5000. Fax 813/823-4797. 333 rms. A/C TV TEL. Winter, $150 double. Off-season, $110 double. Packages available. AE, DC, MC, V.

This 15-story convention hotel has a spacious lobby with a rich decor of marble, crystal, tile, antiques, artwork, and potted trees and plants. The bedrooms are furnished with traditional dark woods, floral fabrics, a king-size bed or two double beds, and an executive desk; many have views of the bay. Charmene's is a full-service restaurant specializing in continental cuisine, while the First Street Deli provides light fare. Brandi's Lobby Bar has piano entertainment. Facilities include an outdoor heated swimming pool, whirlpool, and health club with a sauna.

A NEARBY SPA

Safety Harbor Resort and Spa

105 N. Bayshore Dr., Safety Harbor, FL 34695. ☎ **800/BEST-SPA** or 813/726-1161. Fax 813/726-4268. 170 rms. A/C TV TEL. Packages from $140 per person double occupancy, 2-night minimum stay required. 4- and 7-night packages available. AE, DC, DISC, MC, V.

Sanibel Island's excellent South Seas Resorts Company recently took over this tranquil, waterfront retreat on Old Tampa Bay and gave it a much-needed face-lift and upgrading. The full-service spa offers pampering from massages to hydrotherapy and a full menu of fitness classes from Boxercise to yoga. The resort sits on 22 waterfront acres in the sleepy town of Safety Harbor, north of St. Petersburg. Guests have been enjoying the curative mineral waters for over 50 years, and the water-fitness programs receive acclaim every year.

Dining/Entertainment: Nutritious menus use lots of Florida ingredients in both the Spa Dining Room and the resort's Cafe, which is open to the public for lunch and dinner. The popular "Heart Saver Soup" has five different beans and seven vegetables.

Services: Room service, transportation to the airport.

Facilities: Clarins Skin Institute, spa salon, fitness center, Phil Green Tennis Academy, natural mineral springs.

WHERE TO DINE

Don't overlook the food court at The Pier, where inexpensive chow is accompanied by a very rich—but quite free—view of the bay.

Apropos

300 2nd Ave. NE (at Bayshore Dr.). ☎ **813/823-8934.** Reservations accepted only for dinner. Breakfast $3.50–$6; lunch $5–$9; dinner main courses $9–$16. DC, MC, V. Tues–Sat 7:30–10:30am and 11am–3pm; Tues–Sun 6pm–10pm; Sun brunch 8:30am–2pm. AMERICAN.

Sitting a the foot of The Pier, Apropos is a fine place to breakfast before your tour of downtown, perhaps with a brie-and-bacon omelet, or a seasonal fruit plate, or just plain eggs. At lunch, the view through the masts in the adjacent marina sets the scene for the likes of shrimp and artichoke salad with a sherry mayonnaise dressing. And at dinner, you can choose from a blackboard offering the chef's nightly nouveau-cuisine selections. You'll find as many locals here as tourists.

Bay Gables Tea Room

136 4th Ave. NE (between Beach Dr. and 1st St. N.). ☎ **813/822-0044.** Reservations recommended for lunch, required for afternoon tea. Main courses $6–$12 plus 18% service charge. MC, V. Mon–Sat 11am–2pm, afternoon tea at 3pm; Sun brunch 10am–2pm. AMERICAN.

Set in the beautifully restored 1910 Victorian Bay Gables Bed & Breakfast (see "Where to Stay," above), replete with Old Florida antiques and frilly trimmings, this spot less than two blocks from the bayfront caters mostly to the midday shopping crowd. Meals are served on heirloom china and silver in the cozy atmosphere of three small rooms and a tiny porch upstairs or on a wraparound ground-floor veranda. The menu is simple but freshly prepared, featuring salads, quiches, soups, and finger sandwiches.

✪ Fourth Street Shrimp Store

1006 4th St. N. (at 10th Ave. N.). ☎ **813/822-0325.** Reservations not accepted. Sandwiches $2.50–$6; main courses $4–$12. No credit cards. Mon–Sat 11am–9pm, Sun 11am–8pm. SEAFOOD.

If you're anywhere in the area, don't miss at least driving by to see the colorful, cartoonlike mural on the outside of this eclectic establishment just north of downtown. On first impression it looks like graffiti, but it's actually a gigantic drawing of people eating. Inside, it gets even better, with paraphernalia and murals on two walls making the dining room seem like a warehouse with windows looking out on an early 19th-century seaport (one painted sailor permanently peers in to see what you're eating). You'll pass a seafood market counter when you enter, from which comes the fresh namesake shrimp, the star here. You can also pick from grouper, clam strips, catfish, or oysters fried, broiled, or steamed, all served in heaping portions. This is the best and certainly the most interesting bargain in town.

The Garden Bistro
217 Central Ave. ☎ 813/896-3800. Reservations recommended for dinner. Main courses $8–$14. AE, MC, V. Daily noon–2pm and 5–10pm. MEDITERRANEAN.

A popular hot spot with those in the know, this lively restaurant combines European ambiance with Moroccan cuisine. Choice seats are under huge shade trees in the garden, screened from the street by a trellis fence. Inside, the decor blends the American Southwest with the Mediterranean, with arches, a 19th-century tiled floor, modern local art, and lots of flowers and plants. The creative menu features couscous, a daily *tajin* (a traditional Moroccan stew), pastas such as wild mushrooms with strips of roast duck, and smoked salmon in a light cream sauce. On Friday and Saturday, live jazz adds to the ambiance from 9pm to 1am.

Heritage Grill
256 2nd St. N. (at 3rd Ave. N.). ☎ 813/823-6382. Reservations recommended. Main courses $14.25–$21.95. AE, DC, DISC, MC, V. Mon–Fri 11:30am–2:30pm and 5:30–9:30pm, Sat 5:30–9:30pm. AMERICAN.

Next door to The Heritage/Holiday Inn (see "Where to Stay," above), this 1920s-vintage house has been transformed into a restaurant cum modern art gallery, with the walls displaying for-sale works by local artists. The colorful place mats are hand-painted once a week, and even the waiters are part of the art scene—their tuxedo shirts also are hand-painted. For something old, look behind the bar as you enter: The ornate mahogany liquor and wine cabinet reportedly came from the Mississippi home of Confederate President Jefferson Davis. When you're ready to dine, the menu offers dishes like sautéed macadamia-nut–crusted chicken breast stuffed with prosciutto and sun-dried tomatoes and roasted rack of lamb with a minted mango coulis.

Keystone Club
320 4th St. N. (between 3rd and 4th aves. N.). ☎ 813/822-6600. Reservations recommended. Main courses $11–$20. AE, DC, DISC, MC, V. Mon–Fri 11am–2:30pm and 5–10pm, Sat 4–10pm, Sun 4–9pm. STEAKS/PRIME RIB.

This is the closest thing to a men's club in downtown St. Petersburg, with forest green walls accented by dark wood and etched glass creating an atmosphere that's reminiscent of a Manhattan-style chop house. But women are also welcome to partake of the beef, which is king here. Specialties include roast prime rib, New York strip steak, and filet mignon. Seafood also makes an appearance, with fresh lobster and grouper at market prices.

Nick's on the Water
On The Pier (east end of 2nd Ave. NE). ☎ 813/898-5800. Reservations recommended for dinner. Main courses $8–$18. AE, DC, MC, V. Sun–Thurs 11:30am–10pm, Fri–Sat 11:30am–11pm. ITALIAN/SEAFOOD.

Located on the ground level of The Pier, this informal restaurant offers expansive views of downtown St. Petersburg and the bayfront marina. The menu features a variety of Italian choices, including Nick's tortellini, but the specialty of the house is wood-fired fish, meats, and pizza. The veal dishes also are a big hit, especially the française, with sautéed medaillons.

St. Petersburg After Dark

Good sources of nightlife information are the Friday "Weekend" section of the *St. Petersburg Times* and the "Baylife" and "Friday Extra" sections of the *Tampa Tribune*. The visitor centers usually have copies of the week's newspaper sections (see "Essentials," above).

THE CLUB & MUSIC SCENE   A historic attraction as well as an entertainment venue, the Moorish-style **Coliseum Ballroom,** 535 4th Ave. N. (☎ 813/892-5202), has been hosting dancing, big bands, boxing, and other events since 1924 (it even made an appearance in the 1985 movie *Cocoon*). An acquaintance of mine said it's fun to watch the town's many seniors doing the jitterbug just like it was 1945 again! Call for the schedule and prices.

A much younger set heads to the casual, downtown **Big Catch,** 9 1st St. NE (☎ 813/821-6444), featuring live and danceable rock and Top 40 hits, as well as darts, pool, and hoops. Housed in the landmark Hotel Detroit, the lively **Club Detroit,** 16 2nd St. N. (☎ 813/896-1244), includes a lounge, Channel Zero, and an outdoor courtyard, Jannus Landing. Look for blues, reggae, and progressive DJ dance music indoors and live rock concerts outdoors.

North of downtown, the **Ringside Cafe,** 2742 4th St. N. (☎ 813/894-8465), in a renovated boxing gymnasium, is an informal neighborhood cafe with a decided sports motif. The music focuses on jazz and blues (and sometimes reggae).

PERFORMING-ARTS VENUES   **Tropicana Field,** 1 Stadium Dr. (☎ 813/825-3100), has a capacity of 50,000 for major concerts, but also hosts a variety of smaller events when the Devil Rays aren't playing baseball.

The **Bayfront Center,** 400 1st St. S. (☎ 813/892-5767, or 813/892-5700 for recorded information), houses the 8,100-seat Bayfront Arena and the 2,000-seat Mahaffey Theater. The schedule includes a variety of concerts, Broadway shows, big bands, ice shows, and circus performances.

THE ST. PETE & CLEARWATER BEACHES

If you're looking for sun and sand, you'll find plenty of both on the 28 miles of slim barrier islands that skirt the gulf shore of the Pinellas Peninsula. With some 1 million visitors coming here every year, don't be surprised if you have lots of company. But you'll also discover quieter neighborhoods geared to families, and this area has some of the nation's finest beaches, which are protected from development by parks and nature preserves.

At the southern end of the strip, St. Pete Beach is the granddaddy of the area's resorts. In fact, visitors started coming here nearly a century ago, and they haven't quit. Today St. Pete Beach is heavily developed and often overcrowded during the winter season. If you like high-rises and mile-a-minute action, St. Pete Beach is for you. But even here, Pass-a-Grille, on the island's southern end, is a quiet residential enclave with eclectic shops and a fine public beach.

A more gentle lifestyle begins just to the north on 3¹/₂-mile-long Treasure Island. From there, you cross famous John's Pass to Sand Key, a 12-mile island occupied by primarily residential Madeira Beach, Redington Beach, North Redington Beach, Redington Shores, Indian Shores, Indian Rocks Beach, and Belleair Beach. Finally the road crosses a soaring bridge to Clearwater Beach, whose silky sands attract active families and couples.

If you like your great outdoors unfettered by development, the jewels here are Fort Desoto Park, down below St. Pete Beach at the mouth of Tampa Bay, and Caladesi Island State Park, north of Clearwater Beach. They are consistently rated among America's top beaches. And Sand Key Park, looking at Clearwater Beach from the southern shores of Little Pass, is one of Florida's finest local beach parks.

ESSENTIALS

GETTING THERE   To reach St. Pete Beach and Treasure Island from I-275, take Exit 4 and follow the Pinellas Byway (Fla. 682) west ($1 toll). For Indian Rocks Beach, take Exit 18 and follow Ulmerton Road due west to the gulf. For the

Redington beaches, take Exit 15 and follow Gandy and Park boulevards (Fla. 694) due west (Park Blvd. also is known as 74th Avenue N.). For Clearwater Beach, take the Courtney Campbell Causeway (Fla. 60) west from Tampa; the causeway becomes Gulf to Bay Boulevard (also Fla. 60), which leads straight west into Clearwater.

CITY LAYOUT   These barrier islands are barely wide enough to accommodate **Gulf Boulevard,** the main drag, which runs all the way from St. Pete Beach north to the top of Sand Key. Once you cross Little Pass into Clearwater Beach, **Gulfview Boulevard** and **Mandalay Avenue** become the central north–south arteries.

GETTING AROUND   **BATS City Transit** (☎ 813/367-3086) offers bus service along the St. Pete Beach strip. The fare is $1.

   Treasure Island Transit System (☎ 813/360-0811) runs buses along the Treasure Island strip. The fare is $1.

   The **Jolley Trolley** (☎ 813/445-1200), operated in conjunction with the City of Clearwater, provides service in the Clearwater Beach area, from downtown to the beaches as far south as Sand Key. It also goes to the Belleview Mido resort (see "Where to Stay," below). The ride costs 25¢.

   Along the beach, the major cab company is **BATS Taxi** (☎ 813/367-3702).

HITTING THE BEACH

This entire stretch of coast is one long beach, but since hotels, condominiums, and private homes occupy much of it, you may want to sun and swim at one of the area's public parks. The very best are described below, but there's also the fine **Pass-a-Grille Public Beach,** on the southern end of St. Pete Beach, where you can watch the boats going in and out of Pass-a-Grille Channel. This and all other Pinellas County public beaches have metered parking lots, so bring a supply of quarters.

   Clearwater Beach has beach volleyball, water-sports rentals, lifeguards, rest rooms, showers, and concessions. The swimming is excellent, and there's a children's playground and a pier for fishing. Gated municipal parking lots here cost $1 per hour or $7 a day. The lots are right across the street from Clearwater Beach Marina, a prime base for boating, cruises, and other waterborne activities (see "Outdoor Pursuits," below).

   Connected by a causeway to Dunedin, **Honeymoon Island State Recreation Area** isn't great for swimming, but it's a jumping-off point for Caladesi Island State Park (see below). Honeymoon Island nevertheless has its own rugged beauty and a fascinating nature trail.

CALADESI ISLAND STATE PARK   This 3¹/₂-mile island north of Clearwater Beach has a lovely, relatively secluded beach with fine, soft sand edged in sea grass and palmettos. Dolphins cavort in the waters offshore. In the park itself, there's a nature trail, and you might see one of the rattlesnakes, black racers, raccoons, armadillos, and rabbits that live here. A concession stand, ranger station, and bathhouses (with rest rooms and showers) are available. Caladesi Island is accessible only by **ferries** from Honeymoon Island (☎ 813/734-1501) and downtown Clearwater (☎ 813/442-7433). The rides cost $4 for adults and $2.50 for kids. Admission to the state park is another $4 per person. Call ☎ 813/469-5918 for more information about the park.

FORT DESOTO PARK   South of St. Pete Beach at the very mouth of Tampa Bay, this group of five connected barrier islands has been set aside by Pinellas County as a 900-acre bird, animal, and plant sanctuary. Besides the stunning white-sugar sand beach (where you can watch the manatees and dolphins play), there's a

Spanish-American War–era fort, great fishing from piers, a large playground for kids, and 4 miles of trails wind through the park for in-line skaters, bicyclists, and joggers. The 230-site campground is almost always sold out (sites cost $17.75 a night, but you must make reservations *in person!*). The park is open from 8am to dusk, although campers and persons fishing from the piers can stay later. Admission is free. To get here, take the Pinellas Byway ($1 toll) east from St. Pete Beach and follow Fla. 679 and the signs south to the park. Call ☎ 813/866-2662 for more information.

SAND KEY PARK   This fine county park on the northern tip of Sand Key facing Clearwater Beach is exceptionally nice because its wide beach and gentle surf are relatively off the beaten path in this commercial area. It's great to get out of the hotel for a morning walk or jog here. Open 8am to dark. Admission is free, but the parking lot has meters. For more information call ☎ 813/464-3347.

OUTDOOR PURSUITS

BICYCLING & IN-LINE SKATING   With miles of flat terrain and paved roads, the beach area is ideal for bikers and in-line skaters, and the 47-mile-long Pinellas Trail runs close by on the mainland. **Beach Cyclist,** 7517 Blind Pass Rd. (☎ 813/367-5001), on the northern tip of St. Pete Beach, and **Transportation Station,** 652 Bayway Blvd. (☎ 813/443-3188), on Clearwater Beach, both rent a wide range of bicycles and in-line skates. Prices range from about $10 for 4 hours to $45 for a week.

BOATING, FISHING & OTHER WATER SPORTS   You can indulge in parasailing, boating, deep-sea fishing, Wave Running, sightseeing, dolphin watching, waterskiing, and just about any other waterborne diversion your heart could desire here. All you have to do is head to one of two beach locations: **John's Pass Marina,** at John's Pass Village and Boardwalk, in Madeira Beach on the southern tip of Sand Key; or **Clearwater Beach Marina,** at Coronado Drive and Causeway Boulevard, which is at the beach end of the causeway leading to downtown Clearwater. Agents in booths there will give you the schedules and prices, answer any questions you have, and make reservations if necessary. Go in the early morning to set up today's activities, or in the afternoon to book tomorrow's.

CRUISES   The **Shell Key Shuttle,** Merry Pier, 801 Pass-a-Grille Way in southern St. Pete Beach (☎ 813/360-1348), uses a 57-passenger catamaran to shuttle out to Shell Island, one of Florida's last completely undeveloped barrier islands. It's great for bird-watchers, who could spot a remarkable 88 different species, including some of North America's rarest shorebirds. Boats leave daily at 10am, noon, 2pm, and (summer only) 4pm. Prices are $10 for adults, $5 for children 12 and under. The ride takes 15 minutes, and you can return on any shuttle you wish.

The three-deck *Lady Anderson,* based on the St. Pete Beach Causeway, 3400 Pasadena Ave. S. (☎ 813/367-7804), offers luncheon, dinner-dance, and gospel music cruises around Boca Ciega Bay. The lunch cruises operate Tuesday to Friday and cost $19.50 for adults and $13.50 for children 9 and under. Dinner cruises are offered on Friday and Saturday from 6:30 to 10pm and cost $29.50 for adults, $19.50 for children; cocktails extra. Gospel-music cruises operate on Tuesday and Thursday, boarding at 6:30pm, for $24.50 for adults and $17.50 for children. Reservations are required. The cruises operate from October to mid-May; *Lady Anderson* spends her summers in Panama City Beach.

Captain Memo's Pirate Cruise, at Clearwater Beach Marina (☎ 813/446-2587), sails the *Pirate's Ransom,* an authentic reproduction of a pirate ship, on 2-hour daytime "pirate cruises" as well as sunset and evening champagne cruises. Cruises operate year-round, daily at 10am and 2, 4:30, and 7pm. For adults, daytime or sun-set cruises cost $27; evening cruises, $30; both daytime and evening cruises cost $20 for seniors and juniors 13 to 17, $17 for children 2 to 12, and are free for children under 2.

The *Sea Screamer*, also at Clearwater Beach Marina (☎ 813/447-7200), claims to be the world's largest speedboat. This 73-foot turbo-charged twin-engine vessel provides an exhilarating spin in Gulf of Mexico waters with opportunities to view birds and marine life along the way. Prices are $11.85 for adults, $7.50 for children 5 to 12. Sailings are September to May, daily at noon, 2pm, and 4pm; and June to September, daily at noon, 2pm, 4pm, and 6pm.

SEEING THE SIGHTS

Clearwater Marine Aquarium

249 Windward Passage, Clearwater. ☎ 813/447-0980. Admission $5.75 adults, $3.75 children 3–11, free for children 2 and under. Mon–Fri 9am–5pm, Sat 9am–4pm, Sun 11am–4pm. The aquarium is off the causeway between Clearwater and Clearwater Beach; follow the signs.

This little jewel of an aquarium on Clearwater Harbor is very low-key and friendly; it's dedicated to the rescue and rehabilitation of marine mammals and sea turtles. Exhibits include dolphins, otters, sea turtles, sharks, stingrays, mangroves, and sea grass.

✪ John's Pass Village and Boardwalk

12901 Gulf Blvd. (at John's Pass), Madeira Beach. ☎ 813/391-7373. Free admission. Shops and activities, daily 9am–6pm or later.

Casual and charming, this old Florida fishing village on John's Pass consists of a string of simple wooden structures topped by tin roofs and connected by a 1,000-foot boardwalk. Most of the buildings have been converted into shops, art galleries, and restaurants. The focal point is the large fishing pier and marina, where many water sports are available for visitors (see "Outdoor Pursuits," above).

✪ Suncoast Seabird Sanctuary

18328 Gulf Blvd., Indian Shores. ☎ 813/391-6211. Admission free, donations welcome. Daily 9am–dusk. Free tours Wed and Sun 2pm.

At any one time there are usually more than 500 sea and land birds living at the sanctuary, from cormorants, white herons, and birds of prey to the ubiquitous brown pelican. The nation's largest wild-bird hospital, dedicated to the rescue, repair, recuperation, and release of sick and injured wild birds, is also here.

SHOPPING

In addition to being a sightseeing attraction here, **John's Pass Village and Board-walk,** on John's Pass in Madeira Beach, just north of Treasure Island (☎ 813/391-7373), is the key shopping venue on the beaches. You'll find the **Bronze Lady** here, the world's largest single dealer of works by Red Skelton, the comedian-artist. On the mainland in Clearwater, the **Senior Citizen Craft Center Gift Shop,** 940 Court St. (☎ 813/442-4266), is one of the area's most unique gift shops—an outlet for the work of some 400 local senior citizens.

WHERE TO STAY

St. Pete Beach has national chain hotels and motels of every name and description along Gulf Boulevard. For even more choices, the **St. Petersburg Area Chamber of**

Commerce lists a wide range of hotels, motels, condominiums, and other accommodations in its annual visitors guide (see "Essentials," above). You can also use the St. Petersburg/Clearwater Convention & Visitors Bureau's free **reservations service** (☎ 800/345-6710).

Pricewise, high season runs from January to April. Ask about special discounted packages in the summer. Any time of year, though, it's wise to make reservations early. The hotel tax in Pinellas County is 11%.

I have organized accommodations geographically, starting with the congested St. Pete Beach area on the south end of the strip, then the mostly residential Indian Rocks Beach area, then the relatively quiet but still busy Clearwater Beach at the north.

St. Pete Beach Area

✪ Captain's Quarters Inn

10035 Gulf Blvd. (between 100th and 101st aves.), Treasure Island, FL 33706. ☎ **800/526-9547** or 813/360-1659. Fax 813/363-3074. 6 efficiencies, 3 cottages. A/C TV TEL. Winter, $45–$70 double; $70–$100 suite. Off-season, $50–$75 double. Weekly rates available. MC, V.

This nautically themed property is a real find, offering well-kept accommodations on the gulf at inland rates. All but one of the units sit on 100 yards of beach, an ideal vantage point for sunset-watching. Six units are efficiencies with new minikitchens including microwave oven, coffeemaker, and wet bar or sink; and two beachside cottages have a separate bedroom and a full kitchen (there's a third cottage on the bay side of the island). Facilities include an outdoor solar-heated freshwater swimming pool, a sundeck, guest barbecues, and a library. Pets are accepted.

Colonial Gateway Inn

6300 Gulf Blvd. (at 63rd Ave.), St. Pete Beach, FL 33706. ☎ **800/237-8918** or 813/367-2711. Fax 813/367-7068. 100 rms, 100 efficiencies. A/C TV TEL. Winter, $95–$123 double. Off-season, $71–$113 double. Efficiencies $10 more. AE, DC, DISC, MC, V.

On the beachfront, this U-shaped complex of one- and two-story units is a favorite with families. The rooms, most of which face the pool and a central landscaped courtyard, are contemporary, with light woods and beach tones. About half the units are efficiencies with kitchenettes.

On the premises is a branch of the very good Shells seafood restaurant (see "Where to Dine" under "Tampa," above). Bambooz Lounge and the Swigwam beach bar offer light refreshments. Facilities include an outdoor heated swimming pool with an expansive concrete deck, a kiddie pool, shuffleboard, and a game room. The watersports shack here offers parasailing and equipment rentals and also services the Days Inn Island Beach Resort next door (see below).

Days Inn Island Beach Resort

6200 Gulf Blvd. (at 62nd Ave.), St. Pete Beach, FL 33706. ☎ **800/544-4222** or 813/367-1902. Fax 813/367-4422. 51 doubles, 51 efficiencies. A/C TV TEL. Winter, $118–$148 double. Off-season, $78 double. Efficiencies $10 more. AE, DC, DISC, MC, V.

Two long, gray buildings flank a courtyard with a heated swimming pool at this beachside property popular with young families. Furnished in dark woods and rich tones, guest rooms have picture-window views, most of the courtyard across exterior walkways that are set back far enough to provide sitting areas. About half the units are efficiencies with kitchenettes. Jimmy B.'s beach bar provides outdoor refreshment and evening entertainment, while Players Bar & Grille has sports TVs. Facilities include two outdoor heated swimming pools, volleyball, horseshoes, shuffleboard, and a game room.

○ Don CeSar Beach Resort and Spa

3400 Gulf Blvd. (at 34th Ave./Pinellas Byway), St. Pete Beach, FL 33706. ☎ **800/637-7200,** 800/282-1116, or 813/360-1881. Fax 813/367-3609. 277 rms. A/C MINIBAR TV TEL. Winter, $275–$350 double. Off-season, $175–$240 double. AE, DC, MC, V.

Dating back to 1928 and listed on the National Register of Historic Places, this "Pink Palace" tropical getaway is so romantic you may bump into six or seven honeymooning couples in one weekend. Sitting majestically on $7^1/_2$ acres of beachfront, the landmark sports a lobby of classic high windows and archways, crystal chandeliers, marble floors, and original artwork. Most rooms have high ceilings and offer views of the gulf or Boca Ciega Bay. The service is good, although the front desk can get a bit overwhelmed when groups are checking in.

Dining/Entertainment: The very pricey but intimate Maritana Grille can't be beat for fresh gourmet seafood—and caviar, if your budget can afford a serious splurge. Other outlets include the King Charles Restaurant (offering a sumptuous Sunday brunch), Zelda's Seaside Café, the Lobby Bar, and the Beachcomber Bar and Grille for light snacks and drinks served outdoors.

Services: Concierge, 24-hour room service, valet parking, laundry, newspaper delivery, in-room massage, business services, complimentary coffee in lobby, babysitting, children's program.

Facilities: Beach, outdoor heated swimming pool, exercise room, sauna, steam room, whirlpool, volleyball, gift shops, rentals for water-sports equipment, major shopping arcade.

○ Island's End Resort

1 Pass-a-Grille Way (at 1st Ave.), St. Pete Beach, FL 33706. ☎ **813/360-5023.** Fax 813/367-7890. 6 cottages. A/C TV TEL. Dec 15 to June 1, $80–$170. Off-season, $61–$170. Weekly rates available. MC, V.

A wonderful respite from the maddening crowd, and a great bargain to boot, this little all-cottage hideaway sits right on the southern tip of St. Pete Beach, smack-dab on Pass-a-Grille, where the Gulf of Mexico meets Tampa Bay. You can step from the six contemporary cottages right onto the beach. And since the island curves sharply here, nothing blocks your view of the emerald bay. If you prefer to swim directly in the gulf or grab a brilliant sunset, the Pass-a-Grille public beach is virtually next door. Linked to each other by boardwalks, the comfortable one- or three-bedroom cottages have dining areas, living rooms, VCRs, and kitchens; the one three-bedroom unit also has access to a private pool. Facilities include a fishing dock, patios, decks, barbecues, and hammocks. Owners Jone and Millard Gamble are no fools: they live at this shady, idyllic setting.

The Gambles also own the **Beach Haven,** 4980 Gulf Blvd. (at 49th Ave.), St. Pete Beach, FL 33706 (☎ **813/367-8642;** fax 813/360-8202), an older but updated and affordable art-deco–style beachfront property in St. Pete Beach's busy strip. The pink duplex cottages here contain both motel rooms and efficiencies. Double rates range from $70 to $115 in winter, $55 to $105 off-season.

Radisson Sandpiper Beach Resort

6000 Gulf Blvd. (at 60th Ave.), St. Pete Beach, FL 33706. ☎ **800/333-3333** or 813/360-5551. Fax 813/562-1222. 36 rms, 123 suites. A/C TV TEL. Winter, $149–$197 double, $227–$267 suite. Off-season, $115–$147 double, $157–$197 suite. AE, DC, DISC, MC, V.

Right on the beach, this employee-owned sister of the TradeWinds (see below) has a well-landscaped, tropical courtyard separating its two six-story wings, both set back from the main road. Decorated with light woods, pastel tones, and touches of rattan, most units here have coffeemakers, toasters, small refrigerators, dishwashers, and wet bars. Suites also have a living area with sofa bed.

Dining/Entertainment: Piper's Patio is a casual cafe with indoor/outdoor seating; and the Sandbar offers frozen drinks, snacks, and fine sunsets by the pool. There's a Chili Peppers Mexican restaurant on premises.

Services: Concierge, room service, valet laundry, newspaper delivery, in-room massage, baby-sitting, child care.

Facilities: Beachfront heated swimming pool, another heated swimming pool in its own greenhouse, two air-conditioned sports courts (for racquetball, handball, and squash), exercise room, volleyball, shuffleboard, game room, gift shop/general store.

TradeWinds Resort

5500 Gulf Blvd. (at 55th Ave.), St. Pete Beach, FL 33706. ☎ **800/237-0707** or 813/367-6461. Fax 813/360-3848. 377 units. A/C TV TEL. Winter, $179–$221 double. Off-season, $119–$180 double. Discount packages available in summer. AE, DC, DISC, MC, V.

Don't be dismayed by the outward appearance of this six- and seven-story, concrete-and-steel monstrosity, for underneath and beside it runs a maze of brick walkways, patios, and lily ponds connected by a quarter mile of streams. It all gives surprising charm to this employee-owned hotel. The guest units, which look out on the gulf or the 18 acres of grounds, have up-to-date kitchens or kitchenettes, contemporary furnishings, and private balconies. The children's program and summer packages are a big hit with families from around the world, attracting lots of Europeans.

Dining/Entertainment: The top spot for lunch or dinner is the Palm Court, with an Italian-bistro atmosphere; for dinner, there's also Bermudas, a casual family spot. Other food outlets include the Fountain Square Deli; Pizza Hut; and Tropic Treats. Bars include Reflections piano lounge; B.R. Cuda's, with live entertainment and dancing; and the Flying Bridge, a Florida cracker-house–style beachside bar floating on one of the lily ponds.

Services: With the employees having a stake in the profits as well as the tips, you should get good service here. Room service, valet parking, laundry, baby-sitting, children's program.

Facilities: Four heated swimming pools, whirlpools, sauna, fitness center, four tennis courts, racquetball, croquet, water-sports rentals, gas grills, guest laundry, video-game room, gift shops, full service hair salon with massage and tanning.

Indian Rocks Beach Area

Alpaugh's Gulf Beach Motel Apartments

68 Gulf Blvd. (south of 1st Ave.), Indian Rocks Beach, FL 33785. ☎ 813/595-2589. Fax 813/595-9422. 16 apts. A/C TV TEL. Winter $80–$85 double. Off-season, $60–$72 double. DISC, MC, V. Hotel is 4 blocks south of Fla. 688.

This long-established, family-oriented motel sits at the narrowest section of Indian Rocks Beach, facing the gulf on one side and its own Intracoastal Waterway dock on the other. The buildings flank a pleasantly landscaped central courtyard. The rooms offer modern furnishings, and each unit has a kitchenette and dining area. Facilities include coin-operated laundry, lawn games, and picnic tables.

The owners call this motel "Alpaugh's Number 1." Alpaugh's Number 2 motel is a mile north at Gulf Boulevard and 20th Avenue, also in Indian Rocks Beach (☎ 813/595-9421). The facilities and rates are the same at both, but the courtyard and gulf-to-bay setting makes Number 1 a more pleasant place to stay.

✪ Pelican—East & West

108 21st Ave. (at Gulf Blvd.), Indian Rocks Beach, FL 33785. ☎ **813/595-9741.** 4 suites, 4 apts. A/C TV. Winter, $50–$70 double. Off-season, $40–$50 double. MC, V.

"P.D.I.P." (Perfect Day in Paradise) is the motto at Mike and Carol McGlaughlin's motel complex, which offers a choice of two settings. Their lowest rates are at

Pelican East, in a residential setting 500 feet from the beach, where each of four suites has a bedroom and a separate kitchen. You'll pay more at Pelican West, but it's directly on the beachfront. Each of the four beachside apartments has a living room, bedroom, kitchen, patio, and unbeatable views of the gulf. You don't get phones in your rooms here or a swimming pool to splash around in, but it's clean and modern in all other respects.

Clearwater Beach

✪ Best Western Sea Stone Resort

445 Hamden Dr. (at Coronado Dr.), Clearwater Beach, FL 34630. ☎ **800/444-1919,** 800/ 528-1234, or 813/441-1722. Fax 813/449-1580. 65 rms, 43 suites. A/C TV TEL. Winter, $103–$201 double. Off-season, $72–$140 double. AE, DC, DISC, MC, V.

Located just across the street from the beach in Clearwater's busy south end, the Sea Stone Suites is a six-story building of classic Key West–style architecture containing 43 one-bedroom suites, each with a kitchenette and a living room. Their living-room windows look across external walkways to the harbor. A few steps away, the older five-story Gulfview Wing offers 65 bedrooms. The furnishings are bright and airy, with pastel tones, light woods, and sea scenes on the walls. The on-site Marker 5 Restaurant serves breakfast only. There's valet laundry service, newspaper delivery, and complimentary coffee in the lobby. Facilities include a heated outdoor swimming pool, whirlpool, boat dock, coin-operated laundry, and meeting rooms.

✪ Clearwater Beach Hotel

500 Mandalay Ave. (at Belmont St.), Clearwater Beach, FL 34630. ☎ **800/292-2295,** 813/ 441-2425, or 813/441-2425. Fax 813/449-2083. 157 rms. A/C TV TEL. Winter, $108–$160 double. Off-season, $98–$118 double. AE, DC, MC, V.

Besides the great beach location, you'll enjoy easy access to many nearby shops and restaurants from this old Florida-style hotel. It's been owned and operated by the same family for more than 40 years and attracts an older clientele. Directly on the gulf, the complex consists of a six-story main building and two- and three-story wings. Rooms and rates vary according to location—bay-view or gulf-view, poolside or beachfront. Some but not all rooms have balconies. The dining room is romantic at sunset and offers great views of the gulf, while the nautically themed Schooner Lounge has entertainment nightly. The Pool Bar provides snacks and libations beside an outdoor heated swimming pool. There's valet laundry and parking, and limited room service.

Palm Pavilion Inn

18 Bay Esplanade (at Mandalay Ave.), Clearwater Beach, FL 34630. ☎ **800/433-PALM** or 813/ 446-6777. 24 rms, 4 efficiencies. A/C TV TEL. Winter, $82–$117 double. Off-season, $56–$81 double. AE, DISC, MC, V.

Just north of the tourist area, this quiet beachfront spot is removed from the bustle yet within easy walking distance of all the action. The three-story art-deco building is artfully trimmed in pink and blue. The lobby area and guest rooms, also art deco in design, feature rounded light-wood and rattan furnishings, bright sea-toned fabrics, photographs from the 1920s to 1950s era, and vertical blinds. Rooms in the front of the house face the gulf, while those in back face the bay. Four efficiencies have kitchenettes. Facilities include a rooftop sundeck, beach access, heated swimming pool, complimentary coffee, and beach chair and umbrella rentals. The Beachside Grill & Bar is on premises, and lighted tennis courts and an athletic center are across the street.

✪ Radisson Suite Resort on Sand Key

1201 Gulf Blvd., Clearwater Beach, FL 34630. ☎ **800/333-3333** or 813/596-1100. Fax 813/595-4292. 220 suites. A/C MINIBAR TV TEL. Winter, $169–$269 suite for 2. Off-season, $109–$199 suite for 2. AE, DC, DISC, MC, V. From Clearwater Beach, go south across Little Pass Bridge; hotel is on left.

You'll see the beauty of Sand Key from the suites in this boomerang-shaped, 10-story hotel overlooking Clearwater Bay. The gulf is just beyond the Sheraton Sand Key Resort across the street, and beautiful Sand Key Park is a few steps away. The whole family will enjoy exploring the adjacent boardwalk with 25 shops and restaurants. Each suite has a bedroom with a balcony offering water views, as well as a complete living room with a sofa bed, wet bar, entertainment unit, coffeemaker, and microwave oven.

Dining/Entertainment: The Harbor Grille offers fresh seafood, steaks, and grand bay views. The Harbor Lounge has live entertainment, while Kokomo's serves light fare and tropical drinks.

Services: Room service, laundry, free trolley to the beach, year-round children's activities program at "Lisa's Klubhouse," free valet parking, masseuse.

Facilities: Bayside outdoor heated swimming pool with waterfall, sundeck, sauna, exercise room, guest laundry, waterfront boardwalk with a variety of shops and restaurants.

Sheraton Sand Key Resort

1160 Gulf Blvd., Clearwater Beach, FL 34630. ☎ **800/325-3535** or 813/595-1611. Fax 813/596-8488. 390 rms. A/C TV TEL. Winter, $140–$170 double. Off-season, $130–$160 double. AE, DC, DISC, MC, V. From Clearwater Beach, go south across Little Pass Bridge; hotel is on right.

Away from the honky-tonk of Clearwater, this hotel on 10 acres right next door to Sand Key Park is a big favorite with water-sports enthusiasts. The guest rooms here were recently remodeled; all have coffeemakers, hair dryers, and a balcony or patio with views of the gulf or the bay.

Dining/Entertainment: Rusty's Restaurant serves breakfast and dinner; for lighter fare, try the Island Café, the Sundeck, or Slo Joe's Poolside Bar. The Cook's Corner Deli is open 24 hours.

Services: Limited room service, newspaper delivery, in-room massage, valet parking and laundry, baby-sitting, children's program (summer only).

Facilities: Outdoor heated swimming pool, fitness center, whirlpool, three lighted tennis courts, beach volleyball, newsstand, game room, children's pool, playground, water-sports rentals, 24-hour general store.

✪ Sun West Beach Motel

409 Hamden Dr. (between 4th and 5th sts.), Clearwater Beach, FL 34630. ☎ **813/442-5008.** Fax 813/461-1395. 4 rms, 10 efficiencies. A/C TV TEL. $40–$61 double; $48–$79 efficiency. MC, V.

Overlooking the bay and yet only a 2-block walk from the beach, this well-maintained one-story motel has a heated pool, fishing/boating dock, sundeck, shuffleboard court, and guest laundry. All units, which face either the bay, the pool, or the sundeck, have contemporary resort-style furnishings. The four motel rooms have small refrigerators and the 10 efficiencies have kitchens.

A Historic Hotel on the Mainland

Belleview Mido Resort Hotel

25 Belleview Blvd. (P.O. Box 2317), Clearwater, FL 34617. ☎ **800/237-8947** or 813/442-6171. Fax 813/441-4173 or 813/443-6361. 292 rms. A/C MINIBAR TV TEL. Winter, $190–$260

double. Off-season, $150–$190 double. AE, DC, DISC, MC, V. Resort is 1 mi. south of downtown on Belleview Rd., off U.S. 19 Alt.

The Gulf Coast's oldest operating luxury tourist hotel, this gabled clapboard structure was built in 1896 by Henry B. Plant as the Hotel Belleview to attract customers to his Orange Belt Railroad. Overlooking the bay, it's the largest occupied wooden structure in the world. Today it attracts mostly groups and serious golfers, but there's no denying its Victorian charm and old-fashioned ambiance—once you get past the out-of-place, glass-and-steel foyer added by its present day Japanese owners. The creaky hallways lead to several shops, an art gallery, and a museum explaining the hotel's history. Large, high-ceilinged guest rooms are decorated in Queen Anne style, with dark-wood period furniture.

Dining/Entertainment: The informal indoor/outdoor Terrace Café provides breakfast, lunch, or dinner; the elegant upscale Madame Ma's has gourmet Chinese cuisine. There's also a pub in the basement, a lounge, and a poolside bar.

Services: Room service, dry cleaning and valet laundry, nightly turndown, currency exchange, baby-sitting.

Facilities: Golf privileges at Belleview Mido Country Club, an 18-hole par-72 championship golf course; four red clay tennis courts; indoor and outdoor heated swimming pools (one with a waterfall!); whirlpool; sauna; Swiss showers; workout gym; jogging and walking trails; bicycle rentals; yacht charters; gift shops; art gallery; newsstand; access to a private Cabana Club on the Gulf of Mexico.

WHERE TO DINE

St. Pete Beach and Clearwater Beach both have a wide selection of national chain fast-food and family restaurants. You'll find a bayfront edition of **Shells,** the fine local seafood chain, opposite the Lobster Pot on Gulf Boulevard at 178th Avenue in Redington Shores (☎ **813/393-8990**). See "Where to Dine" under "The Tampa Bay Area," earlier in this chapter, for more information about Shells's menu and prices.

As with the accommodations, above, I have grouped the restaurants by geographic area: St. Pete Beach, including Pass-a-Grille; Indian Rocks Beach, including Madeira Beach, Redington Beach, North Redington Beach, Redington Shores, and Indian Shores; and finally, Clearwater Beach.

St. Pete Beach Area

Hurricane

807 Gulf Way (at 9th Ave.), Pass-a-Grille. ☎ **813/360-9558.** Reservations not accepted. Sandwiches $2.50–$6; main courses $8–$16. MC, V. Daily 8am–1am. SEAFOOD.

An longtime institution overlooking Pass-a-Grille beach, this three-level gray Victorian building with white gingerbread trim is a great place to toast the sunset, especially up on the rooftop. It's more beach bar than fine restaurant, but the grouper sandwiches are a big hit. You can dine inside the knotty-pine paneled dining room or out on the sidewalk terrace, where bathers from across Gulf Way are welcome (there's a walk-up bar for beach libations). The joint jumps at night when one level turns into a virtual dance hall.

Silas Dent's

5501 Gulf Blvd. (at 55th Ave.). ☎ **813/360-6961.** Reservations recommended. Main courses $10–$17. AE, DC, DISC, MC, V. Sun–Thurs 5–10pm, Fri–Sat 5–11pm. STEAK/SEAFOOD.

With a rustic facade of driftwood that makes it look like a ramshackle old Florida fish camp, this restaurant, opposite the TradeWinds Resort, seeks to replicate the home of popular local folk hero Silas Dent. Dent inhabited a nearby island for many years early in this century, and the menu aims to reflect his diet of local fish, using such ingredients as alligator, amberjack, grouper, and squid. Such modern favorites as mahimahi, lobster tails, and scallops are also in evidence. Charcoal-broiled steaks, barbecued ribs, and chicken Silas (with red-bell-pepper sauce) round out the menu. Small portions of some items range from $6.50 to $11.

Indian Rocks Beach Area

✪ Guppy's

1701 Gulf Blvd. (at 17th Ave.), Indian Rocks Beach. ☎ 813/593-2032. Reservations not accepted. Sandwiches $5–$7; main courses $8.25–$19.95. AE, DC, DISC, MC, V. Sun–Thurs 11am–10:30pm; Fri–Sat 11am–11:30pm. SEAFOOD.

Locals love this small bar and grill across from Indian Rocks Public Beach because they know they'll always get terrific chow (it's associated with the excellent Lobster Pot, mentioned below). You won't soon forget the salmon coated with potatoes and lightly fried to brown, then baked with a creamy leek and garlic sauce. Another good choice is lightly cooked tuna (only slightly more done than sushi) finished with a peppercorn sauce. The atmosphere is casual beach friendly, with a fun bar in the rear. Scotty's famous upside-down apple-walnut pie topped with ice cream will require a little extra work on the weights tomorrow. You can dine outside here on a patio beside the main road.

✪ Lobster Pot

17814 Gulf Blvd. (at 178th Ave.), Redington Shores. ☎ 813/391-8592. Reservations recommended. Main courses $13.50–$34.50. AE, DC, MC, V. Mon–Thurs 4:30–10pm, Fri–Sat 4:30–11pm; Sun 4–10pm. SEAFOOD.

Step into this weathered-looking restaurant near the beach and owner Eugen Fuhrmann will tell you to get ready to experience the finest seafood in the area. The prices are high but the variety of lobster dishes is amazing. The lobster américaine is flambéed in brandy with garlic and the bouillabaisse is as authentic as any you'd find in the south of France. In addition to lobster, there's a wide selection of grouper, snapper, salmon, swordfish, shrimp, scallops, crab, and Dover sole, prepared simply or with elaborate sauces.

Omi's Bavarian Inn

14701 Gulf Blvd. (at 147th Ave.), Madeira Beach. ☎ 813/393-9654. Reservations recommended. Main courses $7–$15. AE, DISC, MC, V. Daily 3–9:30pm. GERMAN.

This little restaurant is a small patch of Germany on the gulf, featuring schnitzels, sauerbraten, schweinebraten (roast pork), chicken paprikash, beef goulash, Bavarian bratwurst, and stuffed peppers. Seafood and steak are also on the menu.

Scandia

19829 Gulf Blvd. (between 198th and 199th aves.), Indian Shores. ☎ 813/595-5525. Reservations recommended. Main courses $6–$21. DISC, MC, V. Tues–Sat 11:30am–9pm, Sun noon–8pm. Closed Sept. SCANDINAVIAN.

Unique in decor and menu in these parts, this chalet-style restaurant in the northern fringes of Indian Shores brings a touch of Hans Christian Andersen to the beach strip. The menu offers Scandinavian favorites, from smoked salmon and pickled herring to roast pork, sausages, schnitzels, and Danish lobster tails. There are also a few international dishes such as curried chicken, North Sea flounder, Canadian scallops, Boston scrod, and shrimp and grouper from gulf waters.

✪ The Wine Cellar

17307 Gulf Blvd. (at 173rd Ave.), North Redington Beach. ☎ 813/393-3491. Reservations recommended. Main courses $12.75–$29.50. AE, DC, MC, V. Tues–Sat 4:30–11pm, Sun 4–11pm. CONTINENTAL.

Every evening during the high season and on weekends all year, the cars pack the parking lot at this restaurant, which is highly popular with locals and visitors alike. You'll find an assortment of divided dining rooms, and the cuisine offers the best of Europe and the States. Start off with caviar, move on to a fresh North Carolina rainbow trout or chateaubriand, and top it all off with chocolate velvet torte. There's jazz in the lounge Thursday to Saturday evenings, Dixieland jazz on Sunday, and you'll often find noisy private parties going on.

Clearwater Beach

✪ Bob Heilman's Beachcomber

447 Mandalay Ave. (at Papaya St.). ☎ **813/442-4144.** Reservations recommended. Main courses $12–$24. AE, DC, DISC, MC, V. Mon–Sat 11:30am–11pm, Sun noon–10pm. AMERICAN.

In a restaurant row opposite the beach, this nautically-attired establishment has been popular for more than 45 years. It's the classiest place in Clearwater Beach, with a pianist adding to an elegant but relaxed ambiance. The menu presents a variety of fresh seafood, beef, veal, and lamb selections. The "back-to-the-farm" fried chicken— from an original 1910 Heilman family recipe—is incredible.

✪ Bubby's Bistro & Wine Bar

447 Mandalay Ave. (at Papaya St., behind Bob Heilman's Beachcomber). ☎ **813/446-9463.** Reservations not accepted. Sandwiches and pizzas $6–$12; main courses, $10–$15. AE, DC, DISC, MC, V. Daily 5pm–midnight. AMERICAN.

Bob and Sherri Heilman opened this dark, very urban bistro behind their popular restaurant in 1993, and it's been a local hit ever since. The wine-cellar theme is amply justified by the real thing: a walk-in closet with several thousands of bottles kept at a constant 55°F. Walk through and pick your vintage, then listen to jazz while you dine inside at tall, bar-height tables or outside on a covered patio. The chef specializes in gourmet pizzas on homemade focaccia crust, plus char-grilled veal chops, filet mignon, and fresh fish. There's also an affordable sandwich menu featuring the likes of bronzed grouper and chicken with a spicy Jack cheese.

Frenchy's Cafe

41 Baymont St. ☎ **813/446-3607.** Reservations not accepted. Main courses $4–$15. AE, MC, V. Mon–Thurs 11:30am–11pm; Fri–Sun noon–midnight. SEAFOOD.

Always popular with locals and visitors in the know, this casual cafe makes the best grouper sandwiches in the area—and has all the awards to prove it. They're fresh, thick, juicy, and always delicious. The atmosphere is pure Florida-casual style, and there's always a wait.

Owner Michael "Frenchy" Preston also has the more upscale **Frenchy's Mandalay Seafood Company** at 453 Mandalay Ave. (☎ 813/443-2100). For more casual fare directly on the beach, **Frenchy's Rockaway Grill,** at 7 Rockaway St. (☎ 813/446-4844), has a wonderful outdoor setting.

THE BEACHES AFTER DARK

If you haven't already found it during your sightseeing and shopping excursions, the restored fishing community of **John's Pass Village and Boardwalk,** on Gulf Boulevard at John's Pass in Madeira Beach, has plenty of restaurants, bars, and shops to keep you occupied after the sun sets. Elsewhere, the nightlife scene at the beach revolves around rocking bars, which pump out the music until 2am.

Down south in Pass-a-Grille, there's the popular, always lively **Hurricane,** on Gulf Way at 9th Avenue opposite the public beach (see "Where to Dine," above).

On Treasure Island, **Beach Nutts,** on West Gulf Boulevard at 96th Avenue (☎ 813/367-7427), is perched atop a stilt foundation like a wooden beach cottage on the Gulf of Mexico. The music ranges from Top 40 to reggae and rock. **Manhattans,** Gulf Boulevard at 116th Avenue (☎ 813/363-1500), offers a variety of live music, from country to contemporary and classic rock. Up on the northern tip of Treasure Island, **Gators on the Pass** (☎ 813/367-8951), claims to have the world's longest waterfront bar, with a huge deck overlooking the waters of John's Pass. The complex also includes a nonsmoking sports bar and a three-story tower with a top-level observation deck for panoramic views of the Gulf of Mexico. There's live music, from acoustic and blues to rock, most nights.

In Clearwater Beach, **Jammin'z Dance Shack,** 470 Mandalay Ave. (☎ 813/441-2005, or 813/442-5754 for recorded information), has a beachy atmosphere and a dance floor with state-of-the-art sound, light, video, and laser effects. A deejay spins Top 40 tunes.

If you're into laughs, **Coconuts Comedy Club,** at the Howard Johnson motel, Gulf Boulevard at 61st Avenue in St. Pete Beach (☎ 813/360-5653), charges $12 for its ever-changing program of live stand-up funny men and women. Shows are Wednesday to Sunday at 9:30pm.

For a more highbrow evening, go over to the Clearwater mainland and the 2,200-seat **Ruth Eckerd Hall,** 1111 McMullen–Booth Rd. (☎ 813/791-7400), which hosts a varied program of Broadway shows, ballet, drama, symphonic works, popular music, jazz, and country music.

General Index

ACCOMMODATIONS INDEX

RESTAURANT INDEX

RESTUARANTS

CORAL REEF . WDW .
50'S PRIME TIME CAFE . WDW .
SCI-FI DINE IN THEATRE RESTUARANT . WDW .
RAINFOREST CAFE . MARKETPLACE .

SHOPPING

BELTZ FACTORY OUTLET WORLD .
(5401 W . OAKBRIDGE RD . NORTH INT . DRI .)

FLEA WORLD .
(3 M EAST OF I-4 EXIT 50 ON LAKE MARY
BLVD, 1 M SOUTH ON U.S 17-92 , SANFORD .
FRI — SUN .)

① NAME TAGS .
② "STROLLER" AT EACH PARK .

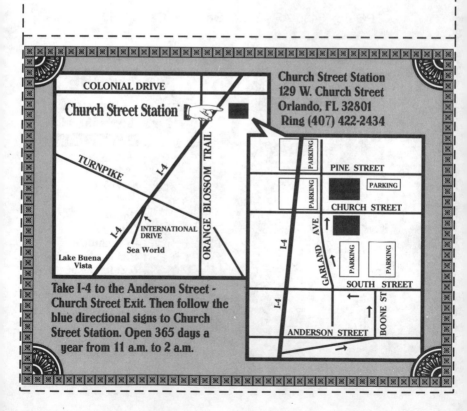

COLONIAL DRIVE

Church Street Station

TURNPIKE

I-4

I-4

ORANGE BLOSSOM TRAIL

INTERNATIONAL DRIVE

Sea World

Lake Buena Vista

Take I-4 to the Anderson Street - Church Street Exit. Then follow the blue directional signs to Church Street Station. Open 365 days a year from 11 a.m. to 2 a.m.

Church Street Station
129 W. Church Street
Orlando, FL 32801
Ring (407) 422-2434

PARKING

PINE STREET

PARKING

PARKING

CHURCH STREET

I-4

GARLAND AVE

PARKING

PARKING

SOUTH STREET

I-4

BOONE ST

ANDERSON STREET

$4.00 off each person

Take advantage of our $24 Value and enjoy 36 fun acres of stimulating slides, adventurous pools and a splashin' wave pool. Bring your own lunch and retreat to 3 acres of beautifully landscaped picnic area.
There's something for the whole family at Water Mania!

Good for up to 6 people
$24.00 value

Receive $10 off your rate on your next rental when you reserve a compact 4-door through full size 4-door car at Hertz Leisure Weekly Rates. Offer available at participating Hertz U.S. Corporate locations through *9/30/98*

Call your travel agent or Hertz at 1-800-654-2210 and just mention PC# 85050.

Receive

$10⁰⁰ Off

A Leisure Weekly Rental

Not valid with other discounts or special events.
Offer expires 12/98

Code: 1232/1233

Hertz rents Fords and other fine cars.

Savings are subject to certain restrictions and availability. Good for domestic and international travel that originates in the U.S. Valid for flights on most airlines worldwide.

Minimum Ticket Price	Save
$200.00	$25.00
$250.00	$50.00
$350.00	$75.00
$450.00	$100.00

MEARS MOTOR SHUTTLE
BOOTH LOCATIONS

2ND LEVEL

- "A" TERMINAL: Exit through the doors in front of American baggage claim carousel #5

- "B" TERMINAL: Exit through the doors in front of United baggage claim carousel #8 or Delta baggage claim carousel #14

THANK YOU FOR USING
MEARS TRANSPORTATION

Gatorland
Orlando

Located on Hwy 441 in South Orlando. From I-4 take exit 26A to 417 north - take exit 11 to Hwy 441 south one mile and Gatorland is on the left.

Call: 800-393-JAWS or 407-855-5496

A World of Orchids
2501 Old Lake Wilson Road
Kissimmee, FL 34747

2 miles west on US 192 from exit 25B off 1-4 then 1 mile south
on Old Lake Wilson Road (CR 545)

FROMMER'S COMPLETE TRAVEL GUIDES

*(Comprehensive guides to destinations around the world, with
selections in all price ranges—from deluxe to budget)*

Acapulco/Ixtapa/Taxco
Alaska
Amsterdam
Arizona
Atlanta
Australia
Austria
Bahamas
Bangkok
Barcelona, Madrid & Seville
Belgium, Holland & Luxembourg
Berlin
Bermuda
Boston
Budapest & the Best of Hungary
California
Canada
Cancún, Cozumel & the Yucatán
Caribbean
Caribbean Cruises & Ports of Call
Caribbean Ports of Call
Carolinas & Georgia
Chicago
Colorado
Costa Rica
Denver, Boulder & Colorado Springs
Dublin
England
Florida
France
Germany
Greece
Hawaii
Hong Kong
Honolulu/Waikiki/Oahu
Ireland
Italy
Jamaica/Barbados
Japan
Las Vegas
London
Los Angeles
Maryland & Delaware
Maui

Mexico
Mexico City
Miami & the Keys
Montana & Wyoming
Montréal & Québec City
Munich & the Bavarian Alps
Nashville & Memphis
Nepal
New England
New Mexico
New Orleans
New York City
Northern New England
Nova Scotia, New Brunswick & Prince
   Edward Island
Paris
Philadelphia & the Amish Country
Portugal
Prague & the Best of the Czech Republic
Puerto Rico
Puerto Vallarta, Manzanillo & Guadalajara
Rome
San Antonio & Austin
San Diego
San Francisco
Santa Fe, Taos & Albuquerque
Scandinavia
Scotland
Seattle & Portland
South Pacific
Spain
Switzerland
Thailand
Tokyo
Toronto
U.S.A.
Utah
Vancouver & Victoria
Vienna
Virgin Islands
Virginia
Walt Disney World & Orlando
Washington, D.C.
Washington & Oregon

FROMMER'S DOLLAR-A-DAY BUDGET GUIDES
(The ultimate guides to low-cost travel)

Australia from $50 a Day	Ireland from $45 a Day
Berlin from $50 a Day	Israel from $45 a Day
California from $60 a Day	Italy from $50 a Day
Caribbean from $60 a Day	London from $60 a Day
Costa Rica & Belize from $35 a Day	Mexico from $35 a Day
England from $60 a Day	New York from $75 a Day
Europe from $50 a Day	New Zealand from $50 a Day
Florida from $50 a Day	Paris from $70 a Day
Greece from $50 a Day	San Francisco from $60 a Day
Hawaii from $60 a Day	Washington, D.C., from $50 a Day
India from $40 a Day	

FROMMER'S PORTABLE GUIDES
(Pocket-size guides for travelers who want everything in a nutshell)

Charleston & Savannah	Puerto Vallarta, Manzanillo & Guadalajara
Dublin	San Francisco
Las Vegas	Venice
Maine Coast	Washington, D.C.
New Orleans	

FROMMER'S IRREVERENT GUIDES
(Wickedly honest guides for sophisticated travelers)

Amsterdam	Miami	Santa Fe
Chicago	New Orleans	U.S. Virgin Islands
London	Paris	Walt Disney World
Manhattan	San Francisco	Washington, D.C.

FROMMER'S AMERICA ON WHEELS
(Everything you need for a successful road trip, including full-color road maps and ratings for every hotel)

California & Nevada	Northwest & Great Plains
Florida	South-Central States & Texas
Great Lakes States & Midwest	Southeast
Mid-Atlantic	Southwest
New England & New York	

FROMMER'S BY NIGHT GUIDES
(The series for those who know that life begins after dark)

Amsterdam	Madrid & Barcelona	Paris
Chicago	Manhattan	Prague
Las Vegas	Miami	San Francisco
London	New Orleans	Washington, D.C.
Los Angeles		

WHEREVER YOU TRAVEL, *H*ELP IS NEVER FAR AWAY.

From planning your trip to providing travel assistance along the way, American Express® Travel Service Offices are always there to help.

Disney

American Express Travel Service
Epcot Center
Walt Disney World Resort
Lake Buena Vista
407/827-7500

American Express Travel Service
2 West Church Street, Suite 1
Sun Bank Center
Orlando
407/843-0004

Travel

http://www.americanexpress.com/travel

For the office nearest you, call 1-800-AXP-3429.